Scott

Lewis

123 LeGrande

Aurora, Illinois 60506

Dan,

Ain't Garage

Sales Great?

The Whodoans

CLEAR FOR ACTION

THE PHOTOGRAPHIC STORY
OF MODERN NAVAL COMBAT
1898—1964

CLEAR FOR ACTION

BY FOSTER HAILEY
AND MILTON LANCELOT

Diagrams by CHARLES G. LANCELOT

BONANZA BOOKS—NEW YORK

This edition published by Bonanza Books,
a division of Crown Publishers, Inc.,
by arrangement with Meredith Press.

C   D   E   F   G

Designed and produced by
Barbara and Dexter Knox and Milton Lancelot

Library of Congress Catalogue Card Number: 64-22646
MANUFACTURED IN THE UNITED STATES OF AMERICA

FOREWORD

Since man first discovered that wood would float and then learned how to make and handle sail so the winds would take him where he wanted to go, there have been battles at sea. Hundreds of years before the Christian era, Crete was the seat of a great sea power that ruled the Aegean, the Adriatic, and the Mediterranean. Then came the Phoenicians, the Persians, and the Greeks. Herodotus, the Greek historian, gave us the oldest written account of one of the first great naval battles when he described how Xerxes' attacking armada was defeated by the defending forces of the Greek states off Salamis in the Aegean in 480 B.C.

The pace of developments was slow for many centuries. Admiral Yi Sun-sin of Korea was the first sea lord to build armored vessels, the so-called "tortoise" ships, with which he defeated the invading Japanese fleet in 1592. From behind iron plates, the Korean sailors shot flaming arrows into the unprotected wooden ships of the Japanese. The explosive shell was not invented until 1819.

The coming of steam in the last century caused a revision of naval strategy. But the last six decades have brought the most revolutionary changes — perhaps they mark the passing of an era.

In two world wars the naval campaigns have become not only battles on the surface of the sea, but in the green depths below and the blue skies above. Now, with the advent of nuclear power, and of missiles capable of mass destruction that can be fired five thousand miles with a considerable degree of accuracy, old concepts of attack and defense must be radically revised. They are in that stage now.

This book is an attempt to tell, in word and photograph and map, the course and development of modern naval warfare through two-thirds of a century — from the Battle of Manila Bay to what probably was the last great surface action of sea warfare, the engagement between the Japanese and the United States fleets off the island of Leyte in the Philippines in October, 1944. And also to have a look at what lies ahead.

So far as the authors have been able to determine, this is the first time that photograph and text have been matched in this fashion to present a connected picture of the era of modern naval warfare. Some of the photographs, it is believed, have not been published in this country before.

The seas probably will remain one of the great avenues of communication despite the advances in aviation. But they no longer are the barrier between nations and continents that they once were, and their control no longer lies with the Admiralty that has the better battleships and captains. It is a great era that is passing. This book is an attempt to present the record of its great moments.

Foster Hailey
Milton Lancelot

New York, March 30, 1964

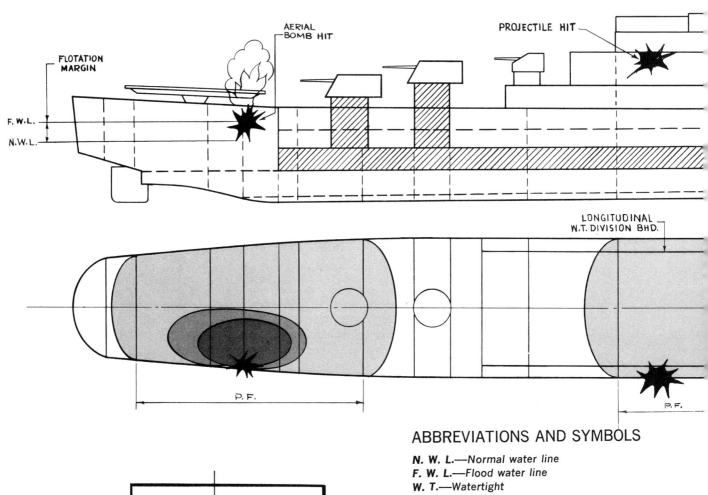
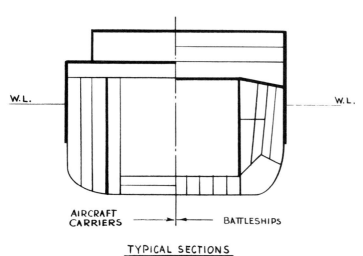

FLOTATION MARGIN

AERIAL BOMB HIT

PROJECTILE HIT

F. W. L.

N.W. L.

LONGITUDINAL W.T. DIVISION BHD.

P. F.

P. F.

W. L.

W. L.

AIRCRAFT CARRIERS

BATTLESHIPS

TYPICAL SECTIONS

ABBREVIATIONS AND SYMBOLS

N. W. L.—*Normal water line*
F. W. L.—*Flood water line*
W. T.—*Watertight*
BHD.—*Bulkhead*
T. F.—*Total flooding*
P. F.—*Partial flooding*
ARMOR—*Cross-sectional*
      —*Profile*

HIT

AREA OF HEAVY DAMAGE

AREA OF MINOR DAMAGE

AREA OF DAMAGE CONTROL ACTION

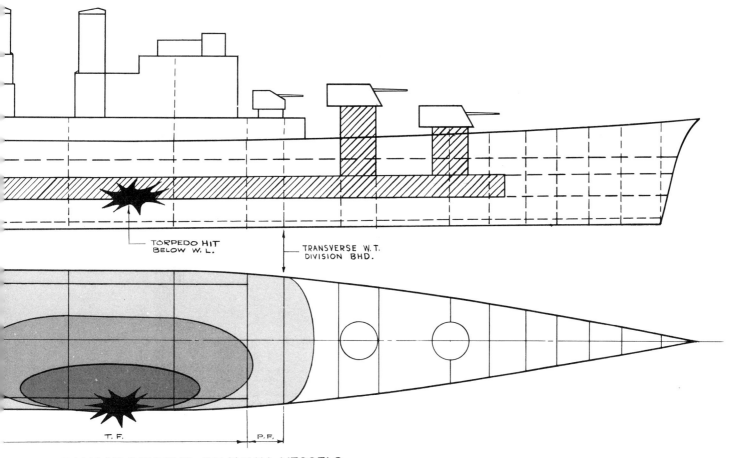

TORPEDO HIT
BELOW W. L.

TRANSVERSE W. T.
DIVISION BHD.

T. F.   P. F.

DAMAGE CONTROL ON NAVAL VESSELS

PROBLEMS IN DESIGN

Armorplating for the protection of vital parts of the ship.
Water-tight compartmentation, transverse and longitudinal,
for the purpose of confining flooding.
Flotation margins to keep ship afloat with flooded compartments—to keep ship on an even keel by flooding opposite
compartments.
Pumping facilities to reduce flooding.
Fire zoning to confine and to prevent the spread of fires.
Fire-fighting facilities.
Facilities for necessary immediate repairs.

EDUCATION OF SHIP'S COMPLEMENT

Extensive training of each individual in specific assignment in
damage control.
Isolating damaged compartments by means of closures.
Making immediate repairs such as shoring, plugging, welding,
etc.
Pumping flooded compartments, fire fighting, and restricting
the spread of fires.

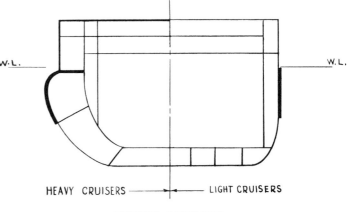

W. L.   W. L.

HEAVY CRUISERS   LIGHT CRUISERS

TYPICAL SECTIONS

Log of U. S. Steamer "Monitor" Lieut. J. L. Worden Comdg

Sunday March 9/62

Comes in fine weather & calm
At ½ past One piped all to quarters, hove up
Anchor, At 2 A.M came to Anchor again

Geo Frederickson

4 to 8 P.M fine weather & calm, at Sunrise saw
3 Steamers lying under Sewals Point, Made one
out to be the Rebel steamer Merrimac, At 1,20
got underweigh & stood towards her & piped all
hands to quarters,

J. Weber

From 8 to Meridian fine clear weather, the Rebel
Steamers advancing & opened fire on the Minnesota
8.20 opened fire on the Merrimac, from that time
until 12, constantly engaged, with the Merrimac

Louis Stodder

From Meridian to 4 P.M. clear weather.
At 12,30 rifled shell struck the Pilot House severely
injuring Commander Worden 1 P.M the
Merrimac hauled off in a disabled condition,
Stood towards the "Minnesota" & received on board
Asst See Fox of the navy. 2 P.M Capt Worden
left for Fort Monroe in charge of Surgeon Logue.

Geo. Frederickson

4 to 6 P.M fine weather. I came to Anchor
alongside the "Minnesota." J. Weber

6 to 8 fine clear weather, sharp lookout kept.

Louis Stodder

8 to 12 weather the same " " " "
10 P.M. Lieut Edwin Flye joined the vessel
as Extra Officer

Geo. Frederickson

Log of the **Monitor** engaging **Merrimac**—Hampton Roads—
9 March 1862.

ACKNOWLEDGMENTS

The authors wish to express their deep appreciation to the following individuals and organizations for their kind assistance in the preparation of this book:

Rear Admiral Ernest M. Eller USN (Ret.) for his advice and permission to use diagrams from the fifteen-volume *History of United States Naval Operations in World War II* by Rear Admiral Samuel Eliot Morison USNR (Ret.) as bases from which to have our modified maps drawn.

Commander Hardy Glenn USN

Lieutenant David Malone USNR

Lieutenant (J.G.) Richard H. Webber USNR

Charlene Lightfoot, Journalist First Class USN

Mr. John Conrad for his diagram on fire and damage control.

Mr. J. F. Golding, Photographic Librarian of the Imperial War Museum, London, England

Mr. Donald Martin, United States Navy Department of Naval History

Mr. William Von Bergen

Mr. Paul White, Audio Visual Division of The National Archives, Washington, D. C.

Australian News and Information Bureau

British Information Service

Brown Brothers, Inc.

European Picture Service

The Imperial War Museum

The Litho Art Corporation, New York, for color positives used in lithographing the jacket from a transparency supplied by the United States Navy.

The National Archives

Netherlands Information Bureau

The Royal Canadian Navy

Charles Scribner's Sons, for permission to adapt maps from *Military History of the World War* (Copyright 1937 Charles Scribner's Sons) by Girard Lindsley McEntee as bases for our diagrams.

United States Air Force

United States Army

United States Army Signal Corps

United States Coast Guard

United States Marine Corps

United States Navy

Wide World, Inc.

NAVPERS-134 (REV. 1-44)   DECK LOG—REMARKS SHEET

UNITED STATES SHIP   LAFFEY (DD724)   Monday   16   April   , 19 45
                                              (Day)   (Date)   (Month)

0 to 4   Steaming on base course 315°t and pgc, 321° psc at 12 knots patrolling
on NW-SE line in Radar Picket Station #1, bearing 002°t, 40 miles from Point Bolo,
Okinawa Jima, Nausei Shoto under boilers #1 and #3. Ship is darkened. Readiness
condition II, material condition "B" set.

                                    S. M. Humphries
                                    S. M. Humphries, Lt. USNR

4 to 8   Steaming as before. 0420 Unidentified aircraft reported; went to General
Quarters. 0455 Lighted fires under boilers #2 and #4. 0508 Cut in boilers #2 and
#4 on main steam line. 0630 Proceeding to day radar picket station. 0710 On sta-
tion. 0744 Commenced firing on enemy aircraft bearing 340°t, distance 11,400 yards.
0747 Ceased firing; enemy aircraft out of effective gunfire range.

                                    G. A. "G" Parolini
                                    G. A. "G" Parolini, Lt.(jg) USN

8 to 12   Steaming as before. Mustered crew on stations; no absentees. 0808
Commenced maneuvering on various courses at various speeds. 0820 Many bandits
closing from general northerly bearing. 0827 Under heavy enemy suicide plane and
five bombing attacks; commenced firing. 0946 Enemy air attack terminated having
been hit by eight suicide planes and four bombs. No steering control due to
rudder being jammed hard left as result of a bomb hit about 0900. 1000 Lying to
awaiting assistance of tugs from Okinawa Jima. (For further information on enemy
air attack, material, and personnel casualties, refer to U.S.S. LAFFEY Action
Report Serial 023 of 29 April 1945.

                                    E. G. Saenz
                                    E. G. Saenz, Lt.(jg) USNR

12 to 16   Steaming as before. 1245 Taken in tow by U.S.S. MACOMB (DMS23). 1345
Cast off tow from U.S.S. MACOMB. 1450 Taken in tow by U.S.S. TAKANA (ATF108) from
ahead using 45 fathoms of LAFFEY's starboard anchor chain proceeding to Okinawa
Jima at about 7 knots. 1450 U.S.S. P.C.E. 851 alongside to starboard. The
following named men were transferred to the U.S.S. P.C.E. 851 for further transfer
to hospitalization:

Name	Service No.	Rate	Branch
BAHME, Jay (n)	267891	Lt. (jg)	USNR (CD)L
SAMP, Edward Joseph Jr.	126521	Lieut.	USNR (D)L
ANDERSON, Mark Gustave	707 50 04	S1c	USNR V6
BALLENGER, Jack Arnold	894 12 52	F1c	USNR SV6
BELL, James Paul	651 55 98	S1c (TM)	USNR V6
BUSSERT, Karl Elsworth	279 99 24	S1c	USN
CARTER, Donald (n)	306 30 39	S1c	USNR V6
EARNST, Jack "O"	342 37 85	TM1c(T)	USN
FERN, Thomas Bernard	825 17 38	S1c	USNR SV6
FAGINSKI, Raymond Henry	666 51 32	Cox(T)	USNR V6
HANSEN, Raymond Andrew	639 43 87	TM2c	USNR V6
JOHNSON, Merle Ray	360 63 85	S2c	USN
LE FEVRE, Walter Thomas	274 46 29	S1c	USN
LILLER, John Francis Jr.	708 37 83	Y3c(T)	USNR V6
MIGUES, Joseph Clestant	644 71 38	Cox	USNR V6
NEWELL, Francis Patrick	650 69 83	Cox(T)	USNR V6
O'SHAUGHNESSY, William John Jr.	707 74 00	S1c	USNR V6
PERRY, Joseph Carvalho	802 61 68	S1c	USNR SV6
PURRICK, Theodore Franklin	706 98 54	SM3c	USNR V6
REMSEN, Herbert Birchell	708 12 57	Cox(T)	USNR V6
RING, Edward Lee Jr.	636 37 23	QM2c	USNR V6
ROBERTSON, Marvin Ganson	930 92 88	S1c	USNR SV6
ROBERTSON, Shirley Dalton	835 62 66	S1c	USNR SV6
ROOKER, Burnard Lee	893 94 74	S1c	USNR SV6
RORIE, Walter (n)	931 87 78	S1c	USNR SV6
ROSANIA, Paul (n)	712 30 43	S2c	USNR V6
SCOTT, Claude Eugene	342 26 79	CEM(AA)(T)	USN
WATERS, Earl Eldridge	876 63 77	PhM3c(T)	USNR SV6
WEISS, Daniel (n)	800 82 56	S1c	USNR SV6
WEISSINGER, George Norbert	805 37 12	S2c(FC)	USNR SV6
WILLIAMS, Richard (n)	818 13 79	MaM3c(T)	USNR SV6
WILSON, Roscoe Simon	844 56 89	StM1c	USNR SV6
ZUPON, Philip Michael	329 07 73	GM1c	USN

APPROVED: EXAMINED:

F. J. Becton   T. W. Runk
F. J. BECTON, Comdr. U.S.N. COMMANDING.   T. W. RUNK, Lieut.   U.S.N.R. NAVIGATOR

TO BE FORWARDED DIRECT TO THE BUREAU OF NAVAL PERSONNEL AT THE END OF EACH MONTH

U.S. GOVERNMENT PRINTING OFFICE 1944 O 617808

Log of Laffey engaging Japanese aircraft off Okinawa—16 April 1945.

CONTENTS

FOREWORD 7

1/ AN ERA 1898 - 1964 13

2/ CONTRAST 1944 AND 1898 29 The Battle of Leyte Gulf and the Battle of Manila Bay

3/ THE BATTLE OF SANTIAGO - 1898 61

4/ THE RUSSO-JAPANESE WAR - 1904 71 Early phases, the Battle of the Tenth of August, the Battle of Tsu Shima Strait

5/ THREE NEW NAVAL POWERS - 1900 81

6/ EARLY PHASES OF WORLD WAR I 87 The Battle of Coronel, the Battle of the Falkland Islands, the Battle of Helgoland, the Battle of the Dogger Bank

7/ THE BATTLE OF JUTLAND - 1916 95

8/ WAR UNDERSEA 1914 - 1918 111

9/ UNITED STATES IN WORLD WAR I 119 Anti-submarine warfare, convoy duty, mine-laying activities, surrender of the German Navy

10/ DISARMAMENT AND REBUILDING 129

11/ ADVENT OF AIR POWER - 1910 137 Early uses of the airplane, its work in World War I, Brigadier General William Mitchell's bombing tests, battleships as air targets, the types of naval planes, development of the aircraft carrier

12/ ENGLAND'S LIFE LINES 1939 - 1941 147 The German Raiders, the action with the *Graf Spee*, the *Scharnhorst* and *Gneisenau* raids, the chase of the *Bismarck*

13/ NORWAY AND DUNKIRK 157 Early engagements off Norway, the battles in the Narvik fjords, the *Glorious* and the German battleships, the evacuation of Dunkirk

14/ ACTION IN THE MEDITERRANEAN 167 The engagement at Oran, the air raid on Taranto, German bombing of British fleet units, the Battle of Cape Matapan, actions off Crete, surrender of the Italian fleet

15/ PEARL HARBOR 177

16/ EARLY RAIDS IN THE PACIFIC 185 The Marshall and Gilbert Islands, Wake and Makin Islands, Rabaul, Lae and Salamaua, the sinking of *Prince of Wales* and *Repulse* off Malaya, Badung Strait, the Battle of the Java Sea, American submarine warfare

17/ THE CORAL SEA AND MIDWAY 199 Japanese advances to the Solomons and American strategy to halt them, the Battle of the Coral Sea, the Battle of Midway, the Battle of the Komandorski Islands

18/ BATTLE FOR A FOOTHOLD 1942 - 1943 209 The Solomon Islands, Guadalcanal, Tulagi, the Battle of Savo Island, the Battle of the Eastern Solomons, the Battle of Cape Esperance, the Battle of Santa Cruz, the Battle of Guadalcanal

19/ WAR IN THE ATLANTIC 1941 - 1943 219 German submarine actions, Allied countermeasures, the sinking of *Scharnhorst*

20/ NORTH AFRICAN LANDINGS - 1943 229 The campaign to secure North Africa, the invasion of Sicily, Salerno and Anzio

21/ NORMANDY AND SOUTHERN FRANCE 239 Sea and air bombardment of the French coast, the establishment of the beachheads, assault and consolidation, the attack on Southern France

22/ ISLAND BARRIERS DOWN 257 The Marianas, the Battle of the Philippine Sea, Saipan, Tinian and Guam

23/ TO TOKYO BAY 269 The Iwo Jima and Okinawa Campaigns, the *kamikaze* suicide plane attacks, the last sortie of *Yamato*, the bombardment of the Japanese islands, Hiroshima and Nagasaki, the surrender of Japan

24/ TOMORROW AND TOMORROW 297

INDEX 307

AN ERA 1898-1964

When the United States Third Fleet sailed into the Philippines in September 1944 to begin the softening-up carrier blows that were followed by the Leyte landings and the subsequent great sea battles, United States sea power was keeping a rendezvous with destiny. For it was in Manila Bay, on May 1, 1898, that the United States Navy asserted itself as a major world force and fought the first battle of modern naval warfare. The difference between the forces that fought the "First Battle of the Philippines" and the Second is an index of the changes that have come through the years.

In 1898 the biggest Navy ship afloat displaced not more than fifteen thousand tons. The biggest gun was 13.5 inches. Effective range was only a few thousand yards. Reports of target practice of those days show little effective hitting beyond three thousand yards, which is only one and one-half sea miles. Many ships still were armed with muzzle-loading guns. Sometimes powder smoke blinded the men operating the batteries for several minutes. Coal smoke was even worse, and although

14 the Russians at that time were equipping some of their ships with oil-burning boilers, the principal fuel used was still coal. Theoretical speeds of as high as twenty-one knots were claimed, but in actual practice the speed was considerably below that, as bottoms fouled quickly. The cruising range of all ships was limited. One thing that made the British Navy strong was its string of coaling stations around the world.

Under Fleet Admiral William F. Halsey's command in the Second Battle of the Philippines were thirty-five-thousand-ton and forty-five-thousand-ton battleships, each with nine sixteen-inch guns that could score accurately on a target thirty-five-thousand to forty-thousand yards away. The Japanese had two even larger and more heavily armed — the sixty-four-thousand-ton *Yamato* and *Musashi*, each carrying nine eighteen-inch naval rifles. The high-pressure oil boilers and high-speed propulsion machinery of these modern dreadnoughts could turn out revolutions resulting in speed of better than thirty knots. More importantly, they were accompanied by aircraft carriers from whose decks patrols flew day and night to make reconnaissance of the seas for three-hundred miles in all directions. These planes could fight as

The slugger—to deal out great punishment and to absorb it—the battleship.

1893, **Oregon,** *United States: 10,288 tons; length 351', beam 69', draught 27'; armament four 13'', eight 8'' guns; hp. 11,110; speed 16.8 knots; complement 473.*

1912, **Iron Duke,** *Great Britain: 25,000 tons; length 623', beam 89'6'', draught 27'6''; armament ten 13'', twelve 6'' guns; hp. 29,000; speed 21 knots; complement 930.*

1942, **New Jersey,** *United States: 45,000 tons; length 887', beam 108', draught 36'; armament nine 16'', twenty 5'' guns; hp. 200,000; speed 30 knots plus; complement 2,700.*

well as scout; the "hitting range" of a battle fleet had been increased from the 3,000 yards of 1898 to 250–300 miles. With fair accuracy at that distance, each air group of sixty to seventy planes could deliver a load of destruction equal to seven or eight broadsides of a battleship. Ahead of the fleet moved a scouting line of submarines, of which there had been none in Commodore Dewey's day, to report on the enemy's fleet movements and to attack if the opportunity was given. The twenty-one-hundred-ton and twenty-two-hundred-ton destroyers of World War II with their five-inch guns, could almost outfight the armored cruisers Dewey had commanded.

The fleet Admiral Halsey led off the Philippines in October 1944 could sail, maneuver, and fight in any kind of weather, day or night. Visual contact no longer was needed in naval actions. Radar penetrates fog and rain and darkness without hindrance. Had the British Grand Fleet and the German High Seas Fleet at the Battle of Jutland, in May, 1916, been equipped as were the ships of the United States Third Fleet, that great surface action would probably have been fought to a more conclusive decision.

The defeated commander today cannot plead that the sun or the visibility was in the enemy's

Flight—and the sea arches its power into the skies, widening the striking range and the eyes of the fleets below—the carrier.

*1922, **Langley,** United States: 11,050 tons; length 542', beam 65'5", draught 16'7"; armament four 5" guns, fifty-five planes; hp. 7,000; speed 15 knots; complement 300.*

*1925, **Saratoga,** United States: 33,000 tons; length 909'5", beam 105'6", draught 32'; armament sixteen 5" guns, ninety planes; hp. 180,000; speed 33.9 knots; complement 2,500 plus.*

*1945, **Midway,** United States: 45,000 tons; length 986', beam 136', draught 36'; armament eighteen 5" guns, one hundred plus planes; hp. 200,000; speed 33 knots plus; complement 3,000 plus.*

*1961, **Enterprise,** United States: 75,700 tons; length 1,040', beam 133', draught 37'; armament two twin Terrier missile launchers, one hundred planes; nuclear hp. 300,000 plus; speed over 35 knots; complement 4,600.*

17

18 favor. They no longer are important. In some of the battles fought in World War II, ships were hit with opening salvos before they even knew a hostile ship or squadron was within a hundred miles of them. In World War II, weather played a part primarily only in plane operation.

The pace of modern warfare had increased far beyond the speed of the ships. Automatic calculators in a fraction of a second solved gunnery problems that would have required twenty-four hours for a mathematician with a slide rule. Sixteen-inch guns could be fired more rapidly than the so-called quick-firing 6-inch batteries of the United States and Spanish fleets of 1898. The penetrating power of shells and their destructiveness had been increased many times. But defensive armament had also been improved. Armor-plate steel a half inch thick in 1944 could turn a shell or bullet that would have penetrated a plate of much greater thickness only twenty years before.

The political implications of naval and fleet developments since 1898 have been even greater than the technical revolution in ship design and the changes in tactics and strategy brought about by the airplane. Britain had to surrender to a friend — the United States — what she never did

Hybrid — speed with heavy striking power, soft over the vitals to save weight—the battle cruiser.

*1908, **Inflexible,** Great Britain: 17,250 tons; length 530', beam 78'6'', draught 26'; armament eight 12'', sixteen 4'' guns; hp. 41,000; speed 26 knots; complement 780.*

*1911, **Von der Tann,** Germany: 18,700 tons; length 561', beam 87', draught 26'6''; armament eight 11'', ten 5'' guns; hp. 71,500; speed 27.6 knots; complement 910.*

*1943, **Alaska,** United States: 27,500 tons; length 808'6'', beam 89'6''; armament nine 12'', twelve 5'' guns; hp. 150,000; speed 30 knots plus; complement 1,500 plus.*

to an enemy — supremacy of the seas. The other two powers that challenged Britain in the first half of the century never were able to come closer than several thousand tons. First it was Germany. Under Kaiser Wilhelm II, who came to the throne in 1888, Germany began a naval race with Britain that, just prior to the First World War, made Germany the second naval power of the world. That fleet was scuttled at Scapa Flow. Then came Japan. In the Russo-Japanese War of 1904–1905, Japan demonstrated, to the satisfaction of her people, that she could challenge the great sea powers of that time.

After the First World War, Japan submitted with poor grace to the 5-5-3 naval ratio with Great Britain and the United States that had been set by the 1921–1922 Washington Disarmament Conference. In 1934 she renounced that agreement and began an accelerated naval building program. By December 7, 1941, she was the world's second naval power, or near it. After ten thirty that morning, when her air attack had put the United States Navy's Pacific Fleet battle line of eight ships out of action, there was no question about it. Three and a half years later the Japanese fleet was only a remnant of unorganized and battered vessels.

Fast fighter — implementing the dreadnought, heading a raiding force, fighting a rugged round—the heavy cruiser.

1892, **Olympia,** United States: 5,800 tons; length 344'1", beam 53', draught 21'6"; armament four 8", ten 5" guns; hp. 17,363; speed 21.7 knots; complement 412.

1909, **Blücher,** Germany: 15,500 tons; length 493', beam 80'4", draught 27'; armament twelve 8.2", eight 6" guns; hp. 32,000; speed 24.5 knots; complement 850.

1943, **Baltimore,** United States: 13,600 tons; length 673'5", beam 69'9", draught 26'; armament nine 8", twelve 5" guns; hp. 120,000; speed 30 knots plus; complement 1,500 plus.

1961, **Long Beach,** United States: 14,200 tons; length 721', beam 73', draught 28'; armament one Regulus launcher, one twin Talos launcher, two advance twin Terrier launchers and one Asroc launcher, two 5" guns; nuclear hp. 80,000; speed 35 knots plus; complement 1,160.

The progress of the United States toward dominance of the seas has been by fits and starts. Until the 1880's, we relied largely on foreign shipyards for ship design and on foreign gunsmiths for arms and armament. During the Civil War, the United States had built up a small shipbuilding and gun-manufacturing industry, but most of the vessels that gave us a claimed parity with Britain at that time had been purchased. In 1875 the United States started to build its own ships, but we still had to go to Europe for design, armament, and guns. In 1887 the Bethlehem Iron Company, as it was called then, was given a contract for armor plate and naval rifles. The United States had begun to build up the building capacity that in 1945 made it the world's greatest sea power.

Captain Alfred T. Mahan's writings on sea power — of which the best known is *The Influence of Sea Power Upon History*, first published in 1890 — and the Spanish-American War gave this trend toward naval thinking the stimulus it needed. The war of 1898 did more even than that. It made the United States a colonial power. It had entered the war primarily to free the persecuted people of Cuba from oppression and to assert on this continent the primacy in the Western Hemisphere that

The screener—maneuver is her forte—running, attacking, running and attacking again—jack of all trades—the light cruiser.

1892, **Raleigh,** *United States: 3,213 tons; length 300', beam 42', draught 19'; armament one 6'', ten 5'' guns; hp. 10,000; speed 19 knots, complement 314.*

1910, **Gloucester,** *Great Britain: 4,800 tons; length 430', beam 47', draught 15'3''; armament two 6'', ten 4'' guns; hp. 23,700; speed 26 knots; complement 376.*

1943, **Birmingham,** *United States: 10,000 tons; length 608'4'', beam 63', draught 20'; armament twelve 6'', twelve 5'' guns; hp. 100,000; speed 33 knots; complement 1,200.*

1960, **Oklahoma City,** *United States: Guided Missile Cruiser; 10,670 tons; length 610', beam 66', draught 25'; armament one twin Talos launcher, anti-submarine warfare torpedo launchers, three 6'', two 5'' guns; hp. 100,000; speed 35 knots; complement 1,400.*

24 | President Monroe had stated sixty-five years before. It came out of the war possessors of Puerto Rico, the Philippines, and Guam. One of the arguments of the proponents of a large navy since 1898 had been the necessity of protecting the possessions gained almost by accident in the war with Spain. United States entry into the affairs of the western Pacific also brought it into close contact with Japan. The former "splendid isolation" from the rest of the world had become only a myth.

The course steered from Manila to Manila and the world's greatest navy was not a straight one. Under the drive of President Theodore Roosevelt, the United States between 1898 and 1906 rose from one of the "also-rans" to the second-greatest navy in the world. Even then the British Navy still was twice as powerful as that of the United States or any other country. At that time the two closest were the United States and Germany. With her continental allies, France and Russia, Britain held an even greater margin of superiority. In the Pacific she had signed an alliance with Japan.

During World War I and the two years immediately following, the United States gained ground rapidly. At the Washington Disarmament Conference of 1921–22, Lord Balfour agreed to parity in

Speed, her greatest weapon—she scouts, convoys, fights, rescues—does a score of tough jobs—the destroyer.

*1896, **Furor,** Spain: 300 tons; length 220', beam 22', draught 5'6"; armament two 12-pounders, two T. Tubes; hp. 6,000; speed 28 knots; complement 67.*

*1920, **Peary,** United States: 1,193 tons; length 310', beam 30', draught 9'3"; armament four 4", twelve 21" T. Tubes; hp. 26,000; speed 35 knots; complement 122.*

*1942, **Nicholas,** United States: 2,050 tons; length 376'6", beam 39'4", draught 18'; armament five 5", ten 21" T. Tubes; hp. 60,000; speed 35 knots plus; complement 300 plus.*

*1962, **Bainbridge,** United States: 7,600 tons; length 564', beam 56', draught 20'; armament one Azroc launcher, two advance Terrier launchers, four 3" guns; nuclear hp. 60,000; speed 35 knots plus; complement 500.*

Endless patrol—a feathery wake, a silent torpedo—the submarine.

1912, **Deutschland,** Germany: 1,700 tons; length 211', beam 29', draught 15'; armament one 5.9'' gun, four T. Tubes; speed 7-9 knots submerged; complement 75.

1938, **Salmon,** United States: 2,198 tons; length 308', beam 26', draught 14'3''; armament one 3'' gun, eight 21'' T. Tubes; hp. 1,600; speed 9 knots submerged; complement 82.

26|

1962, **John Marshall,** United States: 8,000 tons; length 410', beam 34', draught 30'8''; armament four 21'' T. Tubes, sixteen Polaris missile Tubes, nuclear-powered; speed 35 knots submerged; complement 110.

1910, **Salmon D3,** United States: 340 tons; armament two T. Tubes; speed 6 knots submerged; complement 15.

27

big ships with the United States. Later, Prime Minister Ramsay MacDonald extended that to parity to all branches. It was, however, only a paper parity. After sinking, scrapping, or converting most of its modern hulls between 1922 and 1924, the United States did not begin to build to treaty limits until the election of President Franklin D. Roosevelt in 1932 and the passage of the Vinson-Trammel Bill of 1933. It was not until many months after the Japanese attack at Pearl Harbor that parity finally was attained.

World War II saw the United States engaged in the greatest sea campaign of all time. Losses of men and ships during the three and three-quarter years were far beyond those of all United States naval history, from John Paul Jones and the *Bonhomme Richard's* successful fight with the *Serapis* off the English coast in 1779 to December 7, 1941.

Despite its losses, the United States increased its numerical strength in combatant ships five times beyond that of 1941, and by a much greater margin in fighting power. Construction was at a pace that Britain's bomb-damaged shipyards could not match. For good or ill, the United States has within its power the ability to retain indefinitely the sea supremacy it now holds.

Latest technological developments and the introduction of nuclear power have outmoded many of the ships and weapons that give the United States supremacy. But Soviet Russia seems the only real threat to United States leadership.

One thing seems sure. The development of the nuclear-powered submarine and guided missiles makes unlikely any more such surface engagements as the First Manila Bay, the Battle of Jutland, and the Second Battle of the Philippines. Advances in the taming of the weather by the airplane and new detection methods make it highly improbable that surface vessels ever again will be able to steam within big-gun range of each other. The Second Battle of the Philippines marked the closing of an era of modern naval warfare. In the submarine, the airplane, and the radio-controlled ballistic missiles lies the answer to the future of the war at sea.

Yamato *under aerial attack in Tablas Strait.*

CONTRAST 1944 AND 1898

Leyte Gulf - 1944

High over the steaming reaches of the Sibuyan Sea a young American flier in his carrier-borne plane droned along through the cold, clear atmosphere of the upper altitudes the morning of October 24, 1944. His eyes were sweeping the wastes of the ocean under him and the horizon ahead for the betraying smoke ribbon, white bow wave, or streaming wake that would first betray the approaching Japanese fleet for which he was looking.

It was more than a routine dawn patrol. He expected to find something. Before dawn the day before, the American submarines *Darter* and *Dace,* hunting together, had sighted and attacked strong Japanese surface forces steaming northward from the Japanese fleet anchorage of Lingga Roads near Singapore. (*Darter* had sunk the heavy cruiser *Atago,* flagship of the force commander, and heavily damaged the heavy cruiser *Takao; Dace* had sunk the heavy cruiser *Maya.*) It appeared from this contact, and an earlier one of one of our submarines with a Japanese cruiser force, that the Combined Japanese Fleet was gathering to slug it out with the United States Seventh and Third

Fleets covering the landing on Leyte of General MacArthur's Sixth Army, which had hit the beaches on October 20, four days before. It was an engagement eagerly awaited by the American commanders.

At 7:46 A.M., young Lieutenant Max Adams saw what he was looking for, the battleship force *Darter* and *Dace* had attacked. He sent in his contact report, and his mates went into action.

Since the first six months of the Solomons Campaign, the Japanese Admiralty had sent out its fleets in force only once to challenge the Allied advances through the South and Central Pacific toward the inner defense ring around the home islands. On that occasion, four months before, during the early days of the invasion of Saipan, in the Marianas, the Japanese had taken a licking from American carrier groups and submarines. On the first day of that battle, which was fought only at long air range, American fliers shot down one-half of the enemy's air groups — 280 planes — with minor losses of their own. American fliers called it "The Marianas Turkey Shoot." The poorly trained Japanese fliers had been no match.

That same day, the American submarines *Albacore* and *Cuvalla* located the enemy's carrier force and sank two carriers, *Taiho* and *Shokaku*.

The next day, June 20, the American carrier pilots caught the now lightly-protected Japanese fleet units while they were preparing to refuel, sank the carrier *Hiyo* and one tanker, damaged another carrier and two fleet oilers, and strafed many other vessels. Now the Japanese were coming out with all they had left for the showdown fight.

As the sun crossed the yardarm the afternoon of October 24 and started down toward its setting west of the Philippines, the clouded picture on the chart tables of the American admirals came into focus. In addition to the force sighted in the Sibuyan Sea by Lieutenant Adams, another smaller force of enemy surface vessels was to the southward in the Sulu Sea. The two forces were steaming northeastward toward the two passages through the Philippine Islands that would take them into the Pacific and into contact with our invasion fleet off Leyte. (Uncontacted, but also west of Leyte, was still another cruiser force.) To the northeast of Luzon, coming south from the Combined Fleet's home base at Kure on the Inland Sea, was a carrier-battleship force, built around four carriers and two battleship-carriers. In the enemy units converging on Leyte was practically every major combatant ship the Japanese still had in battle condition.

30 | *Cause for naval action—U.S. troops plunge to Leyte. The Japanese fleets must destroy the American navy and cut their supply lines to halt the invasion.*

The United States Pacific Fleet was there in its Sunday suit. In the Third and Seventh Fleets maneuvering east of Leyte were most of the major Pacific Fleet units.

East and north of Samar and Luzon were three fast carrier task groups of the Third Fleet. A fourth group was headed for a refueling rendezvous near Ulithi. These carrier groups were composed of carriers of the *Essex* (twenty-five thousand tons) and *Independence* (ten thousand tons) classes. They were escorted by the newest battleships, cruisers, and destroyers, under the command of Admiral (later Fleet Admiral) William F. Halsey, Jr., the United States Navy's most daring naval tactician.

To the south of the Third Fleet, providing the air and surface protection and bombardment for the Leyte operations, was the Seventh Fleet under Vice Admiral Thomas C. Kinkaid. It included 157 combatant vessels — the older, slower battleships such as *West Virginia* and *Pennsylvania*, of sixteen-inch and fourteen-inch gun armament, respectively, heavy and light cruisers and destroyers, and three groups of slow escort carriers, ships converted from fleet oilers and similar auxiliary vessels. In Leyte Gulf itself were transports, supply ships, and landing craft.

This was it. This was the showdown naval battle of the Pacific war. On one side, the world's greatest and finest carrier forces, supported by her best escort ships. On the other, the world's two greatest battleships, armed with eighteen-inch guns, other, older battleships and escort vessels, and a weak carrier force, backed by six-hundred land-based planes.

The Japanese had long before decided that when the United States attack reached the Philippines, they must throw into the battle every resource they had of men, planes, and ships. Ever since Midway they had been fighting a purely defensive war, committing forces only in small groups and taking heavy losses even so. To save the Philippines, they had to put everything into the scales. The loss of the Philippines would cut their empire in two, and especially cripple their navy. If it stayed to the north, it was cut off from the fuel oil of Southeast Asia. If it stayed south, it was cut off from the repair yards, and particularly the ammunition factories, of the home islands.

After the battle off Saipan, generally called "The First Battle of the Philippines," Admiral Toyada, the Japanese Commander-in-Chief, had regrouped his remaining forces and drawn the plans for the defense of the Philippines. It was called the "Sho" operation. On October 17, he

A B-25 Mitchell cuts out a Japanese destroyer doing convoy duty and . . .

31

destroys it.

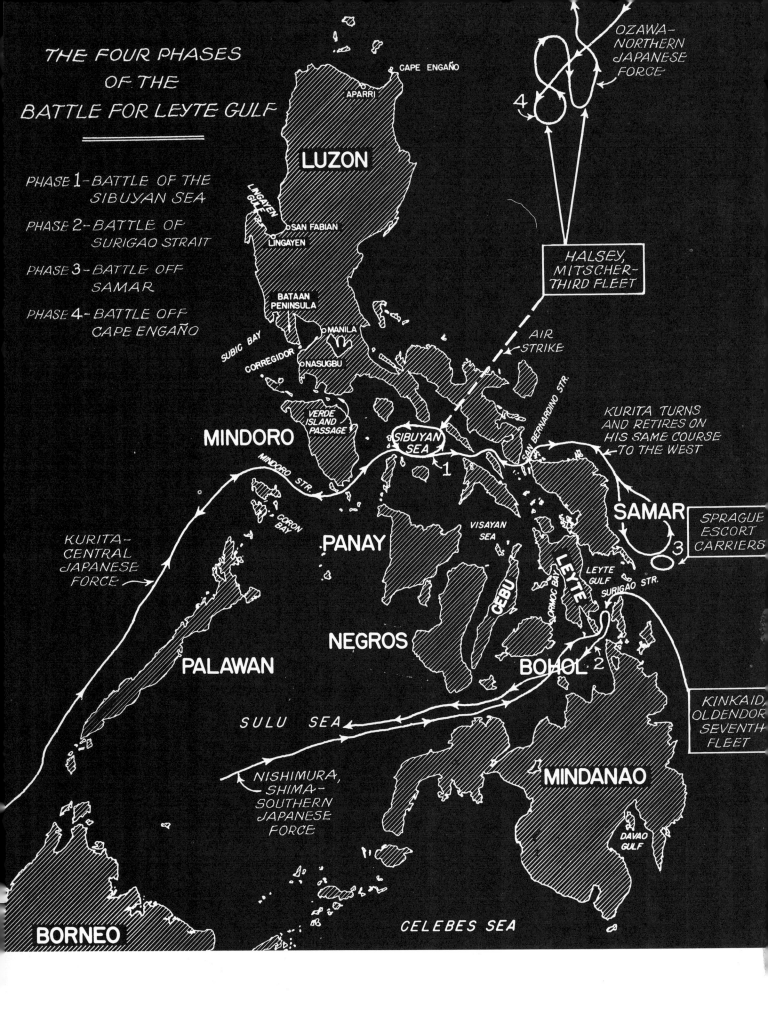

THE FOUR PHASES
OF THE
BATTLE FOR LEYTE GULF

PHASE 1—BATTLE OF THE
SIBUYAN SEA

PHASE 2—BATTLE OF
SURIGAO STRAIT

PHASE 3—BATTLE OFF
SAMAR

PHASE 4—BATTLE OFF
CAPE ENGAÑO

OZAWA—
NORTHERN
JAPANESE
FORCE

CAPE ENGAÑO

APARRI

LUZON

LINGAYEN GULF

SAN FABIAN

LINGAYEN

BATAAN
PENINSULA

SUBIC BAY

MANILA

CORREGIDOR

NASUGBU

VERDE
ISLAND
PASSAGE

MINDORO

MINDORO STR.

CORON
BAY

KURITA—
CENTRAL
JAPANESE
FORCE

PANAY

PALAWAN

NEGROS

SULU SEA

NISHIMURA,
SHIMA—
SOUTHERN
JAPANESE
FORCE

BORNEO

HALSEY,
MITSCHER—
THIRD FLEET

AIR
STRIKE

SIBUYAN
SEA

1

SAN BERNARDINO STR.

KURITA TURNS
AND RETIRES ON
HIS SAME COURSE
TO THE WEST

SAMAR

SPRAGUE
ESCORT
CARRIERS

3

VISAYAN
SEA

CEBU

ORMOC BAY

LEYTE

LEYTE
GULF

SURIGAO
STR.

SURIGAO STR.

BOHOL

2

KINKAID,
OLDENDOR
SEVENTH
FLEET

MINDANAO

DAVAO
GULF

CELEBES SEA

alerted the Combined Fleet. On the day of the American landing at Leyte — October 20 — the Japanese fleet sailed to carry out its orders. In reality, to commit hara-kiri, as most of its high officers later said they soon realized.

The southernmost group of enemy ships, which we can call Force A, was composed of the 29,300-ton fourteen-inch gunned battleships *Fuso* and *Yamashiro*, the heavy cruiser *Mogami*, and four destroyers. Force A was headed for Surigao Strait, a deep-water passage, ten to fifteen miles in width, between the northern tip of Mindanao Island and the smaller islands of Panon and Dinagat, which lie south and southeast, respectively, from Leyte. It was under command of Vice Admiral Shoji Nishimura, like Halsey an old destroyer man and one who believed in night fighting.

Also headed for Surigao Strait was the Fifth Fleet cruiser force of two heavies, one light cruiser, and four destroyers, which had been assigned at the last moment to support the effort to force Surigao Strait. It was under command of Vice Admiral Kiyohide Shima, who was junior to Nishimura in age but senior in rank. This fact apparently played a part in the failure of the latter to keep Shima advised of a change in plans and sent them into the Strait at different hours instead of together, allowing the American forces to engage them separately,

always bad tactics in fleet operations and in this case fatal.

To meet Force A, or perhaps it would be better to designate them A-1 and A-2, Admiral Kinkaid deployed his six old prewar battleships — *West Virginia, Pennsylvania, California, Tennessee, Maryland*, and *Mississippi* — three heavy cruisers, five lights, twenty-one destroyers, and thirty motor torpedo boats. They were deployed, in reverse order, from the western entrance to the Strait to its eastern entry hard by Leyte Gulf.

The central enemy force in the Sibuyan Sea — the one first sighted and attacked by the submarines and then the carrier fliers — let us call Force B. It was under the command of Vice Admiral Takeo Kurita, who was also in over-all command of Forces A-1 and A-2. Force B was headed for San Bernadino Strait, the sea passage between the southern tip of Luzon and the island of Samar. There were five ships in the line. First were the 64,000-ton eighteen-inch gunned *Yamato* and *Musashi*, the most powerful battleships in the world; the United States' biggest were *Iowas* of 52,000 tons, but armed only with sixteen-inch guns. Two of them were with the Third Fleet. Following the two Japanese giants was the 32,700-ton, sixteen-inch gunned *Nagato*, and finally the old but fast and well-tested *Kongo* and *Haruna*, which had

33

Yamashiro and *Fuso* take an aerial pounding in the Sulu Sea.

Musashi goes into evasive action.

been often reported sunk. The battleships — when first sighted by the carrier pilots, after the submarine attack — were accompanied by the heavy cruisers *Chokai, Myoko, Haguro, Kumano, Suzuya, Chikuma* and *Tone,* two light cruisers, and thirteen destroyers. Kurita had his flag on *Yamato* to which he had transferred from the sunken *Atago* the previous evening.

Soon after Force B was sighted by Halsey's fliers, Force A also was picked up. All through October 24, fliers from the Third Fleet's three carrier groups struck at them with bombs, torpedoes, rockets, and machine-gun bullets. The principal strikes were launched at Kurita's main body. With no planes to offer a defense and no assistance forthcoming from land bases, with which communication was poor, the only defense of the Japanese surface vessels was anti-aircraft fire and maneuver.

The planes the United States fliers flew against the Japanese ships that day were the last word in naval aircraft. The fighter pilots were in four-hundred-miles-an-hour Grumman Hellcats, the dive-bomber men in Curtiss Helldivers, the torpedo-plane men in Grumman Avengers. The pilots,

however, were tired. Most of them had been operating for two months in enemy waters, on almost daily strikes or patrols. This pilot fatigue may have been a factor in the attack.

In the absence of carriers, the two new battleships were of course the principal targets. Through the most intensive anti-aircraft fire they had encountered, the Navy pilots poured in to the attack. *Musashi* was the principal target. How many torpedo and bomb hits she received will never be accurately known. Some of her survivors estimated she received at least twenty torpedo hits and probably as many bombs. Whatever the number, the world's greatest battleship was sunk by aerial attack alone. She went down at dusk that night with half of her complement of twenty-four-hundred officers and men.

During the day-long attacks the heavy cruiser *Myoko* also took a torpedo hit and was sent limping toward Manila. *Yamato, Nagato, Kongo* and *Haruna* all took bomb hits as did some of the heavy cruisers and most of the destroyers were strafed by American fighter planes. There were, however, no other torpedo hits — the real killer — on the Japanese ships. And none of them were made un-

*An emperor's pride blows up—**Musashi** never fired her eighteen-inch guns in battle.*

Fateful etching in the Sibuyan Sea — a Japanese ship is pounded.

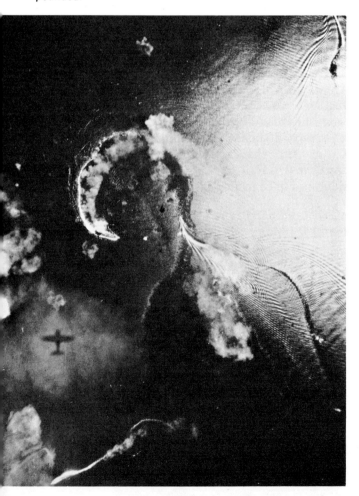

battleworthy, a fact that Admiral Halsey and his staff could hardly credit on the basis of the reports of the returning fliers.

At four hundred miles an hour, or even two hundred miles an hour, in the terrific nervous tension of an attack, it is almost impossible for fliers, any fliers, to correctly evaluate results. It is difficult, too, for a group commander to make his fliers distribute the attack on all targets; the temptation to pick on an already damaged ship and send her down is almost irresistible. It was a trait our commanders had noticed among the Japanese. That is apparently what happened to *Musashi*. Many of the torpedoes that should have been aimed at other ships apparently were dropped at her once she was seen to be in trouble.

During the attacks of late afternoon, Admiral Kurita, without air cover and seeing one of his two major ships badly hurt, reversed his course while yelling for help from the shore-based planes. The last American attacking group sighted him several miles west of the first position and still heading westward away from San Bernadino Strait.

Far to the south, in the Sulu Sea, Admiral Nishimura's Force A also was under air attack but not in such intensity. The captain of the only surviving ship of his force, Commander Shigeru Nishino, of the destroyer *Shigure,* said only the battleship *Fuso,* and his destroyer, were hit by bombs. Neither was slowed, nor was the fighting efficiency of either appreciably impaired. Other ships of the force were only slightly damaged topside by rocket and machine-gun fire in strafing runs.

*A Hellcat takes off as **Princeton** burns.*

While all this was going on west of Leyte, in the Sulu and Sibuyan seas, the United States Third Fleet carrier groups also were under air attack. The light carrier *Princeton* was hit, and after daylong efforts to save her, which resulted in heavy damage to the cruiser *Birmingham* and destroyers who were aiding her own crew in fighting fires, she finally was abandoned in late afternoon and sunk. The decision to sink her came after an air patrol that had been sent to the north in search for what Halsey called the "missing piece in the puzzle" — the Japanese carriers — had found them. The

search was ordered after carrier planes were identified as among the Japanese craft attacking our carriers. The composition of the Northern Force, which can be called Force C, was inaccurately reported at first, but there was little question in the American Admirals' minds that this was Admiral Jisaburo Ozawa's "Main Force," coming down from the Inland Sea for the all-out attack.

Aboard Halsey's flagship *New Jersey,* east of Luzon with the carriers, and aboard Kinkaid's flagship *Wasatch,* in Leyte Gulf, important decisions had to be made. Force A, heading for Surigao

*A bomb penetrates to her stowed torpedoes and **Princeton** explodes.*

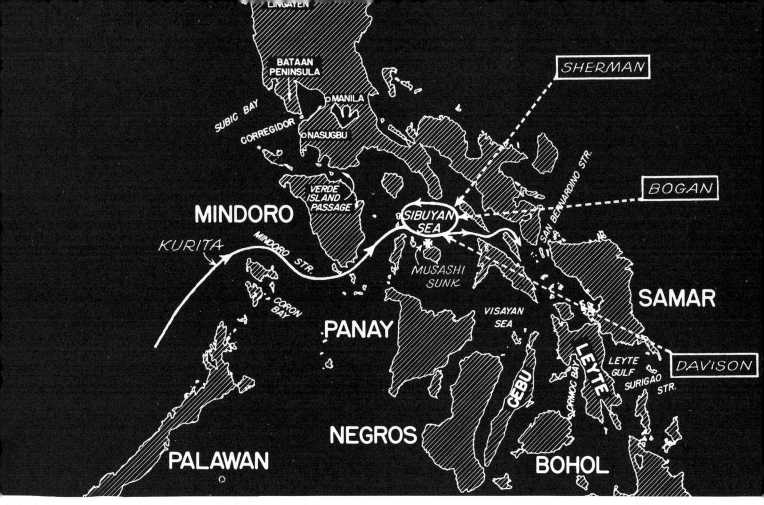

Phase one—the Battle of the Sibuyan Sea.

Victim of accurate dive bombing—a Japanese battleship is damaged.

Strait, was Kinkaid's responsibility. He deployed his forces in the Strait for night battle. Force B, heading for San Bernadino Strait, and Force C, coming down from the north and to the eastward of the Philippines, were Halsey's and the Third Fleet's task to stop. Kinkaid's decision was simple. Halsey's was complex.

As Halsey wrote in January, 1945, three months later, in making his report for the record of the battle, he was faced with three choices: keep his whole force off San Bernadino Strait to protect Leyte Gulf; divide his forces, leaving the battleships off the Gulf and sending his carriers north to attack Force C; take the Third Fleet north to meet and overwhelm Force C. In making his decision, he had the overoptimistic report of his fliers that they had so punished Force B that it could not possibly carry out its mission. This seemed substantiated by the last daylight report that Force B was on a westerly course, with most of its ships in bad shape. The contact report on Force C had identified it as containing both battleships and carriers. Previous code breaks — the so-called "magic" of United States intelligence — also had identified Force C as "Main Force," which it had been but now was not.

"Commander Third Fleet," wrote Halsey in his report, "decided to (a) strike the Northern Force suddenly and in full force; (b) keep all his forces concentrated and (c) trust to his judgment as to the fatally weakened condition of the Center Force — judgment which happily was vindicated by the Japs' inability to deal with the CVE's and small fry which stood toe to toe with them and stopped them in their tracks." This was written, it should be noted, before the war was over and before the Japanese Admirals had been questioned as to the motivation of their decisions and the extent of damage to their ships.

In fact, Halsey did exactly what the Japanese high command wanted him to do, steam north to engage Admiral Ozawa's "Main Force" and clear the way for Admiral Kurita with his battleships to penetrate Leyte Gulf.

Originally, the plan had been for the Japanese forces converging on Leyte to operate as a combined fleet, under their own carrier-based air cover. But the landings coming before they were expected and heavy losses in previous engagements, especially in the air battles in the South China Sea and around Formosa with Halsey's forces that had preceded the Leyte landings, brought a change in plans. Admiral Ozawa's carrier groups had been so weakened that any hope the carriers could play a decisive part were aban-

doned. Ozawa steamed south with the sole objective of luring Halsey away from Leyte Gulf.

"I expected complete destruction of my fleet," Admiral Ozawa told American questioners after the end of the war, "but if Kurita's mission was carried out, that was all I wished."

As darkness enveloped the Philippines and its adjacent waters the night of October 24, this was the situation: Force A-1, attacked by air but not badly hurt, was headed for Surigao Strait. Fifty miles behind it was Force A-2, also headed for the strait. In the Strait waiting for them was the combatant surface force of the Seventh Fleet. The two opposing groups lined up as follows:

Japanese: Battleships — *Fuso, Yamashiro;* Heavy Cruisers—*Mogami, Nachi, Ashigara;* Light Cruisers — *Abukuma;* Destroyers — Eight; PT Boats — None.

U.S. Seventh Fleet: Battleships—*Mississippi, West Virginia, Tennessee, Maryland, California, Pennsylvania;* Heavy Cruisers — *Louisville, Portland, Minneapolis;* Light Cruisers — *Denver, Columbia, Phoenix, Boise, Shropshire* (Australian); Destroyers — Twenty-six; PT Boats — Thirty.

Admiral Kurita's Center Force, or Force B, which had again reversed its course after the last American fliers had left and headed through treacherous San Bernadino Strait in darkness, was opposed only by an unsuspecting United States force of escort carriers, destroyers, and destroyer escorts. The strength was as follows:

Japanese: Battleships — *Yamato, Nagato, Kongo, Haruna;* Carriers — None; Heavy Cruisers — *Chokai, Haguro, Kumano, Suzuya, Chikuma, Tone;* Light Cruisers — *Noshiro, Yahagi;* Destroyers — Ten; Destroyer Escorts — None.

U.S. Seventh Fleet: Battleships — None; Escort Carriers — *Fanshaw Bay, Saint Lo, White Plains, Kalinin Bay, Kitkun Bay, Sangamon, Sewanee, Chennango, Santee, Saginaw Bay, Petrof Bay, Natoma Bay, Manila Bay, Marcus Island, Kadashan Bay, Savo Island, Ommaney Bay;* Heavy Cruisers — None; Light Cruisers — None; Destroyers — Three; Destroyer Escorts — Four.

To the east of Luzon, Halsey was heading northward with the Third Fleet to meet and attack Force C. Their relative strengths were:

Japanese: Carriers — *Zuikaku, Chitose, Chiyoda, Zuiho;* Battleships — *Ise, Hyuga;* Heavy Cruisers — None; Light Cruisers — *Oyodo, Tama, Isuzu;* Destroyers — Ten.

U.S. Third Fleet: Carriers — *Lexington, Essex, Intrepid, Enterprise, Franklin, Langley, Cabot, Independence, San Jacinto, Belleau Wood;* Battleships — *New Jersey, Iowa, Massachusetts,*

One of Oldendorf's old Pearl Harbor "ghosts" — **West Virginia's** guns flash in the Suriago trap.

Washington, South Dakota, Alabama; Heavy Cruisers — *Wichita, New Orleans;* Light Cruisers — *Vincennes, Miami, Biloxi, Santa Fe, Mobile;* Destroyers — Forty.

The stage was set for the greatest sea fight since the Battle of Jutland, twenty-eight years before.

Enemy Force A-1 was the first to be brought to action.

Admiral Nishimura, who had not been in touch with Admiral Shima, steamed into Surigao Strait ahead of schedule shortly after midnight, after successfully beating off two attacks by torpedo boats that Admiral Kinkaid had stationed along the expected route of approach. The moon had gone down, and the strait lay ahead of them dark and silent. Nishimura, however, knew that his intentions must be known. He had his force in column, his four destroyers in the lead, then *Yamashiro,* in which he wore his flag, *Fuso* and *Mogami.*

In the confused fighting of the night battle, no one knows exactly what happened. According to Commander Nishino of the *Shigure,* it was not until three twenty-five, when the force was halfway up the strait, that any of the ships were hit, although American reports indicated several hits in early attacks. At that time, Nishino said, in a simultaneous attack by destroyers from both sides, the three leading destroyers and *Fuso* were hit almost simultaneously. One enemy destroyer sank. The other two, and *Fuso,* dropped out of column, afire, to sink or be sunk hours later, under further torpedo attacks and shell fire of United States cruisers and destroyers. *Yamashiro, Mogami,* and *Shigure* steamed doggedly ahead.

At 3:51 A.M., the remaining ships of Nishimura's force came within range of the Seventh Fleet battleships and cruisers lying in wait across the eastern end of Surigao Strait. *Louisville,* which was Admiral Oldendorf's flagship, was first to open fire, followed by the other cruisers and then, in succession, the battleships.

Both Commander Nishino and American destroyer captains who were just making their attacks or retiring from them when the battle line opened fire, said the sky was a terrible pattern of lightning-like flashes of the guns, and a Roman-candle effect of red-hot shells arching through the night to explode against Japanese targets.

For twenty minutes the unequal gun duel went on. Then, running low on ammunition and with some of the ships unable to find any targets left on their radar screens, the American commanders began to check fire. *Fuso* was gone, with hardly a survivor left. So was the second crippled destroyer. *Mogami* was limping back down the strait, battered to a worse shape than at the Battle of Midway. Commander Nishino, in *Shigure*, a badly confused man, was retiring at full speed.

With the sinking *Yamashiro* and two enemy destroyers still burning brightly in the Strait, Admiral Shima steamed in. His flagship, *Nachi*, exchanged signals with *Shigure*, but he neither asked for, nor was given, information as to the fate of Nishimura's force. Shortly after entering the strait, the light cruiser *Abukuma* was hit by a torpedo from one of the American torpedo boats and dropped out of line badly hurt. Shima, in *Nachi*, steamed ahead at high speed. He never made contact with the American battle line, only with American destroyers. In turning to retire, *Nachi* collided with *Mogami*, further hurting both of them.

Admiral Oldendorf sent his cruisers and destroyers down the strait to polish off cripples. Not quite certain of the strength the enemy had left, however, he soon broke off pursuit to wait for the airmen to take up the battle. *Mogami* was fired on again during this chase, and one crippled enemy destroyer was sunk. In air attacks during the twenty-fifth by our carrier planes and by Army B-25's, both *Mogami* and crippled *Abukuma* were sunk. Admiral Shima, in *Nachi* and with *Ashigara* and two destroyers, escaped to Coron Bay, as did the damaged destroyers that had stood by *Mogami* and *Abukuma*. *Shigure* limped on down to Brunei. The two cruisers did not survive the war. *Nachi* was sunk off Manila by planes ten days later and *Ashigara* off Singapore by a British submarine the next June.

Of the two enemy battleships, three heavy cruisers, one light cruiser, and eight destroyers that had sortied through Surigao Strait the early morning of October 25, the two battleships, one heavy cruiser, one light cruiser, and three destroyers were sunk and every other ship damaged. United States losses were one PT boat sunk, one beached, and one destroyer, *Albert W. Grant*, badly battered by Allied, as well as enemy, shellfire, when

40 | *An American destroyer lays its screen for the running baby carriers.*

Gambier Bay

she was caught between the lines while making a torpedo attack. No American battleship or cruiser was even touched by an enemy shell or torpedo.

To the north the battle did not go so well for the rest of the Seventh Fleet. No further contacts had been made the night of October 24 with enemy Force B after our attacking pilots had reported it retiring westward through the Sibuyan Sea. The three escort carrier groups guarding the northern entrance to Leyte Gulf, not far from the eastern entrance to San Bernadino Strait, were on the alert the next morning, but they were not expecting surface action. They had instead, at 5:00 A.M., launched an air strike against the survivors of Force A-1 and A-2. At five forty-five — a half hour before sunrise in those latitudes in October — they sent up their own topside guard of fighter planes. The patrol had been airborne an hour when one of the pilots excitedly reported that an enemy force of four battleships, eight cruisers, and ten destroyers was steaming out of the strait toward the little American flattops.

Admiral C. A. F. Sprague, whose northern group of six small carriers was nearest to the enemy, ordered all available planes launched to attack the oncoming enemy ships, and sent his escort of destroyers and smaller destroyer escorts toward the enemy to make smoke and later to launch a torpedo attack. Then he headed east at his best speed — eighteen to twenty knots against the twenty-five knots or better of the enemy battleships and cruisers — into the wind, to launch his planes, and also into a providential rain squall. He was, of course, calling for help by radio.

Against the sixteen-inch and eighteen-inch guns of the battleships and eight-inch rifles of the enemy cruisers, Admiral Sprague had as a counter only his few planes and the five-inch guns of his destroyers and carriers. The new American battleships, which could have slugged it out on fairly even terms with the Japanese capital vessels, were far to the north with Halsey. The American battleships and cruisers that had turned back enemy Force A in Surigao Strait were too far to the south to aid. The only help immediately forthcoming was from the other two escort carrier groups, Admiral Thomas Sprague's force, which was seven miles to the south, and Admiral Felix B. Stump's force, thirty miles to the southeast. Like the escort force under attack, however, they already had committed part of their air groups to attacks on the southern forces and to the usual daily missions over Leyte Gulf. They sent what planes they had on their decks.

When the enemy force first was sighted, Admiral Sprague turned east, away from them. That, fortunately, was the direction from which the wind was coming, the wind he needed across his decks to launch his planes. On that course, however, he was drawing away from any possible help from the battleships and cruisers in Leyte Gulf, so as he neared the eastern limit of the rain squall, he turned his carriers south, a course change of ninety degrees. Admiral Kurita, who should have foreseen the effort to run south, did not anticipate it and lost an opportunity to cut across the corner and close the range on the slower American ships as they came out of the squall. He followed them through it. Kurita explained after the war that he was attempting to keep to windward of the American carriers to prohibit plane launching.

It was an unequal fight. The carrier fighters, bombers, and torpedo planes attacked the enemy force again and again through heavy anti-aircraft

41

fire, even making "dry" runs on the enemy ships after they had exhausted their torpedoes, bombs, and ammunition. They scored some hits, but not enough to stop the Japanese.

The three destroyers and three destroyer escorts with Admiral C. A. F. Sprague's force fought heroically. Outstanding was the U.S.S. *Johnston*, one of the 2100-ton *Fletcher* Class destroyers, mounting ten torpedo tubes and five five-inch guns. She made an unordered torpedo attack early in the battle, scoring possibly two hits on an enemy cruiser, and then fought on bravely with her five-inch guns against the overwhelmingly superior fire power of the enemy ships. Finally, surrounded by enemy ships and almost dead in the water, she was sunk by enemy gunfire after almost three and a half hours of fighting. Another destroyer, *Hoel*, and a destroyer escort, *Samuel B. Roberts*, also were lost in this vastly unequal engagement at close quarters.

Steaming out of the rain squall after the American ships, the Japanese columns continued to close and, despite poor gunnery, soon began to score on the thin-sided American escort carriers. One sixteen-inch or eighteen-inch shell hit *Gambier Bay* below the water line, flooding one of her engine rooms, and she fell out of line to wallow in the glassy sea, an almost helpless target, as the enemy ships steamed by on either side of her and poured in a hailstorm of shells of all caliber to sink her.

The other carriers also were being hit heavily. *Kalinin Bay* took several hits of various caliber, as did *Fanshaw Bay*, Admiral Sprague's flagship. *White Plains* was damaged by a near miss. Only *Kitkun Bay* of the six under attack escaped damage.

At nine o'clock, over two hours after the start of the engagement, the situation looked hopeless for the slow, out-gunned little American force. The Japanese were steaming in three columns in pursuit of the fleeing American ships, closing the range with every turn of their propellers. To starboard was a column of enemy destroyers, to port the heavy and light cruisers, and dead astern the four battleships. Each American captain was on his own, chasing the enemy salvos as they fell short or over. The varicolored splashes (each ship of such a force has a distinctive dye in its shell charge so it can spot its own misses and correct the range and deflection) provided an eerie and terribly beautiful setting for the deadly game of tag being played.

Just when most of the American commanders and their crews had resigned themselves to the same fate as that of *Gambier Bay*, whose funeral

42

One of the escort carriers, missed by a salvo, is luckier than her sister . . .

Gambier Bay—crippled and dropping out of line.

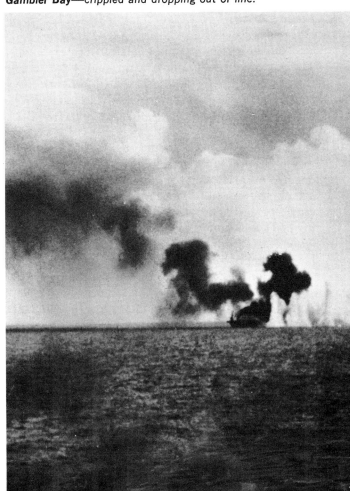

St. Lo *is hit by bombs and abandoned.*

Hoel *went down in gallant efforts to protect the carriers.*

pyre of smoke hung on the horizon, the Japanese force turned away. A final torpedo attack by the enemy destroyers was launched from so far out the torpedoes had almost expended their motive power before reaching the American ships. None struck home. In five more minutes Admiral Kurita well might have wiped out all six United States carriers and their escorts.

In questioning after the war, Admiral Kurita and his Chief of Staff, Rear Admiral Tomiji Koyanagi, said that the attack against the American light carriers was broken off just as it was at the point of greatest success because the Japanese ships, maneuvering independently, had become scattered and they wanted to close their formation, assess damage, and decide on their future course.

After milling around for two hours in the area, during which time they were under intermittent attack from American planes, Admiral Kurita decided to abandon his plans to enter Leyte Gulf — which was now open to him — and to go north to join Admiral Ozawa. He hoped, he said, to find the Third Fleet on the way, a fleet of whose whereabouts he did not know and of whose presence far to the north he had not been advised, either by Ozawa or by Japanese air headquarters ashore.

The little American carriers and their planes and destroyers and destroyer escorts, despite the odds, had given more punishment than they had taken. The Japanese heavy cruiser *Suzuya* had been hit by bombs causing fires that reached her torpedo locker, which exploded and sank her. The heavy cruisers *Chokai* and *Chikuma* both were disabled and dead in the water from torpedo and bomb damage, and were sunk by their own destroyer escorts. The heavy cruiser *Kumano* had

43

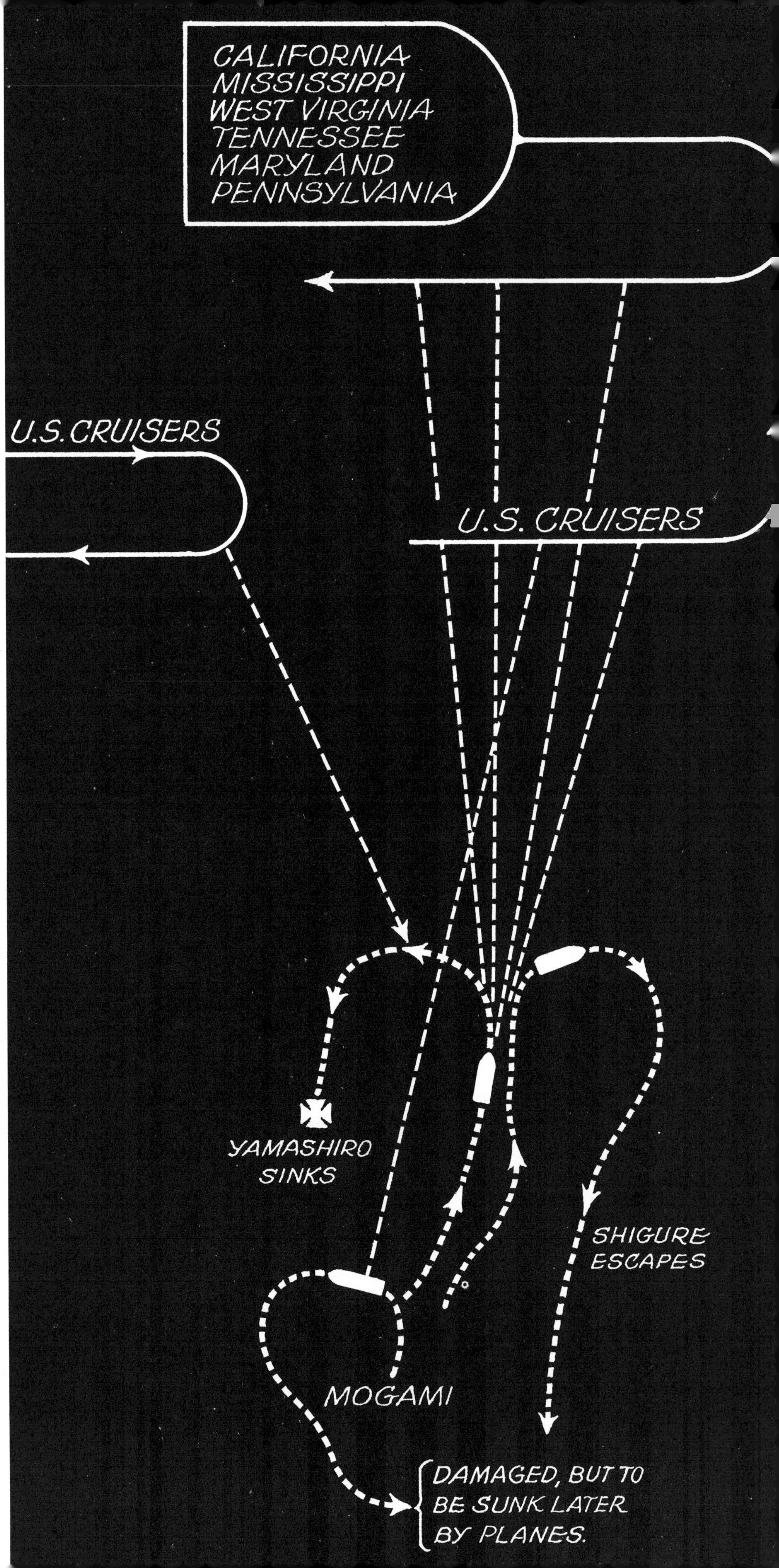

CALIFORNIA
MISSISSIPPI
WEST VIRGINIA
TENNESSEE
MARYLAND
PENNSYLVANIA

U.S. CRUISERS

U.S. CRUISERS

YAMASHIRO
SINKS

SHIGURE
ESCAPES

MOGAMI

DAMAGED, BUT TO
BE SUNK LATER
BY PLANES.

44 | Phase two—
the Battle of Surigao Strait.

been hit by a torpedo from a destroyer and slowed to a speed of sixteen knots.

The Seventh Fleet's losses were the escort carriers *Gambier Bay* and *Saint Lo,* the latter from air attack by land-based planes, the destroyers *Johnston* and *Hoel,* and the destroyer escort *Samuel B. Roberts.* Other carriers were damaged, but were still operating. It was Kurita's decision to go looking for bigger targets, rather than their efforts, however, that saved them from annihilation. They had fought their fight, and Kurita's force still had overwhelming gun superiority when it broke off the action.

A short time before the battle off Samar had begun, planes of the Third Fleet carrier groups had located Admiral Ozawa's Force C 350 miles to the north and had attacked. The high-speed run north through the night had been made in copybook style, the battleship-cruiser force in the van, some ten miles ahead of the carriers. The attack was to be made also by the book, with the carrier planes attacking over the battle line, which then would steam on in to take on the damaged enemy carriers and battleships in a gun duel. It was the first time in the war that this had been possible.

Halsey was almost in sight of the enemy force, with annihilating victory in sight, when frantic

messages began to pour in from Kinkaid and from Admiral Nimitz back in Pearl Harbor. The enemy's Central Force had come on and was attacking the Seventh Fleet carriers, so the messages said. Leyte Gulf was open to him. Where were the six new battleships and the heavy cruisers of the Third Fleet that, Kinkaid assumed from intercepted messages, had been formed into a task force to meet the enemy off San Bernardino Strait? They were, of course, with Halsey.

Never was there a better example of the failure of divided command. Although operating in adjacent waters, defending a common objective, the Seventh Fleet and the Third Fleet were under different tactical and strategical control. Halsey reported to Nimitz back at Pearl Harbor. Kinkaid reported to General MacArthur on Leyte. The only link was through MacArthur and Nimitz, except as one or the other fleet commander intercepted messages from the other. Kinkaid had not been advised of Halsey's decision to take the whole Third Fleet north with him. He assumed — on the basis of an intercepted message — that the battleships and cruisers of Halsey's force were somewhere off Leyte.

Halsey was faced, when word came of the action off Samar, with one of the hardest decisions

Victim of Mitscher's flyers—burning **Zuikaku** *races to her doom.*

Her poorly camouflaged flight deck riddled and buckled, *Zuiho* will be sunk by half-ton bombs and two torpedoes.

ever posed a United States naval commander. His battle plans had worked out perfectly. He had the northern force of enemy carriers and battleships almost under the guns of his fine new battleships. He was many hours steaming away from the battle 350 miles to the south. But as the frantic appeals for aid continued to pour in, he reluctantly detached his battleships and one of his carrier groups and turn back south to answer the appeals for help. He also ordered Vice Admiral John S. McCain, who was refueling the Third Fleet's fourth carrier group 250 miles to the east of Samar, to knock off and go to the aid of the Seventh Fleet.

As Halsey sped south, first with all six battleships and three carriers, then finally only with his two fastest and newest big boys, *Iowa* and *New Jersey*, Vice Admiral Marc A. Mitscher, with his remaining two carrier groups, pressed the attack against Force C:

The American attack on Admiral Ozawa's ships was a slaughter. The four carriers, with only twenty fighter planes to protect them, were almost sitting ducks for the attacking American pilots. *Zuikaku*, *Chitose*, and *Chiyoda* all were hit and damaged in the first major attack, and one destroyer was sunk, almost instantaneously. An hour later, when the second and heaviest attack wave bored in, all four Japanese carriers received their death blows. All sank within minutes of each other three hours later.

In midafternoon, with his four carriers destroyed, Admiral Ozawa turned north in an attempt to escape. Had Halsey been there with his fast battleships, none of Force C might ever have

A Japanese cruiser is hit by Halsey's Helldivers.

reached the Inland Sea. As it was, *Tama* and two destroyers, which had been rescuing personnel from the sunken carriers, were overtaken and sunk in attacks by United States submarines and a cruiser force that Admiral Mitscher sent in at nightfall to do the clean-up job that Halsey's battleships had been assigned. Only *Ise, Hyuga, Oyodo* — the light cruiser to which Ozawa had transferred his flag from *Zuikaku* — and five destroyers escaped.

Admiral Halsey and his force of battleships and heavy cruisers never did get in the battle, except to sink a damaged destroyer off Samar shortly after midnight. Admiral McCain's carrier fliers arrived off Samar on the twenty-fifth, in time to join in air attacks on Admiral Kurita's Force B, inflicting new but not lethal damage on several ships. The next day they hit and sank the light

cruiser *Noshiro* and blew the bow off a destroyer, which was beached and abandoned. At the same time, fliers from the escort carrier groups of the Seventh Fleet found a transport group west of Leyte and sank the light cruiser *Kinu* and a destroyer with machine-gun and rocket fire. By dawn of the twenty-seventh there was not a Japanese force within three hundred miles of Leyte Gulf. From that day to the end of the war, the United States Pacific Fleet had only land-based airplanes to oppose it. Repaired *Yamato* made an abortive sortie from the Inland Sea on April 7, 1945, during the invasion of Okinawa, but was quickly caught and sunk by Third Fleet carrier pilots.

In list of vessels sunk in the Second Battle of the Philippines, the score was Japan: twenty-six, United States: six. In tonnage, the margin was much greater, for the largest American vessel sunk

47

An Avenger has another torpedo shot at **Zuikaku**.

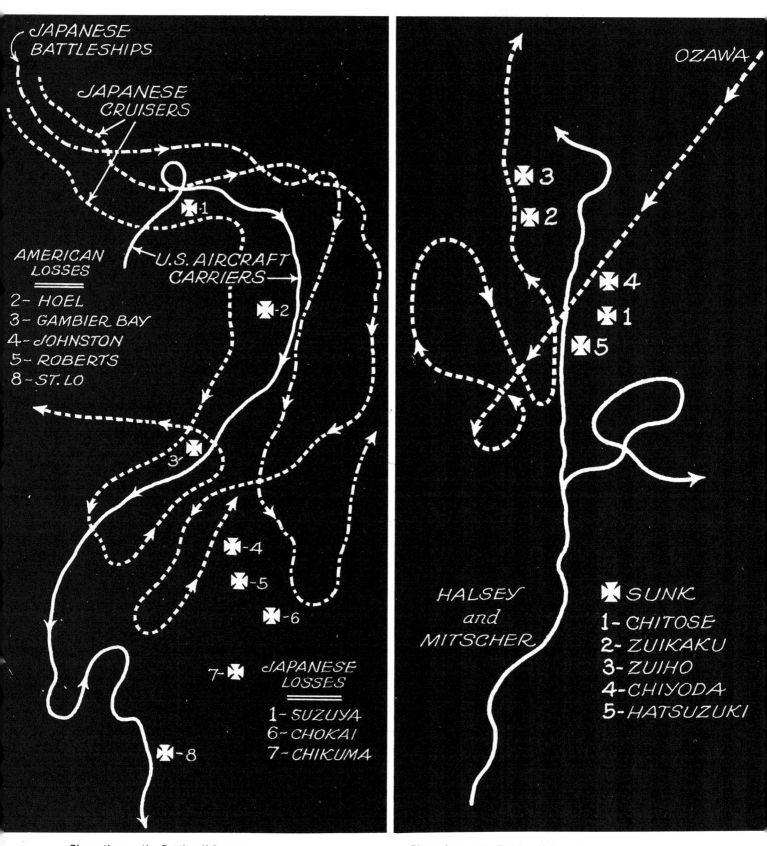

JAPANESE
BATTLESHIPS

JAPANESE
CRUISERS

✠ 1

U.S. AIRCRAFT
CARRIERS

AMERICAN
LOSSES
2 – HOEL
3 – GAMBIER BAY
4 – JOHNSTON
5 – ROBERTS
8 – ST. LO

✠ -2

✠
3 -

✠ -4

✠ -5

✠ -6

7 - ✠   JAPANESE
LOSSES

1 – SUZUYA
6 – CHOKAI
7 – CHIKUMA

✠ - 8

OZAWA

✠ 3

✠ 2

✠ 4

✠ 1

✠ 5

HALSEY
and
MITSCHER

✠ SUNK
1 – CHITOSE
2 – ZUIKAKU
3 – ZUIHO
4 – CHIYODA
5 – HATSUZUKI

Phase three—the Battle off Samar.

Phase four—the Battle off Cape Engano.

was the ten-thousand-ton light carrier *Princeton*. The detailed losses were:

JAPAN: Battleships — *Musashi, Yamashiro, Fuso;* Carriers — *Zuikaku, Chitose, Chiyoda, Zuiho;* Heavy Cruisers — *Atago, Maya, Chokai, Suzuya, Chikuma, Mogami;* Light Cruisers — *Abukuma, Tama, Noshiro, Kinu;* Destroyers — *Wakaba, Yamagumo, Michishio, Asagumo, Hatsutsuki, Akitsuki, Nowake, Hayashimo, Uranami;* Destroyer escorts — none.

UNITED STATES: Battleships—None; Carriers — *Princeton, Gambier Bay, Saint Lo;* Heavy Cruisers—none; Light Cruisers—none; Destroyers — *Johnston, Hoel;* Destroyer Escorts — *Samuel B. Roberts.*

Because the Japanese Sho Operation came so close to being a success, it will be studied by naval students for years. What was the main cause of its failure? Was it poor communications, which were atrocious by American standards all through the approach and the engagement? Was it because of excess timidity on Admiral Kurita's part, when he went north with Force B "looking for the Third Fleet" instead of into Leyte Gulf when the way was open to him? Was it lack of co-ordination between Japanese fleet and Japanese land-based air? Did the American admirals win the battle, or did the Japanese admirals just lose it?

Whatever the answers to the above questions — and there can be almost as many as there will be students of the tactical problems involved — there can be no question as to the result of the Japanese defeat or United States victory, whichever way you wish to put it; the battle finished the Imperial Japanese Navy as a factor in the Pacific War.

Admiral Ozawa, questioned as to the Japanese Navy's role after the Battle for Leyte Gulf, said:

"After this battle, the surface force became strictly auxiliary, so that we relied on land forces, special (Kamikaze) attack, and air power."

The Second Battle of the Philippines, probably the last great surface fight of history, not only marked the end of an era of naval warfare, it also put a period to the story, "The Rise and Fall of Japan as a Sea Power, 1905–1945."

49

Ise, a battleship-carrier, runs for home after a bad mauling.

Musashi leaves her Brunei base, to sink in the Sibuyan Sea.

Missouri receives the surrender of Japan and goes home.

Baltimore—number two in Dewey's line.

Manila Bay - 1898

Stem to stern, like elephants in a circus parade, each officer of the deck conning his ship in the white wake of the preceding vessel, the Asiatic Squadron of the United States Fleet headed through the south passage that led into Manila Bay the dark night of April 30–May 1, 1898. Corregidor Island rose dark and silent out of the water to the north. To the south, across the five-mile-wide passage, could be dimly made out the small island of El Fraile and the Spanish fort that perched atop it. A formal decree of Imperial Spain, then one of the world's leading maritime powers, declaring the existence of a state of war with the United States, had been signed in Madrid six days before. Now the upstart commodore of the upstart navy of the upstart nation that had presumed to tell Spain how it should treat its Cuban subjects was headed in to challenge the Spanish ships that stood guard over another of Spain's far-flung possessions. The night hung like a dark curtain across the stage where was to be enacted the first act of one of the world's great sea dramas.

Spain's declaration of war had been long anticipated. It had found the United States Squadron, under command of Commodore George Dewey, lying ready in the British naval base of Hong Kong. Dewey sent three of his ships steaming north toward Manila the same afternoon he received the message informing him a state of war existed. He followed with the remainder the next morning. He had left Hong Kong Harbor well within the twenty-four-hour limitation imposed by Britain's neutrality.

Commodore Dewey had his flag on the *Olympia*, a so-called "protected cruiser" mounting four eight-inch breech-loading guns, a secondary battery of ten five-inch rapid-fire rifles, fourteen six-pounders, seven one-pounders, a field gun, and four Gatling machine guns. Her classification as a "protected cruiser" was predicated on the four and three-quarter-inch steel plates of her decks that protected her magazines and engine room. She displaced 5,870 tons of water. *Olympia* was one of the first American-designed, American-built, and American-armed vessels constructed in the program for a modern navy that was initiated in 1883 and which paid off such high dividends in the war against Spain.

Next in line to *Olympia* was the cruiser *Baltimore*, British-designed but American-built, slightly smaller and slightly older than *Olympia* but armed with four eight-inch guns, six six-inch, four six-pounders, two three-pounders, two one-pounders, four 37-mm Hotchkiss rapid-fire guns, a field gun, and two Colt machine guns. Behind them came the *Raleigh* and *Boston*, of 3,213 tons and 3,000 tons displacement, respectively. The *Boston* carried two 8-inchers, but *Raleigh's* biggest gun was a six-inch breechloader, a slow-firing rifle. The *Raleigh* had a secondary battery of ten five-inch rapid-fire rifles and the *Boston* six six-inch breechloaders. Both had the usual smaller guns. The gunboats *Concord* and *Petrel* brought up the rear of Dewey's "battle line." They were of 1,710 tons (the size of a modern destroyer) and 892 tons, respectively, and mounted six-inch breech-loading guns. The little fleet was completed with the revenue cutter *Hugh McCulloch*, assigned as a dispatch boat, and two transports, the *Nanshau* and *Zafiro*. The two latter were loaded with provisions for the squadron and 3,600 tons of coal.

The delay of two days between Spain's formal rejection of the United States' ultimatum regarding Cuba and the declaration of war had permitted

Olympia led, flying Dewey's flag.

Reina Cristina waited, flying Montojo's flag.

Dewey to prepare his fleet for battle, especially *Baltimore*, which had steamed down from Shanghai to join him when Spanish-American relations became strained. She had arrived at Hong Kong with a fouled bottom and in need of coal and other supplies. The forty-eight-hour grace period had permitted her dry-docking, scraping, painting, and replenishment of stores so she was ready to sail when war finally was declared.

Within four hours of receipt of word that the United States was at war, one hot Sunday morning in Hong Kong, the *Boston, Concord,* and *Petrel* put to sea. Dewey did not want to take a chance on being caught with his whole force in a neutral harbor in the event the Spanish squadron at Manila had already put to sea. After taking on additional stores during the night, he followed them at ten o'clock the next morning in *Olympia,* with the *Raleigh, Baltimore, Hugh McCulloch,* and the two transports.

"You will surely win," shouted the captain of the British *Immortalité* as the little squadron stood past his ship toward the open sea. "I have seen too much of your target practice to doubt it." His judgment of the situation was in contrast to that of Russian, German, and French naval officers in the port, who, Gunner Joel C. Evans of the *Boston* said, believed the Spanish would win. They could not conceive of Dewey's ability to run the Spanish

forts at Corregidor and, in a period of hours, not only destroy the Spanish squadron, but silence most of the superior guns of the Cavite and Manila forts.

Boston, Concord, and *Petrel* had only sailed as far north as Mirs Bay on the China coast, thirty miles from Hong Kong. Dewey rendezvoused with them there on Monday evening, and two days later, Wednesday, April 27, sailed for Manila to seek out the Spanish fleet. The *Olympia* band played the march "El Capitán" as the little United States fleet put to sea.

Because of the necessity of conserving coal and for the additional reason that he felt sure the Spanish authorities in Hong Kong had apprised Manila of his departure and there would be no chance of surprising the Spanish commanders, Dewey steamed northeast at a conservative eight knots, about half speed for his ships.

The American squadron raised the west coast of Luzon at dawn the morning of April 30. The landfall was Point Bolinao several miles northwest of the entrance to Manila Bay. Commodore Dewey wanted to sweep Lingayen Gulf and Subic Bay to assure himself that the Spanish squadron had not left its anchorage and was lying in wait for him where it would not be expected.

The American ships had been stripped for action. All the way north from Hong Kong the

53

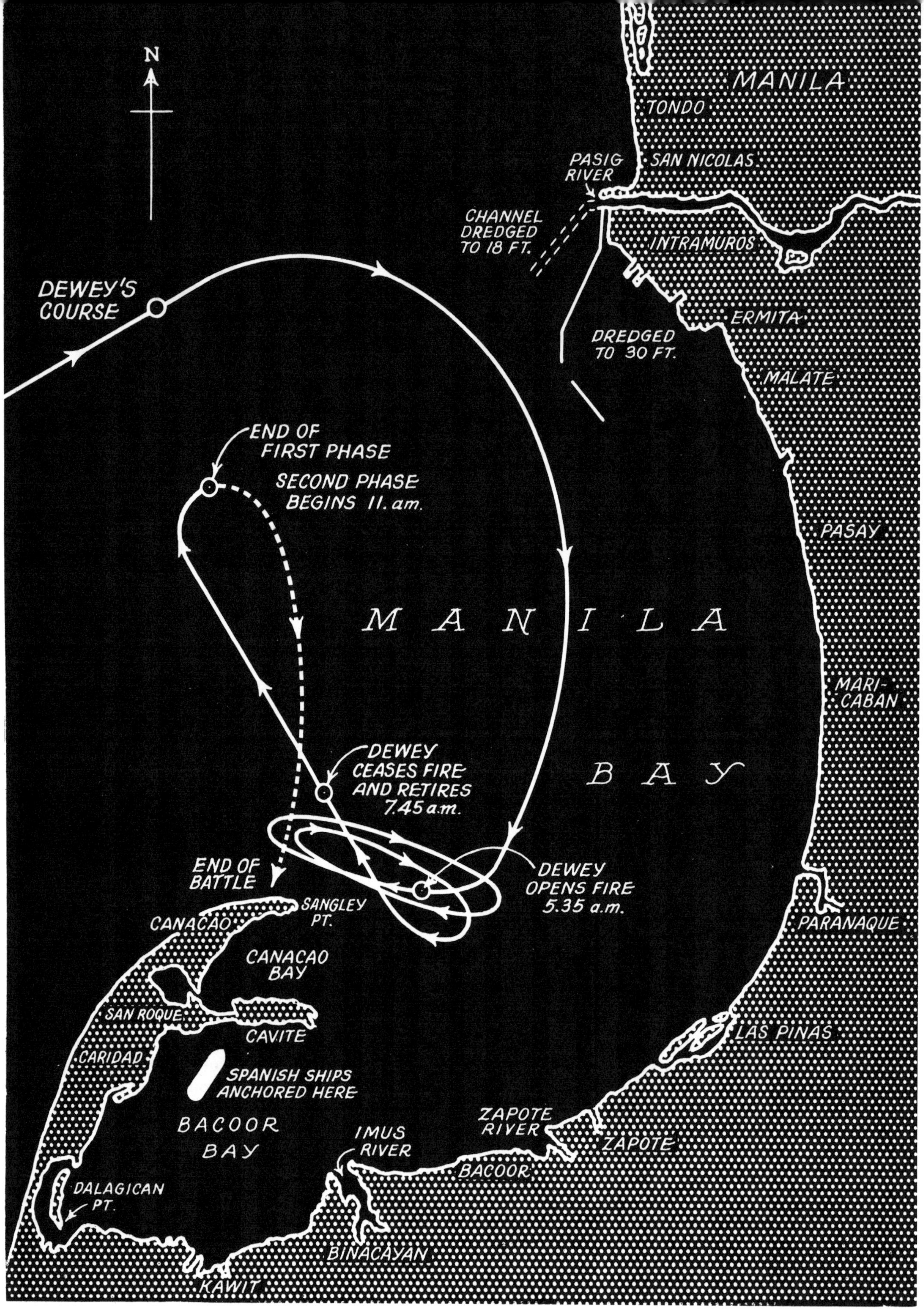
N
MANILA
TONDO
PASIG RIVER
SAN NICOLAS
CHANNEL DREDGED TO 18 FT.
INTRAMUROS
DEWEY'S COURSE
ERMITA
DREDGED TO 30 FT.
MALATE
END OF FIRST PHASE
SECOND PHASE BEGINS 11. am.
PASAY
M A N I L A
MARI-CABAN
B A Y
DEWEY CEASES FIRE AND RETIRES 7.45 a.m.
END OF BATTLE
DEWEY OPENS FIRE 5.35 a.m.
SANGLEY PT.
CANACAO
CANACAO BAY
PARANAQUE
SAN ROQUE
CAVITE
LAS PINAS
CARIDAD
SPANISH SHIPS ANCHORED HERE
BACOOR BAY
ZAPOTE RIVER
ZAPOTE
IMUS RIVER
BACOOR
DALAGICAN PT.
BINACAYAN
KAWIT

54

crews had been kept busy ripping out the ornamental woodwork and partitions that make for more comfortable peacetime living but are a hazard in war because of the danger of fire and of splinters. (Forty-three years later, similar scenes were to be enacted on other United States war vessels in the days immediately following the Japanese attack on Pearl Harbor.) Dewey's ships were ready for battle when they sighted the Luzon coast that morning.

The quickening light failed to reveal any Spanish warships in the northern anchorages, so Dewey detached *Boston, Concord,* and *Baltimore,* and sent them ahead at full speed to reconnoiter Subic Bay. He followed with the remainder of his ships. The Spanish fleet not having been found there, Dewey again reformed his force in the bay, told his captains of his plans, and continued on south at dusk. The Spanish squadron obviously had chosen to remain in Manila, and he proposed to go in after them. He set his course and his speed to arrive off the entrance at midnight. With only guide lights shining at the taffrails, the squadron ghosted south through the dark tropic evening.

The entrance to Manila Harbor was then, as now, dominated by Corregidor, a square-mile rock from whose six-hundred-foot eminence emplaced guns cover the entrance on either side. On the other side of the entrance was El Fraile. No matter how black the night, no squadron of ships could hope to steam through the channel without detection. The Spanish were also known to have a signal station on Point Bolinao, and Dewey had no reason to doubt that Admiral Montojo, the Spanish commander, had known of his presence since early morning and was expecting him.

As Dewey led his column of ships toward the entrance, the Spaniards appeared to be either asleep or unwilling to believe their eyes. The leading ships were well on their way through the narrows when the coal heavers on the *Hugh McCulloch* found it necessary to stoke their fires. Sparks and flame poured out of her stack when the coal hit the firebox, and the Spanish sentries no longer could ignore the American ships. A signal rocket swished up from Corregidor, an answering one from El Fraile. Then came the flash of one of the eight-inch German-made guns from El Fraile. Obeying the old rule to fire at any ship or fort that fires at you, *Boston, Concord,* and *McCulloch* all opened on the bearing of the Spanish gun. If there had been any question before of the presence of the United States ships, there could be none now. But, inexplicably, there was no further firing from either El Fraile or Corregidor. The American force sailed on into the bay, untouched.

The forts passed, the American crews stood easy at their battle stations, the gunners sleeping on the deck beside their mounts as the squadron proceeded slowly up the bay toward Cavite and Manila. At daybreak Dewey had his squadron seven miles due west of Manila itself and northwest of Cavite, a sandy peninsula that protrudes from the mainland seven miles southwest of Manila city to form a sheltered anchorage.

The island shore and Cavite form a great sickle, of which Manila is the handle and Cavite Peninsula the sharp point. Behind Cavite lay the Spanish ships. They had not even raised steam. As Admiral Montojo explained later, two of his ships were undergoing repairs and were not ready for battle, and he had every reason to feel secure, pro-

55

Don Juan de Austria—one of the gunboats in Cavite.

Boston—*number four in the line*

tected as he was by the eight-inch rifles of the forts on Cavite and at Manila. He knew Commodore Dewey had no larger rifles on his ships and that he would have to come within range of the shore batteries if he were to engage the Spanish vessels. In addition, shore-controlled sea mines protected his anchorage.

Admiral Montojo had under his command the 1,970-ton steel cruiser *Reina Maria Christina,* mounting ten 6.2-inch guns; the 3,342-ton wooden cruiser *Castillo,* mounting four 5.9-inch Krupp rifles in addition to the usual lesser batteries; the three light cruisers *Don Antonio de Ulloa, Don Juan de Austria,* and *Velasco;* the gunboats *Isla de Luzon* and *Isla de Cuba;* the gun vessels *General Lezo* and *Elcano;* the dispatch vessel *Marquis de Duero;* the auxiliary cruiser *Isla de Mindanao;* and two torpedo boats, precursors of the small but deadly PT boats of World War II. One of the cruisers, *Velasco,* had a main battery of three 5.9-inch English naval rifles. The other cruisers, the gunboats, and the gun vessel *Elcano* mounted 4.7-inch guns as their main armament.

It is obvious that, compared with the eight-inch and six-inch rifles of Admiral Dewey's four cruisers and two gunboats, the Spanish squadron was outgunned and outranged. But the Spanish forts more than evened the balance, and if the ten largest Spanish war vessels had had steam up and had chosen to maneuver against the United States squadron, they could have equalized further this disadvantage of fire power. The British proved at the battle of the River Plate, where they had only cruisers and destroyers against the German pocket battleship *Graf Spee,* that lighter ships, if audaciously and skillfully handled, often can outfight a bigger vessel.

As the light increased, one of the eight-inch guns of the Manila forts fired a shot at the United States ships. It fell two-thousand yards short (a sea mile) of the *Olympia.* No American vessel answered. The morning fog, or haze, that customarily intercedes between the cool dampness of the night and the sticky heat of the day in the tropics, still shrouded most of the shore line and the Spanish ships off Cavite, which Dewey was sure were there, but which he could not see. Radar was more than forty years away. He had only the testimony of his long glasses to go by. The sun, however, soon burned away the mist and revealed the Spanish ships as he had pictured them.

The men of the United States squadron were fed, the dishes cleared away, and then, leaving the dispatch boat and the two transports in the center of the bay out of range of the shore guns, Dewey formed his battle line and opened the action. He led, in *Olympia.* As they turned toward shore, he hoisted the signal. "Fire as convenient."

The shore batteries at Cavite and Manila opened fire as soon as the American ships came in range, but Dewey pressed steadily in without replying until *Olympia* was within two miles of the fort of Cavite and the anchored Spanish ships. Then he turned to Captain Charles V. Gridley,

Reina Cristina abandoned—a hulk destroyed by concentrated fire.

commanding officer of the *Olympia*, and delivered his famous order: "When you are ready, you may fire, Gridley."

As *Olympia* neared Cavite, Dewey had turned the column to starboard to unmask his squadron's full port broadside, and the opening salvo of *Olympia* was followed almost immediately by those of the other ships. It was 5:35 A.M. The surface of the bay was smooth as a sheet of plate glass, and the squadron turned on its first firing course at slow speed to give the gunners as steady a platform as possible.

Don Antonio de Ulloa, burned out and settled by the stern.

The American gunners concentrated first on the guns of the forts at the point-blank range of three thousand yards. Every Spanish gun was firing. From the transports and the dispatch boat in the bay it seemed the American ships could not live through the rain of shells falling around them. Incredibly not a ship of Dewey's squadron was scratched. As they cleared the fort, he turned his column in a wide circle and retraced his firing course to give the fresh batteries on the starboard sides of his ships an opportunity to enter the engagement. As the range was closing, the Spaniards prematurely exploded a mine field half a mile or so ahead of *Olympia*. It did no damage.

Admiral Montojo, seeing the forts could not protect him from the American fire, ordered his squadron to get underway. As *Olympia* neared firing range, his flagship, the *Reina Christina*, slipped the cables of her anchors and steamed out to meet the American flagship. All the American ships immediately concentrated their fire on her. She was hit time and again and soon was on fire forward. One of the hits, too, Admiral Montojo later reported, damaged her steering gear, making her unmanageable.

She turned, still under terrible fire, and was abandoned by both Admiral and men at seven thirty, less than two hours after the battle had started. One report was that she had been struck no less than seventy times. Of her crew of 250 to 300 men, 52 were killed and 150 wounded.

When he was forced to abandon *Reina Christina*, Admiral Montojo went by small boat to the *Isla de Cuba*. The sharp-eyed American lookouts and gunners spied his Admiral's flag at *Isla de Cuba's* yardarm, he complained later, and followed him there with their fire. At this time he ordered the torpedo boats to attack. They raced out of the harbor toward *Olympia*, but one of them was blown out of the water, and the other turned and scurried for safety, both without having scored a hit or, apparently, having launched their torpedoes.

Five times Dewey led his squadron across the bay in front of the forts and the Spanish vessels. In addition to *Reina Christina*, now a blazing hulk, the *Don Antonio de Ulloa* and the *Castillo*, the latter the large wooden cruiser, were set afire, and others were damaged. At seven forty-five the order to cease fire was sent from *Olympia*, and the squadron withdrew out of range of the forts. A few minor hits had been received by the American vessels, but no men had been killed, nor had any guns been put out of action. Dewey wished to assess the damage done the Spanish ships and check a report, found to be erroneous, that *Olympia* was short on five-inch ammunition. The cool night had been succeeded by a burning hot day, and some of the American crews, especially the coal stokers and water tenders, were near exhaustion in the 150- to 160-degree heat of the fire rooms and engine rooms.

It is an amusing commentary on how differently such an action is viewed, depending on the perspective, that a message was sent to Madrid at about that time triumphantly announcing that the enemy had been so outmaneuvered and so heavily punished that it had been forced to withdraw.

Comfortably at anchor outside the range of the Spanish batteries, the men ate and rested until eleven o'clock, lying in the shadows of their guns and their ships' superstructure, enjoying a breeze that had made up. At eleven o'clock Commodore Dewey ordered the action resumed.

This time, instead of forming in column, he sent his ships in individually, each to deal with a particular target. *Baltimore* steamed in first, soon followed by the other five, all again concentrating their fire at the onset on the forts. The two largest Spanish ships, *Reina Christina* and *Castillo*, had already been put out of action.

*Admiral Dewey, **Olympia's** Captain Gridley, and Chief of Staff Commander Lamberton discuss the battle before going back in to finish off the Spanish fleet.*

*Cease fire—and **Olympia's** men come topside for air and to clear their eyes.*

Raleigh—number three in the line.

The Spanish ships were not ignored, but they lay in such shallow water behind Cavite that some of them could not be brought within effective range. The *Boston* went so close inshore that she stuck her stern in the mud and was some time working herself free, her guns continuing to fire meanwhile. The shallow-draft *Petrel*, however, could navigate the shoal water, and she went in where Dewey's cruisers could not go. Spouting fire like a garden hose does water, she soon had scored hits on every remaining Spanish cruiser and gunboat and won for herself the title "the baby battleship" from the other vessels.

For almost an hour and a half the battle continued. Then Admiral Montojo, who had failed to find refuge with the *Isla de Cuba* even behind the Cavite dock, ordered his ships scuttled and abandoned and a white flag hoisted on Cavite Fort. Commodore Dewey gave the "cease-fire" order from *Olympia* at twelve thirty. Every Spanish ship except two tugs and a few small launches had either been sunk or was on fire and sinking.

The accuracy of the United States gunners, which had been noted by the British captain and on which he had based his prophecy of success for the American squadron, had been more than fulfilled. The American ships had destroyed the Span-

ish squadron with the expenditure of not more than half of their ammunition. Practically every shell fired apparently had found a target.

The inaccuracy of the Spanish gunners was as appalling as that of the Americans was astounding. Not a single American officer or man had been killed, only eight had been wounded by flying splinters and those only slightly, and no American ship had suffered any material damage to make her either unseaworthy or unbattleworthy. The Commodore could have fought another battle the next day with no loss of efficiency of ships or men.

Secretary of the Navy Long cabled Dewey:

THE PRESIDENT, IN THE NAME OF THE AMERICAN PEOPLE, THANKS YOU AND YOUR OFFICERS AND MEN FOR YOUR SPLENDID ACHIEVEMENT AND OVERWHELMING VICTORIES. IN RECOGNITION HE HAS APPOINTED YOU ACTING [REAR] ADMIRAL AND WILL RECOMMEND A VOTE OF THANKS TO YOU BY CONGRESS AS A FOUNDATION FOR FURTHER PROMOTION.

No commendation and promotion ever was more deserved. It was several months before the Spaniards finally were driven out of Manila, but the issue was decided in the blazing action of the hot morning of May 1 off Cavite.

In the fifth volume of *The History of Our Navy*, an authoritative contemporary history of that time, John R. Spears closed his report of the First Battle of the Philippines with this assessment of the factors of victory:

"Many comments on the Battle of Manila have been written by naval men," he wrote in 1898, a few months after the engagement. "Of them all, none is so valuable as those which point out the fact that while the Spaniards were utterly reckless of danger, the Americans showed cool courage; where the Spaniards fought in a frenzy of rage, the Americans made and maintained the attack with deliberate and relentless determination."

The description of the officers and men, fighting with cool courage, was as true of the Second Battle of the Philippines, forty-six years later, as it was of the First. In 1944, as in 1898, it was the real margin of victory.

Concord, number five, brought up the rear with **Petrel.**

Maine enters Havana Harbor.

THE BATTLE OF SANTIAGO - 1898

At Manila on May 1, 1898, Commodore George Dewey and his small Far Eastern Squadron fought the first battle of the Spanish-American War. The distinction of firing the first shot in the war, however, had fallen to the gunboat *Nashville,* in command of Captain Washburn Maynard. It was fired across the bow of the Spanish freighter *Buenaventura* just outside Key West as our squadron left its anchorage there the morning of April 22 to set up a blockade of Cuban ports, two days before the formal declaration of war by the Spanish Cortes in Madrid. The Spanish captain at first thought he was being saluted. Disillusioned by the second shot, he submitted to boarding, and his ship, bound from Pascagoula, Mississippi, to Rotterdam with twenty thousand dollars' worth of lumber, was taken into Key West as a prize.

That first warlike act followed by two months and six days the explosion of a shore-controlled mine under the United States battleship *Maine,*

Cause célèbre—*Maine* on the bottom of Havana Harbor.

in Havana Harbor, which had resulted in the death of 266 of her crew. The *Maine* had been sent to Havana in January to protect the lives of the few hundred United States citizens there who were being increasingly threatened by supernationalist Spaniards as relations between Washington and Madrid steadily deteriorated.

There was little doubt that the mine had been exploded deliberately, although by whom and at whose orders was never officially determined. The United States did not take immediate action to avenge the act. Captain Robley D. (later Rear Admiral "Fighting Bob") Evans probably expressed the feeling of most Americans when he said that if he had been in Rear Admiral Sicard's place (then commander of our North Atlantic Squadron at Key West) he would have taken his ships into Havana Harbor the next day and told the Spaniards: "Now, we'll investigate this matter and let you know what we think about it at once." President McKinley apparently still was hopeful of avoiding war. While the newspapers popularized the slogan "Remember the *Maine*," and demanded war, the President ordered convened a Navy board of inquiry to investigate the explosion. It made its report to Congress on March 28. It found that the *Maine* had been destroyed by a mine.

Congress had not waited for the board's report. On March 8 it appropriated fifty million dollars for "national defense," and the energetic young Assistant Secretary of the Navy, Theodore Roosevelt, began preparing the Navy for war by sending a naval officer to England to buy two cruisers being built there for Brazil and by purchasing and converting every merchant vessel,

yacht, and tug he could find for sale in American waters.

On April 22, a United States Squadron under Rear Admiral William Sampson had been engaging in target practice at Key West for several months and had been steadily increased. It included the battleships *Iowa* and *Indiana*, the armored cruiser *New York*, the cruisers or gunboats *Marblehead*, *Montgomery*, *Nashville*, *Wilmington*, and *Helena*, the monitors *Puritan*, *Amphitrite*, *Miantonomoh*, and *Terror*, and several smaller craft. At Hampton Roads were the battleship *Massachusetts*, the armored cruisers *Brooklyn* and *Texas*, and the light cruisers *Minneapolis* and *Columbia*. They were under Captain (later Commodore) W. S.

Nashville fired the first shot.

62

Iowa

Indiana

New York flew Sampson's flag.

Schley. They had been stationed there to guard against any possible raid on the United States East Coast by any Spanish ships, for there were recurring alarms that such raids were imminent. Every coastal city was demanding that it be given protection, as had been done and acceded to so disastrously during the war with England in 1812, when the British Fleet was able to force its way through Hampton Roads and on to Washington to burn the capital. Captain Mahan's exposition of how disastrous was such a policy — a fleet split up into many squadrons is no fleet at all — had been read, however, by our Navy Department. Assistant Secretary Roosevelt, the dominant force there, refused to listen to the pleas and kept increasing the Sampson Squadron instead of further weakening it. The battleship *Oregon* was ordered to make the fourteen-thousand-mile voyage to Key West from San Francisco, and our small South American Squadron of the *Cincinnati, Bancroft,* and *Castine* steamed north to join.

Contrary to popular misconceptions of the time in both Spain and the United States, neither country had an overwhelming superiority at sea. The United States had five battleships to one for Spain. The Spaniards had seven fast, armored cruisers to our four, and her torpedo boats were theoretically far superior to those of the United States Navy. However, our naval vessels were in a much better state of readiness than were those of Spain, and our crews were better trained. The Spanish Admiralty knew this, but the Spanish people did not. It was only under protest that Admiral Cervera left his Cape Verde anchorage and sailed for the West Indies with his squadron.

The decision to use the weapon of blockade instead of attempting a landing in Cuba was dictated by the compelling fact that we had too small an army to challenge the hundred thousand troops Spain had there. Too, as long as there was a danger

Ericsson

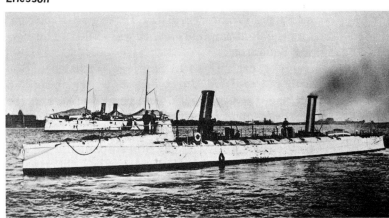

Oregon raced around the Horn in time to fight.

of interception of a transport train by a fast Spanish battle force, our Army generals feared to load their troops in Florida and sail. It was not until after the bottling up of Cervera's squadron at Santiago that we began to move our troops to Cuba.

The first few weeks of the war were relieved from monotony for the blockading forces only by a few prizes seized attempting to run the blockade, a few minor shore bombardments, and constant watchfulness for the appearance in the Caribbean of Cervera's squadron. It finally arrived off Martinique on May 11 and, after coaling at Curaçao, proceeded to Santiago. News of its arrival off Martinique was reported to United States authorities, and Commodore Schley, whose force had been ordered south from Hampton Roads, left Key West on May 19 with orders to proceed around the west end of Cuba and sweep the south coast to Cienfuegos in search of the Spanish ships. Schley's squadron consisted of the battleship *Massachusetts*, the armored cruisers *Texas* and *Brooklyn*, and the gunboat *Scorpion*. It was called "The Flying Squadron."

Cervera's force in Santiago consisted of the armored cruisers *Maria Teresa*, on which he had his flag, the *Cristobal Colon*, the *Viscaya*, and the *Oquendo*, and two torpedo boats, *Furor* and *Pluton*. At San Juan, Puerto Rico, over eight hundred miles to the east, were the only other Spanish warships of any size in West Indian waters, the light cruisers *Isabel II* and *Concha* and the torpedo boat *Terror*.

Commodore Schley arrived off Cienfuegos on May 22 and, despite the apparently confirmed re-

ports that Cervera was at Santiago, remained there three days before finally assuring himself the Spanish squadron was not inside. Then he sailed on eastward, arriving off Santiago on the twenty-sixth. Although newspaper correspondents with the fleet reported the stacks of the Spanish ships could be plainly seen, Commodore Schley appeared not to be satisfied. On May 27, he dispatched a message to Admiral Sampson, who had ordered him to blockade the port if he found Cervera there, that he would have to return to Key West for coal, since a heavy seaway made it impossible to refuel at sea. Before he had put his plan into effect, however, the sea subsided, his battleships were able to refuel, and he took up a blockading position off the port. Two days later he reported Cervera's ships definitely were inside the harbor. Admiral Sampson, who had not doubted their presence and who had sent the newly purchased cruiser *New Orleans* to

Control of the seas—vital need of the troops.

Maria Teresa flew Cervera's flag.

Vizcaya

Cristobal Colon

Oquendo

reinforce Schley, hurriedly refueled at Key West and sailed on May 30 to take command of the blockade. He arrived off Santiago on June 1.

For a month and three days Sampson maintained his watch. By day the United States vessels patroled off the harbor entrance outside the range of the two Spanish forts. By night they moved in and turned their searchlights on the channel. A British observer, when he saw it for the first time, is said to have exclaimed: "What a damned impertinence!" The Spanish forts seldom fired, however.

On the seventh day of the blockade, June 3, occurred one of the bravest and most publicized individual acts of heroism in United States naval history. In an effort to block the harbor and prevent Cervera from escaping, a young naval constructor, Richmond Pearson Hobson, and six volunteer seamen, sailed the collier *Merrimac* in under the guns of the Spanish fort and sank her in the harbor mouth. Unfortunately, the run of the tide swung her out of the main channel, and when she went down it still was open. Hobson and his men were taken off the sunken vessel at daylight by Admiral Cervera himself. None of them was so much as scratched despite the heavy fire they had been under.

Once it was certain that the principal Spanish ships were bottled up at Santiago and San Juan, plans were completed for opening the land cam-

Furor   *Pluton*

Bottleneck—the entrance to Santiago Harbor.

paign. The first movement, however, was naval. In need of a sheltered anchorage in which to coal his vessels, Admiral Sampson sent the marines ashore at Guantánamo Bay on June 10 to drive the Spaniards off the commanding heights. On June 21, Army troops were landed near Santiago. In the jungle the land campaign bogged down, and there were several harsh passages between Army and Navy commanders. The Navy hoped the troops would push on and capture the port. The Army thought the Navy should force the entrance and take the harbor from the sea. Cervera solved the dilemma for them.

Hobson's **Merrimac** fails to seal it.

On Sunday morning, July 3, Santiago was sunny and warm. The blockade had settled down to routine, varied only by an occasional bombardment of the forts. That morning the ships deployed in a semicircle outside the harbor, and the usual Sunday calm prevailed. Reading from west to east around the semicircle, the blockading ships were the converted tug *Vixen*, two miles offshore at the western tip; next was *Brooklyn*, then *Texas*, *Iowa*, *Oregon*, *Resolute*, and *Ericsson*. Closer in shore were *Gloucester* and *Indiana*. *Massachusetts* had been in line next to *Iowa*, but was short of coal and had been ordered to Guantanamo to refuel. She had left at 4:00 A.M. At eight thirty Admiral Sampson in his flagship, the *New York*, also sailed away, bound for the Army beachhead to the east to confer with General Shafter, the Army commander. Commodore Schley, in the *Brooklyn*, was left in command of the force.

At nine o'clock a column of smoke rose from behind the hills that screened the Spanish harbor anchorage from the blockading ships. But it was

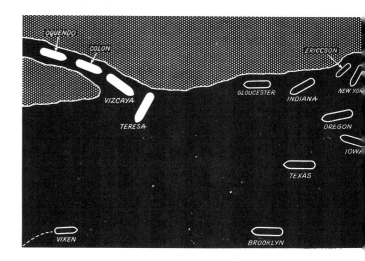

not certain if it was from a ship's stack and no alarm was sounded. The lookouts, however, had been alerted. When the sharp prow of the *Maria Teresa* showed around the headland at nine thirty-one, it was sighted simultaneously by practically every ship in the fleet. The *New York* was still in visual distance. Seeing the flash of the warning gun from the *Oregon*, she turned back at full speed to rejoin.

Admiral Cervera, because of the narrowness of the channel, had to sortie his ships in column. He led in *Maria Teresa*, followed in order at eight-hundred-yard intervals by *Viscaya, Colón, Oquendo, Furor,* and *Pluton*. His plan was to come out at full speed to catch the blockading ships unaware and then outrun them and put in at Havana. The Spaniards had miscalculated both the ability

Vizcaya explodes against the shore.

of the American firemen to get up steam and the accuracy of the naval gunners.

As *Maria Teresa* cleared the channel and turned west to run along the shore, she fired one gun at *Brooklyn* and a full broadside at *Indiana*, which, at the first sight of the enemy's prow, had headed for the harbor entrance under heavy fire from the shore batteries, which had opened rapid fire on the American vessels to help cover the sortie from the harbor of the Spanish squadron.

Indiana was first of the United States ships to hit. At least one shell from her broadside was seen to strike *Maria Teresa*, causing a fire amidships. Then every ship in the American squadron that could reach opened fire. As the faster Spanish ships moved on out of range of an American ship, the latter would shift her fire to the one following. Lightly-skinned *Pluton* was the first enemy vessel to go down. As the also lightly-armored *Gloucester* closed with her and *Furor* to screen the larger ships, for which they were heading with their crippling torpedoes, a large-caliber shell from one of the American battleships or cruisers hit *Pluton* amidships and literally cut her in two. She had been in the fight less than a quarter of an hour. Five minutes later *Furor*, raked by *Gloucester's* small guns and the secondary batteries of the larger American ships, turned, crippled, toward shore and ran herself aground.

The four Spanish cruisers, meanwhile, were steaming westward at their best speed under the concentrated fire of the American cruisers and battleships. The fight had begun at a range of approximately two miles. But as the United States vessels, forming a gantlet line down which the Spanish cruisers had to run, got up speed, they closed to sometimes less than a mile. At that range every gun could reach. At ten fifteen, forty-five

67

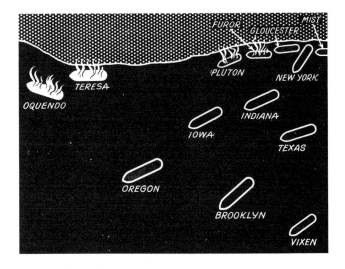

minutes after she had first appeared, *Maria Teresa* piled on a reef, a blazing wreck.

The second and third enemy cruisers in column, *Viscaya* and *Colón*, steadily had drawn out of range of the battleships' guns as our ships centered their attention on *Maria Teresa*, but the last one out of the channel, *Oquendo*, was not so fortunate. As she turned west to follow the fleeing ships ahead of her, she came under the fire of all four of the American battleships at once. Hit repeatedly and set afire, she staggered on for a few more miles but finally turned and ran ashore only a half mile beyond *Maria Teresa*. As she struck, she broke in two.

Most courageously maneuvered of the Spanish cruisers was *Viscaya*. Second in line to the *Maria Teresa*, when she saw damage being done to the flagship by the American guns, she turned out of line and headed directly toward the *Brooklyn*, westernmost of the American vessels, as though to ram. The *Brooklyn* turned hard a-port to present only her stern to the Spanish vessel, and the *Viscaya* then turned back in line. The maneuver, however, had cost her the advantage she had gained by her speed over the battleships. The *Oregon*, coming up fast under the drive of the beautifully-tuned engines that had brought her on the fourteen thousand-mile trip from San Francisco, brought her under fire. When the *Viscaya* turned back on course, she had opened up the batteries of the *Brooklyn*, and the two American ships made short shrift of the third Spanish cruiser. At eleven five she turned toward the beach

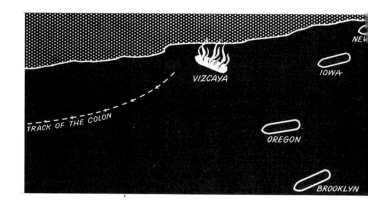

and also ran aground. Only one Spanish ship still remained afloat, the *Colón*.

Although third in line, *Colón* appeared to have escaped the heavy fire poured on her three sister vessels as they ran the American gantlet line, and she cleared *Brooklyn* to the westward still relatively unscarred. She turned toward the open sea with *Brooklyn* and *Oregon* in close stern chase and, several miles behind them, *New York*, *Texas*, and *Vixen*. For two hours the contending vessels steamed west, with the theoretically slower *Brooklyn* and *Oregon* gradually closing the range. At twelve fifty *Oregon* opened fire at nine thousand yards, four and one-half sea miles. Although the American shells were falling astern of *Colón*, they were gradually walking up on her, and at one fifteen Captain Dias Moreau hauled down the blood-and-gold banner of Spain and, heading his vessel toward shore, ran her aground.

Oregon *pounds the shore batteries.*

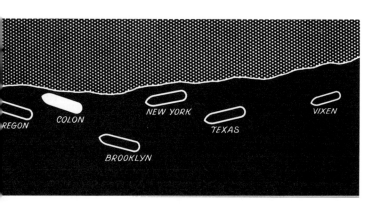

In three hours and forty-five minutes the entire Spanish squadron had been destroyed, with a loss of 350 men killed, 160 wounded, and 70 officers and 1,600 men taken prisoner. Only 150 made their way back to the Spanish lines at Santiago. United States losses were Chief Yeoman George H. Ellis of the *Brooklyn*, killed, and another man wounded by enemy fire. Several of the United States sailors also suffered punctured eardrums from the concussion of their own guns. United States fire was poor, with only 123 certain hits of 8,060 rounds fired, but the badly-trained Spanish

Privilege of imminent victory—even the boys watch the fight.

69

sailors did far worse. Only some thirty hits were counted on American vessels, most of them from small-caliber guns at ranges of less than a mile.

The war dragged on for another six weeks, but the only other naval action, except for short bombardments and some minor brushes with Spanish gunboats in various small harbors, occurred off San Juan. There the auxiliary cruisers *St. Paul* and *Yosemite* twice engaged *Isabel II* and *Terror,* the *St. Paul* scoring several hits on the latter. She also forced aground the merchantman *Luzon,* which was attempting to run the blockade.

Santiago surrendered on July 17, after a renewal had been threatened of a severe shore bombardment of ten days before, and as the American Army was closing in. On August 12, Spain sued for an armistice. Another expedition that had been convoyed to Puerto Rico was rapidly overrunning that island under the protection of naval guns when the cease-fire order came.

The Spanish home squadron, led by the only battleship, *Pelayo,* and including the armored cruiser *Carlos II,* the torpedo boat *Rapido,* three gunboats, the steamer *Patriota,* and some colliers, had sailed from Cádiz on June 16 and transited the Suez Canal as though bound for Manila. The move served only to cause some nervousness to Commodore Dewey at Manila and to the Navy Department in Washington. After passing through the canal, the squadron was recalled. Later information was that it had been in no condition to fight.

From the perspective of two-thirds of a century, it might appear to many that the Spanish-American War was the most minor of conflicts in which this country has engaged and the one that has had the least effect on United States history. A closer study shows how important a part it has played in national and international development.

The battles of Santiago and Manila Bay proved that American sailors and American ships were capable of more than holding their own with those of one of the former great naval powers of Europe. The acquisition of the Philippines and Guam, which came as an offhand by-product of the war, turned American attention toward the Pacific. The patriotic fervor aroused enabled the proponents of the Panama Canal to push through that project. It made this country conscious of its strength. It turned American eyes outward toward the rest of the world. United as a nation by the Civil War, its continental boundaries established, the brief war of 1898 made of the United States not only the major power of the Western Hemisphere but a great world power as well.

After the Spanish War America still was not, as Champ Clark had boasted after the successful conclusion in 1897 of our ultimatum to England on the Venezuelan boundary, "the most puissant nation on the globe," but it definitely was on the way. United States isolationism received its death blow in 1898. In the two great world wars since 1898 this nation each time has assumed its obligation as the arbiter of Europe and the balance of power in the world.

*Symbol of shattered Spanish power—the wreck of **Vizcaya**.*

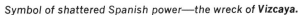

Nelson's *Victory* and *Katori* flank incoming *Kashima*—portent of things to come.

THE RUSSO-JAPANESE WAR-1904

A cold, wintry blanket of darkness hung over the Russian Far Eastern Fleet the night of February 8, 1904, as it swung at anchor in the roads outside the entrance to Port Arthur, the Manchurian naval base it had secured from China. Russia had forced Japan, in the Treaty of Shimonoseki, to relinquish its claim for the port for a like use.

Admiral Stark, the Russian commander, was expecting war but not that night. There had been no declaration of such intentions. Relations between Russia and Japan had been deteriorating for some time, and diplomatic relations had been broken. But Admiral Stark, like other Russian commanders and officials, believed the old rules still applied and that a country would give a gentlemanly warning before it made an attack. Like the United States commanders thirty-six years later, he underestimated the Japanese.

Just before the sounding of eight bells to mark the hour of midnight and the changing of the watch on the slumbering Russian ships, a fast Japanese torpedo boat flotilla darted in from the sea and attacked. Before the Russian crews could be routed out of their bunks to man their guns, the battleships *Tsarevitch* and *Retsivan* and the armored cruiser *Pallada* had been torpedoed. Without a declaration, the Russo-Japanese War had begun. In a year and four months of war from that night, a numerically inferior Japanese fleet swept the Russian Navy from the seas of the Far East in a series of sea fights and bombardments culminating on May 27–28, 1905, in the Battle of Tsushima Strait, which was the most one-sided naval victory since Nelson's rout of the French at Trafalgar a hundred years before. The war dealt Russian sea power a blow from which it had not recovered forty years later.

In the expectation of war with Japan, Russia had been strengthening her Far Eastern Fleet for many months. One of her best battleships, the *Oslabya*, was en route with an escort of smaller vessels to join Admiral Stark the night the Japanese launched their torpedo-boat attack. The Russians already had in the Far East seven battleships, nine armored and light cruisers, and several squadrons of gunboats, torpedo craft, and auxiliary vessels. In the Black Sea and the Baltic were two other fleets. In Russian shipyards several other battleships and cruisers were being fitted out.

Against this imposing, if divided, battle array of seventeen battleships, nineteen coastal defense ships mounting large-caliber guns, nine armored cruisers, and twenty-one lighter cruisers, Admiral Togo, the supreme Japanese commander, had but eight battleships, two coastal defense ships, nine

armored cruisers, and twenty-one light cruisers. The Japanese had the advantage, however, of making the Russians come twenty thousand miles to them. Too, Russia's Black Sea Fleet that included four battleships and three heavy-gunned turret ships was locked by treaty in that inland sea, forbidden to transit the Dardenelles. Even so, the odds on paper were heavily in favor of the Russian fleets. Most foreign observers expected the country whose symbol was a great bear to send down to quick defeat the upstart oriental nation of Japan.

The sympathies of the United States quite obviously were with the Japanese. At the Battle of Manila Bay, the Japanese ships there had arrayed themselves alongside the British squadron when it appeared the large German squadron might take a hand for Spain, and cheered the United States victory. Japan's open pretensions to dominance in the western Pacific had been viewed as amusing, but little else. Her protest that our annexation of Hawaii in 1898 would "upset the balance of power" in the Pacific had been received with astonishment and disbelief and had been ignored. What in the word could Japan be talking about? was the American reaction. What balance? Only the United States and the European nations were great sea powers. It still was a white man's world. Then, too, Americans had been irked by Russian restrictions on trade in her zones of influence in China in contravention of the principle of the Open Door.

The United States did even more than cheer for the Japanese. Two of Japan's warships had been built in United States shipyards. Americans had loaned Japanese firms money. American technical advice had helped Japan build up her heavy industries to the point where in the sixteen months

Retsivan—*victim of the first Japanese sneak attack at Port Arthur.*

Korietz blows up at Chemulpo.

between Port Arthur and Tsushima she was able to improve her fleet so that ship for ship it was far superior to the Russian. It was thirty-six years before these benevolence-hatched chickens came home to roost. The Japanese Navy's unheralded attack on the Russian Fleet at Port Arthur brought no outcry from the United States. Americans probably thought it somewhat unchivalrous, but necessary when a David was attacking a Goliath.

The Japanese did not delay in taking advantage of the efficacy of the Port Arthur attack and the stunning impact on the Russian Admiralty. As at Pearl Harbor three and a half decades later, the torpedoed Russian ships were not irretrievably lost, all three being able to get inside the harbor in shallow water before they sank. But the audacity of the Japanese move seemed to stun the Russian admirals. After that they seemed never able to do anything right.

The Russian Far Eastern Fleet had been attacked while divided. Instead of being concentrated at Port Arthur, three of the Russians' best armored cruisers — the *Gromoboi*, *Rossia*, and the *Rurik* — and the protected cruiser, *Bogatyr*, were stationed at Vladivostok, twelve hundred miles by sea to the northeast. The protected cruiser *Varyag* and the gunboat *Korietz* were in the Korean port of Chemulpo (Inchon).

Port Arthur was just the first of the Russian disasters. The Japanese followed up the night torpedo-boat sortie with a daylight attack by heavier vessels, during which the Russian battleship *Poltava* and the Russian cruisers *Diana*, *Askold*, and *Novik* suffered extensive shell-fire damage. On the same day, February 9, 1904, a Japanese squadron attacked and sank the *Varyag* in Chemulpo Harbor (the Japanese later raised her and added her to their fleet), and destroyed the *Korietz*. A few days later, the Russian mine-laying vessel *Yenessi* accidentally discharged a mine she was laying and was destroyed. Admiral Stark, although still possessing superiority to the Japanese forces opposing him, allowed himself to be partially blockaded in Port Arthur and made no effort to sortie or to interfere with Japanese movement of troops for a land attack.

Admiral Makharoff, one of the Russians' best admirals, was dispatched to supersede the inept Stark. But on his first sortie from Port Arthur on April 13 with the now repaired fleet, his flagship, the battleship *Petropavlosk*, struck a drifting mine, blew up, and sank. Most of the crew, and most disastrously the Admiral, too, were lost. The fleet returned again to anchorage in Port Arthur, where it was under fire of Japanese land batteries moving up behind the contracting siege arc around the port.

In August, a new Russian Admiral, Witjeft, decided to abandon the port and move to Vladivostok, and he led the fleet to sea in the repaired *Tsare-*

vitch, at the same time ordering the cruiser-led force in Vladivostok to sortie from there and meet him in the Sea of Japan.

Admiral Togo in the meantime also had suffered grievous losses to his fleet. On May 15, while cruising off Port Arthur inviting the Russian fleet to come out, he led his battle line into a field of drift mines. In quick succession the battleships *Hatsuse* and *Yashima* and the cruiser *Yoshino* hit mines and were destroyed.

Admiral Witjeft led to sea then, in August, a far more powerful fleet, on paper, than Togo had under his command. In addition to *Tsarevitch*, in the Russian line were the battleships *Retsivan*, which also had been raised and repaired in the seven months since the first attack, *Sevastopol*, *Pobieda*, *Poltava*, and *Peresviet*. They were escorted by four cruisers and eight destroyers.

Undaunted by the odds, the Japanese Fleet accepted the battle and closed with the Russian ships only a few miles outside Port Arthur in what is called the Battle of the Tenth of August. It opened at long range shortly after noon and continued without a letup until after 7:00 P.M. To bolster his weakened battle line, now reduced to four capital ships, Togo deployed the two new British-built armored cruisers, *Nisshin* and *Kasuga*, which had been purchased from Argentina just prior to the start of the war.

Showing a much higher degree of accuracy than the Russians and using high-explosive shells far superior to those of their enemy, the Japanese gunners severely mauled the Russian vessels. *Tsarevitch*, leading the Russian battle line, suffered grievously. One of the Japanese shells that exploded on her deck killed Admiral Witjeft. Here again, it seems the loss of one man counted for more than any ship damage. Admiral Witjeft had planned to push on to Vladivostok, no matter the cost, to join the cruiser and destroyer squadrons there. He reiterated the order just before he was killed. His second in command, Rear Admiral Prince Okhtomsky, was a man of another kidney.

When Admiral Witjeft was killed, the Russian Fleet fell into disorder, and Prince Okhtomsky ordered it back to Port Arthur. The cruiser commander, Rear Admiral Reitzenstein, in the *Askhold*, attempted to carry out Witjeft's last order, but the *Pallada* deserted him to follow Okhtomsky, and the Japanese ships made it impossible for the remaining Russian vessels to push on northeast. Only the *Bovik*, badly battered, finally got through to the Sea of Japan, and she was tracked down and destroyed. The *Askold* and a destroyer reached Shanghai, the *Diana* fled southward to the friendly French Indochina port of Saigon, and the battered *Tsarevitch*, with three destroyers, put in at Kiaochau, a port in German-leased Shantung Province. All were disarmed and their crews interned until the end of the war.

On August 10, the squadron at Vladivostok had sailed south from there, on Admiral Witjeft's orders, and was as far south as Fusan, approaching the Strait of Tsushima when it was intercepted by a Japanese squadron led by Admiral Kamimura. *Rurik* was sunk. *Gromoboi* and *Rossia* were hit many times before they could disengage to limp back to Vladivostok. Neither the Vladivostok

The Japanese open fire—Battle of August 10th.

*Built in Great Britain, bought from Argentina—**Kasuga**, one of Togo's cruisers.*

squadron nor the surviving ships at Port Arthur played any further part in the war. Most of those in the Manchurian harbor were sunk by Japanese land batteries before the capitulation of the port.

The outbreak of war found the Russians with the backbone of their Baltic Fleet — five new battleships — still being fitted out in Russian shipyards. Plans were immediately made to hurry this work and dispatch the entire available force to the Far East. But it was October 15 before it finally got under way. At the head of the fleet was one of Russia's finest naval officers, Admiral Rojdestvensky, in the battleship *Kniaz Souvaroff*. Ahead of it was a twenty-thousand-mile journey and the rapidly expanding Japanese Fleet.

The voyage almost came to disaster at the start. There had been rumors that Japan had bought in Europe and kept there a squadron of torpedo boats which was to attack the Russian Fleet before it could get well under way. Nervous Russian gunners first fired on a Swedish fishing vessel in the Skagerrak and then opened fire on the British trawling fleet off the Dogger Bank, sinking several vessels and killing many sailors. Britain demanded full reparations, and for a time relations between her and Russia were strained and tense.

Largely through the generously tendered use of French ports — France and Russia were long-time allies — Rojdestvensky made a slow voyage down the African west coast (sending part of his force

through the Mediterranean and the Suez Canal), around the Cape of Good Hope, and thence through the Indian Ocean and the South China and Yellow Seas to a point off Shanghai on May 25. He had been joined en route by another Baltic division of a turret ship, four coastal defense vessels, and a cruiser under Admiral Nebogatoff. Off Shanghai, Rojdestvensky detached all of his auxiliaries except four store ships, two repair vessels, and two hospital liners, and sent them in to anchorage in the Yangtze River. This, most observers at that time believed, was his first major strategic error.

Until the Russian service train appeared in the Yangtze, Admiral Togo could not know for sure just what passage into the Sea of Japan the Russians would attempt to force on their way to Vladivostok; there were three. Admiral Togo received word of the Russians only when they touched a port or were sighted at sea by a vessel friendly to Japan. With the appearance of the auxiliaries in Shanghai, however, he could be reasonably certain Admiral Rojdestvensky was bound for the passage between Korea and Japan. Either of the others, being much longer routes, would have required a refueling and reprovisioning at sea. Togo deployed his forces behind Tsushima and waited.

The weather was thick and worsening as the Russian Fleet steamed northeastward on May 25 from Shanghai, a distinct advantage to the Russians, as it lowered the chances of the fleet's being

Mikasa flew Togo's flag. Here she mothers several torpedo boats.

sighted and reported by Japanese scouts. The weather cleared somewhat the next day, but the following night was misty, and it was a late sunrise the morning of May 27. Admiral Rojdestvensky made his plans to pass through the narrowest part of the strait at noon. At 7:00 A.M., he was twenty-five miles northwest of Ukeshima, steering a northeasterly course for the strait, when he was first definitely sighted and identified by the Japanese cruiser *Idzumo*. An hour before, four Japanese cruisers had crossed astern of the Russian force but apparently had failed to see the enemy ships because of the mist. The *Idzumo* flashed the news to Togo's flagship, *Mikasa*, some one hundred miles to the north.

The Russian Fleet was deployed with its battle force in two parallel lines. To starboard was the stronger, the battleships *Kniaz Souvaroff, Imperator Alexander III, Borodino, Orel, Oslabya, Sissoi Veliky, Navarin,* and the cruiser *Admiral Nakhimoff.* In the port line were the turret ship *Imperator Nikolai,* on which Admiral Nebogatoff had his flag, and the three coastal defense vessels that had steamed with it from the Baltic — the *Admiral Senyaim, Apraxin,* and *Ushakoff.* Behind them was a cruiser division of four ships — the *Oleg, Amora, Dimitri Donski,* and the *Alexander Monormach.* Out ahead were three fast scout cruisers — the *Svietlana, Almaz,* and *Ural* — and there was a cruiser with two torpedo-boat destroyers on either flank. Bringing up the rear in the column were the four supply vessels, the two repair ships, and the two hospital liners.

Admiral Togo had four battleships, *Mikasa,* his flagship, the *Shikishima, Asahi,* and *Fuji,* the new armored cruisers *Sisshin* and *Kasuga,* and six other armored cruisers, the *Idzumo, Iwate, Adzuno, Asama, Tokiawa,* and *Yokumo.* Then he had in addition three squadrons of auxiliary cruisers and coastal defense vessels and a whole swarm of torpedo craft. The odds against him were more apparent than real. In addition, he had the incalculable advantage of knowing through his scouts exactly where the Russian Fleet was all the morning, how it was deployed, its course, and speed. Until Rojdestvensky sighted the Japanese battle line at 2:15 P.M. on a course to cross his bow, the Russian had no idea as to the location of Togo's main force. All he had seen were the cruiser scouts.

Admiral Togo led his battle line across the Russians' course at ninety-five hundred yards' range, then swung in a tight circle to port to recross in the maneuver known as "crossing the T." At the same time he sent his light cruiser divisions to the rear of the Russian line to attack the supply vessels.

As the Japanese ships circled to straighten out on an easterly course, Admiral Rojdestvensky turned his force to starboard on a parallel course and both fleets opened fire, the *Mikasa* and the *Kniaz Souvaroff* giving the signal to the other vessels by their opening broadsides. The first few Japanese salvos were over but the Japanese gunners soon corrected the range and began to get hits with stunning regularity. The Russian Admiral was slightly wounded with one of the first

Oslabya went down first under devastating fire from the Japanese gunners.

Admiral Nakhimoff, soon to follow Oslabya.

Shikishima—one of the four battleships under Togo's command.

shells to explode on his vessel. The Russians also were scoring on the Japanese ships, but not in equal measure. After the first twenty minutes during which the Russians were taking such punishment, their fire became, understandably, erratic.

The *Oslabya*, fifth ship in the starboard line, was the first Russian vessel to go down. A twelve-inch shell in one of the first enemy salvos penetrated her forward, just above the water line. It would not have been serious under ordinary circumstances but she, like all the Russian ships, had topside loads of coal. In the heavy sea, she began to take water through the shell hole. This flooded her portside bunkers and as she continued to take punishment, she dropped out of line, heeled over, and sank. The three following ships, the *Sissoi Veliky*, *Navarin*, and *Admiral Nakhimoff*, their upper works ablaze, also slowed and temporarily left the Russian battle line. The Japanese then concentrated their fire on the four leading battleships, all of which already were battered and on fire in many places.

As the *Oslabya* was sinking, the *Kniaz Souvaroff* suffered a hit aft, lost steering control, sheered off, and left the fight. The *Imperator Alexander III* thus became the leading ship. Aboard her, Captain Buchvostoff, with no orders from the wounded Admiral on the blazing wreck astern, led the three surviving Russian battleships in a great circle to starboard (south) and then turned back north. Admiral Togo started to follow them around, then seeing Buchvostoff's intention, countermarched to reverse his course and again "cross the T." As the two lines converged on a collision course, the fire of every one of the twelve Japanese vessels in the main battle force was concentrated on the *Alexander III*. She turned eastward in an attempt to escape but soon dropped out of line, leaking badly and afire. The *Borodino* now had the dangerous role as leader. She continued on an eastward course as Admiral Togo drew up on a parallel course to outmaneuver the Russians, using the superior speed his fleet possessed by virtue of his clean-bottomed, almost untouched vessels, as opposed to the seven-month-old fouled hulls and leaking sides of the Russians.

While the main battle between the armored ships was under way, the lighter Japanese cruisers closed with the supply ships to the south. In a running fight they badly damaged several of them, although suffering considerable losses themselves in the process. Admiral Dewa's cruiser flagship, *Kasagi*, was holed below the water line and had to head for port. The *Naniwa Kan* was also hit below the water line and had to drop out of the fight.

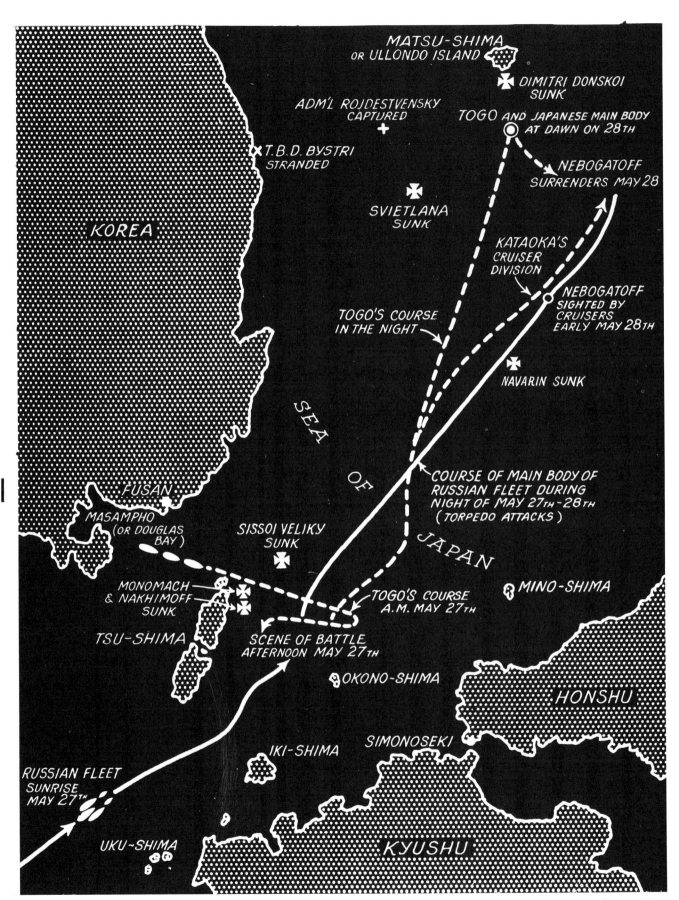

MATSU-SHIMA
OR ULLONDO ISLAND

DIMITRI DONSKOI
SUNK

ADM'L ROJDESTVENSKY
CAPTURED

TOGO AND JAPANESE MAIN BODY
AT DAWN ON 28TH

T.B.D. BYSTRI
STRANDED

NEBOGATOFF
SURRENDERS MAY 28

KOREA

SVIETLANA
SUNK

KATAOKA'S
CRUISER
DIVISION

NEBOGATOFF
SIGHTED BY
CRUISERS
EARLY MAY 28TH

TOGO'S COURSE
IN THE NIGHT

NAVARIN SUNK

SEA

OF

COURSE OF MAIN BODY OF
RUSSIAN FLEET DURING
NIGHT OF MAY 27TH-28TH
(TORPEDO ATTACKS)

78|

FUSAN

JAPAN

MASAMPHO
(OR DOUGLAS
BAY)

SISSOI VELIKY
SUNK

MINO-SHIMA

MONOMACH
& NAKHIMOFF
SUNK

TOGO'S COURSE
A.M. MAY 27TH

TSU-SHIMA

SCENE OF BATTLE
AFTERNOON MAY 27TH

OKONO-SHIMA

HONSHU

IKI-SHIMA

SIMONOSEKI

RUSSIAN FLEET
SUNRISE
MAY 27TH

UKU-SHIMA

KYUSHU

The Rising Sun begins its ill-starred ascent—Battle of Tsu
Shima Strait.

Navarin keeled over the following morning.

Some of the Russian vessels, however, were almost riddled with enemy shells and limped northward, herded like a flock of sheep by the darting Japanese cruisers and destroyers.

The whole Russian fleet by late afternoon was in an almost helpless huddle, under fire from Togo's twelve armored ships to the east and harassed from the south by the enemy's lighter cruiser squadron. Togo might have closed at any time to finish them off, but he chose to wait. He was like a hunter stalking a wounded bear. He still had his torpedo squadrons in reserve.

Admiral Rojdestvensky, again wounded, so that he could barely speak, had turned over command of the force to Admiral Nebogatoff in the *Imperator Nikolai* before being taken off the soon-to-sink *Kniaz Souvaroff*. He ordered Nebogatoff to push on through to Vladivostok. Admiral Nebogatoff's division had been largely ignored by Togo while he concentrated on the bigger battleships.

The *Borodino* still led the Russian battleship line. Behind her limped the *Orel*, then the *Alexander*, the damage to which had been partially repaired. Behind them the other Russian ships were in a confused group. As darkness came, the *Alexander*, hit many times again, finally gave up the ghost. She turned on her side and went down. A few minutes later the fires aboard the *Borodino* apparently reached her magazines, for she blew up and sank. Far astern a squadron of Japanese torpedo boats gave the *coup de grâce* to the *Kniaz Souvaroff*. The cruiser *Ural*, abandoned by her crew, was sunk by a few casual shots from a Japanese battleship.

Night found the remnants of the once proud Russian Baltic Fleet still struggling northward, with the Japanese battle line sheering away to the east. Admiral Togo had ordered his heavy ships to leave the area for a reason that soon became apparent to the Russian ships. With his battle force Togo had twenty-one destroyers, carrying torpedoes. In the sheltered bays of Tsushima were some eighty smaller torpedo boats that he had not ordered into action because of the high seas. At sunset he gave orders to the destroyer divisions to pursue the Russian ships and harass them during the night. Unknown to him, sixty-four of the torpedo boats, acting on previous orders, also sallied forth to join the fight. Just after eight o'clock they fell on the disorganized Russian ships from all sides.

When the major Japanese ships had left, to rendezvous to the northeastward off Ullondo Island at daybreak, the Russian commanders and crews must have believed it possible that now they might reach Vladivostok. Then came the destroyers and torpedo boats. All through the night the running fight continued. Only the darkness and the heavy sea saved the Russians from complete disaster then. The *Navarin* was hit by two torpedoes and sank the next day. Other ships also were hit and damaged but did not go down. The Japanese lost two torpedo boats to Russian fire and several others were hit or damaged in collisions.

What Russian formations remained were broken up during the night. Daybreak found them

79

*Russian torpedo boat **Biedovoi**—Admiral Rojdestvensky transferred from his flagship, was captured aboard one of her sisters.*

scattered all over the Sea of Japan. The only organized group was that of three turret and coastal defense ships and the armored cruiser *Orel*, in which was Nebogatoff, to which two cruisers had attached themselves. The four larger vessels were quickly surrounded, and after a few salvos from the Japanese at long range, Nebogatoff surrendered.

There remained only the stragglers to be mopped up. Some of the Russian ships refused to surrender and went down with guns blazing. Among these were the cruiser *Svietlana* and the coastal defense vessel *Admiral Oushhokoff*. Others were so badly hurt they sank without further enemy action during the day of the twenty-eighth or the following night, and others were scuttled by their crews. One cruiser division, composed of the *Oleg*, *Aurora*, and *Jemschug*, escaped during the night of the twenty-seventh and finally found safety and internment in Manila. The repair ship *Swir* and the supply vessel *Anadir* went to Shanghai. The cruiser *Izumrud* fled during the maneuvers that finally led to Nebogatoff's surrender on May 28, but she ran on a reef attempting to enter the Russian harbor of Vladmir Bay in Siberia and was destroyed to avoid capture. Seven of the nine torpedo boats that Admiral Rojdestvensky had with him were hunted down May 28 and 29 by the Japanese and sunk or captured. Among those captured was the *Buiny*, which had taken off the wounded Admiral Rojdestvensky from the sinking *Kniaz Souvaroff*. The transport *Korea* escaped to Madagascar. The only

ships of the Russian armada finally to reach Vladivostok were the cruiser *Almaz* and the destroyers *Brawy* and *Gresny*.

Thus, of the thirty war vessels and eight auxiliaries with which Admiral Rojdestvensky had entered the battle, only six of the smaller warships and three of the auxiliaries escaped, five of those to neutral ports for internment. Admiral Togo lost only two torpedo boats and suffered no major damage to any of his large vessels. The captured Russian ships were added to the Japanese Navy.

With their Far Eastern Fleet destroyed and their Far Eastern Army defeated on land, the Russians were willing to listen to President Theodore Roosevelt's peace proposals. Negotiations were begun in June. On August 23, 1904, at Portsmouth, New Hampshire, was signed the treaty that ended the war, which had been finally decided in those blazing hours in Tsushima Strait and the Sea of Japan.

The overwhelming victory over Russia, far more sweeping than the United States victory over Spain, had a similar stimulating effect on the Japanese people. The nation that had been forcibly "rescued" from barbarism by Commodore Perry discovered in the war with Russia that it could be, at times, more than a match for the superior-acting white countries. The sun that rose over the Russian wreckage of the Battle of Tsushima cast a shadow that eventually reached across the Pacific to Pearl Harbor.

Admiral Nebogatoff surrenders, and the Russo-Japanese War is almost ended.

80

THREE NEW NAVAL POWERS-1900

In column of divisions, four abreast, sixteen gleaming white battleships headed southward past the Virginia Capes through the late afternoon sunlight of December 16, 1907, obedient to the signal hoists transmitting the orders of "the old man" on the flagship, the new and stately sixteen-thousand-ton *Connecticut.*

Rear Admiral Robley Dunglison (Fighting Bob) Evans had led them out of Hampton Roads that morning, past the presidential yacht *Mayflower,* on whose afterdeck stood the President who said he believed in talking softly but in always carrying a big stick — Theodore Roosevelt. The fleet was going out to shake a big stick under the collective nose of the rest of the world, and especially of Japan.

From the joke navy of twenty years before, the United States Fleet had grown until now it was second in the world only to that of Great Britain. The projected cruise was the greatest naval ma-

Dreadnought—Britain continues her search for sea supremacy.

neuver ever undertaken by such a fleet. It was announced only as a cruise to San Francisco. It was intended from the start for the ships to go on around the world, and especially to visit Far Eastern waters, with or without an invitation from Japan.

There was not a ship in Evans' battle line over nine years old. Nine of them hardly had begun to stain their commission pennants with sea brine. They were the fruit of a "golden era" of naval expansion. Instead of contentment with the probability of the second-largest fleet on the seas, there now was serious discussion of a navy second to none. When England two years before had revealed the characteristics of its new revolutionary-type battleship, *Dreadnought,* with its main battery of ten twelve-inch guns, our Congress had been quick to answer by laying the keels for two matching vessels and proposing two more. Our construction program was part of a naval building race such as there had not been before in modern times. It was a race in which Germany and Japan had grimly joined, and even led for a while. The authoritative Brassey's *Naval Annual* (British) in 1899 included the United States and Japan in its comparative tables for the first time.

The ships that steamed southward in four columns through the late sunlight that December afternoon, therefore, were not the result of a growing tension with Japan that had quickly intruded after we had so wholeheartedly cheered the Japanese Fleet to victory over Russia at the Battle of Tsushima. The cruise of the fleet to the Pacific was, though.

Dissolution of the beautiful dream of everlasting friendship with Japan had been rapid after August, 1905. The Japanese were dissatisfied with their increments from the Treaty of Portsmouth, whose terms they felt had been largely dictated by President Roosevelt. They voiced their feelings. On our part we soon learned that Japan had no more intention of abiding by either the letter or the spirit of the policy of the Open Door in China than had Russia. Japanese–United States relations reached a crisis in 1906 with adoption by the city of San Francisco of a California statute that permitted segregation of children of "Mongolian or Chinese descent." Japan protested vigorously. The President, in a message to Congress, made what amounted to a public apology. But at the same time he ordered Fighting Bob Evans to pull back our battle units from Far Eastern waters, where they might have been trapped by superior Japanese forces, and asked if the Navy had a plan in case of hostilities. Of course it had one.

One of the lessons Navy men had learned from the Russo-Japanese War was that a fleet divided into several units, as had been the Russian, could be met and destroyed in detail by a basically in-

1906, **Dreadnought,** Great Britain: 17,900 tons; length 520', beam 82', draught 31'; armament ten 12'' guns, twenty-seven 12-pounders; speed 21.3 knots; complement 800.

ferior foe. It applied particularly to us because at that time we massed our fleet in the North Atlantic and kept only relatively inferior forces in the Pacific, and even those scattered in various squadrons. Great Britain had read the lesson plain, too, and had withdrawn many of her vessels from other oceans to augment the Home Fleet, to make it capable of overpowering the growing German Navy. This probably was one of the principal motivations for her secret alliance with Japan. This left the United States as the only strong nation whose interests conflicted in the Pacific with the growing insular people of Nippon. Instead of looking fearfully to the east, toward Europe, as Americans had for so long, they now turned their eyes to the west.

Rioting against orientals in San Francisco in 1907 again had increased the tension with Japan. The President sent William Howard Taft to Tokyo to explain matters to the Japanese and to talk of the horrors of war, but at the same time he stepped up the plans for the cruise of the fleet. When those plans finally were announced, Japan ordered Ambassador Aoki home for a "routine" consultation, using the same adjective the President had employed in describing the projected cruise. At a banquet at the Lotus Club in New York in his honor a few days before the fleet sailed, Admiral Evans said he and his men on the trip would be ready "for a feast, a frolic, or a fight."

Technical justification for the cruise was found in the Russo-Japanese War, where the difficulties of the long trip from the Baltic to the Far East by Admiral Rojdestvensky's fleet had set our Navy Department wondering what would happen if we should have to send our fleet from its North Atlantic bases to the Pacific. The four old battleships we had in the Pacific were no match for the Japanese. At that time the Panama Canal had not been built, and the only route for reinforcement was around the tip of South America.

The trip was an unqualified success. Admiral Evans led his sixteen battleships into San Francisco Harbor the following May in as good condition as when they had left Hampton Roads, with four and a half months of large-scale maneuvers under battle conditions behind them. "Fighting Bob" had to relinquish command in San Francisco because of failing health, but the fleet went on around the world as planned. Allegedly in accession to a Japanese suggestion, only part of the fleet made a formal visit to China — the Japanese didn't want the Chinese actually to see what a fine Navy we had, or so the story went. The extreme cordiality shown in New Zealand and Australia toward our officers and men strengthened ties that over thirty years later were to become ironclad in a common battle against Japan. It was freely stated that the two British Dominions and the United States were determined to see to it that the Pacific remained a white man's ocean.

The sixteen first-class battleships parading around the world in 1907–1908 were the backbone, but not the entire substance, of the great Navy

83

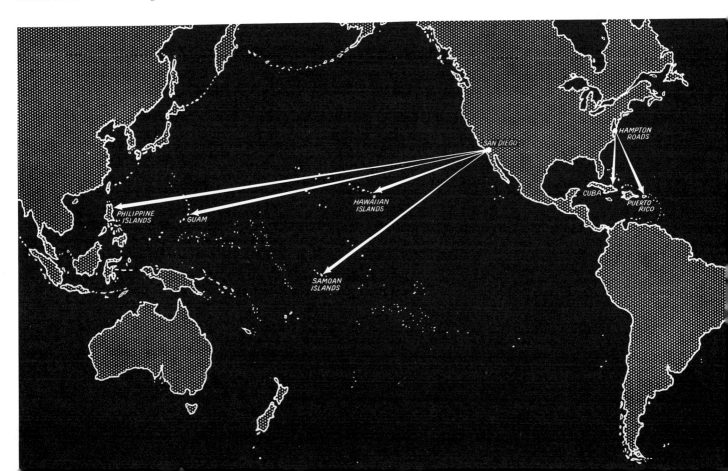

Delaware—the United States bids to stay in the race.

built or building. *Brassey's Annual* noted in 1908 that the United States had many fast heavy and scout cruisers, ships of eight-inch, six-inch and five-inch guns such as had proved so effective in the Battle of Tsushima in blanketing the superstructure of the Russian vessels and interfering with their big-gun fire. In other words, our Navy men had taken a middle position between the extremists who insisted on the one hand that it was the Japanese big guns that did the greatest destruction and that therefore we should build only battleships, and those at the other end of the line who thought the battleship reasoning was a fallacy and that smaller, faster, vessels with nothing bigger than eight-inch guns were the answer. In his message of December 3, 1907, to Congress, President Roosevelt made plain his philosophy of a balanced fleet. He also pointed out that a fleet was only as good as its fleet train (of supply) and its bases.

The attitude for a balanced fleet is reflected in the program laid before Congress by the Secretary of the Navy for 1908. It asked for the laying of keels of four battleships of the *Delaware* class (ten twelve-inch guns to make them worthy to "lay in line" with the British *Dreadnought*), four scout cruisers of the twenty-four-knot *Chester* class (two five-inch guns, six three-inch), ten destroyers, four

submarines, one ammunition ship, one repair ship, two mine-laying ships and four fleet colliers; this was before the day of oil. Except for battleships, the program was adopted. Appropriations were made for only two of the *Delawares*. President Roosevelt confided to a friend that that was satisfactory, as in asking for four he had been willing to compromise for half that number.

An equally important service of the Roosevelt administration in making and keeping the United States a great sea power was the construction of the Panama Canal. Canals between the Atlantic and Pacific, both for peace and for war purposes, had long been projected. In 1902, President Roosevelt secured from Congress the necessary authorization (the Spooner Act), and he immediately concluded, supporting the cession of Panama from Colombia, a treaty for the cession of territory to build it. The canal was completed and opened to travel on August 15, 1914.

Its locks, by which vessels are raised from sea level to the inland lakes across which they steam and then dropped down to sea level again,

1909, **Delaware**, United States: 18,000 tons; length 510', beam 85'6'', draught 27'6''; armament ten 12'', fourteen 5'' guns, four 1-pounders; speed 22.3 knots; complement 937.

were constructed with warships in mind. They were made 1,000 feet long and 110 feet wide. That was wide enough then to accommodate any naval or commercial vessel and was thought to provide for the foreseeable future.

The canal more than halved the distance between the fleet base at Hampton Roads and that at San Diego, cutting it from thirteen thousand miles to five thousand. It enabled us theoretically to guard both oceans with one fleet. Later calculations, based on the speeding up of war and the possibility that a hostile fleet or air force might be able to block the canal by attack, changed this viewpoint. In the 1930's we began talking of a two-ocean navy.

The Panama Canal was one of the great engineering feats of all time. Chief engineer was Lieutenant Colonel George Washington Goethals, later promoted to major general. His achievements have been somewhat overshadowed by great engineering projects done since. But considering the machines with which he had to work, the building of the canal in seven years was a major achievement. In the early days, slides in the cuts through which the canal passed, especially the great Culebra Cut, hampered both construction and operation. In recent years, with advances in engineering, such difficulties have been few.

No longer will an **Oregon** *race around the Horn—Miraflores locks of the Panama Canal.*

85

Led by Representative R. C. Hobson, of Santiago fame, in the House and by Senator Henry Cabot Lodge and other Republican stalwarts in the Senate, the Big Navy group, mostly Republicans, was able to maintain the program of construction through the four years of the Taft administration and even into the first year of the administration of President Woodrow Wilson, which began in 1913. The next year, however, the two-battleships-a-year program was cut in half.

Even this building rate was not sufficient to maintain superiority over or even equality with Germany, which was building ships of all kinds at a pace accelerating from year to year. Russia, which had sunk back to a third-rate power after the terrible defeats of the Russo-Japanese War, also was fully embarked on a building program by 1914, and France was rapidly overhauling the United States position.

In 1908, when our Atlantic Fleet steamed around the world as the second-finest navy, the comparative tables listed the battleship strength of the various sea powers as follows:

	G.B.	U.S.	Germany	France	Japan	Italy	Russia
Built	54	24	22	18	12	10	8
Building	6	5	6	6	4	3	4
	60	29	28	24	16	13	12

In 1914, on the eve of the First World War, the comparative tables showed this strength:

	G.B.	Germany	U.S.	France	Japan	Russia	Italy
Built	68	37	31	21	16	8	11
Building	14	11	5	10	4	11	4
	82	48	36	31	20	19	15

The United States building program was not even as up to date as it looked. Some of the five ships building were from authorizations of three years before.

In a fight at sea, however, it could be seen that Great Britain had nothing particularly to fear from Germany, unless Italy — then a member of the Triple Alliance with Germany and Austria-Hungary — went to war with her ill-suited diplomatic allies. Great Britain had maintained her two-navy standard, that is, a navy greater than that of any other two powers, and her diplomatic partners in the Entente Cordiale — Russia and France — both were building battleships at a comparable rate with Germany. When Great Britain was able to bring Italy in on her side, the balance at sea was swung overwhelmingly. Austria, with eleven old battleships, all bottled up in the Adriatic, was of little use at sea to her ally. World War I, however, was to see something new added, unrestricted war under the sea, by a fleet of German submarines that almost won the war.

86 | *Nassau—Germany accepts the challenge and gathers her strength.*

*1908, **Nassau**, Germany: 18,500 tons; length 470′, beam 89′, draught 27′6″; armament twelve 11″, twelve 6″ guns, sixteen 24-pounders; speed 20 knots; complement 963.*

Blücher—to be caught by Beatty.

EARLY PHASES OF WORLD WAR I

On August 4, 1914, began the greatest naval war in over one hundred years, and the third of modern times; our own war with Spain was the first, the Russo-Japanese the second. It saw arrayed against each other fleets far beyond even the dreams, perhaps, of Nelson at Trafalgar in 1805. Before it was concluded, with the armistice of November 11, 1918, every great power of the world was involved — Britain, Germany, the United States, France, Japan, Italy, and Russia. Britain, as the leading naval power, with a force almost twice as powerful in battleships as the navies of any two other countries, including the United States, bore the principal burden for the Allies. The German Navy did nearly all the fighting for the other side.

In the years between 1898, when armored fleets first opposed each other at Manila Bay and Santiago, and 1914, the capital ships of the world's fleets had grown from the 10,000- and 12,000-ton "battleships" of the turn of the century to such steel-clad monsters of their day as the 27,500-ton *Queen Elizabeth's* of the British Navy with their eight fifteen-inch guns and thirteen-inch armor plate; *Haruna* of the Japanese Navy (under construction), with eight fourteen-inch guns; *Borodino* of the Russian Navy — 32,200 tons and twelve fourteen-inchers; *Nevada* of the United States Navy — 27,500 tons and ten fourteen-inch Naval rifles. Germany had two fifteen-inch gun ships under construction, but at the start of the war the remainder of her first-line ships carried no bigger than twelve-inch rifles. Most of them, however, were faster than the British vessels.

Great Britain had two great problems at sea when the war began. The first was to contain the German High Seas Fleet in the North Sea. The second was to protect her life lines of empire against commerce raiders. In the first few days of the war, there was a food scare in Britain that might have had serious consequences had the German cruisers then at sea gone into action immediately in the steamer lanes, or had Germany unloosed her wolf packs of submarines, as she did two years later.

While the British Home Fleet deployed in the North Sea from its newly selected anchorage at Scapa Flow in the Orkneys, Britain's far-flung cruiser squadrons began their task of running down the German vessels at large in the outer seas. Most potent of these enemy groups was the German Far Eastern Squadron composed of the armored cruisers *Scharnhorst* and *Gneisenau* and the light cruisers *Leipzig*, *Emden*, and *Nürnberg*. Also in the Pacific was the light cruiser *Dresden*. The Far Eastern Squadron was under command of Rear Admiral Graf von Spee. It had bases at Tsingtao, in Germany's concession on the Shantung Peninsula, in the Caroline, Marshall, and Mariana Islands — all of which figured so prominently in World War II — at German Samoa and at Rabaul, New Britain. The ships were all at sea on August 4. It was not until November 1 that the British cruiser squadrons finally caught up with von Spee and the bulk of the German squadron. Then it was to their sorrow. The meeting took place in the southeastern Pacific off the Chilean port of Coronel.

Rear Admiral Sir Christopher Cradock, with his base in the Falkland Islands off the coast of Argentina, in October had been ordered to round Cape Horn and search the south Pacific for von Spee's squadron. Cruisers from the German squadron, particularly the *Emden*, had been raiding commerce in the Pacific and had served as a constant threat to movement of any merchant vessels of belligerent nations in that ocean. Late in September von Spee had bombarded the French port of Tahiti.

Japan had come into the war on the allied side on August 24, 1914, on the promise, it was learned later, of most of the German possessions in the Pacific, and was guarding the western and northern Pacific. Von Spee's presence at Tahiti had led the British to believe he was headed for the west coast of South America, perhaps to halt the Chilean nitrate trade or to stop other South American vessels carrying valuable war cargoes. The British Admiral went out to intercept him.

Admiral Cradock had as the backbone of his force the armored cruisers *Good Hope* and *Monmouth*, the former mounting two 9.2-inch and sixteen six-inch guns. The *Monmouth* carried only

Scharnhorst flew von Spee's Flag.

Leipzig

six-inch guns. With them were the second-class cruiser *Glasgow* and the auxiliary cruiser *Otranto*. Plodding along behind, escorting the colliers, was the seventeen-year-old battleship *Canopus*, the main battery of which was four twelve-inch guns. It was a force considerably inferior to that under von Spee's command, whose 8.2-inch-gun cruisers, the *Scharnhorst* and the *Gneisenau*, had two of the best firing records in the German Navy. At long range, and without the *Canopus*, it would be the German's sixteen large-caliber guns against the British squadron's two. Despite this enemy superiority, Admiral Cradock started his sweep of the Chilean coast with his cruisers, leaving the *Canopus* plodding along some two hundred miles astern.

At four thirty the afternoon of November 1, 1914, the *Glasgow*, scouting ahead, made contact with von Spee's force. After being sure she was seen, she retired toward the *Good Hope*, several miles away. Although overmatched, instead of attempting to join the *Canopus* before attempting to bring the German squadron to action, Admiral Cradock maneuvered for a decision then. It was surmised he did not want to lose contact, once gained, and he was hopeful he might so damage the German ships, or some of them, that they would be easier to find than they had been before. Whatever the reason, he attempted to close.

The sea was high, but the sky was clear as the two squadrons neared each other, the British to the westward, with the setting sun shining in the German gunners' eyes to give the British a momentary advantage. Admiral von Spee used his ships' superior speed to stay outside of range

until the sun had gone down. Then conditions were changed. Now it was the German gunners who had the advantage. The British ships were sharply outlined against the afterglow, while the German ships became mere shadows against the darkening sky and the Chilean coast. Von Spee closed for action.

It proved an unequal contest from the start. The relatively untrained British crews, many of them reservists, were no match at the guns for the Germans. They would not have been under equal conditions. Under the disadvantage of not being able to see the fall of their shot, they were hopelessly outclassed. In a matter of minutes, both the

89

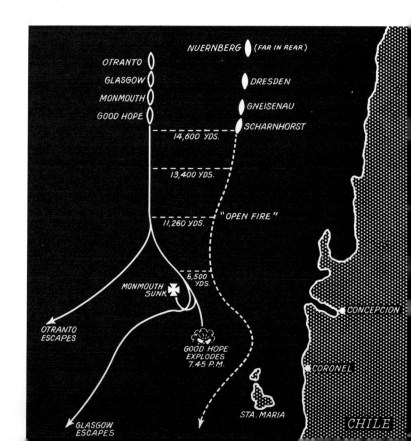

*Famed **Emden** was to run free later—but only for a while.*

Good Hope and the *Monmouth,* on which the two German armored cruisers were concentrating their fire, were badly hurt, holed, and aflame. At seven forty-five a great explosion tore the *Good Hope* in two as she was limping directly toward the Germans, apparently determined to sell herself dearly. A few minutes later, under cover of the rain squalls that had swept across the battle area, the battered *Monmouth* and the practically untouched *Glasgow* and *Otranto* broke off firing and attempted to flee to the west. Quite by accident the *Nürnberg,* which had been too far astern to get in the fight, while steaming to rejoin von Spee passed close enough to the crippled *Monmouth* to identify her and sink her without getting a reply from the British cruiser's guns. In the darkness, the *Glasgow* and the *Otranto* escaped to join the *Canopus.*

There were no survivors from either British cruiser, Admiral Cradock perishing on his flagship.

The defeat off Coronel was a serious blow to British prestige. Even more, it still left at large a formidable German squadron. The battle cruisers *Inflexible* and *Invincible* were detached from Jellicoe's Grand Fleet, and with them, and a further augmented squadron, Vice Admiral F. Doveton Sturdee was sent out to track down and destroy the German squadron and the German commerce raiders. He arrived at the Falkland Islands to coal on December 7.

Shortly after the Battle of Coronel, von Spee was ordered by Berlin to break through the British screen and return home. He decided to look in at the Falklands on the way, destroy the signal station and what ships he found there. With him as he

*Flying Craddock's Flag, she sacrificed herself—**Good Hope.***

90

And now **Invincible**, flying Sturdee's flag, leads the chase.

She and **Inflexible** near their quarry . . .

transited the Strait of Magellan from the Pacific to the South Atlantic were the same ships he had at Coronel — the *Scharnhorst* (his flagship) and *Gneisenau*, and the *Leipzig, Nürnberg,* and *Dresden*. The *Prinz Eitel Friedrich* had been with him off Chile, after Coronel, but he had detached her for raider work. On the morning of December 8, as he steamed north, he sent the *Gneisenau* and the *Nürnberg* ahead to scout the harbor and destroy the British wireless station on the point of land that screened the harbor from the south.

Admiral Sturdee, instead of giving his ships on arrival the expected long notice to coal and make repairs, had put them instead on two-hour notice. When the German ships were sighted, the British quickly got underway. The first shot was fired by the *Canopus*, which had an officer ashore at the signal tower to spot for her. When the Germans came within what this officer estimated to be his guns' range, eleven thousand yards, and as they deployed to begin shelling the wireless station, the *Canopus* fired. The shells fell short, but the German ships turned away and sped south to rejoin von Spee as Admiral Sturdee led his force out to battle.

The German squadron had a good head start, but an unexpectedly clear day, the superior speed of the British battle cruisers, with their top speed of 26 knots compared to the *Scharnhorst's* and *Gneisenau's* 22.5 — which they never were able to make because of their long months without overhaul — soon closed the distance between the two squadrons.

Admiral Sturdee, with his flag in *Invincible* — eight twelve-inch guns — led a vastly superior force. *Inflexible* had a similar armament. Then there were the armored cruisers, *Cornwall, Carnarvon,* and *Kent,* with guns up to 7.5 inches, the second-class cruisers *Glasgow* and *Bristol,* and the auxiliary cruiser *Macedonia.* The old battleship *Canopus* was left behind to guard the harbor.

The German light cruiser *Leipzig* was the rear guard of the German squadron. She apparently was unable to keep up speed. At about one o'clock, after the chase had been underway for three hours, the British flagship opened on her, and von Spee made the brave decision to sacrifice his flagship and the *Gneisenau* in an effort to shake free his light cruisers to continue their effective raiding of commerce. He sent the signal to the latter to scatter and head southeast, while he turned to the northeastward on a converging course with the two British battle cruisers. The British cruisers, *Cornwall, Kent,* and *Glasgow,* turned to follow the German light cruisers, and Admiral Sturdee closed with *Inflexible* and *Invincible* to engage the German heavies. At about one thirty the British ships opened fire with their twelve-inch guns.

For almost three hours, in which the slower *Carnarvon* finally came up to join, the unequal fight was carried on. Outgunned at long range, von Spee attempted to close with the British ships to blanket their decks and turrets with his superior secondary batteries of 5.9-inch guns, as the Japanese had done so effectively against the Russian ships at Tsushima. Admiral Sturdee had the speed on him, however, which Rojdestvensky had not had on Togo nine years before, and the British battle cruisers were enabled to maneuver at long range and tear apart the German ships with their twelve-inch shells.

At four seventeen the *Scharnhorst* went down with Admiral von Spee and every man of her crew. For almost two hours longer the *Gneisenau,* now subject to the fire of both the battle cruisers

and **Invincible** *opens fire off the Falklands.*

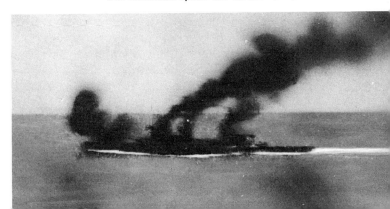

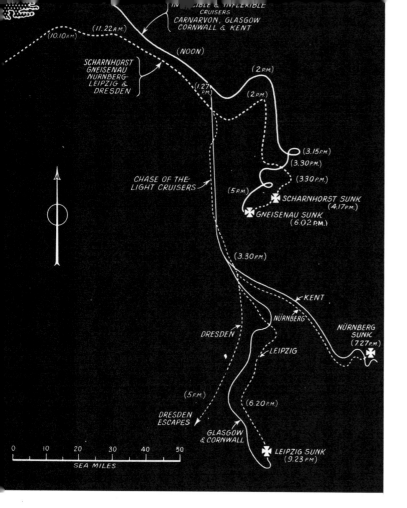

CARNARVON, GLASGOW
CORNWALL & KENT

(11.22 A.M.)

(10.10 A.M.)

(NOON)

SCHARNHORST
GNEISENAU
NÜRNBERG
LEIPZIG &
DRESDEN

(1.27 P.M.)

(2 P.M.)

(2 P.M.)

(3.15 P.M.)
(3.30 P.M.)

CHASE OF THE
LIGHT CRUISERS

(3.30 P.M.)

(5 P.M.)

SCHARNHORST SUNK
(4.17 P.M.)

GNEISENAU SUNK
(6.02 P.M.)

(3.30 P.M.)

KENT

NÜRNBERG

DRESDEN

NÜRNBERG
SUNK
(7.27 P.M.)

LEIPZIG

(5 P.M.)

(6.20 P.M.)

DRESDEN
ESCAPES

GLASGOW
& CORNWALL

LEIPZIG SUNK
(9.23 P.M.)

0 10 20 30 40 50
SEA MILES

92

Dresden is finished in the Juan Fernandez Islands.

in the Juan Fernandez Islands west of Coronel on March 14 and sunk by *Glasgow*.

The destruction of von Spee's squadron eliminated the only sizable German force at sea. Other commerce raiders were finally run down and either sunk or forced into neutral harbors for internment. The spectacular *Emden* was caught in the Cocos Islands on November 9 and sunk by the Australian armored cruiser *Sydney*. The *Karlsruhe* blew up off the West Indies in November. The *Prinz Eitel Friedrich* and the *Kronprinz Wilhelm* found sanctuary, but internment, in Newport News. Within nine months of the start of the war the British Navy had full control of the outer seas, except for submarines. The scene was set for the Battle of Jutland and unrestricted submarine warfare, which finally was to bring the United States into the war against Germany to tip the scales definitely in favor of the Allies and against the Central Powers.

The two years that passed before the Battle of Jutland brought many lesser naval actions between units of the British Grand Fleet and the German High Seas Fleet. Both fleets were to suffer grievous losses.

One of the first and worst to befall the British was the sinking of the three armored cruisers *Cressy*, *Hogue*, and *Aboukir* by a single German submarine, the *U-9*, on September 22, 1914, while

Inflexible picks up all those left of **Gneisenau's** crew.

Inflexible picks up all those left of **Gneisenau's** crew.

and the *Carnarvon*, fought on. Finally, dead in the water, all but one of her guns out of action, afire from stem to stern, her crew opened her sea cocks, and she too sank. The British ships picked up some 200 of her complement of 850 officers and men, but many of them were wounded and died within a few hours of rescue. Speed and trigger-sharp gunnery had decided the issue, as they always must in a surface fight in the open sea, other conditions being equal.

While the main battle was going on, the British and German cruisers were dueling far astern and to the southeastward. The *Glasgow*, being the fastest of the British ships, harried the German vessels until the two armored cruisers, *Kent* and *Cornwall*, could come up. Then she turned the task of destruction over to them. *Kent* caught and destroyed the *Nürnberg* shortly after seven o'clock. *Glasgow* and *Cornwall* engaged *Leipzig*, which finally sank at 9:23 P.M. No men were saved from the *Nürnberg*, only a few from *Leipzig*. *Dresden*, meanwhile, had outrun the British cruisers and made her escape. She was to prowl the steamer lanes for three months more before being caught

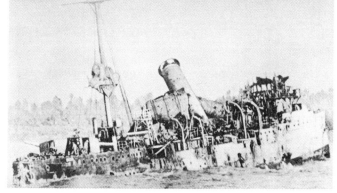

Emden—run down in the Cocos Islands.

Beatty's ships go into action off the Dogger Bank.

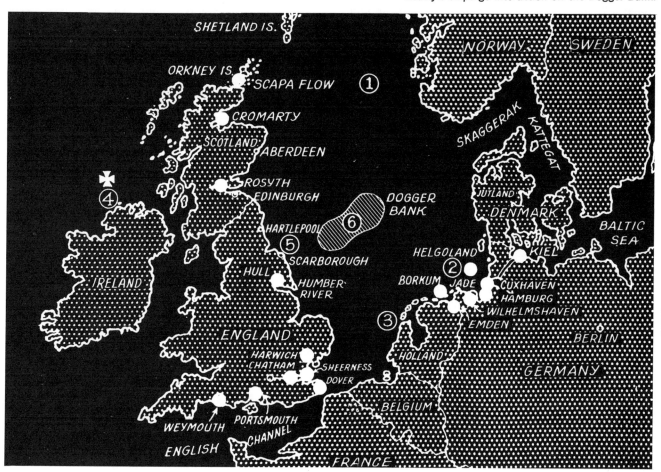

93

1—Waters of the British Home Fleet based at Scapa Flow.
2—British surprise sweep off Helgoland, sinking German light cruisers **Koln, Ariadne, Mainz,** and a destroyer.
3—German submarine **U-9** sinks British armored cruisers **Cressy, Hogue,** and **Aboukir.**

4—British battleship **Audacious** strikes a mine and sinks.
5—German battle-cruiser squadron bombards English coast at Scarborough, Whitby, and Hartlepool.
6—Beatty catches a German squadron off the Dogger Bank and sinks the cruiser **Blücher.**

Beatty scores and **Blücher** rolls over off the Dogger Bank.

they were maintaining a screening station off the Hook of Holland to the east of Dover and the English Channel, across which Channel steamers were moving the British Expeditionary Force to France and Belgium. All three sank within half an hour with a loss of over fifty officers and fourteen hundred men. A month and five days later, on October 27, the new battleship *Audacious*, while maneuvering for target practice off the northwest coast of Ireland, struck a submarine-laid mine and sank while under tow for port.

One of the most audacious early moves of the British fleet against the Germans was a sweep off Helgoland on August 28 of the first year of the war by Commodore Roger Keyes, Commodore R. Y. Tyrwhitt, and Commodore W. E. Goodenough with light cruisers, supported by Vice Admiral Sir David Beatty and his battle cruisers. The Germans had not had time to mine their home waters and were depending on light cruisers and destroyers to patrol the approaches to the main High Sea Fleet anchorages and berths at Helgoland and the Jade Bay. On a misty morning the sweep was made. It appeared to have caught the Germans completely by surprise. In poor visibility, the British groups met and destroyed the light cruisers *Köln*, *Ariadne*, and *Mainz*, and a destroyer, the *V-187*, and damaged several other ships. The only British ship to suffer any considerable damage was the light cruiser *Arethusa*, which was safely towed to port. The sweep was the conception of Commodore Keyes.

The Germans were active themselves, in addition to being a constant menace to the troop ships moving across the Channel. On December 16, 1914, a squadron led by the battle cruisers *Seydlitz*, *Moltke*, *Derfflinger*, and *Von der Tann* bombarded the Yorkshire coast, hitting Scarborough, Whitby, and Hartlepool, and then evading an attempt at interception by Beatty and Jellicoe. The High Seas Fleet came out to support the raiding force, which was under command of Rear Admiral Franz von Hipper, but it turned away after a night contact of

its cruiser screen, and a general action was averted.

On the following January 24, off the Dogger Bank, the fishing grounds to the east of England in the North Sea, Beatty got part of his revenge for the failure to intercept off Yorkshire. Apprised by British agents in Germany that the original raiding squadron, minus the *Von der Tann*, apparently was again getting ready for sea, Beatty was sent out to sweep for them. In the misty early morning hours of January 24, he contacted the German ships and, in a running fight of several hours, sank the German heavy cruiser *Blücher* and seriously damaged the *Seydlitz* and the *Moltke*. Beatty's own flagship, the battle cruiser *Lion*, was put out of action just as it appeared the whole German squadron might be cut off from Helgoland and destroyed — Beatty having superior forces to command. In the confusion that followed one of his last maneuvers and the misreading of his last message before the *Lion* dropped out of line, the chase was dropped. Beatty transferred from the crippled *Lion* to a destroyer and overtook his battle squadron, but by that time the German ships were safely away. The *Lion* was towed to port and repaired.

The Dogger Bank action was the last major action before Jutland. The Home Fleet settled down to constant sweeps of the North Sea, to keep the German High Seas Fleet contained and to combat the growing submarine menace. In the Mediterranean, the British forces were active in support of the campaign against Turkey, which had joined the Central Powers in the war, taking a large part in the landings at Gallipoli and the attempt to seize or force the Dardanelles. The Dardanelles expedition had the twofold purpose of securing the Suez Canal from an overland attack through the Near East and of joining forces with the Russians in the Black Sea, thus splitting Turkey. The old battleship *Goliath* was torpedoed and sunk during these operations, and the Dardanelles campaign finally was abandoned.

*Mine victim—**Audacious** sinks off North Ireland.*

Seydlitz, listing badly, races for the shore.

THE BATTLE OF JUTLAND - 1916

The Danish steamer *N. J. Fjord* was traveling placidly along through the North Sea some hundred miles west of the Danish province of Jutland the bright afternoon of May 31, 1916, minding her own business, when the column of black coal smoke from her stack was sighted almost simultaneously by light scouting units of the British Grand Fleet and the German High Seas Fleet, which were at sea unbeknownst to the other, attempting to entice some of the enemy's units within range of their battleships' big guns. Neither had expected to meet the other's main force. The Germans had not even entertained that hope. They were too heavily outnumbered and outgunned — thirty-seven British battleships and battle cruisers to the German's twenty-seven and 12-inch, 13.5- and 15-inch guns against their 11-inch and 12-inch main batteries. The British were definitely aware only of a sortie by the German battle cruisers.

While investigating the little Danish steamer, each hostile unit sighted the other, spread the alarm, and led the battle cruisers of the opposing forces to contact for the first phase of the greatest sea battle to that time. It is probable the two fleets would have met that night or the next day, even had it not been for this circumstance. But there always was the possibility that they might not have. They both had been to sea before without joining action. The little neutral ship served as the instrument of destiny to bring them together.

It seems incredible that on May 31, 1916, after almost two years of bitter war, the first- and second-ranking fleets of the world had not yet joined battle, especially since they were based only a few hundred miles apart, the German fleet on Helgoland and the British fleet in Scotland and at Scapa Flow in the Orkneys. The latter anchorage is only 440 sea miles as a plane flies from Helgoland Bight. In the Battle of the Dogger Bank on January 24, 1916, the two opposing battle cruiser squadrons had met, but inconclusively. Until the end of May, 1916, naval action in the North Sea had been largely submarine versus surface ship, an occasional brush between light cruisers or destroyers, and the laying of mine fields.

A raid by German battle cruisers on Lowestoft and Yarmouth on April 25, 1916, helped bring about the Jutland battle. The raid, by the *Lützow, Derfflinger, Moltke,* and *Von der Tann* on the two British east-coast towns had not done a great deal of damage. It had, however, aroused public opinion and led to public announcement by Lord Balfour that steps were being taken to make a recurrence improbable. This had led Vice Admiral Reinhard Scheer — who, only a few months before, had been named Commander in Chief of the High Seas Fleet — to believe his chances of bringing the Brit-

Lion—Beatty's flag.

ish Grand Fleet to action piecemeal were enhanced, as the announced British plan indicated a splitting of the battle squadrons between various ports along the English and Scottish coasts instead of leaving them concentrated at Scapa Flow.

Other political considerations also had led to the decision on both sides to seek a decisive engagement. The war on land was practically stalemated for the Central Powers — Germany and Austria-Hungary — in the summer of 1916. The German Army and people were demanding that the fleet break the British blockade, which was slowly strangling their country of both home-front and war-making supplies. Chancellor T. von Bethmann-Hollweg, in April, 1916, again had secured from the Kaiser an order forbidding unrestricted submarine warfare, against which the United States had so strongly protested in 1915, after the sinking of the *Lusitania,* and had renewed in the spring of 1916 when one of the first fruits of its resumption was the loss of American lives on the cross-Channel steamer *Sussex.* German naval lead-

Iron Duke—Jellicoe's flag.

Lützow—von Hipper's flag.

ers realized that submarine warfare was ineffectual if it was waged under the rules of international law, which made it necessary for the submarine to surface and stop any suspected vessel. So they had recalled most of the undersea boats to operate with the High Seas Fleet. The recall coincided with the projected raid on Lowestoft and Yarmouth, which was planned to coincide with the opening of an Irish rebellion.

Admiral Sir John Jellicoe, the British naval Commander in Chief, also was under political pressure to bring to battle and destroy the German High Seas Fleet. The Russians — the Bolshevik Revolution had not yet exploded — had demanded that the British open up a supply route to them through the Baltic. Admiral Jellicoe realized this could not be done as long as the High Seas Fleet was in being. He hoped, like his opposite number, that he could catch the enemy's scouting groups unsupported or some of his battle squadrons out alone and thus begin the task of defeating the enemy in detail instead of in one fleet engagement. This better suited his cautious nature.

The British fleet had just completed a sweep to the Skagerrak and was back home coaling when the German battle cruisers, supported by the High

Friedrich der Grosse—von Scheer's flag.

Seas Fleet, made the Lowestoft-Yarmouth raid. Jellicoe could not get back out in time to intercept them. The Admiralty did, however, at that time accede to the clamor to give more protection to the coasts — Scapa Flow was too far distant — and not only made the dispositions but announced them by inference.

The Fifth Battle Squadron, composed of Britain's four newest and biggest battleships, the *Queen Elizabeth's*, was attached to Vice Admiral

Jutland—the fleets and the battle area.

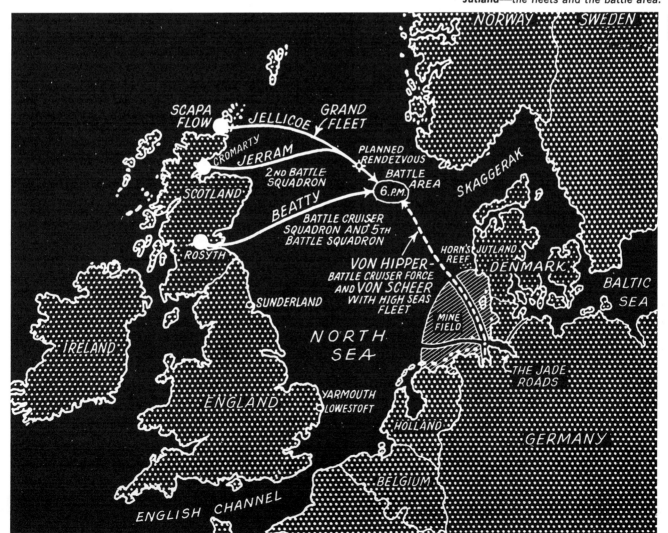

Inflexible—she was to lose three sisters later.

Seydlitz scored heavily in the opening moments.

Sir David Beatty's Battle Cruiser Squadron at Rosyth in the Firth of Forth. The *Queen Elizabeth* class were of 27,500 tons, with eight fifteen-inch guns and with a speed of twenty-five knots, not far enough below the twenty-eight knots of the newest battle cruisers of Beatty to make cruising with them impracticable.

The Second Battle Squadron under Vice Admiral T. H. M. Jerram was at Cromarty in Moray Firth, halfway between Rosyth and the main fleet base at Scapa. With Jellicoe at the home base was the Third Battle Cruiser Squadron of *Invincible*, *Indomitable*, and *Inflexible* under Rear Admiral H. L. A. Hood, the son of another famous British admiral. As will be seen later, this disposition of forces had considerable influence on the outcome of the battle.

In mid-May, Scheer decided on another raid, against Sunderland, by his battle cruisers supported by the main fleet, but bad weather over the North Sea made reconnaissance by Zeppelin impossible, and he decided on a less ambitious plan — a sweep of the Skagerrak, where British sea patrols were operating. Accordingly, he gathered his forces in the Jade Roads, which lie just to the west of the Weser estuary on the German North Sea coast and due south of Helgoland. This fact British Intelligence learned and transmitted to Jellicoe. When the German battle cruisers put to sea the morning of May 31, that fact was also reported. Intelligence on their movements was secured by interception of German wireless messages and their decoding through the key that had been captured by the Russians on the wreck of the *Magdeburg*. For some reason the Germans seldom changed their code and apparently had no idea the British were breaking it. The British, however, did not know that Scheer had followed Hipper,

commander of the cruiser forces and now a Vice Admiral, with the main fleet.

When the German fleet began concentrating in the Jade Roads the afternoon of May 30, Admiral Jellicoe and Vice Admiral Beatty — who had an autonomous status — were ordered to put to sea and rendezvous in the "Long Forties" the next day: Beatty from Rosyth with his battle cruisers and the Fifth Battle Squadron under Rear Admiral H. Evan-Thomas, who had not been operating with Beatty and was unfamiliar with his practices or tactics; Jellicoe from Scapa Flow with the First and Fourth Battle Squadrons and the Third Battle Cruiser Squadron; and Jerram from Cromarty with the Second Battle Squadron and the First Armored Cruiser Squadron. All had light cruisers and destroyer flotillas with them. Jellicoe ordered Jeram to join him next day at noon and set a rendezvous with Beatty, at a point not definitely defined, somewhere between what would be their 2 P.M. positions, from which they would steer on courses he had assigned so as to meet. Everything went as planned, except that Jellicoe was delayed in reaching his position, and Beatty's navigating officer gave him an incorrect position when he made his turn north to join Jellicoe shortly after two o'clock the afternoon of May 31.

Scheer meanwhile was carrying out his plan, which was to proceed almost due north from Helgoland to where the Skagerrak opened into the North Sea off Jutland. In anticipation that his movements eventually would become known to the British — he did not know how well they actually were surmised before he ever set sail — he had deployed his submarines off the various British bases to report on the British fleet. Unfortunately, these gave him little information. Two opened fire on the advancing screen of Jellicoe's force and

Gloucester—her type sighted von Hipper.

Revenge, Hercules, Agincourt, Colossus, Colling-wood, Neptune, St. Vincent, King George V, Ajax, Centurion, Erin, Orion, Monarch, Conqueror, and *Thunderer;* three battle cruisers: *Invincible, Indomitable,* and *Inflexible;* eight armored cruisers: *Defense, Duke of Edinburgh, Warrior, Black Prince, Minotaur, Cochrane, Hampshire,* and *Shannon;* twelve light cruisers; fifty-one destroyers and destroyer leaders; and the fast mine layer, *Abdiel.*

With Beatty were six battle cruisers: *Lion, Princess Royal, Queen Mary, Tiger, New Zealand,* and *Indefatigable;* four battleships: *Barham, Warspite, Valiant,* and *Cordelia;* fourteen light cruisers; one seaplane ship, *Engadine;* and twenty-seven destroyers. The two forces totaled 151 warships.

Jellicoe's flagship was *Iron Duke;* Beatty's was *Lion.* Rear Admiral Evan-Thomas had his flag in *Barham,* and Vice Admiral Jeram had his flag in *King George V.* Rear Admiral Hood was riding *Invincible.*

Scheer led a force of ninety-nine ships, divided as follows: With Hipper, who had his flag in *Lützow;* were the other battle cruisers, *Derfflinger, Seydlitz, Moltke,* and *Von der Tann;* ten light cruisers and thirty destroyers. With Scheer were the battleships *Friedrich der Grosse,* in which he had his flag, *König, Grosser Kurfürst, Markgraf, Kronprinz, Kaiser, Prinz Regent Luitpold, Kaiserin, Ostfriesland, Thüringen, Helgoland, Old-*

then had to dive while the major vessels they had not seen passed overhead, all unknown to them. Another submarine captain sighted Beatty's force, also after attacking the screen, but saw them steering a southerly course in an evasive maneuver taken because of his attack. This misled Scheer, who could not visualize from this information a British fleet concentration off Jutland the next day. It appeared to him to be independent sweeps of fleet units, which was just what he desired.

Under Jellicoe's command as he steered toward the rendezvous with Beatty the afternoon of May 31, 1916, were twenty-four battleships: *Iron Duke, Benbow, Bellerophon, Temeraire, Vanguard, Superb, Royal Oak, Canada, Marlborough,*

99

Superb opens fire as **Canada** follows.

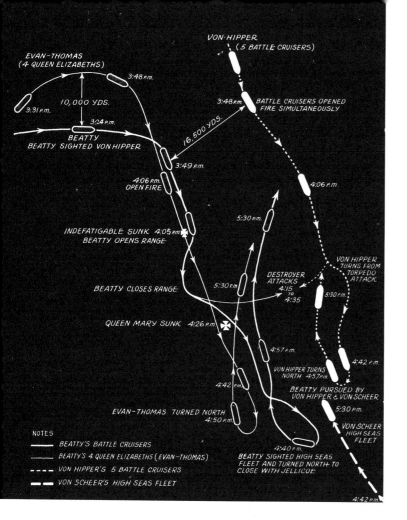

EVAN-THOMAS
(4 QUEEN ELIZABETHS)

VON-HIPPER
(5 BATTLE CRUISERS)

3:48 P.M.

3:31 P.M.

10,000 YDS.

3:24 P.M.

BEATTY
BEATTY SIGHTED VON HIPPER

3:48 P.M. BATTLE CRUISERS OPENED
FIRE SIMULTANEOUSLY

16,500 YDS.

3:49 P.M.

4:06 P.M.
OPEN FIRE

4:06 P.M.

INDEFATIGABLE SUNK 4:05 P.M.
BEATTY OPENS RANGE

5:30 P.M.

VON HIPPER
TURNS FROM
TORPEDO
ATTACK

BEATTY CLOSES RANGE

DESTROYER
ATTACKS
4:15
TO
4:35

5:30 P.M.

5:30 P.M.

QUEEN MARY SUNK 4:26 P.M.

4:57 P.M.

4:42 P.M.

VON HIPPER TURNS
NORTH 4:57 P.M.

4:42 P.M.

BEATTY PURSUED BY
VON HIPPER & VON SCHEER

EVAN-THOMAS TURNED NORTH
4:50 P.M.

5:30 P.M.

VON SCHEER
HIGH SEAS
FLEET

NOTES

———— BEATTY'S BATTLE CRUISERS
–––––– BEATTY'S 4 QUEEN ELIZABETHS (EVAN-THOMAS)
- - - - VON HIPPER'S 5 BATTLE CRUISERS
═══ VON SCHEER'S HIGH SEAS FLEET

4:40 P.M.
BEATTY SIGHTED HIGH SEAS
FLEET AND TURNED NORTH TO
CLOSE WITH JELLICOE

4:42 P.M.

100 | enburg, *Posen, Rheinland, Nassau, Westfalen, Deutschland, Pommern, Schlesien, Hannover, Schleswig-Holstein* and *Hessen* (the last six second-line battleships of eighteen-knots speed and mounting only four eleven-inch guns each in their main batteries); one light cruiser and thirty-one destroyers.

As probably was natural, since it was the smaller, the German fleet was more tightly knit than the British. The battleship organization was the same, each four ships being organized as a division under a rear admiral and two divisions to a squadron. Britain's nine battle cruisers were split into three squadrons to the Germans' one, her light cruisers into four squadrons to the Germans' two, and her destroyers into seven flotillas under different commands instead of into two flotilla groups, as were the Germans'.

At 2:15 P.M. on the fateful afternoon, the two fleets were in cruising order, with the battle cruisers ahead in each case, Beatty steering for a rendezvous with Jellicoe, who was sixty miles to the north, and Hipper leading Scheer and the German battle line by fifty-five miles. Both admirals knew hostile forces were cruising somewhere in the North Sea, but they did not know their course, their speed, or their ultimate objective.

The little Danish steamer, blundering along between the paths of the two great fleets, precipitated the engagement. She had been sighted by both light cruiser scouts before Beatty turned to the north to meet Jellicoe and the Grand Fleet, which has been joined as previously arranged by the battleship-cruiser force from Cromarty. The British light cruisers *Galatea* and *Phaeton* had continued on eastward, away from Beatty's northerly course, to investigate the Danish steamer, when they saw two German destroyers, which were mistaken for light cruisers, near the steamer. The British ships opened fire, then turned northwest to rejoin Beatty. They were followed by the German destroyers and the German light cruisers to which they were attached. The Battle of Jutland had entered the first of the four great phases into which it is customarily divided.

When Beatty and Hipper received the report of their light cruisers, both turned from their parallel northerly courses toward the point of contact, Beatty turning to the southeast so as to interpose himself between the German force, the strength of which he did not yet know, and the German bases. Hipper turned to the west. Neither was in sight of the other.

They steamed in that general direction for forty-five minutes, Hipper swinging to the northwest to follow his light forces that were engaging the British light cruisers. The Germans sighted and identified Beatty's ships at three twenty, and the latter identified the German battle cruisers at three twenty-four. Hipper turned about to the southeastward, and Beatty turned first east-southeast and then almost southeast on a slightly converging course. At three forty-eight, Hipper opened fire with all ships. The British vessels, in a turn, followed one by one *Lion's* opening salvo of three forty-nine as they squared away on their new course. Jellicoe at this time was fifty-two and one-half miles to the north.

Von der Tann

Indefatigable, target of **Von der Tann** . . .

vanishes under her plunging salvos.

The battle began with the two battle-cruiser forces on almost parallel courses to the southeast, with the Germans to the eastward of the British ships. Since the odds were six against five in favor of the British, Beatty ordered the *Princess Royal*, next in line to *Lion*, to concentrate with her on the leading German ship — Hipper's flagship, *Lützow* — and all others to take their opposite number. Through some error, the third British ship, *Queen Mary*, apparently did not understand, and she took under fire the third German ship, instead of the *Derfflinger*. The latter was left unfired on for several minutes.

This first phase of the battle went badly for the British. Firing with beautiful accuracy, the German battle cruisers soon were dropping salvos around all the British ships, and scoring hits; *Lion* and *Tiger* were hit within the first three minutes. The German fire was so heavy that at three fifty-two Beatty turned slightly more to southward in order to open the range and take advantage of his bigger guns — all twelve-inch to the Germans' twelve-inch and eleven-inch — and at 4:05 P.M. he turned even farther away. And well he might. By four o'clock, twelve minutes after opening fire, the Germans had scored twelve hits to four for the British.

The accuracy of the German fire paid its first major dividend at 4:05 P.M. when *Indefatigable* was hit in quick succession by two plunging salvos from *Von der Tann*. She exploded and sank.

Until the loss of *Indefatigable*, only Beatty's battle cruisers had been engaging the Germans. At 4:06 P.M. the Fifth Battle Squadron of four new British battleships, under Rear Admiral H. Evan-Thomas, finally got up to join the fight. They had engaged the German Second Cruiser Group of light cruisers, the ones that had first opened the battle, at three fifty-eight, but the Germans had turned away behind a smoke screen, and Evan-Thomas then had turned south, somewhat to the eastward and astern of Beatty's line, and almost due west of Hipper's force. The Germans now were in a precarious position, with five battle

Moltke—*her guns and* **Derfflinger's** *sank* **Queen Mary.**

cruisers and four battleships aligned against them. At four-fifteen Hipper ordered a destroyer attack, at the same time turning away to open the range between himself and the British ships. Beatty, at almost the same time, ordered his destroyer squadrons to attack, and turned back to the eastward to resume the fight, which his ships had largely abandoned when Evan-Thomas came up.

It was a disastrous resumption of the fight for Beatty's force. At four twenty-six *Queen Mary*, third in line, was hit much as *Indefatigable* had been, by a plunging salvo of twelve-inch shells from the *Derfflinger*, and she too turned away as her magazines began exploding, and sank. In thirty-eight minutes of action against a superior force, the German gunners had sunk two of the enemy's ten principal ships engaged.

The German battle cruisers also had been taking punishment, especially the rear ships of the line, which were under the fire both of Beatty's battle cruisers and Evan-Thomas' battleships. *Von der Tann* had only one of her four turrets still in action. At four twenty-seven, Hipper ordered a turnaway together, apparently deciding to wait for Scheer and the battle fleet to come up before resuming action. The first phase of the action, however, had gone in his favor beyond all expectations. The British squadrons had been badly outmaneuvered, Hipper had been allowed to close the range inside the maximum of the heavier British guns, and the German gunnery had been far superior. Lack of co-operation between the lighter British units and poor communications had been of help to the outnumbered German forces.

During the lull in the fighting between the bigger ships — Evan-Thomas also had turned away at 4:27 P.M. instead of following Hipper — the destroyer flotillas of both sides met in a free-for-all between the lines. It was not conclusive. Two destroyers were lost on both sides — the first German losses. One of the British destroyers scored a torpedo hit on the *Seydlitz*. Lack of organization and leadership among the stronger British forces, however, made even this engagement a tactical victory for the Germans.

Scheer, with the German fleet, and Jellicoe, with the British main body, meanwhile were steaming at their best speed to join the action. Scheer still did not know that the British battleship squadrons were at sea. Nor did the British know of his presence. Commodore W. E. Goodenough, scouting to the south of the battle, was

Queen Mary explodes.

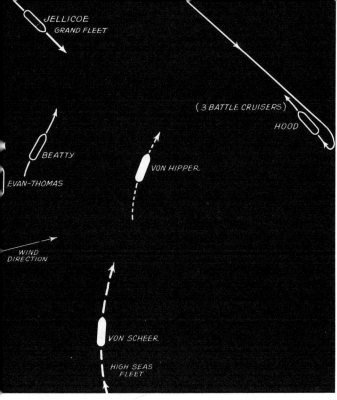

JELLICOE
GRAND FLEET

(3 BATTLE CRUISERS)

HOOD

BEATTY

VON HIPPER

EVAN-THOMAS

WIND
DIRECTION

VON SCHEER

HIGH SEAS
FLEET

first to sight the German battleships. This was at four thirty-three. Despite the heavy fire they rained on him, he maintained touch and was able to give Beatty and Jellicoe invaluable information.

Beatty did not turn back north immediately on receiving Goodenough's report but continued on south until he too sighted the Germans at four forty. Then he ordered a turnabout to starboard and steamed back north to lead them under the fire of Jellicoe's battle line. The German battleships opened fire on him but scored no hits. Evan-Thomas led the Fifth Battle Squadron on south until he too at four fifty came under fire of the Germans, and then he followed Beatty north, fighting a rear-guard action.

Hipper, meanwhile, had turned back west as Scheer approached, to take his place with the battle cruisers at the head of the German battle line. The German battleships were in a division front, with First Division, led by *Koenig*, the farthest north. Scheer was in the middle, in *Friedrich der Grosse*. They were steering northwest. Jellicoe was steering southeast. Thus the two great fleets

moved majestically toward each other at a combined speed of almost forty knots. Scheer apparently still was of the opinion that he had only Beatty's force with which to deal.

In the early stages of the battle-cruiser action, the visibility had been somewhat in favor of the Germans, they being to the eastward in poor light, but at about five o'clock the sun came out. With the sun in the Germans' eyes, range finding and spotting were hampered. The British Fifth Battle Squadron had much the advantage of the rear guard action, scoring an estimated fifteen hits to four received.

First contact between elements of the British main body and the Germans was to the northeastward, when Rear Admiral Hood's Third Battle Cruiser Squadron of *Invincible, Indomitable,* and *Inflexible,* and accompanying light forces, ran out of misty seeing within less than ten thousand yards range of the German Second Scouting Group of light cruisers and destroyers. The German light cruiser *Wiesbaden* was almost immediately crippled and had to be abandoned during the night. She sank the next day. Other German ships were hit but were able to get away behind a smoke screen.

During the crucial phase of the pre-action maneuvering between five and six o'clock, Jellicoe was left almost entirely without information as to the position, course, and speed of the German fleet. What information he received during most of the afternoon and evening was garbled and often incorrect. Lack of proper indoctrination on communications — the nerve system of any fleet — could have been costly. It did delay his decision as to his deployment for some time. Had he received the information that was available but not sent, he might have taken action that would have led to far more decisive results.

The base courses steered by the two fleets — Scheer to the northwest and then northeast, Jellicoe to the southeast — brought Jellicoe and his battle line to a position to the northeastward of the German fleet as they finally came together. To

103

Lion *is hit amidships.*

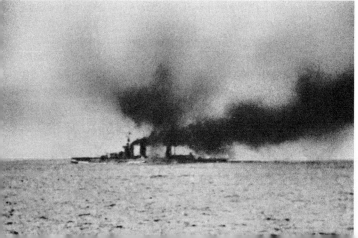

Southampton, *advance scout for Beatty, sighted von Scheer.*

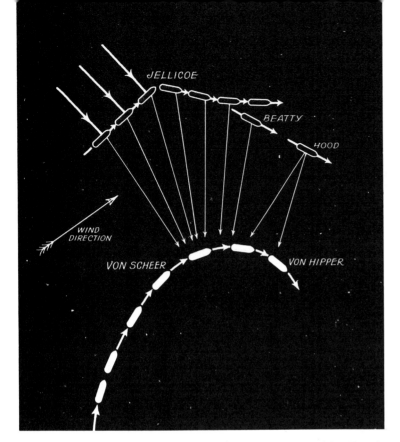

WIND
DIRECTION

JELLICOE

BEATTY

HOOD

VON SCHEER

VON HIPPER

Defense, *no match for* **Lützow's** *heavy guns, blew up.*

the northwestward of Scheer was the Fifth Battle Squadron under Evan-Thomas, and some miles ahead of the British battle line was Admiral Hood with his three battle cruisers. Scheer was headed straight into a cul-de-sac of superior ships.

104 Jellicoe had deployed his battle divisions to the east, with *King George V* as the guide, as he prepared to go into action. Beatty, coming up from the southwest, cut across the track of his own fleet to take position ahead of the battleships. Evan-Thomas wisely decided not to follow him, since that would put him between Jellicoe and the Germans. He dropped in astern. Hood, instead of continuing on south to operate independently to eastward of the Germans, turned west to join Beatty. Firing between the main fleets began at six thirty.

In the meantime, the British had lost another ship, the armored cruiser *Defense*. When Hood had contacted the German scouting force and Jellicoe began his deployment, the British armored cruisers cut across the head of the fleet to attack. They were brought under the fire of the German battle cruisers. Like *Indefatigable* and *Queen Mary*, *Defense* could not stand the hits of the German twelve-inch and eleven-inch guns, and she too blew up and sank. Two other British ships, the armored cruiser *Warrior* and the battleship *Warspite*, also were put out of the fight during this preliminary stage, the latter with a jammed rudder which had caused her to circle under full fire of the whole

German fleet. Badly holed, *Warrior* sank the next day while en route home under tow. *Warspite* was safely taken home and repaired to fight another day.

While Jellicoe, at six fifteen, was making his battle dispositions, Scheer turned from northwest to north and then to northeast, Hipper's battle cruisers in the van. Had he continued until six thirty, he would have sent his ships in a line directly into the center of the British line, thus "crossing the T" for Jellicoe. But when the German scouting group had run into Admiral Hood's battle cruisers, German Rear Admiral Boedicker had reported them as battleships and Hipper had turned ninety degrees through east to south to unmask his own guns and to clear the line of fire for the battleships following him. The position of the whole German fleet, however, still was precarious.

As the British battleships opened fire, everything was in their favor. They were indistinguishable to the German fire control officers against the darkening eastern sky, except by their gun flashes, and the coal smoke pouring from the German stacks and blowing to the eastward added to the German gun pointers' difficulties. The head of the German column was brought under heavy fire from ships they could not see. As one of them described it later, it seemed as though the whole northeastern sky was afire. It was folly to push on. In ten minutes the German vessels took twelve hits.

Scheer did not hesitate for long. At six forty-five he executed one of the most difficult of all battle movements, what the Germans call a *Gefechtskehrtwendung*, a battle turn of all ships through 180 degrees to a course the reverse of the one they were steering. Before this was taken, the German battle cruisers, which had fought so valiantly against heavy odds for so long, inflicted one

Derfflinger—her guns hammered . . .

and ***Invincible's*** magazines are hit . . .

more tragedy on the British fleet. Hood in *Invincible,* having contacted Beatty and taken up his position ahead of the latter's battle cruisers, was heavily engaging the turning German battle cruisers when salvos from both *Lützow* and *Derfflinger* appeared to hit his flagship as she steamed into a spot of good visibility for the Germans. *Invincible* exploded and broke in half. What the loss of Hood, who went down on his ship, meant to the future course of the action cannot be known, but he was one of Britain's most daring and courageous admirals.

Scheer's desperate disengaging maneuver was carried out as though at battle practice, instead of in a fight. His destroyers advanced toward the British battleships as though to attack, but were recalled before the attack was developed and fired only four torpedoes. During the engagement the *V-48* was hit and crippled by a shot from a crippled British destroyer, *Shark,* and was sunk later in the evening by two other British destroyers. Two accompanying German destroyers sank *Shark.*

As soon as his ships were steadied on their new course, Scheer turned even farther away, to a westerly course. He said later in his report he believed the main British fleet was directly to the east, instead of northeast, as they were. Both main bodies by this time were out of sight of each other. Jellicoe had not turned after the retreating German ships, as a more audacious commander might have done, because of fear of floating mines the Germans might have left in their wake. When the battleship *Marlborough* reported at six fifty-seven that she had been hit, either by a torpedo or a

105

and the broken ship goes down.

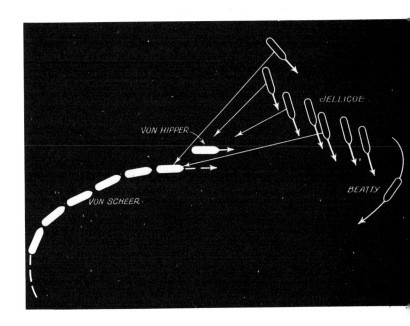

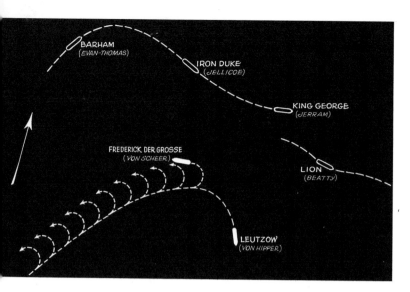

Frankfurt—led torpedo attacks against Hood's ships.

mine, Jellicoe thought his fears were confirmed. Anyway he continued with his plan of working to the southward of the German ships, so he turned due south.

Scheer did not stay long on his westerly course. At six fifty-five he again made a battle turn to a reverse course and headed back toward the British fleet. Without any effort of its own, the British fleet again was being given an opportunity to join the issue with a numerically inferior enemy. Contact was again established at seven o'clock. At 7:04 P.M. the firing began at about ten thousand yards. Again the British had everything in their favor. The German ships were silhouetted against the western sky, while the British ships still were only indistinct shapes to the German gunners. The Germans were coming toward them in a line which would mask all but the forward batteries and would allow British concentration of fire on the leading enemy ships, while they themselves still were far out of range of the guns of the German rear ships. Hipper's battle cruisers also were in bad shape, his own flagship, *Lützow*, being crippled and out of the battle. The others were badly mauled, and their crews were exhausted. Captain Hartzog in *Derfflinger* was the senior officer in command. He led the squadron, followed by *Seydlitz*, *Moltke*, and *Von der Tann*. They felt the first effects of the British battleships' fire.

At seven thirteen Scheer was in the most precarious situation of the battle. His van was heavily engaged by an enemy it could not see, except for the gun flashes. He could not know at what minute the vastly superior British light forces might come steaming out of the mist in a torpedo attack. That he realized the seriousness of the situation is certified by his orders. Again he ordered the battle turn to a reverse course southwest and at the same time ordered his battle cruisers to attack the British battle line, a suicidal task.

Again the German fleet executed its radical maneuver almost without a flaw. Not a ship fouled another. As the maneuver was completed, the German battle cruisers gradually swung away from their headlong drive at the British battle line and finally turned away. Many of the German ships had taken further heavy punishment during these sixteen minutes of renewed full-scale action. The British claimed no less than twenty-nine hits during the period. Among those receiving another hit was the crippled *Lützow*, from which Hipper had been taken by a destroyer and put aboard *Moltke*.

As he again disengaged, Scheer ordered his destroyer flotillas in to the attack, and to make smoke. In the maneuvering to avoid the torpedoes fired, Jellicoe turned away from the Germans instead of toward them, and for a time the two fleets steamed on opposite courses. With darkness coming on, Jellicoe had lost another fine opportunity to follow the enemy while he was disorganized. A little of Farragut's philosophy of "Damn the torpedoes, full speed ahead" might have paid big dividends. His actions certainly were not in the tradition of Nelson. Jellicoe's fear of mines dropped by the retiring German ships and his mania for a "fleet in being" seem to have dictated practically all of his battle decisions.

Scheer did not stay long on his westerly course. He apparently came to a decision soon after this to attempt to fight his way home, via Horns Reef, which lies about halfway up the Danish pe-

Shark *sank a destroyer and later was herself sunk.*

Lützow *lists and von Hipper transfers.*

ninsula. The German mine fields, through which there were clear channels for his passage, began there. He turned south.

Jellicoe meanwhile had turned southwesterly to put the two fleets, each unbeknownst to the other, again on converging courses. In the van of the German fleet were the battered battle cruisers and the six over-age battleships which Scheer had had at the rear of his line, but which by his maneuvers he had made the lead ships. Ahead of the British fleet and out of sight of Jerram in *King George V* with the Second Battle Squadron, which was leading the British battle line, was Beatty with his three squadrons of battle cruisers, which now were minus *Invincible*, *Indefatigable*, and *Queen Mary*.

Shortly after eight o'clock Beatty sighted the German battle cruisers and the van of the German battle line. He opened fire. The Germans turned away to the southwestward. When the firing began, Jellicoe first turned his battleship divisions to the west as though to close, but soon went back again to a southwesterly course. He was not sure of the position of the German fleet. Jerram saw the Germans, but, in the dim light, thought they were Beatty's battle cruisers and did not open fire or close to identify. Several British destroyers also contacted German battleships, but they did not attack in force and soon lost contact. Some critics have said Jellicoe's supercautiousness had transmitted itself to all officer ranks.

As the afterglow faded, despite continuing contacts between the parallel-steaming fleets, Jellicoe decided against any further effort to engage that night. He set a cruising order and turned south for the six hours of darkness. Scheer, at

107

Royal Oak—*to fight and die another day, and* **Hercules**

B98 led destroyer flotillas striking for von Scheer—and Jellicoe turned away.

When Scheer changed his course to southeast, the British battle fleet, steaming south, was almost due east of his main body. But it was gradually drawing ahead because of an excess of one knot speed over the sixteen being made by the German ships. The turning away of the German battle cruisers to avoid Beatty's fire also had slowed up the German line. As Scheer steamed southeastward, therefore, he passed astern of the British battleship squadrons, and he thus had to fight his way only through the British light forces, which Jellicoe had grouped five miles astern of him.

All through the short night, there was flaming action in Jellicoe's rear as first one British group and then another made contact with the German ships. In the misty darkness, it was difficult to tell friend from foe, and most ships did not open fire until within two thousand to one thousand yards of each other. The British light cruiser *Southampton*, battered by German battleships, fired a torpedo that hit and sank the German light cruiser *Frauenlob*. Each side also lost destroyers in the night's fighting. At dawn, attacking British destroyers hit the old German battleship *Pommern* with a torpedo, and she, too, quickly turned over and sank. *Lützow* and *Elbing* were abandoned and sunk by their own men, who then were rescued by friendly destroyers. *Rostock*, under tow, also had to be abandoned at daylight. The principal British

almost the same time, set his fleet course southeast for Horns Reef's light, ordering his ships to hold to course regardless. He knew the British fleet was somewhere to the eastward of him, but he had decided to push on through, abandoning his three crippled ships, hoping to get at least the major portion of his fleet home safely. He succeeded, except for three more major vessels. The crippled *Wiesbaden*, the *Elbing*, and *Lützow* were sunk or due to be sunk during the night or the next morning.

108

Close call for a British cruiser.

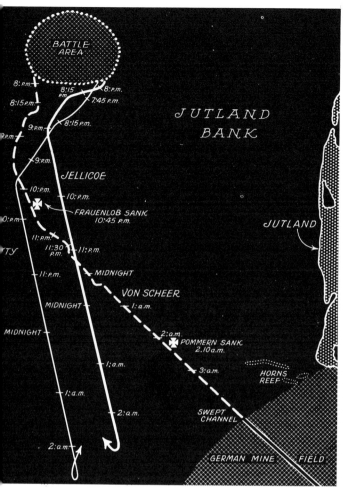

The German High Seas Fleet returns to base.

loss was the armored cruiser *Black Prince*, destroyed by gunfire. There was no more contact between the main bodies of the two fleets. The last damage done to either side was when the battleship *Ostfriesland* struck a mine near Horns Reef. She was not critically damaged.

By full daylight, Scheer was safely past Horns Reef and steering for home behind the protection of the German mine fields. He had a full report of his fleet condition by that time — including the fact that none of the battle cruisers were fit to fight — and he knew he was in no condition to renew the action even had he been so inclined. Jellicoe did not attempt to intercept him, but instead steered back north on the lookout for his light cruisers and destroyers. At eleven o'clock he was informed by the Admiralty that Scheer was safely back home, and he ordered his own fleet to return to its bases.

The strategy and tactics of Jutland, and the consequences of the battle, probably will be the subject of heated controversy until there are no more navies, or naval men. In ships lost, the score was eleven to fourteen in favor of the Germans. In men, it was much higher: 6,097 British officers and sailors lost to 2,545 Germans. The surviving German ships suffered more hits and greater damage than did the British ships, but all were repairable.

The British ships lost were: battle cruisers — *Queen Mary*, *Indefatigable*, and *Invincible;* armored cruisers — *Defense*, *Warrior*, and *Black Prince;* destroyers — *Tipperary*, *Turbulent*, *Fortune*, *Ardent*, *Shark*, *Sparrowhawk*, *Nestor*, and *Nomad*.

109

Minotaur screened Jellicoe and fought the destroyers.

Pommern turned over at night and sank.

The German losses were: battleships — *Pommern;* battle cruisers — *Lützow;* light cruisers — *Wiesbaden, Elbing, Rostock, Frauenlob;* destroyers — *V-27, 29, 48,* and *4,* and *S-35.*

One of the reasons for the high British losses, especially those of the three battle cruisers, apparently was the light armor which had been made necessary by the desire for speed and also perhaps a lack of good damage-control practice. Most of the German battle cruisers received heavier punishment than did *Queen Mary, Indefatigable,* or *Invincible,* yet stood up to it. They suffered direct hits in their turrets, causing powder fires there, but none reached the magazines. Only the heroic work of a wounded officer in one of *Lion's* turrets saved her from a fate similar to that of her sisters.

With both legs shot away, the turret officer, Major F. J. W. Harvey, closed the doors of the ammunition hoist and ordered the magazine flooded.

The naval aspects of the battle might be said to have been about equal; the losses were in proportion to the strengths of the two navies, eight to five, and did not change the over-all situation. The political results of the battle were considerable. It convinced Scheer that the British fleet was still too formidable for him to hold any hope of decisively defeating it. He made only one more sortie in force, in August, and at that time turned back before contact. He urged an unrestricted submarine war, which was begun the following February, the final act that brought the United States into the war.

110

Seydlitz *just makes the shore—in flames.*

WAR UNDERSEA 1914-1918

In October, 1916, five and one-half months after the Battle of Jutland, Admiral Jellicoe wrote to the British Admiralty that the loss of Allied and neutral shipping to the German submarines was rising to such alarming monthly totals that unless something was done about it, submarine warfare "may, by the early Summer of 1917, have such a serious effect upon the import of food and other necessaries into the Allied countries as to force us into accepting peace terms which the military position on the Continent would not justify, and which would fall short of our desires."

Britannia ruled the seas, but only the surface. A new element had been added to warfare. The instrument itself was not new. David Bushnell of Connecticut built a submarine called "The American Turtle" in 1775 and with it exploded a one-hundred-pound bomb near the British sixty-four-gun ship *Eagle* in New York harbor. The U.S.S. *Housatonic*, a Union sloop of war, was sunk by a

S.S. Lusitania's fate . . .

submarine-attached mine off Charleston in 1864. The Germans were the first to develop the submarine as a really effective instrument of war. They were the first, too, to use it ruthlessly where it was most effective, against unarmed merchant vessels. The result of the Battle of Jutland was one of the factors that decided the Germans to try to cut the bridge of ships on which Britain always has depended, in peace and in war. It was the one most vulnerable spot of Shakespeare's England: "this fortress built by Nature for herself."

At the beginning of the war, in August 1914, England was ahead of Germany in commissioned submarines as she was in commissioned surface vessels. She had thirty-six submarines to twenty-eight for Germany. Only ten of the German boats were ocean-going. Both countries, at that time, conceived of the submarine as a scouting vessel or one to station in front of the enemy's harbors or at the entrance to his mine fields to attack outbound and inbound warships. Germany also used them in the early days to attack on the surface with gunfire the British fishing fleets, on whose catch the British Isles so heavily depended. They also used them effectively against British war vessels, as has been related in a previous chapter. It was not until 1915, however, that the German Admiralty sent them out into the steamer lanes to attack British and Allied shipping or neutral shipping bound for British or French ports. The culmination of this phase was the sinking on May 7, 1915, of the liner *Lusitania*, with the loss of 1,198 men, women, and children, and the torpedoing without warning in the same month of the United States merchantmen *Gullflight* and *Nebraska*. United States protests were so heated — we also had protested against the British surface blockade of Germany, but not in such strenuous terms, because it was carried on without loss of life, ships being stopped and searched for contraband — that on June 5, 1915, Germany revised its notice of the previous February and announced that thereafter passenger liners were not to be fired on unless they took action first against the submarine.

The great vulnerability of the submarine made it impossible for the Germans to carry on any war on commerce, or impose a blockade, without violating the generally accepted conventions of so-called civilized war, that is: not to attack without warning. Through a hazy periscope, it is difficult for a submarine captain to identify a ship he plans to attack. Certainly he seldom has a clear enough view to see what flag she is flying. If he brings his ship to the surface to investigate, he may be sunk before he can decide whether the approaching vessel is armed, a neutral, or a friend. The only effective way in which the submarine can be used is to fire first and ask questions afterward.

The German Admiralty had no delusions that it could conduct a civilized war with submarines. It had been restrained only by Chancellor T. von Bethmann-Hollwegg, who in 1915 and 1916 still had hopes the United States would not enter the war. After the Battle of Jutland, Admiral Scheer finally convinced the Chancellor and the Kaiser that there was little hope left that the High Seas Fleet could win control of the seas, and that the best chance to knock Britain out of the war before the United States came in was to wage an unrestricted campaign against merchant shipping with the submarine. The German surface raiders had been eliminated by the British Navy long before. Anyway, their exploits had been more publicized than crippling on British commerce. The submarine was the only answer. On February 1, 1917, began the second unrestricted German submarine campaign.

Until the beginning of the second unrestricted submarine campaign in 1917, British ship losses had been 519 merchant vessels and 300 fishing craft. More than two-thirds of these had been sunk in 1916. Allied and neutral losses brought the total to 1,666. German submarines lost were 24 in 1914–15 and 25 in 1916. Major sufferers among the neutrals had been the Scandinavian countries, whose sea trade routes were easy for the German submarines to reach and whose cargoes of ore and dairy products were prime targets. When Germany's political leaders had placed successive restrictions on the submarine commanders because of protests from the United States in 1915, and again in 1916, the Norwegian, Swedish, and Danish vessels apparently had been exempted from the rules.

If Jellicoe had believed, in October, 1916, that the German submarine campaign might succeed in forcing Britain to ask for terms, his thoughts in the spring of 1917 must have been very dark indeed. In January, 1917, the last month of restrictions for submarine commanders, 96 British and Allied merchant vessels were sunk, and 65 neutrals. In the first month of unrestricted warfare, the totals were 171 and 66, respectively. Gross tonnage of ships lost rose from 293,000 to 468,000. This was beyond Britain's capacity to replace.

When the unrestricted submarine campaign was launched, Germany's submarine fleet had grown from the 10 ocean-going submarines, with which she had begun the war, to 111, of which

streaks through the water off the coast of Ireland.

Hove to for German inspection . . .

some were *UC*, or mine-laying type, but which also carried deck guns and torpedoes and used them when the opportunity offered, off the British ports or in the English and Irish Channels. Cruising ranges had also increased. Techniques had been developed steadily. The officer corps of the High Seas Fleet had provided a fertile source of submarine commanders and the more adventurous of its men, who faced with the fleet a life of almost complete inactivity, volunteered for submarine duty. The submarine captains and crews in 1917 were the cream of the German Navy.

How close the submarines came to winning the war for Germany never will be known. The Allied commanders in their memoirs probably never have been completely honest in recording what must have been their feelings during the dark days of the spring of 1917. Had it not been for the entry of the United States as a belligerent on the side of the Allied Powers on April 6, 1917, it is quite probable England might have been forced to ask for terms, as Jellicoe had prophesized.

Four factors combined to defeat the German submarine campaign. Not necessarily in the order of importance, they were: a remarkable increase in United States and British shipbuilding capacity, especially that of the United States; establishment of the convoy system; construction of the needed

and an officer makes ready to board.

No ship was safe in shaded areas—unrestricted submarine war of 1917.

Another kill—ten minutes to abandon ship.

Dangerous wait for one last man.

American merchant convoy under way.

anti-submarine vessels and development of the methods of detection; development of the depth charge, or "ash can" as it was commonly called by the sailors of World War I, a mine that could be exploded at various depths with such force as to disable the submarine near which it exploded.

One of Admiral Jellicoe's recommendations, when he made his dire prediction as to the submarine war and, as First Sea Lord, was called to London to take charge of the Admiralty program for dealing with it, was the detachment of some of the Grand Fleet's destroyer-boat flotillas to augment the smaller vessels then used on anti-submarine patrol. He and all his high naval conferees, suffering from what Prime Minister David Lloyd George called "hardening of the professional arteries," stubbornly opposed the establishment of a convoy system. This, despite the fact that the convoy system already had been tried with the coal ships to France and found highly satisfactory.

According to Lloyd George, Rear Admiral William S. Sims, who had been sent to England by President Wilson to confer with the British Admiralty, quoted Admiral Jellicoe as saying, in April, 1917, that Britain was losing the war to the submarines and he did not know what to do about it. Admiral Sims and Admiral Beatty, who had succeeded Admiral Jellicoe as Commander in Chief of the Grand Fleet, however, saw the value of convoys, and finally Lloyd George practically forced the Admiralty to accept their views and establish a system. The first experimental North Atlantic convoy was sent from Gibraltar to New York in May, 1917, and another sailed from Hampton Roads, Virginia, to England. Both got through safely.

Convoy was not a new development. In ancient days, when piracy on the high seas was an honored profession and any ship of one country was fair game for a stronger ship of any other, the ship captains themselves organized convoys. They had no armed ship escort, for each ship in those days carried its own simple weapons. Convoy was even a well-tried British Navy function. After Trafalgar, the principal task of the British fleet, until the war with France was ended, was the escorting of merchant vessels by ships of war to protect them from the French privateers. Up until May of 1917, except for the coal convoys to France, convoy had been used by the British only of ships

A "Y" gun tosses out its "ash cans."

A U-Boat is destroyed.

Depth charges rigged for dropping astern.

carrying troops across the Channel and to the Mediterranean and from the Dominions and the colonies to Europe and the Near East. These convoys had been established primarily to protect the ships from possible enemy surface raiders, not from submarines.

Establishment of convoy was a tremendous paper task, since it necessitated issuance of orders for the gathering in convenient ports of twenty to forty ships of a similar speed and then sending them to sea at one time with protecting destroyers or cruisers. As it was finally worked out, it was relatively simple. The difficulties of organization did not prove as great as expected, and the merchant skippers quickly disabused the Admirals of the idea that they could not keep station in foul weather. Only a light escort was furnished most of the way across the North Atlantic, being augmented only in the danger zones — approaching the British Isles, Gibraltar, or the French coast — by increased destroyer protection.

The various methods evolved to deal with the submarine began almost immediately to turn the tide. In April, 1917, German submarines reached their peak of effectiveness when they sank 277

British and Allied vessels and 118 flying the flags of neutrals. The gross tonnage sunk was 840,000 tons. It decreased through the months to a low for 1917 of 95 British and Allied ships and 21 neutrals sunk in November, rose again and remained over the hundred mark for December, 1917, January, February, March, and May of 1918, and then steadily declined during the closing months of the war. At the same time, German submarine losses rose. Whereas the Germans lost only 49 undersea boats in 1914–16, in 1917 the total was 66, and for the ten months and eleven days of 1918, it was 88. During all this time, Allied ship construction was increasing from month to month. During 1916, Britain produced 608,000 gross tons, in 1917, 1,163,000, and in 1918, 1,348,000. The figures for the United States are even more impressive: 1,560,000 in 1916, 2,733,000 in 1917, and 4,697,000 in 1918. During 1918 the rate of production was almost three times that of losses.

The German submarine campaign had come so close to success, however, that it was a certainty the German Admiralty would try it again in their war of revenge. They came even closer to succeeding in 1939–41 than they had in 1914–1918.

More fortunate, another German comes back to port.

UNITED STATES IN WORLD WAR I

Six storm-battered destroyers, one with its fireroom ventilator missing, steamed in column through the submarine nets and up to an assigned anchorage in Queenstown Harbor, on the southeast coast of Ireland, on May 3, 1917. In a few minutes, Lieutenant Commander (later Vice Admiral) Joseph K. Taussig, U.S.N., was reporting to Vice Admiral Sir Lewis Bayly, R.N., for duty.

"When will you be ready to go to sea?" was the Admiral's first question.

"We are ready now, sir; that is, as soon as we finish refueling," answered the commodore of the first United States Navy squadron to arrive in European waters.

"I will give you four days from the time of arrival," said Admiral Bayly, smiling.

"Thank you, sir. That will be more than ample time," Commander Taussig answered.

The destroyers were, of course, in no condition to go to sea after their rough North Atlantic

The United States Sixth Battle Squadron reports for duty.

British smoke protects four U.S. mine-layers.

crossing. Taussig was not going to admit that to a British Admiral, however. The story of his answer was told quickly on both sides of the Atlantic. It helped cement a friendship between the United States and British navies that had been growing for many years and has held firm through two long wars against common enemies.

The Admiral's question and the answer of the slightly-built American Lieutenant Commander were not spoken as jokes on either side. The need was great and growing. No later additions to the Allied fleets in the North Atlantic, the Mediterranean, and the North Sea were more welcome than those six little one-thousand-ton, four-stacked United States destroyers — *Wadsworth, Wainwright, Conyngham, Davis, McDougal,* and *Porter* — which reported at Queenstown thirty days after the United States had joined Great Britain, France, Italy, and the other Allies in the war against the Central Powers. The previous month, submarine sinkings had reached the total of 860,000 tons. They never again reached that level. The United States Navy, especially the destroyers, played a prominent part in providing a satisfactory answer as to why they did not.

The United States made four major contributions at sea during the First World War. First, there was that of the destroyers, the number of which increased to thirty-five within two months of the first arrival, and which totaled seventy on active duty at the three main stations — Queenstown, Brest, and Gibraltar — at the end of the war. Joined with them in this anti-submarine work were a score of converted yachts, 120 smaller submarine chasers that were sent to Europe and the Mediterranean, some 20 submarines, and the Navy planes and blimps that operated out of England, France, and Italy on anti-submarine patrol.

A second important precautionary aid was the disposition of our battle fleet to deal with any German commerce raiders that might slip out of the North Sea. One group of five battleships, *New York, Wyoming, Florida, Texas,* and *Delaware* (later relieved by *Arkansas*), served under Rear Admiral Hugh Rodman with the British Grand Fleet out of Scapa as the Sixth Battle Squadron. Three more battleships, *Nevada, Oklahoma,* and *Utah,* were based at Berehaven, Ireland, under Rear Admiral Thomas S. Rodgers. The remainder stayed on the western side of the Atlantic.

A third major contribution was the laying, with the help of the British, of the North Sea Mine Barrage across the 240 miles of North Sea from the Orkneys to the coast of Norway.

The fourth, and most important task, was the moving of two million troops to France, of which

Dropping the mines at full speed. 121

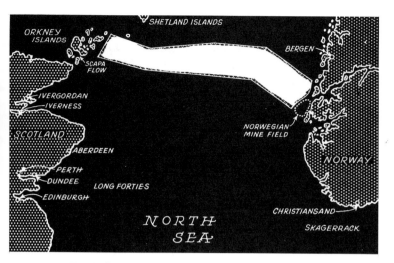

North Sea Mine Barrage laid by United States and British ships.

the United States Navy carried 45 per cent in Navy transports and provided escort for over 80 per cent of all.

Other chores done by the Navy were the usual ones of operation of foreign stations, where our squadrons were serviced and repaired, and operation of a battery of fourteen-inch naval guns, which did effective work along the Western Front for several months.

At the end of the war, there were more than eighty thousand officers and men of the United States Navy serving in European waters or on European stations. This was almost as many as were enrolled in the Navy on April 7, 1917. Our European forces were in general command of Rear Admiral William S. Sims, the stormy petrel of the American Navy.

One of the most grueling naval tasks of the war was that of the destroyers on escort duty, especially those of the Queenstown and Brest patrols. There are few weeks in the year when there are not one or two storms moving somewhere along the steamer lanes across the North Atlantic. The Bay of Biscay, through which most of the troop convoys sailed en route to French ports, is, because of its relatively shallow water, one of the most uneasy large bodies of sea in the world. The little destroyers with their narrow beam and low freeboard were not fit to live on in a North Atlantic storm. It was not uncommon for a wave to sweep along them halfway up their stacks from stem to stern.

Because there was never enough of them to do all the convoy tasks that had to be done, they and their crews got little rest. Their only guarantee for a few days in port was to take such a pounding from the waves that they required an overhaul before putting to sea again. The usual procedure for them was to put to sea in escort of small groups of returning transports or supply ships, escort them through the danger zone that was set at twenty-five degrees west longitude, approximately one thousand miles west of Brest. Then they would meet an incoming convoy of fifteen to twenty ships and escort them to Brest, St. Nazaire, Bordeaux, or perhaps a British port. They then were given an opportunity to refuel and take aboard stores, by which time — sometimes only a few hours — other ships would be ready to start the return voyage, and they would put to sea with them. Within a year, five months, and five days from that first arrival, they escorted 710 convoys without loss and more than 600 ships sailing singly.

Despite the hardships, destroyer duty was a coveted assignment among Navy men. The destroyer crews were lucky to get hot coffee and cold food at sea. But when they were in port, nothing

Camouflaged convoy.

within reason was denied them, and they ate very good rations indeed. Vice Admiral Bayly became so fond of the destroyers under his command that he called them "my destroyers," their crews "my Americans." He took their part in many a dispute with the British Admiralty and British captains and British crews.

American destroyers and converted yachts had a reported 150 contacts with German submarines during the war. They were officially credited with sinking only two, seriously damaging three, and possibly damaging sixteen. The total may have been larger, since the Germans lost 203, more than three-fourths of these during the last two years of the war. Two of our destroyers were torpedoed but made port, two were sunk in collision, and one was seriously damaged in collision.

The most remarkable job of the Navy, in which of course the destroyers played their part, was the safe transportation of two million men to France. They were carried mostly in what were known as fifteen-knot convoys, although thousands traveled in the faster ships such as *Leviathan*, *America*, and *George Washington* — all interned German liners that were converted to transports. Those generally went alone. They had enough speed to make it difficult for a submarine, even if it sighted one of them, to get in a position to attack.

A typical convoy was one that sailed from New York during the summer of 1918, with one of the authors of this book as a signal quartermaster on one of the ships, the eighteen-thousand-ton *Mongolia*. A former Pacific mail passenger liner, the *Mongolia* was taken over as a transport by the Navy in the spring of 1918. Three-tiered bunks, contrived of canvas stretched between gas pipe, were installed in her holds. Fully loaded, she carried sixty-five hundred troops. She had a crew of six hundred. Her top speed was around eighteen knots.

In midafternoon the loaded transports began sliding down the river from their Hoboken piers. Clearing Ambrose Light before dark, the twenty loaded transports, all approximately of the same size, all with a top speed of between eighteen and twenty knots, formed up in four columns abreast, five ships to a column. In command was the auxiliary cruiser *Von Steuben*, which also carried troops. As escort were three destroyers, which had to refuel en route from the oil-burning *Wilhelmina*, one of the convoy. Most of the ships in the convoy still burned coal, of which enough was taken on in New York for the round trip.

Taussig's **Wadsworth**.

123

Zig-zag—the convoy's maneuver to confuse the plotted course of the submarine's pursuit.

Ready for trouble—with the wash on the line.

*Britain's **Tempest** sows her charges.*

By nightfall the convoy was in regular formation, steaming along on a zigzag course at fifteen knots. Such convoys used the zigzag from earliest daylight to full dark, and even during the night when it was bright moonlight. There are many different zigzag patterns. In one you might change ten degrees to the right, then ten more ten minutes later. Eventually you got from one point to another, but much on the pattern of a hunting dog trotting along ahead of his master in search of quail. The reason for the zigzag was that if a submarine skipper out ahead sighted the convoy and then submerged to get in position to attack, he had to guess just where the convoy was going to be after it had done one of its zigs or zags.

All of the ships were brilliantly camouflaged, some with what appeared to be most of the colors of the rainbow. On a clear day, when both sky and sea were blue, they truly were "painted ships upon a painted ocean," as quoth "The Ancient Mariner." The reason for camouflage was to make it difficult for a submarine commander, catching sight of the convoy off on the horizon, to determine in just what direction it was going. Camouflage does little to hide a ship. A blue-gray ship will fade into a misty horizon much more quickly than one adorned like Solomon's wives. But oddly-painted patterns do disguise the true course being steered.

From sunset until an hour after dark each night, and from an hour before sunrise until full light, all hands — both crew and troops — were ordered topside at what is called "general quarters" or "battle stations." Those two periods of all the day are the most favorable for a submarine attack. Men caught below decks when a torpedo hits in an unarmored ship have little chance of escaping death. On deck it is only a step into the water. Much deck space was taken up with wooden and composition rafts. In the cold waters of the North Atlantic, a man would not survive long adrift on one of them, but at least it would give every man a fighting chance for his life.

Through the long days and dark nights, steering roughly a great-circle course for Brest, the convoy plowed along. Off the Newfoundland Banks it ran in fog for three straight days. The zigzag had to be abandoned; there was no need for changing course in a fog. For three days the merchant skippers — commissioned officers in the Naval Reserve — whose ability Admiral Jellicoe and other members of the British Admiralty had questioned, kept perfect station on each other through the use of their ships' whistles. When the convoy finally emerged from the fog, well on its way to France, each ship was right in line.

The approach to the twenty-fifth longitude, the limit of the danger zone where the Germans concentrated their submarines on the sea approaches to England and France, was timed to be at dawn of the fourth day away from journey's end. Lookouts on the leading ships that morning reported ships approaching dead ahead. Then, out

124

A member of the American Mine Patrol finds the going rugged.

of the early morning mists, came tearing six destroyers of the Queenstown patrol that were assigned to take the convoy the rest of the way. If an armored cruiser or battleship was along as convoy leader, she generally would turn back at this point. The *Von Steuben*, carrying troops, naturally went along with the rest of us.

During the last four days there were frequent alarms. Sometimes one or two of the tossing little escorts, spread out ahead of the columns of transports and on either flank, went dashing off toward the horizons. Soon there came the underwater shocks of depth charges exploding as a German undersea boat, or what the destroyer's captain thought was one, was attacked. Even if the submarine was not sunk, such attacks kept it down below periscope level, and the convoy could soon outrun a submerged U-boat, most of which could make only six to eight knots under the surface.

The arrival at Brest came in early morning. First appeared the rocks outside the entrance, called "The Sisters," then the opening between the hills that led into the deep water harbor where a hundred transports could swing safely at anchor at one time.

Because dock space was limited, the transports generally unloaded their troops, and what little cargo they carried, aboard lighters. Sometimes the transports would leave the same night for the return trip; sometimes they would lie in the harbor overnight. The return trip always was

much faster than the outgoing one. The ships would leave two or three at a time, often with wounded men aboard, and under escort would steam west for three days. The evening of the third day, the escorts would leave, to join up with the rest of their patrol and pick up an incoming convoy, and the transports then would steam full speed for home. Arrived back in Hoboken, they would immediately begin to load supplies and coal. As soon as that job was completed, the troops would again start coming aboard. In four or five days, *Mongolia* and her sister ships would be heading down the North River again, outbound for France or England. That was the manner in which two million United States soldiers went to France in 1917 and 1918. Only two

125

Blimp off the French coast—early aerial anti-sub patrol.

A seaplane turns to take off in search of U-boats.

The menace beaten, the men arrive.

*Last British casualty—**Britannia** torpedoed November 9, 1918.*

of the transports were torpedoed and sunk, *Covington* and *President Lincoln*. They were both hit on the trip home, when they were carrying only a few hundred. Few men were lost in either one.

An even nastier job from the point of weather than that of the destroyer and transport fleet was the laying of the North Sea Mine Barrage, and, after the war, collecting it. Participating American mine layers laid more than fifty thousand mines across the North Sea, or 80 per cent of the total. The barrage was intended, as was a companion one laid outside the German harbors and across the Strait of Dover, to pen in the submarines and also to act as a guard against any sorties by the High Seas Fleet, in case it eluded the combined British–United States Grand Fleet and the Dover patrol. Only one ship of the mine-laying fleet was lost to enemy action. One of the mine-layers was torpedoed and sunk by a German submarine. Not more than five or six German submarines were believed to have been lost in running through the mine fields, but German Navy men admitted after the war that it was a great mental hazard and helped to break down German Fleet morale. The mine field was not laid until the summer of 1918. Even more ambitious projects, there and in the Mediterranean, the Aegean and the Adriatic, were not yet in operation

when the Armistice of November 11, 1918, ended the war.

Naval air power, which was practically non-existent at the start of the war, was just getting into full operation in the European war when the Armistice came. Even so, twenty-seven stations had been established, with a flight and ground personnel of fifteen thousand men. Attacks were made on some two-score submarines that were sighted, and several bombing missions were flown against the German U-boat bases along the Flanders coast of Belgium.

Although the United States Navy's part in the naval phases of the First World War were more useful than spectacular — it fought no Jutlands — the war-building program from 1916 on did push it to unquestioned second rank by the date of the Armistice. With the surrender of the German fleet at Scapa Flow, and its scuttling there by its men, there was no other sea power even approaching the strength of the United States and British navies.

In 1919 the battleship score was: Britain, thirty-five battleships built, none building; United States, seventeen battleships built, six building. In lesser craft, especially destroyers, the United States had an even stronger position. Then came the disarmament conference.

The Imperial German Navy steams out of Kiel . . .

and scuttles itself at Scapa Flow.

5-5-3 victim—and **Washington's** punishment starts . . .

DISARMAMENT AND REBUILDING

Thirty miles astern, against a towering bank of black clouds, we could see the flashes of the guns as a United States South Pacific Task Force of cruisers and destroyers engaged a group of Japanese destroyers attempting the enemy's last large-scale reinforcement of his dwindling forces on Guadalcanal. It was just after eleven o'clock the night of November 30, 1942.

"Eighteen years ago this month," said Commander Frederick Bell, captain of the destroyer *Grayson* that was escorting some of our own transports away from Guadalcanal and from the deck of whose ship we were watching the fight, "we towed the *Washington* out to the drill grounds off the Virginia Capes and sank her in conformity with the terms of the 1921–22 Washington Disarmament Conference. How Admiral Wright could use her in there tonight!"

Commander Bell was one of many naval officers serving in the Pacific during the dark days of

CHAPTER 10

guns, bombs, and torpedoes complete their work . . .

and a part of our pact is finished.

1942 and 1943 who could remember when the United States voluntarily had relinquished its place as the second-greatest sea power in the world. It had sunk its ships and completed hulls. Great Britain and Japan largely tore up blueprints. When the crisis came in 1941, America had not yet been able fully to retrieve, since 1933, the mistaken naval policies it had pursued blindly from 1922 to 1932, while Japan rearmed.

Even without the hindsight that the years permit, it is difficult to understand how three successive national administrations could, while keeping this country out of the only international organization that had a remote chance of staving off disaster — the League of Nations — so misread Japanese history and contemporary actions as to believe it could indefinitely live in peace in the Pacific with that nation. Our skimpy naval appropriations reversed a national policy that had been carried on by administrations of both parties, Democratic and Republican, since the 1880's. On March 4, 1933, when President Franklin D. Roosevelt took office, this country's navy was no better than third, if that, behind Great Britain and Japan.

Eight years was too short a time, in the middle of a depression, to retrieve the mistakes of the previous twelve years. It is much easier to recruit, train, and equip a great army than it is to build a navy. To do the latter takes time.

During World War I, 1914–18, the United States suspended its big-ship program to turn out the smaller vessels that were so urgently needed to combat the German submarines. In 1919, with new designs to take advantage of the experiences of Jutland, it resumed its Big Navy building program. On November 12, 1921, when the Disarmament Conference which had been called by President Harding convened in Washington, the United States had under construction a navy second to none.

Charles Evans Hughes, President Harding's Secretary of State, exploded a bombshell in the conference with his opening speech when he proposed that the great sea powers immediately scrap most of their post-Jutland ships and programs and limit themselves to capital ship replacement of 500,000 tons for Great Britain and the United States and 300,000 tons for Japan. That was the famous 5-5-3 ratio around which all naval discussions and arguments were to center for the next ten years. Secretary Hughes' ideas were enthusiastically received by a world weary of war and of armament burdens. Japan and Great Britain accepted the proposition, in principle, as to capital ships. Then began the technical discussions.

What finally evolved was something probably entirely different from what Secretary Hughes had envisioned when he made his proposal. It certainly was something much different from what the people of the world, and particularly those of the United States, believed it to be. The 5-5-3 ratio finally was accepted as to capital ships — that is, ships above the cruiser class, which was limited to ten thousand tons — but all ships below the battleships and battle cruiser class were exempted from the ratio. Different agreements were reached as to those. Even the 5-5-3 ratio was not to come into final balance for twenty years, or until 1942. All building was prohibited until 1931. Japan first argued for a 10-10-7 ratio for capital ships, but finally agreed to the 5-5-3 ratio as a price for concessions that will be outlined later.

The Washington agreement, as finally negotiated, resulted in the following scrapping program:

Great Britain to scrap twenty-two prewar battleships and tear up the plans for two super battleships; Japan to scrap two post-Jutland and nine prewar battleships and three cruisers, convert two battle cruiser hulls to carriers and tear up the plans for two more battle cruisers; the United States to scrap or sell 19 prewar battleships and thirteen post-Jutland ships, battleships and battle cruisers, some of them the most powerful ships in the world, with twelve sixteen-inch guns and all in an advanced stage of construction. (The *Washington* was one of the sixteen-inch gun battleships that it destroyed.) By 1942, under the replacement program for obsolescent ships, Great Britain and the United States were to have fifteen first-line battleships each and Japan was to have nine.

The only United States vessels of the 1916 and 1919 programs that were saved by the treaty were the *West Virginia, Colorado,* and *Maryland,* all of 32,600 tons, with eight sixteen-inch guns, and the aircraft carriers *Saratoga* and *Lexington,* which had been converted from battle-cruiser hulls. The Japanese likewise saved the *Matsu* and *Nagato* and the two 26,900-ton aircraft carriers, *Akagi* and *Kaga,* the latter two being built on battle cruiser and battleship hulls, respectively. *(Akagi* and

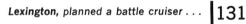

Lexington, *planned a battle cruiser . . .* **131**

emerges like sister **Saratoga—***a flat-top.*

Kaga were in the Japanese carrier force that attacked Pearl Harbor on December 7, 1941. They were sunk on June 4, 1942, the first day of the Battle of Midway.)

One of the concessions that was given the Japanese in 1922, to wean them from their 10-10-7 ratio demands, was the promise of the United States not to fortify the Philippines or Guam. The Japanese in turn agreed to maintain the *status quo* in the Ryukyus, the Bonins, the Kuriles, and the Mandated Islands. When the Japanese renounced the Washington agreements in 1935, they hurried to make up for lost time in all those islands. Even after Washington knew what Japan was doing, the United States Congress several times declined to take countermeasures at Manila and Guam, decisions that had such tragic consequences in the first few months of the Second World War.

Many youngsters still unborn when the 1921–22 conference was held paid with their lives during 1942 and 1943, while America's belated building program was materializing into ships at sea, for the mistakes made in the post-World War I years.

Two political questions developed as a corollary of the Washington Disarmament Conference. One of these was the abrogation of the Anglo-Japanese Alliance, by which Great Britain rid herself during the early years of this century of the burden of maintaining a large navy in the Far East. With the era of good feeling between the United States and Britain that had steadily grown during the pre-1914 years, little danger to this country had been seen in its existence. With the question of sea-power ratios, however, it came very much to the fore. Even though Americans still were great and good friends of the British, they did not like the idea of having two of the three leading sea powers joined by such an alliance. In the event of trouble, that would make the naval ratio 8-5 against them, instead of 5-5-3. To take its place, a Four-Power Treaty was entered into, with the United States and France joining Great Britain and Japan in an agreement on the Pacific. At the same time, a Nine-Power Treaty, between the United States, Great Britain, Japan, France, Italy, China, Belgium, the Netherlands, and Portugal as signatories was signed, guaranteeing the Open Door in China and restricting Japanese expansion there.

The naval agreement of the Washington Disarmament Conference, which finally was ratified and took effect in 1924, would not have left the United States, in 1933, in its actual position of inferiority had this country built up to treaty re-

quirements each year. It did not. To the disadvantages inherent in the naval agreement, such as the failure to include smaller vessels and auxiliaries — which are just as necessary to a fleet as battleships — and abandonment of plans for the building up of the Philippines and Guam as naval bases, there was the growing yearly failure to lay down the keels of the ships that were allowed under the agreement. Successive Secretaries of the Navy continued to ask for appropriations. They got only half-hearted support from President Coolidge and none at all from President Hoover. The Navy got only a bare subsistence from Congress. Admiral Mahan was a prophet honored everywhere except in his own country.

One issue that confused the post-Washington Conference Congressional arguments was the inclination of so many opponents of the agreement, the so-called Big Navy men, to emphasize the disadvantage in which it placed the United States vis-à-vis the British Navy. Japan never slackened in her building program, even when the 1923 earthquake destroyed many of her shipyards. Each year saw a growing disparity with Japan as well as with Britain in the categories of cruisers, destroyers, and auxiliaries. Too many Americans were swayed by the same psychology that led Big Bill Thompson, Chicago's perennial buffoon of a mayor, to threaten to punch King George V in the snoot if he ever came to this country. Americans looked east, where no danger lay. They should have looked westward.

In the spring of 1933, when President Roosevelt took office, the status of the United States fleet in comparison with that of Japan was far from the 5-3 ratio agreed on at the Washington Conference. Three succeeding so-called disarmament or naval conferences — at Geneva in 1927 and 1932 and at London in 1930 — had resulted only in the winning by Japan of agreement to a 10-10-7 ratio in cruisers and destroyers with Great Britain and the United States. The West gained no concessions in return. At London in 1930, the United States had no bar-

Spared by the treaty—Maryland.

gaining margin, such as the great one she had owned at Washington eight years before. President Hoover's proposal at Geneva in 1932 for a revision downward of the tonnages of the 1922 Washington Conference was almost drowned out by the noise of the riveting hammers in Japanese shipyards.

By 1933, events on the European Continent were moving rapidly toward a crisis. Hitler had come to power to start the acceleration of the German naval building program. Mussolini was building up his big, if imperfect, fleet in the Mediterranean, preparing for his African adventures and war with Britain. France was only belatedly moving to meet the growing German and Italian naval menace. Formation of the Rome-Berlin Axis and the Tri-Partite Alliance among Germany, Italy, and Japan was just around the corner. As in the period 1910–1914, Britain was concentrating more and more of her fleet in the Mediterranean and the North Sea to meet this new Continental menace. America was left alone in the Pacific to deal with Japan. The rulers of Nippon were conscious of the changed conditions. They had brazenly begun the Manchurian conquest in 1931.

The actual naval standing between Japan and the United States in the spring of 1933 was: battleships, United States fifteen and Japan nine (eleven of ours were to become overage before 1941); aircraft carriers, four and five; heavy cruisers, fifteen and ten; light cruisers, United States ten and Japan twenty-three. In two important categories the United States was outnumbered. In destroyer strength, Japan was about the 10-7 ratio. In addition, she was building her merchant ships with an eye to quick conversion to war use. Her seventeen-thousand-ton twenty-three-knot *Yawata* class passenger liners were designed in the 1930's for quick metamorphosis into aircraft carriers.

Whatever else one may think of President Roosevelt's first two terms, one accomplishment cannot be denied his administration. A beginning was made in catching up in the naval race with Japan. His first step, in November, 1933, was to earmark $238,000,000 of National Industrial Recovery Act funds for the construction of two aircraft carriers *(Enterprise* and the first *Yorktown,* that did such heroic fighting against Japan in the early months of the war), four heavy cruisers, and twenty destroyers. The following spring, in March of 1934, the Vinson-Trammel Act was passed. It authorized the construction, before 1941, of enough vessels of all categories to bring the United States Navy up to the full strength allowed under the Washington (1922) and London (1930) naval agreements.

The Vinson-Trammel Act, however, and this cannot be too often emphasized, was only a program. There was not shipbuilding capacity in this country even to allow the beginning of the program for some time. It required, too, the voting of appropriations in succeeding years for individual ship construction. As has been pointed out before, time is one factor that plays a vital part in any shipbuilding program; before the war vastly speeded all such processes, the minimum construction time for a battleship was two and one-half to three years, two years for a carrier, a year and one-half for a cruiser, and nine months to a year for a destroyer. A man-of-war is the most intricate and costly of all fighting machines. It also ages very rapidly.

|133

The Vinson-Trammel Act was passed while preliminary conversations were under way looking toward another naval conference at London. Japan quickly showed her hand. She demanded parity in tonnage in all categories. Washington, only now embarked on a program to bring the United States Navy up to 1922 treaty strength, refused to consider such a proposition. A suggested British compromise to give Japan parity on paper, with

Iowa of '98—a target

Iowa of '22—a drawing

the understanding she would not attempt to achieve it at sea, was met with equal scorn on both sides of the Pacific. On December 31, 1934, Japan gave the required two years notice of abrogation of the naval agreements she had entered into at Washington and London. The armament race between the United States and Japan was under full steam.

The British meanwhile, having bowed to Hitler's demands on land by declining to back up the French and bar his re-entry to the Rhineland, signed a treaty with him regarding naval building (which Hitler renounced as soon as Germany was strong enough, in 1939), and then went ahead with plans to convene another world naval conference. Held in December–January 1935–36, against the background of Mussolini's war in Africa, League sanctions, and an increasingly strident Hitler, it led only to a three-power agreement among Great Britain, France, and the United States to hold battleships to a tonnage of thirty-five thousand and guns to fourteen-inch and to exchange information on building programs. Japan attended the opening sessions of the conference but soon withdrew.

No further naval conferences were held, or even attempted, prior to the outbreak of war in Europe in 1939 and its spread to the Pacific in 1941. The United States went ahead with its building program, under the Vinson-Trammel Act of 1934. In January, 1938, after passage of a naval appropriation measure providing for construction of two battleships, two light cruisers, eight destroyers, six submarines, and other auxiliary craft, in line with the 1934 Act, Representative Carl Vinson introduced a measure in the House providing for an increase in United States naval strength of 20 per cent beyond that previously authorized. It is commonly known as the Second Vinson Act. It met the most bitter opposition. While hearings were under way, three United States cruisers joined in the ceremonies of dedication of Britain's new Singapore base, February 4, 1938. That provided the Anglophobes with fresh ammunition. The bill's chief supporters were Vinson, Wadsworth, and Martin in the House. In the Senate the fight for the bill was led by Senators David Walsh, Key Pittman, and Eugene Hale. The leading Senate opponents were Borah, Johnson,

134

Iowa of '43—a reality.

Vandenberg, King, La Follette, and Nye.

While the debates were under way in Congress, Japan notified Great Britain she had no intention of abiding by the qualitative limit on tonnage and gun size agreed to at the 1935 London Conference. To meet the threat of forty-five thousand-ton Japanese battleships, mounting sixteen-inch guns, specifications for the armament of two American battleships just voted *(North Carolina and Washington)* was changed from fourteen-inch to sixteen-inch guns. It also raised the question of alteration of the Panama Canal, if America was to counter the Japanese threat. The canal locks could not handle a ship of forty-five thousand tons. That increased the task of argument of the Big Navy proponents. With President Roosevelt putting his full political weight behind the measure, however, the Act finally was passed in May.

Despite these successes in gaining naval appropriations of sufficient size to enable the building of a fleet capable of meeting Japan on even terms, much that could have been done to prepare for the war that Japan long had been planning was blocked by Congressional action. It refused again and again to do anything about Guam. Congress did, however, appropriate $65,000,000 for construction of naval aviation bases in the Hawaiian Islands, at Midway, Wake, Johnston, Palmyra, Kodiak, and Sitka in the Pacific, and at seven locations in the Caribbean and eastern United States. Increasing funds also were voted for aviation, both Navy and Army, and for an expansion of the pilot-training program.

Explosion of the European powder keg on September 1, 1939, accelerated the United States naval program. But the time lost through the years could not be regained. When the Japanese attacked Pearl Harbor on December 7, 1941, the U.S. did not have parity with her in any single important category except submarines. Furthermore, the fleet was divided between the Atlantic and Pacific Oceans. The only two modern battleships — *North Carolina* and *Washington* — were in the Atlantic. They were the first battleships commissioned in seventeen years. Fifteen more were under construction, or on order. But a ship on the ways was of no use in the first dark days. There were eight battleships at Pearl Harbor, and one on the Pacific Coast in dry dock. Only three of the seven aircraft carriers in commission were in the Pacific. Eleven carriers were building and two more were authorized ten days after the start of the war, but it was not until 1943 that any of these went into action. Of eighteen heavy cruisers in commission, thirteen were in the Pacific. Fourteen more were building. There were nineteen light cruisers. Many of these were on duty in the Atlantic. Forty-two more were under construction or on order. Like the battleships and carriers, most of these saw no action until 1943. One hundred and seventy-one destroyers were in commission on December 7, 1941, but over half of these were in the Atlantic already engaged in "a shooting war" with the German submarines, while convoying ships to Iceland.

At the beginning of the war, the Japanese had (and all of their ships in the Pacific, of course): fifteen battleships, of which even the oldest had been vastly improved; fifteen aircraft carriers; twenty to thirty heavy cruisers mounting eight-inch guns, and most of them superior in speed to America's heavy cruisers; twenty-two light cruisers; 150 to 200 destroyers.

There are many reasons, of course, why Japan struck when she did. One of them must have been because she realized that if she waited many more months, or another year, America would overtake her with its belated building program. Events might even have led to a belated start on construction of real naval bases in the Philippines and at Guam, bases which the Navy was unable to build until 1944–45, after three and a half years of bloody fighting.

135

North Carolina—*planned, started, and scrapped.*

One factor on which the Japanese did not count was the ability of the great industrial machine of the United States to swing so quickly into high gear and begin turning out ships and planes far beyond her ability to match. By the end of May, 1945, the Navy had increased from a total of 338 combatant ships at the start of the war, to 1,150, this despite the loss of 309 vessels to that date. Including auxiliaries and amphibious craft, the Navy had 107,386 ships, and 19,882 more of all sizes were on order. United States naval strength was greater than that of all the other countries of the world, the Japanese, German,

Italian, and French navies largely having been either destroyed in the war or scuttled. The U.S. had such a navy because for the first two years in the Pacific it had men manning the ships there who were not afraid to die. They bought with their lives the time we needed to build this great fleet. The innocents paid the price for peacetime folly, when Americans talked in pious platitudes, such as those of the Kellogg-Briand Pact against war, when they held aloof from international organization but were too blind to see that one of the costs of isolationism was a navy second to none in the world.

North Carolina—*planned, completed, and tested in battle.*

1923—the Navy brings torpedoes to the air.

ADVENT OF AIR POWER-1910

Over the slumbering Italian battle fleet in Taranto Harbor near the toe of the Italian boot burst a line of brilliant flares at eleven o'clock the night of November 11, Armistice Day, 1940. Minutes later the two flare-dropping British planes and a dive bomber peeled off from their 7,500-foot level to lay their bombs on an oil tank, a seaplane hangar, and cruisers, destroyers, and supply ships in Mar Piccolo, the inner harbor. Then came the torpedo planes, five old Swordfish biplanes, each with a fifteen hundred-pound aerial torpedo suspended between the fixed wheels of its undercarriage. Skimming in over the water at thirty feet altitude, they launched their torpedoes at the six battleships lying in the Mar Grande, the outer harbor. Three more dive bombers and another torpedo plane, which had lost formation, attacked independently. An hour later four more torpedo planes came fishtailing in to the attack, accompanied by four more dive bombers, and then, finally,

A *Cavour* class battleship bleeds her oil away at Taranto.

a lone wolf whose take-off had been delayed but who had flown alone through the night from the British aircraft carrier *Illustrious* to carry out his mission.

When *Illustrious* launched her two flights of planes from 170 miles to the southward, all of Italy's six battleships were in the harbor — *Littorio, Vittorio Veneto, Conte di Cavour, Guilio Cesare, Caio Duilio* and *Andrea Doria*. There also were several heavy and light cruisers, destroyers, and fleet auxiliaries. In the excitement of maneuvering through the heavy anti-aircraft fire, the British fliers could not be sure what they had hit. A photograph taken from a reconnaissance plane the next day showed one of the *Littorio's* lying with a heavy list and her fo'c'sle awash, a *Cavour* class with her stern under water, and a *Duilio* beached and abandoned. Two cruisers were shown listing and surrounded by oil. Two auxiliaries had their sterns under water. The oil-storage depot and the

seaplane hangar both were wrecked. British losses had been two planes, in which one officer was killed, three others taken prisoner. Never had so great a blow been struck with such an economy of loss — of fleet danger, of effort. The rest of the Italian fleet retired to a more northern base. It never used Taranto again.

The British attack on Taranto was the first effective application by the British Fleet Air Arm of the new weapon that had been added to the sea arsenal since World War I. It was the most spectacular exemplification in the first war years of the new long-range striking power of the fleet. Before Taranto, planes from *Ark Royal* had aided in the immobilizing attack by British naval force from Gibraltar on the French fleet at Oran. But the main reliance there had been on surface fire. Taranto was all air.

The early plane-ship encounters in the Mediterranean, even Taranto, however, were only a pale shadow of the great sea-air battles that were to be fought in the Pacific after the United States had suffered, from Japanese fliers at Pearl Harbor, its Pacific Taranto.

The United States and Japan, even more than Great Britain, had accepted the airplane as an indispensable weapon of naval warfare, forming the carrier-striking forces that played so great a part in the war in the Pacific. Despite the claims of many air force enthusiasts that the airplane was a distinctive weapon that could best be operated under a separate command, the United States and Japan from the first had developed it as an integral part of fleet operations. The British had been slow to follow. It was not until 1938 that the British Admiralty was given undivided control of the Fleet Air Arm. Even so, the British had six aircraft carriers to our five at the start of the war in 1939, and they also had two seaplane carriers, the *Argus* and *Albatross*. Japan had the greatest number of carriers, seven. By 1941, this had been increased to fifteen.

The experience of the British in the first two years of the war served as a great stimulus to United States naval thinking. The Japanese success at Pearl Harbor and our own experience in the carrier battles in the Coral Sea and at Midway confirmed earlier impressions. The aircraft carrier was given first priority in construction. After two years the United States gained superiority at sea in that class and then steadily increased it. By the spring of 1945, American carrier forces were superior enough to go anywhere they wished to go and slug it out with either sea-based or land-based air power.

In addition to the larger carriers for fleet operations, the United States also converted scores of smaller vessels for the escort carrier class. It was their operations in the North Atlantic in convoy protection that finally nullified the German submarine campaign and kept open the lifeline to Britain and then later to North Africa and the European Continent.

Ely in the first take-off from a ship—Birmingham ...

and landing for the first time on Pennsylvania.

It was only justice that the United States should have won the air supremacy of the world in World War II. For the airplane, and especially its development as a navy weapon, was largely pioneered by Americans. Just as the Wright brothers were the first to make a successful flight, from a sand dune at Kitty Hawk, North Carolina, on December 17, 1903, so it also was an American, Eugene Ely, who first flew a plane off the deck of a Navy vessel and then landed a plane on deck. It was an American, Glenn Curtiss, who first made a successful flight in a hydroplane, on January 26, 1911. Curtiss also was the first man to land a plane on the water alongside a naval vessel and be hoisted aboard by a crane. This was done in San Diego Harbor on February 17, 1911.

It was United States Navy fliers who developed the dive-bombing technique. The first torpedo specifically designed for release from a plane was developed by an American, Frank A. Leavitt, during the early days of World War I. Rear Admiral Bradley A. Fiske, USN, in 1912 patented for the United States Navy the first "torpedo plane," which, he said, "might, under favorable conditions, make a twenty-thousand-dollar airplane a worthy match for a twenty-million-dollar battle cruiser." It did. The first recorded successful use of aerial-borne torpedoes was in July, 1916, in the Sea of Marmara during the Dardanelles Campaign, when a British Navy lieutenant, carrying 14-inch, 731-pound torpedoes in his plane, sank four Turkish ships in successive flights.

Philadelphia, 1918—an early seaplane lands.

*1917—a Sopwith Pup lands on a carrier convert (from a cruiser)—Britain's **Furious.***

All during World War I, though, the airplane was used more or less experimentally, instead of as a standard naval weapon. Its chief mission was considered to be that of a scout, rather than that of an attacker in its own right. It was not until much later that the Navy plane, flying from land or a carrier's deck, came to be considered a "long-range gun."

As a scout, and as an anti-submarine weapon, the airplane was widely used in World War I. Had the seaplane sent up by the tender *Engadine,* at the Battle of Jutland, been more successful in its work in finding the German High Seas Fleet and reporting its position to Jellicoe, it might have given a stimulus to air thinking by the big-ship admirals.

Probably the most famous of World War I naval planes was the Sopwith Pup, the standard scout seaplane of the British Navy. Late in the war the Germans, realizing the vulnerability of the big Zeppelins, filled as they were with explosive hydrogen, began the development of big, long-range seaplanes to carry on the bombing of England.

Ironically, it was an Army Air officer, Brigadier General William (Billy) Mitchell, who first dramatized the vulnerability of heavily armored surface ships to attack from the air. Outspoken proponent of air power over sea power, General Mitchell carried out several bombing tests against surrendered German naval vessels and United States battleships in 1921 and 1923. In the first tests, in 1921 off the Virginia Capes, Army bombers sank the submarine *U-117,* the German destroyer *G-102,* the cruiser *Frankfurt,* and the battleship *Ostfriesland.* The latter two were survivors of the Battle of Jutland. In later tests, the obsolete American battleships *New Jersey* and *Virginia* were sunk.

Mitchell's tests, although they showed that an airplane could carry a missile large enough and powerful enough to sink ships, hardly were definitive and in a way were misleading. The bombings were done on anchored vessels and carried out without opposition, either from enemy planes or from anti-aircraft fire. They led many Army men to the conclusion that the same type of plane that was efficacious against fixed land targets also would be successful in attacks on moving ships at sea. They never were. It was not until skip-bombing was developed, in which the bombing plane makes a run in much as does a torpedo plane and releases its bombs at low level and high speed against the side of the target ship, that United States Air Force bombers had any success against naval vessels. It was this technique that was used in the Bismarck Sea in 1943, where General Mac-Arthur's fliers intercepted and destroyed a convoy of transports bound for the reinforcement of New Guinea.

After Mitchell's tests on the older battleships and captured German vessels, the Navy had target practice on the new *Washington,* the big battleship

*One of Mitchell's planes zooms past a captured Jutland veteran—the sinking **Frankfurt.***

140

141

Alabama feeds the growing Air Arm.

Unintentional—but a curve works on old **Arkansas.**

that was ordered scrapped after the Washington Disarmament Conference. They took her to sea off the Virginia Capes, in November, 1924, and tried out all naval weapons against her hull and heavily-armored topside structure. Planes, submarines, and surface vessels took turns pounding her. Much more highly compartmented and more heavily armed than were the German vessels or the old American battleships, she stood up well to her pounding. Big-gun fire from the battleship *Texas* was credited with doing the most damage to her.

For many years after World War I, both Navy Air and Army Air had a hard struggle to survive. Mitchell was court-martialed for being years ahead of his time, and for saying so in public. Our Navy fliers, developing the techniques of dive bombing and torpedo plane attack, got along on short rations. A few spectacular stunts, like the flight of the NC-4 across the Atlantic to Lisbon in 1919 and the round-the-world flight of Army planes in 1924, were about all the sop the fliers were allowed or the only information on aircraft development for sea warfare that was given the public.

First transatlantic flight—NC-4 sixty miles out to sea, May 16, 1919 . . .

It remained for World War II to witness the full flowering of the naval arm of air power, much as the submarine had proved itself in the sea warfare of the first world struggle. The dive bomber, the torpedo plane, and their carriers, some of which were of a greater tonnage than most battleships, were the decisive factor of the war at sea.

For months in the Mediterranean before Taranto, the British Mediterranean Fleet under Admiral Sir Andrew Cunningham (later Admiral of the Fleet and First Sea Lord) had been proving that warships, if properly fought and handled, had little to fear from horizontal bombing attack. Failure of the Italian fleet on at least two occasions to risk the issue of a surface battle with inferior British forces was believed to have been based on the belief that the overwhelming bomber power Italy had deployed at many land bases around the Mediterranean Basin would take care of the British fleet. The Italian fliers failed dismally. Different planes and different techniques were needed for the war at sea.

Properly to understand the difference between the sea and land air arms, some knowledge of the differences in the planes used is necessary. All navies have developed these distinctive weapons of the air.

The Dive Bomber. Any plane that can stand the strain can dive at a target from a high altitude and lay its bomb. The conventional type of World War II was a strongly-built, single-wing, single-motored plane carrying two men and capable of pulling out safely from a dive as great as twenty thousand feet. It was equipped with large flaps on the wings that were lowered just before the bomb was dropped to slow the speed and steady on the target. The pilot aimed his plane at the target ship just as anyone aims a gun. As he dived, he could

and she lands off Portugal on May 27.

The dive bomber—a Helldiver points its bomb.

follow to some extent the course of his target. If he was "on" at dropping height — one thousand to two thousand feet — it was almost a sure hit.

A bomb dropped from a plane in level flight at twenty thousand feet is easy to avoid if the captain of the ship under attack maneuvers properly. Terminal velocity of a falling body is approximately 550 feet a second, and it takes several seconds for a bomb to reach full speed. From five thousand feet, it requires nineteen seconds for a bomb to reach the ground. From twenty thousand feet the time required is well over a minute. A ship making thirty knots will have traveled over half a mile while the bomb is falling. If a turn is made when the bomb is dropped, it can't possibly hit close enough to do any harm. The better the bombsight, the farther the miss. Even when a mass attack was made, and the bombs were dropped in a pattern, hits were few. The British Navy has a photograph of the carrier *Ark Royal* emerging safely from the spray thrown up by thirty bombs that fell in a pattern all around her. The dive bomber and dive-bombing technique were pioneered by the United States Navy. At the battle of Midway, a flight of sixteen dive bombers scored fifteen hits on the Japanese carrier *Kaga*.

The Torpedo Bomber. This also was a single-wing, single-motored plane, capable of flying from, and landing on, a carrier's deck, although it could fly from a land field just as well. It showed a great development during the war. The first standard torpedo bomber of the war was the Grumman Avenger. It was used by both the United States and British navies. It had a speed probably twice that of the 150 knots of the ancient Swordfish

143

The torpedo plane—an Avenger's tin fish is launched.

The fighter—a Hellcat takes off in a hurry.

The scout—the eyes of the fleet below.

planes with which the British fliers attacked the Italian ships at Taranto.

In a torpedo run, the bombers go in low at top speed and attempt to lay a pattern, so that in whatever direction the target turns, she will get hit. The torpedo bomber was the real killer of the fleet air force. Ships with protected decks could stand hits from dropped bombs. No ship, even a battleship, could withstand much underwater damage, such as was delivered by a torpedo. If it did nothing else, it so slowed the surface vessel that it could be overtaken and destroyed by an enemy surface ship.

The Carrier Fighter. More strongly built — to withstand the shock landings on a pitching carrier deck — than the land-based fighter, and with smaller wing load to allow for a quick take-off, the carrier fighters were so improved during World War II that the two leading American models, the Grumman and the Chance-Vought Corsair, were a match at medium altitudes for any land-based fighter except the German jets. They had a more limited range, however, than some of the better American land fighters, such as the Lightning and the Mustang. They provided fighter cover for the fleet, escorted dive bombers and torpedo bombers to the attack, and did diversionary strafing. They were themselves capable of doing dive bombing. At war's end, most were armed with rockets.

The Scout Seaplane. A relatively slow, sturdy plane that was catapulted by an explosive charge from the deck of a cruiser or battleship, they spotted fire for their ships, did anti-submarine patrols and reconnaissance jobs. The scout seaplanes played an important part in spotting shore bombardments and were effectively used against submarines.

The Patrol Bomber, Seaplane. Largely superseded in the latter stages of the war against Japan by the land-based naval versions of medium and

heavy bombers perfected by the Army Air Force, the old seaplanes such as the PBY's and the PBM's played a heroic role in the early days of the war against Japan, as did the Sunderland flying boats of the British in the campaign against the German submarines. The PBY's and the PBM's, needing only a protected body of water from which to take off, often operated far ahead of even the forward land bases in the Pacific, flying from sheltered coves in which their tenders were anchored. The only four-motored plane of the Japanese was the Kawanishi patrol bomber, which they used for long-range reconnaissance work and night nuisance-bombing attacks on forward bases.

The British and United States Army Air Force, hampered in some ocean areas in the early years of the war at sea by lack of naval air support, adopted what is known as skip-bombing. For this type of bombing, any plane could be used. A level

The patrol bomber—searches and stalks, as one did the **Bismarck.**

Kamikaze—one of the Jap suicide planes, the **Baka Bomb.**

or shallow glide approach was made abeam of the ship to be attacked. The bombs were dropped close in, so as to hit at the water line or just above. These methods proved effacacious against lightly-armed transports or supply ships, even when such big targets as B-17's and B-24's, both four-motored bombers, were used. Because the plane had to go in close before dropping its load, it was a hazardous operation against a warship.

The aircraft carrier, from whose decks the fliers of the United States, Britain, and Japan took off for so many crippling attacks against enemy ships and bases, was a development of the years since the close of World War I.

The first United States carrier was the *Langley,* converted from the collier *Jupiter* and commissioned in 1922. In World War II, the aircraft car-

riers were counted in squadrons and ranged in size from the ten-thousand-tons of the smallest escort class to the forty-five-thousand-tons of the United States Navy super carriers on which construction was begun in 1943. No admiral would think of going to sea without air cover, either provided from land bases or from accompanying carriers.

The carrier is a mobile base that can go anywhere the fleet can go and against which an enemy must set up a defensive patrol for hundreds of miles out from his coasts. An island must stay where it is. Its position is marked on all charts. A carrier force may hit from any direction. It was from a carrier's deck that Lieutenant General Jimmy Doolittle, then a Lieutenant Colonel, led off his two-motored Mitchell Army bombers for the first air attack on Tokyo on April 18, 1942.

145

Converted from a collier—**Langley** was the first operational American carrier.

Through air reconnaissance and intelligence furnished by submarine scouts, it is possible, when the distances are not too great, for the naval command of any country to learn of the approach of a hostile fleet and, with its air power, to attack it long before it can come within range of its ship's guns. Weather is still the great enemy of the plane, but the great developments in electronics in recent years, particularly the adaptation of radar to airplane use, have made it possible to operate air fleets by day or by night, in fog or clear weather, and detect and bomb any target encountered.

The development of the airplane and of long-range guided missiles does not mean that surface ships are entirely outmoded for non-nuclear wars. In amphibious warfare, surface warships have provided the artillery support without which the landing waves could not have advanced against emplaced enemy artillery. In the latter stages of the war against Japan, United States battleships, cruisers, and destroyers even were used for strategic bombardments against Japanese shore-line factories. Supply ships still must be escorted to island bases, and the airplane still has not entirely taken the place of the surface ship in anti-submarine work. Too, there always is the chance that the enemy surface fleet may be able to withstand any punishment given by air and keep on coming until it is in big-gun range, such as was the case

with the Japanese columns that attacked in the Second Battle of the Philippines. Anti-aircraft defense also has improved, but some of the enemy planes generally got through to do their damage no matter how good the defense. Air attack reached its epitome in the Japanese Kamikaze Corps, the suicide pilots who flew bomb-laden planes directly into United States ships in the closing phases of World War II.

Anti-aircraft defense has not kept pace with the attacking power of the plane. The best defense is another airplane. Air supply has also so increased in efficiency that in the future an air force should be able to go anywhere it wants to go and take along its own supply of bombs and gasoline and mechanics and spare parts. When the day comes that that is possible, then control of the sea will be held by the nation that has the biggest and best submarines and the best air fleet, not the best surface fleet. The airplane and the submarine accounted for the principal ship losses of the Japanese fleet. Had Japan had the submarines, the planes, and the pilots that the United States had, it would not have been driven from the seas, it might not have lost the war.

Any war of the future, one fought with conventional weapons, not the nuclear monsters, will be decided above the sea and under it, not on its surface.

146

*American war effort — fifty **Casablanca** class escort carriers were built in '43 and '44.*

Graf Spee puts to sea.

ENGLAND'S LIFE LINES 1939-1941

CHAPTER 12

Late in August, 1939, a week before the Stukas began screaming down on Warsaw and Hitler's legions moved across the Polish border, a trim gray warship of twelve thousand tons displacement steamed northward through the North Sea, then turned westward to pass north of Iceland and enter the North Atlantic by the wide passage between Iceland and Greenland. Waiting for her at a predetermined area in the North Atlantic was the tanker and supply ship *Altmark.*

The warship was the German armored ship *Admiral Graf Spee,* popularly called a "pocket battleship," one of three built by the Weimar Republic during the postwar years when Germany was limited to vessels of ten thousand tons displacement. She mounted six eleven-inch guns in fore and aft turrets, was intricately compartmented and heavily armored for a ship of her class, and had a speed of twenty-six knots. She was going out to raid the steamer lanes as soon as Hitler moved and war came with France and Britain.

Designed for the very mission she was on, the *Graf Spee* had a cruising range at fifteen knots of twenty thousand miles, which was twice her official rating. She carried, appropriately enough, the name of the German Admiral who had led a raiding squadron in the Pacific in World War I and who had gone down on his flagship December 8, 1914 in the Battle of the Falkland Islands.

The *Graf Spee* was one of the major units of a small but potent navy that Germany had built, first through violation of the Treaty of Versailles and then under a naval treaty with Britain. Hitler had denounced the latter as soon as he felt he was strong enough. It included four battleships, the thirty-five thousand-ton *Bismarck* and *Tirpitz*, with eight fifteen-inch guns, the latter of which had been launched in April, 1939, and was not yet in commission, and the twenty-six thousand-ton *Scharnhorst* and *Gneisenau*. The main batteries of the latter two were nine eleven-inch guns. There were three "pocket battleships," the *Spee*, the *Deutschland* (later renamed the *Lützow*), and the *Admiral Scheer*, named for the leader of the High Seas Fleet at Jutland. An aircraft carrier was under construction, but it never was completed. There were five heavy cruisers, *Blücher*, *Admiral Hipper*, *Prinz Eugen*, *Seydlitz*, and *Lützow*. They were of ten thousand tons displacement and mounted eight eight-inch guns each. There were four light cruisers, numerous destroyers, hundreds of smaller craft, and between seventy-five and one hundred submarines.

The German Navy was no match for the British Home Fleet in a surface action, but it had a nuisance value far beyond its numerical strength. Until the very end of the war, it tied up a large number of Allied ships, both British and American, which could have been used to great advantage in the Pacific. In the Baltic, and especially in the campaign for Norway, it played, on the small scale of those actions, a prominent part.

The German fleet, however, never fully lived up to the fears of the Allied admiralties. One of these fears was that the fast German ships would slip past the blockade in the North Sea and fall on the lightly-guarded convoys that composed the bridge of ships from the rest of the world to England, a bridge without which Britain would die. Several of them did, but each foray was of short duration. The *Graf Spee* was the only one of the major German vessels at sea when the war began.

For reasons that remain obscure, the *Graf Spee* did not immediately strike at merchant shipping. After two refueling rendezvous with *Altmark*

Harwood in **Ajax** *plows after* **Graf Spee.**

in mid-Atlantic, she crossed the equator and began her commerce raiding off the South American coast, but not until September 30. The first victim was the five-thousand-ton British freighter *Clement*. She was sunk by gunfire and her crew set adrift in a lifeboat.

Then occurred one of the paradoxes that were to distinguish the brief career left her commanding officer, Captain Hans Langsdorff. It was a calm sea. The coast of Brazil was only fifty miles away. But Langsdorff broke radio silence to ask the radio station at Recife to notify ships in the vicinity of the drifting lifeboat. He thus compromised his own security. It was the first notice the British South Atlantic Squadron, led by Commodore (later Rear Admiral) H. H. Harwood, had that *Graf Spee* was loose in its ocean.

The Commodore took steps to intercept her. He had under his command the heavy cruiser

Exeter, badly damaged, fought gallantly with **Achilles.**

Cumberland of 10,000 tons and eight eight-inch guns, *Exeter* of 8,390 tons and six eight-inch guns, and the light cruisers *Ajax* and *Achilles* of 6,985 tons and 7,030 tons, respectively. Each of the latter carried eight six-inch guns. The Commodore wore his broad pennant in *Ajax*.

For two more months, while *Graf Spee* continued raiding in the South Atlantic — interlarded with one foray around the Cape of Good Hope — with only moderate success, the British Squadron had no luck. Then, on December 13, they caught her, but at a time when the biggest British ship of the squadron, *Cumberland*, was in the Falklands for an overhaul. Captain Langsdorff had captured and sunk eight vessels in the meantime, transferring most of their men to the tanker *Altmark* (which later was boarded by the British in Norwegian waters to release the prisoners), and keeping the officers aboard *Graf Spee*.

Commodore Harwood, correctly guessing the possible plans of Captain Langsdorff, was cruising to the northeastward off the coast of southern Brazil with *Ajax*, *Achilles*, and *Exeter* the morning of December 13, 1939, when they sighted *Graf Spee* to the north. Despite the heavier armament of the German ship, the British squadron closed for action. Using tactics at sea that Hitler had found so useful on land in Europe, Commodore Harwood sent *Exeter* to attack *Graf Spee* from one quarter, while *Ajax* and *Achilles* attacked from the other. That forced Langsdorff to divide the fire of his two turrets. The British cruisers' extra speed — thirty-two knots to *Graf Spee's* top of twenty-six — helped further to reduce the odds.

Captain Langsdorff turned away when he sighted the British cruisers, opening fire on them at 6:18 A.M. at a range of about ten miles. *Exeter* returned the fire two minutes later from her forward four eight-inch guns, and *Ajax* and *Achilles*, crossing to the other side of *Graf Spee*, which was turning away to the west, opened fire a short time later. It was extreme range for the light cruiser's six-inch guns.

The German gunners used their advantage of range to good advantage and also showed the efficiency that had made them the prize shooting ship of the German Navy. Concentrating on *Exeter*, they quickly scored two damaging hits, the second of which knocked out one of the forward turrets and all the bridge controls. A short time later *Exeter* suffered two more hits.

All three British ships were closing the range all this time and, as the *Graf Spee* finally completed her maneuvers and squared away for her run to the southwest at six twenty-six, two or more British

Overhauled **Cumberland** missed the fight.

salvos of six-inch shells hit her. *Graf Spee's* fire control system was knocked out, and the topside damage done demoralized her crew, most of them young Nazis who probably were quite willing to die for their *Führer* but did not have the experience or fortitude to stand up under the long-range engagement of the guns. The British sailors noted the erratic fire of the German ship at about this point but did not learn its cause until later.

The running fight continued until eight o'clock with *Graf Spee* frequently laying a smoke screen in an attempt to escape the fire of her nimbler adversaries, who were harrying her like a pack of hunting dogs pursuing a bear. By that time, *Exeter* had received two more hits and was out of the battle, limping for the Falklands with sixty-one killed and twenty-three wounded. *Ajax* also had received two hits and *Achilles* one. Ammunition, too, was running low on the British ships after the

149

Graf Spee destroys herself in the River Plate off Montevideo.

*Deutschland, sister to **Graf Spee**.*

one-and-a-half-hour fight, and Commodore Harwood dropped back to trail *Graf Spee* and await the *Cumberland*, which had started to raise steam as soon as word of the action was flashed to her.

Captain Langsdorff ran his crippled ship into Montevideo, the Uruguayan port and capital city, where he was given three days to make his ship seaworthy. With his fire control gone and Commodore Harwood and his cruisers outside — *Cumberland* had joined up — Captain Langsdorff obeyed the orders from Hitler not to attempt to escape. Having buried his thirty-six dead and put ashore the sixty-one captive British seamen he held, Captain Langsdorff left Montevideo late on Sunday afternoon, and in the Río de la Plata, off the Argentine coast, he destroyed his ship. The message from the seaplane of *Ajax* to Commodore Harwood was timed 8:54 P.M. It said *"Spee* has blown herself up." A few days later Captain Langsdorff, interned with his crew by the Argentine government, wrapped himself in the old flag of the Imperial German Navy and blew out his brains with his pistol.

In its first test the Nazi Navy had been proved to be something less than the perfect instrument Hitler had believed it to be.

150

Three weeks before *Graf Spee* was run to aground at Montevideo, two even more powerful German ships, *Scharnhorst* and *Gneisenau*, slipped past the British North Sea blockade and sailed into the North Atlantic by the same route *Spee* had taken, between Greenland and Iceland. On the way down, they ran into the British armed merchant cruiser *Rawalpindi*. The former India luxury liner, of 16,697 tons, had been armed with several six-inch guns and sent out to do scout and convoy duty. It was not expected that she would have to fight two of the world's best battleships.

Despite the odds against her, *Rawalpindi's* captain apparently had no thought of surrender. In retirement for two years, Captain Edward Coverly Kennedy, sixty years of age, had come back to help out when war began. Civilian life had not dimmed his fighting ardor. When the two German battleships (one of which was mistakenly identified as *Deutschland*) came over the horizon at his ship the afternoon of November 23, he ordered his crew to battle stations and tried to make a running fight of it. The second German salvo bracketed the lightly-skinned liner. The third salvo hit squarely. For thirty-five minutes the unequal battle went on. By that time every gun on the *Rawalpindi* was silenced. She was afire from one end to the other. The survivors of her crew, some forty men, took to three small boats that remained in a fairly seaworthy condition. Thirty of them were picked up by the Germans, who left hurriedly when a British cruiser was seen coming up fast in response to *Rawalpindi's* signals. Eleven more were rescued from their waterlogged boat.

The brush with *Rawalpindi* apparently dissuaded the two German battleships from continuing on into the North Atlantic, for they steamed back to port and did not return until the spring of 1941. They got in among a convoy on that occasion and sank an estimated one hundred thousand tons

Gneisenau—to raid—but never to fight her equal in decisive combat.

Duke of York will later sink Scharnhorst.

Scharnhorst and Gneisenau start out on a raid.

of shipping, but then were caught in Brest and heavily bombed for several months until they escaped through the English Channel to a home port. There Gneisenau was found to be so badly hurt she was taken to the Polish port of Gdynia and finished out the war ingloriously as a blockship. Scharnhorst met her end in the North Sea at the guns of the British battleship Duke of York and the guns and torpedoes of cruisers and destroyers. But that was not until December 26, 1943. Another

of her sisters was to receive her death blow long before that date.

Since the destruction of Jervis Bay, another British armed merchant cruiser, before the guns of a German "armored ship" — as the British officially described her, and which probably was one of the German heavy cruisers of the Admiral Hipper class — on November 5, 1940, in the North Atlantic, the German surface ships had not taken to the high seas. They had remained at base through the winter of 1939–40. In the spring of 1940, they had been kept busy in the campaign against Norway.

Many of them suffered damage there. The task of patrol by the British Home Fleet through the winter, and that of the detached squadrons and Force H at Gibraltar, had been one of weary days in North Sea and North Atlantic weather, without sight of an enemy. In March, Scharnhorst and Gneisenau made their last sortie in the steamer lanes together. Planes of Force H once sighted them, but they got into Brest without a surface fight.

In May, out came Bismarck, the 35,000-ton, fifteen-inch-gunned battleship that was a match for anything then afloat except the United States'

Cruiser Sheffield fights fifty-foot waves on a raider sweep.

151

Bismarck slips quietly out of the haze of the fjords . . .

with her cruiser escort *Prinz Eugen* . . .

and heads out to sea.

sixteen-inch gunned *North Carolina* and the British *Nelson* and *Rodney*. She carried the flag of Admiral Günther Lütjens.

Like most of the German big ships, *Bismarck* had been basing in the Norwegian fjords. On May 22, 1941, a reconnaissance aircraft reported *Bismarck* had left her berth at Bergen. All British squadrons were alerted. Late in the afternoon of the next day, the heavy cruisers *Norfolk* and *Suffolk* sighted her headed south through Denmark Strait, the familiar passage between Greenland and Iceland, in company with the heavy cruiser *Prinz Eugen*. They held doggedly to her through the short night of those latitudes, and at dawn of May 24 guided to the position of the German ships the 42,000-ton, fifteen-inch-gunned battle cruiser *Hood*, the biggest Allied warship afloat, and the battleship *Prince of Wales*, later to be sunk by Japanese planes in the South China Sea.

The two British battleships, *Hood* in the lead, sighted the German battleship and cruiser at fifteen miles distance. They began to close at full speed. *Hood* was first to open fire, at the low range

for her guns of about thirteen thousand yards. The *Prince* followed a moment later. Then *Bismarck* answered. As at Jutland, twenty-four years before, the German gunnery was far superior to that of the British. The first few British salvos all were wide of the mark. *Bismarck*, either because of superior visual range-finding equipment, or perhaps because of the fine radar equipment the Germans were known to have even at that time, was "on" the target with at least two of her first three salvos.

Suffolk, with Norfolk, made the first contact.

Hood—at full speed—is followed by . . .

153

Prince of Wales, to close in action with Bismarck.

Bismarck fires her opening salvos . . .

*and **Hood** is quickly destroyed.*

A great fire mushroomed amidships on *Hood,* and then, like her smaller sisters at Jutland, she disappeared in a great explosion. Great pieces of her spattered the sea for a radius of more than half a mile. Of her 1,418 officers and men, only three survived.

*A Catalina will find **Bismarck** later . . .*

Brought under fire of both German ships — at the start *Prinz Eugen* had concentrated on *Prince of Wales* — the second British battleship also sustained hits which caused her to break off the action. Her men, however, saw at least one of her fifteen-inch shells hit *Bismarck* on the fo'c'sle, starting a fire. It was the first of many hits *Bismarck* was to take before she finally went down.

By the time of this first action, every ship the British could muster was on the move toward the German vessels. Converging on their track, which was to the southeastward toward France, were the carriers *Victorious* and *Ark Royal,* the battleships *King George V, Rodney,* and *Ramilles,* the battle cruiser *Renown,* and many smaller vessels. In visual contact still were *Norfolk* and *Suffolk* and *Prince of Wales.* They resumed action briefly late the same afternoon. That night a flight of Swordfish planes from *Victorious* hit *Bismarck* with at least one torpedo. Then contact was lost. For thirty-one hours none of the many planes and ships searching the wastes of water caught a sight

154

and guide Fairey Swordfish torpedo planes to damage her rudder and slow her down.

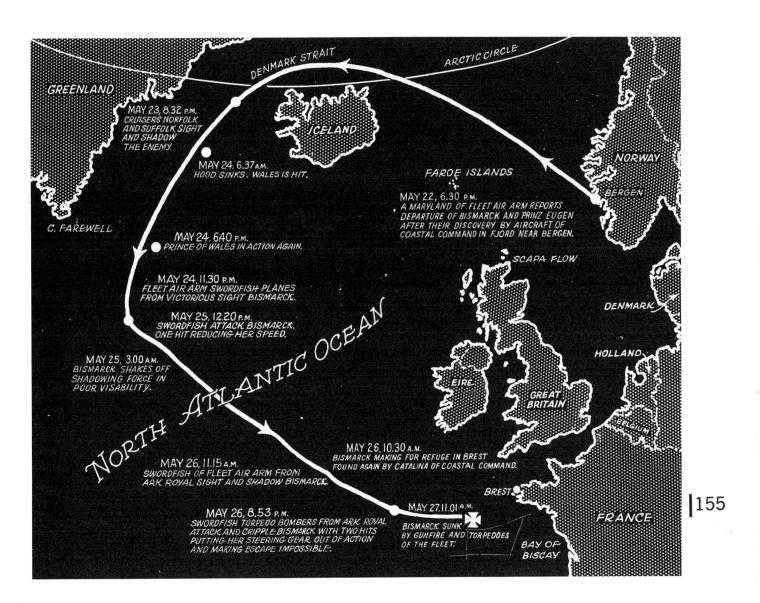

DENMARK STRAIT

ARCTIC CIRCLE

GREENLAND

ICELAND

MAY 23, 8.32 P.M.
CRUISERS NORFOLK
AND SUFFOLK SIGHT
AND SHADOW
THE ENEMY.

MAY 24, 6.37 A.M.
HOOD SINKS. WALES IS HIT.

FAROE ISLANDS

NORWAY

BERGEN

MAY 22, 6.30 P.M.
A MARYLAND OF FLEET AIR ARM REPORTS
DEPARTURE OF BISMARCK AND PRINZ EUGEN
AFTER THEIR DISCOVERY BY AIRCRAFT OF
COASTAL COMMAND IN FJORD NEAR BERGEN.

C. FAREWELL

MAY 24, 6.40 P.M.
PRINCE OF WALES IN ACTION AGAIN.

SCAPA FLOW

MAY 24, 11.30 P.M.
FLEET AIR ARM SWORDFISH PLANES
FROM VICTORIOUS SIGHT BISMARCK.

DENMARK

MAY 25, 12.20 P.M.
SWORDFISH ATTACK BISMARCK.
ONE HIT REDUCING HER SPEED.

MAY 25, 3.00 A.M.
BISMARCK SHAKES OFF
SHADOWING FORCE IN
POOR VISABILITY.

HOLLAND

EIRE

GREAT
BRITAIN

NORTH ATLANTIC OCEAN

BELGIUM

MAY 26, 11.15 A.M.
SWORDFISH OF FLEET AIR ARM FROM
ARK ROYAL SIGHT AND SHADOW BISMARCK.

MAY 26, 10.30 A.M.
BISMARCK MAKING FOR REFUGE IN BREST
FOUND AGAIN BY CATALINA OF COASTAL COMMAND.

BREST

MAY 26, 8.53 P.M.
SWORDFISH TORPEDO BOMBERS FROM ARK ROYAL
ATTACK AND CRIPPLE BISMARCK WITH TWO HITS
PUTTING HER STEERING GEAR OUT OF ACTION
AND MAKING ESCAPE IMPOSSIBLE.

MAY 27, 11.01 A.M.
BISMARCK SUNK
BY GUNFIRE AND TORPEDOES
OF THE FLEET.

BAY OF
BISCAY

FRANCE

155

King George V, with the main British units, catches **Bismarck**...

and concentrated gunfire on the helpless ship fails to sink her.

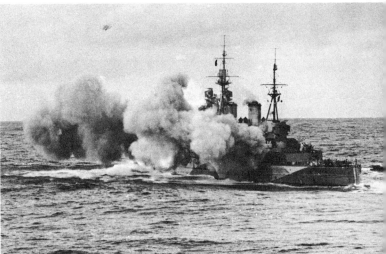

of her now somewhat battered 791-foot-long, 118-foot-wide hull. It was an American-built patrol bomber that found her.

The big, slow Catalina — the "PBY" made famous later in the Pacific — was droning along through a cloud layer at 10:30 A.M., May 26, an American observer at the controls, when the plane suddenly broke out into clear weather. There down below was *Bismarck*, now alone. She opened fire immediately, apparently having tracked the plane in with her radar, and it ducked back into the clouds. The German ship was lost again for a few moments, but the alarm had spread. Forty-five minutes later aircraft from *Ark Royal* spotted the German ship. Contact was not lost again. The British ships in the area closed in for the kill.

Vice Admiral Sir James Somerville, in charge of Force H, which had steamed out from Gibraltar with *Renown* and *Ark Royal* to join the hunt, was closest to the southward. He ordered a strike of torpedo planes sent out against her and sent ahead the light cruiser *Sheffield* to establish and maintain surface contact. Closing in from the north were the aircraft carrier *Victorious* and the battleships *King George V* and *Rodney*, under Admiral Sir John C. Tovey.

The first attack by *Ark's* planes made in poor visibility and high seas was unsuccessful. On a second try, two torpedoes went home, one near the stern that crippled *Bismarck's* rudder and sent her circling wildly to starboard. It also apparently knocked out a propeller, for she never again was able to make more than eight to ten knots. As darkness closed down, the British squadrons were rapidly overhauling the stricken giant. Shortly after midnight, the destroyers began to attack. At least two hits with twenty-one-inch torpedoes were scored. Still the German battleship kept going.

Shortly after dawn, four hundred miles west of France, *Norfolk* and *Suffolk* sighted her, and then *King George V* and *Rodney*.

The *Norfolk* was the first to engage and scored some hits. Then *Rodney* opened up, followed by *King George*. For over an hour, finally at the point-blank range of two to three miles, the two British battleships pumped their sixteen-inch and fourteen-inch shells into the battered and burning hulk. Seven hundred shells were fired. Probably few missed. No ship in history ever took punishment such as that and stayed afloat. As near as anyone ever came to it, the German naval architects had built an unsinkable ship. She was dead in the water, being abandoned by her crew, but with her flag still flying. Some of the survivors later said the scene aboard the ship was indescribable. Admiral Lütjens had locked himself in his cabin, and there was no one left to surrender the ship.

With *Bismarck* only a burning hulk and the fuel in his own ships running low because of the long chase, Admiral Tovey led his battleships away toward home, leaving *Bismarck* to be finished off with torpedoes from the cruisers. At 10:27 A.M., May 27, 1941, she finally went down by the stern. One hundred and one men of her estimated crew of twenty-four hundred were saved.

Bought at the price of *Hood* and her men, it was a costly victory, but one of the few triumphs Prime Minister Churchill had to offer his countrymen in the summer of 1941, one of the blackest of the war for the tight little islands that alone stood between Hitler and the conquest of Europe. It was the last foray of the German fleet into the North Atlantic. It partly redressed the humiliations of the year before, when Britain had to give up the campaign to keep Hitler and the Nazis out of Norway.

156

Cruiser torpedoes must finish the job, and . . .

after a fighting career of only five days, **Bismarck** slides down.

British Commandos raid a Norwegian harbor.

NORWAY AND DUNKIRK

In 1919, the hospitable people of Denmark, Norway, and Sweden took into their homes many German children made orphans by World War I. They nursed them back to health, then sent them back to the Reich. On April 9, 1940, these recipients of Scandinavian bounty, or at least many of them, returned to Denmark and Norway. They went back at the head of an army and a navy, to seize those two would-be neutral countries.

Germany threw into the struggle for command of Norwegian waters nearly every available ship she had afloat. Of her major units only *Bismarck* was not identified as participating.

The war on the Western Front was still in its "phony stage" with the armies of the Netherlands, Belgium, France, and Britain lined up behind fortified borders, the former two in a state only of armed neutrality. Hitler apparently wanted to try out his *Luftwaffe*, his army, and his navy on an easier foe than faced him in the west. More importantly, he needed the Norwegian fjords as bases for his ships and submarines. And he needed the Norwegian airfields from which to fly his bombers against Allied and neutral shipping.

Before Hitler moved in the spring of 1940, Britain and France began taking steps to make more effective the sea blockade with which they hoped to strangle the Nazis. One of the biggest loopholes was in the Baltic and along the North Sea Coast of Norway. Norway and Sweden were selling Germany the vital ores she needed to keep her war machine going. Prime Minister Churchill, then First Lord of the Admiralty, warned the two countries the Allies would not stand idly by and see the trade continued. Hitler was bringing equally strong pressure to keep the materials flowing. Norway and Sweden, still hoping to maintain their neutrality, as they had in World War I, answered sharply the Allied warning.

The British did embark in late March an expedition whose objective was the seizure of the Narvik mines. It was an expeditionary force organized originally to aid Finland against Soviet Russia, but which had not been formed in time to carry through that purpose. The force did not go to Norway. It was diverted instead to strengthen the British-French lines along the German border. But it did serve as an excuse for Hitler to move. He announced his expedition against Norway as a protective measure. His spies and Norwegian quislings had prepared the ground.

The German naval units began to move on April 6. First intimation given the outside world that something was stirring in Norwegian waters was the announcement of the British Admiralty on April 8 that mines had been sown at three points off the North Sea Coast of Norway to disrupt the ore trade from Narvik. The mine fields, incidentally, apparently caused the Germans no trouble. The next morning, German troops moved across the border of Denmark, and simultaneous attacks from the sea and from the air were launched by

the German Navy and the *Luftwaffe* on eight Norwegian ports and all its main airfields.

The first phases of the campaign, although highly successful for the Germans, were not carried through without losses. On April 8, the British submarine *Orzel* torpedoed and sank the small German transport *Rio de Janeiro*. Another British undersea craft sank the oiler *Poseidon*. The heavy cruiser *Blücher* went down under the guns of the Norwegian forts guarding Oslo. The light cruiser *Karlsruhe* was damaged by shore batteries at Kristiansund April 9 and was sunk by the British submarine *Truant* while attempting to limp back to Kiel. Her sister ship, *Königsberg*, was damaged by shore batteries at Bergen and was destroyed the next day by a direct hit from a British bomber, the first armed surface vessel to succumb to air power in the war. It was not a fair test, however: *Königsberg*, without an armored deck, was a fixed target alongside a dock.

The principal naval actions of the brief Norwegian campaign were fought in and off the northern ore port of Narvik. The Germans sent their most powerful naval force there, led by *Scharnhorst* and *Gneisenau*, accompanied by the heavy cruiser *Admiral Hipper* and *Graf Spee's* sister ship, *Admiral Scheer*. On the way north, the force ran over the British destroyer *Glowworm*, which had been set to guard one of the mine fields laid the day before. She was sunk by the guns of *Hipper* and two destroyers. Later in the day, in a snowstorm, and with high seas running, *Scharnhorst* and *Admiral Hipper* were intercepted off Narvik by the British battle cruiser *Renown*, but escaped in the poor seeing after *Scharnhorst* had received two hits and *Renown* had been pierced by a shell that failed to explode. A British submarine picked up *Admiral Scheer* in her periscope sights two days later and hit her with one torpedo.

The British Home Fleet had put to sea from Scapa Flow on first receiving word of the German naval movement on April 6. The German attack

158

The five destroyers slide up the fjord.

had been so well planned, however, that the occupation of most of Norway's principal ports was complete before any of the British squadrons could interfere. The more difficult task then faced the British of going into the fjords after the enemy's ships.

Stationed off Narvik, after the German capital ships had withdrawn, was a squadron of British destroyers under Captain A. W. Warburton-Lee. They were *Hardy, Hunter, Hostile, Hotspur,* and *Havock.* A friendly Norwegian pilot told them of the presence of ten German destroyers inside. Captain Warburton-Lee asked London for instructions. They told him to use his own judgment. "Going into action," was his terse answer. It was then dark. A snowstorm was raging. Visibility was zero.

Commodore Friedrich Bonte, the German in command of the sea forces that had just put ashore General Eduard Dietl and his force of two thousand men, had distributed his ten destroyers at various strategic posts, leading three of them into Narvik Harbor with him. The British destroyers escaped detection in the miserable seeing until they were at the mouth of the harbor, deep up in the fjord. Warburton-Lee went in alone in *Hardy* to scout the harbor. The little British destroyer was on top of the three German destroyers and the cluster of merchant ships at the dock before the

Germans were aware of its presence. With guns blazing, she made two runs up the line of ships, firing her torpedoes. Commodore Bonte's flagship, *Wilhelm Heidkamp,* had her stern blown off. The Commodore was killed. As *Hardy* left the harbor, the other four British destroyers went in. The destroyer *Anton Schmitt* was sunk by a torpedo. *Dieter von Roeder* was badly hit. The already damaged supply ships and transports on which General Dietl's force had arrived all were further punished.

The British destroyers to that point had escaped damage. But as they circled outside the harbor, preparing for another attack, five of the remaining seven ships of Bonte's original force came up to join the action. In a few minutes, they had sunk *Hardy,* fatally wounding Captain Warburton-Lee in the attack, and *Hunter; Hotspur* and *Hostile* also were hit. With *Havock* as escort, the two damaged destroyers began a slow retirement down the fjord, a retirement with which the German destroyers, strangely enough, did not interfere. On the way out, they met and sank the German ammunition ship *Raunfels.* Captain Warburton-Lee was posthumously awarded Britain's highest award for valor, the Victoria Cross.

For three days, the Germans were left alone to consolidate their positions ashore. Then they got such a visitation as they probably never had expected. Survivors of *Hardy,* who had made shore

159

and a German destroyer drifts helplessly afire . . .

and joined with some British merchant seamen to await rescue, could not believe their eyes the squally morning of April 13 when they saw steaming into the narrow fjord the 30,600-ton *Warspite*, screened by nine destroyers. Ahead of them, as a scout, cruised one of *Warspite's* planes, a bomb-laden Swordfish. One of its pilot's first accomplishments was to sink a submarine at anchor in the fjord.

The first German destroyer met fled into a swirling snow squall, spreading the alarm. Lieutenant Commander W. L. M. Brown in the Swordfish spotted another hiding in a cove five miles ahead. It was sunk by a torpedo from the destroyers and by shells from *Warspite's* secondary battery. Two more German destroyers, one the flotilla leader *Wolfgang Zenker,* appeared but also fled under heavy fire. The British force plowed steadily on toward Narvik Harbor as a spread of torpedoes fired by the retiring enemy destroyers passed harmlessly to one side and exploded against the sides of the fjord.

With *Warspite* pounding ships in the harbor and coastal batteries the Germans had installed, and the destroyers darting here and there to attack German destroyers and shore howitzers, the British ships leisurely proceeded to the task of razing the port's defenses. It was like an ice-clad scene from Dante's Inferno. One German destroyer, *Giese,* already crippled in the previous attack by the Warburton-Lee force, was disabled and abandoned by her crew. Another was sunk in the harbor. The new German destroyer commander, Commander Bey, at this time decided to beach his ships to save them from destruction in deep water and ordered them run aground in a small fjord to the northward of Narvik Harbor. They proceeded there, closely pursued by the British destroyers *Forester* and *Hero.* One of the enemy vessels was put aground before she reached the rendezvous. She was destroyed by Swordfish's remaining bomb and destroyer gunfire. The remaining three German destroyers entered the narrow fjord and were run up on the icy shore. The British destroyers,

as another runs herself ashore.

fearing ambush, milled around outside and wirelessed Admiral Whitworth for orders.

"The torpedo menace must be accepted," he answered. "Enemy must be destroyed without delay. Organize attack, sending most serviceable destroyers first. Ram or board if necessary."

The British destroyers roared into the narrow mouth of the fjord, but there was no resistance. All the German ships had been abandoned. Two were sinking. The third was sunk by a torpedo from *Hero*. All seven German destroyers in the fjords around Narvik and in Narvik Harbor now had been destroyed. The wrecks of the damaged German ships in the port had been further blasted. Many shore batteries had been silenced. The only British damage received was to the destroyer *Eskimo*, which had her bow blown off by a torpedo, and the destroyer *Cossack*, which bent some of her plates when she ran aground in Narvik Harbor. Both, however, were seaworthy and left Narvik with *Warspite*.

In his official report on the action, Admiral Whitworth said: "The cumulative effect of the roar of *Warspite's* fifteen-inch guns reverberating down and around the high mountains of the fjord, the bursts and splashes of these great shells, the sight of their ships sinking and burning around them, must have been terrifying to the enemy." Then he added: "The reports on the enemy made by *Warspite's* aircraft were invaluable. I doubt if ever a ship-borne aircraft has been used to such good purpose as it was in this operation."

If *Warspite's* audacious sortie did not terrify the Germans, it at least upset their defenses. In May, the British Army was able to take the port after a stubborn fight, but it was abandoned when the disasters on the Western Front forced England to call back home every ship and man she had. The savage advance of the panzer armies through the Netherlands, Belgium, and France in a period of a month and a half after Hitler started his drive, knocked France out of the war and left England the only remaining bulwark in Europe against the New Order. Before the miracle of the evacuation at Dunkirk, however, the British Navy was to suffer a new disaster.

When it was decided late in May to evacuate the British forces in Norway, the aircraft carrier *Glorious*, sister ship of *Courageous*, which had been sunk off Ireland by a submarine in the early days of the war, was sent to provide air cover for the operation and to take home a squadron of fighter planes that had been based at Narvik. With only two destroyers as escort, she was headed home with the planes on her deck when she was intercepted in the North Sea by a German surface force composed of the thirty-five-thousand-ton battleships *Scharnhorst* and *Gneisenau*, the pocket battleships *Lützow* and *Admiral Scheer* (which apparently had been quickly repaired) and screening cruisers and destroyers.

The Germans said they had learned of *Glorious'* plans, although they did not say by what means, and that the mission of the force was her interception and destruction. On the run north, the German task force met and sank the British tanker *Oil Pioneer*, the empty troop transport *Orama*, and the Navy tug *Juniper*. In midmorning, June 8, 1940, they came up on *Glorious* and her two-destroyer escort in misty weather.

The battle did not last long. *Glorious*, believing friendly battleships were in the area, had let the Germans steam up to close range before she recognized them as enemy. Then it was too late to escape. Armed only with 4.7-inch guns for defense against hostile aircraft, protected only by the two destroyers, *Ardent* and *Acasta*, and at too close quarters to launch her planes, she was an easy target for the German gunners with their eleven-inch rifles. In a few minutes, the two little destroyers and the big carrier had been torn to pieces by the German shells. Thirty-six survivors of the fif-

Cossack and *Forester* survey the wreckage and turn to leave.

Britain continues her attacks with famed Commandos—darting in, wrecking, dashing out.

162 | teen hundred men aboard the three ships were picked up by a Norwegian ship fleeing toward Britain. As a United States admiral was later to describe a carrier, they are "Joe Louises with glass jaws." They can give punishment, but they can't take it.

The loss of *Glorious* taught Allied commanders one lesson. In areas where enemy surface ships are likely to be met, a carrier should not go to sea without strong escort of armored vessels — especially in bad weather, where the value of wide reconnaissance their planes can give them is lost.

The Norwegian campaign, which had begun in futility with the laying of the mine field, ended in disaster with the loss of *Glorious*. In the evacuation of the belated British Expeditionary Force that had been sent to Norway, the British were under continual harassing attacks by the German Air Force, which forced them to abandon on the beaches much of the equipment they had landed. Norway was too far away for air cover to be provided from England, and the British Navy did not have the aircraft carriers available to go in and slug it out with land-based air power, as the United States Third Fleet was able to do four years later off the Philippines.

Disaster was following disaster in such quick succession in the spring and summer of 1940 that the Norwegian campaign soon was almost forgotten in England. (It is easier to remember victories than defeats.) From whatever side of the fence you view the Norwegian campaign, the German Navy, with the powerful support of the German Air Force, had been able to accomplish its mission. It had suffered some losses, but not crippling ones.

While the echoes of the guns still were bouncing around in the rock-walled fjords of Norway, events were building up in France to one of the greatest small-boat feats in naval history, the evacuation of Dunkirk, where was met what Kipling called "those two impostors" — triumph and disaster.

While the Norwegian campaign was still in a fluctuating stage, although with the odds in favor of the Germans, Hitler, on May 10, 1940, hurled his *Panzer* divisions and his *Luftwaffe* against the neutral Low Countries and the armies of Britain and France along the Western Front. Defense line after defense line was overrun or breached. When the German tanks broke through at Sedan, the situation of the French and British armies in the west became precarious. In full control of the air, the

Germans appeared to be in a position to cut the Allied troops into small groups and defeat them in detail. By mid-May it became obvious Britain would have to attempt to save what she could. The retirement on Dunkirk was ordered. In the dynamo room of a Dover Hotel were set up headquarters of what must always remain one of the great amphibious operations of World War II. It was an improvisation of an amphibious force such as the world never before had witnessed.

In command of the Sea Frontier at Dover was Vice Admiral Sir Bertram Home Ramsey, who had been called out of retirement in Scotland at the beginning of the war to set up again the command he had headed in World War I, when from H.M.S. *Broke* he led the Dover Patrol. He probably never had imagined that such a task as this would be handed him. If he could evacuate thirty thousand of the five hundred thousand British and French troops retiring toward Dunkirk, it would be a good job. To him and to Vice Admiral Jean Marie Charles Arbrial were allotted some two hundred small British naval craft, none bigger than a destroyer, and about three hundred like French naval craft. Admiral Ramsey knew that would not be enough. He sent a questionnaire to small-boat-owners along the coast and advertised in the London papers for men with a knowledge of the sea who would volunteer for work "dangerous in the extreme."

When the vanguard of the British-French armies reached Dunkirk, the harbor area, in which the water was controlled by gates at low tide, still was usable. The first night, May 28, the evacuation craft went in there to embark the exhausted troops direct from the piers. During the

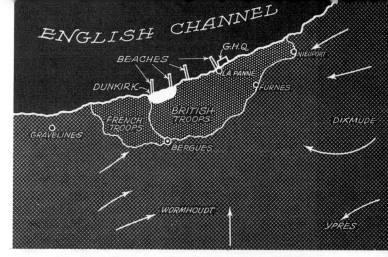

Under constant pressure from the advancing enemy, 337,131 British and French soldiers were taken from this constricted area—one of the greatest feats of courage and skill in military history.

first ten hours of darkness, thirteen thousand were taken off. The next day the German bombers came in force. They knocked out the tide gates, making the harbor area unnavigable at low water. They bombed and strafed the docks. Operations were transferred to an emergency pier which, as Admiral Ramsey said, was "never intended in the wildest imagination as a place for a ship to go alongside." It was a five-foot-wide stone jetty, made of two rows of piles and filled with stone ballast. It was obvious that was not going to suffice, although on the second night by that and other means twenty thousand more troops were taken off.

163

Ramsey called for every craft along the Thames and the Channel coast that could float to evacuate the men from the beaches. Tugs chugged across the Channel towing long strings of five-shilling-an-hour motorboats, which went in across reefs and sand spits to pick up the men on the

Running for the beaches . . .

hundreds of ships pick up thousands of men.

beaches and transfer them to larger ships lying offshore. The Royal Air Force gathered on the South England fields and kept a constant umbrella over the evacuation flotilla.

164 During the first forty-eight hours, the evacuation had to be done largely at night; the *Luftwaffe* made it too costly an operation in the daytime. Then a blessed fog came in. For two days it blanketed the Dunkirk beaches. It was weather through which English and French sailors could operate, but through which the Germans could not fly. When it finally lifted, the Royal Air Force was there to give protection, and the gallant fight went on. German E-boats, fast torpedo-carrying craft, moved down to the newly-conquered Belgian har-

bors and began operating against the evacuation fleet. War vessels of the force had to be detached to screen the unarmed craft.

For ten days the strangest armada that ever sailed for England plied back and forth between the white cliffs of Dover and Dunkirk. Old men, young men, women, and boys were at the tillers. How many died no one ever will know exactly. The deeds they did will never die. On the peak day, 66,000 men crossed the Channel in this splinter navy. Finally, with only dead Britons and Frenchmen and live Germans on the beaches and in the burning ruins of Dunkirk, Admiral Ramsey gave his great fleet of small ships the most heartfelt "Well done" that any commander ever penned.

The Royal Navy strains to protect them.

And still there are more who must be picked up.

Aboard and back to England . . .

Instead of the estimated 30,000 or, perhaps, 60,000 men that headquarters had hoped to save, a total of 224,585 British soldiers and 112,546 French soldiers had been carried safely to England. It was estimated that as many as seven hundred non-naval vessels had joined the armada from England and perhaps half as many from France, a total force of perhaps fifteen hundred craft of all kinds. No one ever will know exactly how many, just as no one will ever know how many were lost. Several days after the operation was completed — it was called "Operation Dynamo," after the small room from which it was directed — Admiral Ramsey said in an interview that of thirty-four motor lifeboats and eighty-eight ships and boats sent out by the Port of London Authority, only six had returned as of that date. "If they get back another dozen, they will be lucky," he said. Official British naval losses were announced as six destroyers, one gunboat, one aircraft tender, six mine sweepers, eight trawlers, three drifters, and four miscellaneous craft. The French officially announced the loss only of seven destroyers and one supply ship. Practically every ship engaged was damaged.

Cold calculation proves that the last days of the B.E.F. in France and Dunkirk were a disaster. But the retreat, and especially the evacuation, were so brilliantly executed, it was almost a victory. Psychologically, it was a victory. If 75 per cent of the B.E.F. had been left on the beaches to die or surrender, would Britain have summoned the courage to fight on through the summer and fall of 1940 and the winter of 1940–41, with the *Luftwaffe* overhead and Hitler only twenty miles away across the Channel? Perhaps. Perhaps not. The "victory" of Dunkirk helped give them the courage to fight on.

Many of the men Ramsey's "Navy" of Dunkirk took off the beaches in 1940 went back under his protection four years later when, as Deputy Commander for Sea Forces under General Dwight D. Eisenhower, he directed the amphibious phase of the invasion of Normandy.

For the British Mediterranean Fleet, the disasters on land that culminated in Dunkirk, the Italian entry into the war, and the armistice signed by Vichy France also brought grim days, and years of fighting against great odds.

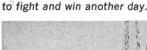

to fight and win another day.

166

*Torpedoed **Barham**, still moving forward, heels over.*

ACTION IN THE MEDITERRANEAN

Until June 10, 1940, the Mediterranean was in war only what it was in peacetime — a nineteen-hundred-mile-long seaway from the Suez Canal to the Strait of Gibraltar and one of the many attenuated life lines that stretched from the tight little islands of Britain, twenty miles off the European Continent, to the ends of the earth. The day that Mussolini delivered his "stab in the back" to defeated France and joined Hitler in the war on the democracies it became one of the war's sea battlegrounds.

In the first uneasy days immediately following September 1, 1939, the British Mediterranean Fleet maintained a wary watch on Italy. When it appeared that her entry into the war on the side of her Axis partner was not imminent, the major units of the fleet were sent to other areas. Admiral Sir Andrew Cunningham, later made Admiral of the Fleet, First Sea Lord and Chief of Naval Staff, then Commander in Chief Mediterranean Fleet, flew his flag ashore for several months. The only fleet units retained in the Mediterranean were light forces to deal with any German submarines that might venture into their waters.

Italy's declaration of war on June 10, 1940, changed all that. The final step was not unexpected. In preparation the Admiralty had sent back to the Mediterranean several major units. In Alexandria, under Admiral Cunningham's command, were the battleships *Warspite* and *Malaya*, to which later was added the old battleship *Royal Sovereign*, the small carrier *Eagle*, and several cruisers and destroyers. At Gibraltar, under Admiral Sir James Somerville, was Force H, composed of the battle cruiser *Hood*, later to be sunk by the *Bismarck*, the battleships *Resolution* and *Barham*, cruisers, destroyers, and the aircraft carrier *Ark Royal*. Sailing with the British was the considerable French fleet, including the battleships *Lorraine*, *Bretagne*, *Provence*, the new battle cruisers *Dunkerque* and *Strasbourg*, the seaplane carrier *Commandat Teste*, heavy and light cruisers, and destroyers. *Lorraine* and most of the cruisers were at Alexandria. The others were at Oran on the Algerian coast. Together the two Allied fleets were far superior to the Italian Navy, which was built around six battleships and some of the fastest, but most vulnerable, cruisers afloat.

168 | On June 11, Admiral Cunningham began a series of sweeps that it was hoped would lure the Italians into battle. Tobruk Harbor was shelled. Several Italian submarines were located in the clear Mediterranean waters, and had the life beaten out of them with depth charges. The situation seemed well in hand until June 25.

On June 25, Marshal Pétain surrendered France and ordered all French fleet units in the Mediterranean to return to Toulon. That, the British could not allow. Prime Minister Churchill, who

*Three units of Force H—battle cruiser **Renown**, carrier **Ark Royal**, and cruiser **Sheffield** off Gibraltar.*

had taken over the government from the shaking hands of Neville Chamberlain the day that Hitler struck, May 10, offered the French four choices: sail with the British against Germany and Italy; intern and demilitarize in British ports; sail to a French colonial or neutral port for internment; sink your ships or have them sunk by us. Only a few small units took the first choice. The French ships at Alexandria, under command of Vice Admiral Godefroy and including *Lorraine*, took the second. Vice Admiral Marcel Bruno Gensoul, at Oran, declined all the British offers and prepared to obey Vichy's orders.

*The **Strasbourg**, shelled in Oran, was later to scuttle herself at Toulon.*

*French battleship **Lorraine**.*

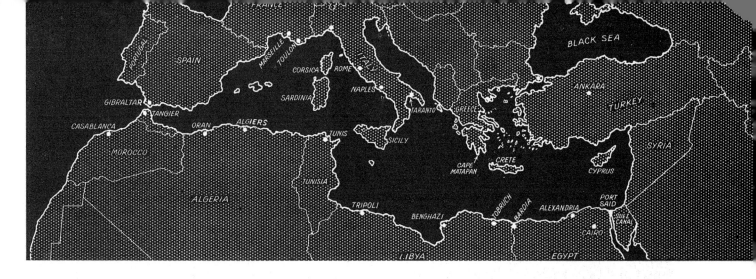

When it became evident the French at Oran were going to resist, Admiral Somerville sailed with Force H. Late in the afternoon of July 3, after last-minute negotiations had failed to bring a satisfactory answer from the French and while they were raising steam to leave the port, the British battleships opened bombardment. *Bretagne, Dunkerque,* and *Provence* were quickly hit and put out of action. Only *Strasbourg* was able to get underway and clear the harbor. She was attacked by Swordfish planes carrying bombs and after sunset by torpedo-carrying planes. But she was able to continue to Toulon despite at least one torpedo hit and shell damage. (She was scuttled there with other French ships when the Allied invasion of France began in June, 1944.) To make sure *Dunkerque* was disabled, on July 4, two flights of Swordfish went in and drove home a torpedo attack. Prime Minister Churchill described it as a "melancholy action." It was. But it removed the French fleet from all but the late stages of the war in the Mediterranean when, under a rebirth of French freedom, its remnants again sailed with the British.

*Bad Italian bombing—**Valiant** (center), **Hood** (right), **Resolution** (behind Valiant), and a cruiser sail through the futile splashes.*

All through the summer, Admiral Cunningham swept the eastern Mediterranean without being able to bring about a large-scale fleet action. And as long as the Italian fleet remained in being, even if it would not fight, it was dangerous to move convoys through those land-girt waters. The Italians might suddenly change their minds about engaging.

On July 8, a part of the Italian fleet was contacted off Sicily, but it fled behind a smoke screen after a few exchanges at extreme range. *Warspite* did have the satisfaction of scoring a hit at twenty-six thousand yards on the Italian battleship *Cesare.* Its principal effect apparently was to strengthen the resolution of the Italian commanders not to risk a large-scale action, even though they could mass gun superiority over both the main Mediterranean Fleet and Force H together had they chosen to do so.

Both before and after this inconclusive fleet engagement — the first time since Jutland a British admiral had been able to signal the Admiralty, "Enemy battle fleet in sight" — land-based air power had an opportunity to prove what it could

169

Cruiser **Bartolomeo Colleoni** blows up after action with Australian cruiser **Sydney** and two destroyers.

do. In a period of six hours the afternoon of July 7, no less than seven attacks were made on Admiral Cunningham's force. Over 130 bombs were dropped from medium altitudes at the British ships. Only one hit was scored. The light cruiser *Gloucester* received a bomb on her bridge that killed her captain and seventeen others but did not put her out of action. While pursuing the retreating Italian ships the next day, the British were subjected to an even heavier attack, nine runs being made at them by over one hundred Italian bombers. This time no British ship was struck. In the open sea a "near miss," and no matter how "near," seldom does any harm to a modern vessel unless bomb fragments fly aboard. This Italian attack was typical of many more that were to be made in the following years, typical both as to technique and as to results. It was not until the Germans with their dive bombers arrived that the British began to lose ships to air power.

Several minor clashes between light units of the two opposing fleets occurred during the remainder of the summer of 1940 and early fall. In one of these, on July 18, the heavy cruiser *Sydney* met and destroyed one of Mussolini's prize cruisers, the thirty-seven knot *Bartolomeo Colleoni*. *Sydney* also severely mauled another before it escaped. Most Italian major ships, however, stayed discreetly out of range. In November it was decided that if they would not come out and fight, the Fleet Air Arm would go in after them at their bases. Meanwhile, on September 1, the carrier *Illustrious* had joined the fleet. To her was entrusted the task of attacking the Italian ships at their southern base at Taranto, in the instep of the Italian boot.

Such an operation had long been planned. When, in 1938, it became evident that a showdown

Italian flagship **Vittorio Veneto**

Italian cruiser **Eugenio Di Savola**

Italian destroyer **Avieri**

Italian battleship **Italia**

170

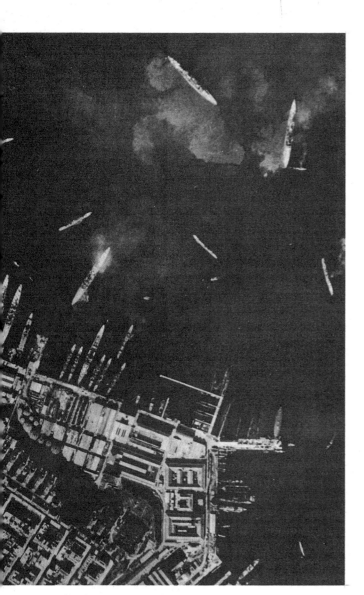

The Taranto raid—damaged Italian ships in the harbor.

with Italy must some day come, Rear Admiral (then Captain) A. L. St. G. Lyster had been instructed to draw up plans for attacking the Italian fleet in Taranto. Detailed plans were worked out and practiced. On November 11, 1940, the right man was at the right spot. Admiral Lyster, as Commander Mediterranean Aircraft Carriers, was afloat, with his flag in *Illustrious*. At dusk of Armistice Day of the second year of World War II, the big carrier, escorted by cruisers and destroyers, left the main force and steamed off to carry out orders. "Good luck, then, to your lads in their enterprise," Admiral Cunningham signaled to Admiral Lyster as their flagships parted company.

171

The tactics used in the raid, and the results, have been told in a previous chapter. In a period of an hour and a half over Taranto Harbor, the planes from *Illustrious* swung the balance of sea power in the Mediterranean. It was an operation the Japanese must have been watching carefully. They duplicated it at Pearl Harbor, even to fitting their aerial torpedoes with fins so they would not bury themselves in the mud of the shallow harbor. It was learned after the Armistice with Italy of September 3, 1943, that the damage done the Italian battleships was repairable. But they were immobilized for many months. One of them, *Conte de Cavour*, still was under repair at Taranto when the Allies moved in.

"Well executed," was the Commander in Chief's laconic salute to *Illustrious* as she rejoined *Warspite* the next morning.

The only air surface engagement in which large units of the Italian fleet were forced to put their fate to the touch was that of March 28–29, 1941, when an Italian force that included a battleship, cruisers, and destroyers steamed into dis-

Two British cruisers prepare to fire as shells fall near.

aster off Cape Matapan, the southernmost point of the Peloponnesus Peninsula of Greece.

Before that stirring engagement took place, however, the complexion of the Mediterranean campaign had changed. In January, Hitler sent his dive bombers to Italy to show the inept Italian Regia Aeronautica how ships should be attacked. On January 10, while the British fleet was covering a convoy movement from Gibraltar to Malta and Greece, the Stukas struck. They had been guided to the fleet by a shadower, who apparently got his precious information away before *Illustrious'* new fighter planes, Fulmars, could shoot him down.

The first attack came shortly after noon. *Illustrious* was just launching a flight when out of the north came a flight of forty to fifty JU-87's and 88's, the feared Stukas that had so terrorized the French countryside ahead of the advancing German armies seven months before. The German fliers were a far more formidable adversary than were the Italians. They screamed down on *Illustrious* with a fury that would not be denied. A damaging hit that rendered the flight deck of *Illustrious* unusable was scored in the first attack. All through the afternoon the Germans kept coming, although in smaller force. A badly battered *Illustrious* finally made Malta late that afternoon. Under intermittent bombing attack at a Malta dock, she finally was sufficiently repaired to limp off to Alexandria and then, via the Suez Canal and around Good Hope, to Newport, Virginia, for repairs. She was, however, lost to the fight for almost a year.

The day after the attack on *Illustrious*, the cruisers *Southampton* and *Gloucester* were attacked by the Stukas. The *Southampton* was sunk. After January 10, 1941, convoys and the fleet moved in the Mediterranean only in great peril

and with constant losses. All except military convoys to the Eastern Mediterranean were shifted to the long voyage around Africa and up through the Suez Canal. But the fleet stayed on. The Mediterranean was not to become Italy's *mare nostrum* even with the German Air Force over it.

Even with half of the Italian battle line out of action as a result of the Taranto attack, Mussolini's fleet still was a formidable one. Admiral Cunningham had to be on constant lookout to prevent it from getting to sea and in among the supply and troop ships moving to Greece. On March 27, 1941, acting on a report that enemy cruisers and destroyers had been sighted steering southeastward from Taranto, he put to sea. The carrier *Formidable* had joined up to replace *Illustrious*, *Eagle* having been shifted to the Indian Ocean, and the battleships *Barham* and *Valiant* were with *Warspite* as the backbone of the Mediterranean Fleet. Admiral Cunningham had split his forces. With the battleships and carriers he had two small flotillas of destroyers. Four cruisers were sent out ahead of the Battle Force, also with a destroyer screen.

Early in the morning of March 28, an aircraft from *Formidable* sighted three enemy cruisers and four destroyers about thirty miles from the British cruiser force, which was under command of Vice Admiral H. D. Pridham-Wippell. He advised Admiral Cunningham of their presence. Shortly thereafter the surface vessels sighted them. Noting they were eight-inch gun cruisers, Admiral Pridham-Wippell turned away toward Admiral Cunningham's position, in the hope of luring them under the battleship's big guns. When they turned back after a short chase, he also reversed course and soon came on an Italian battleship of the *Littorio* class, which was discovered to be the flagship of the Italian fleet, *Vittorio Veneto*. Both she and

Action off Cape Matapan—a torpedo is launched at an Italian cruiser.

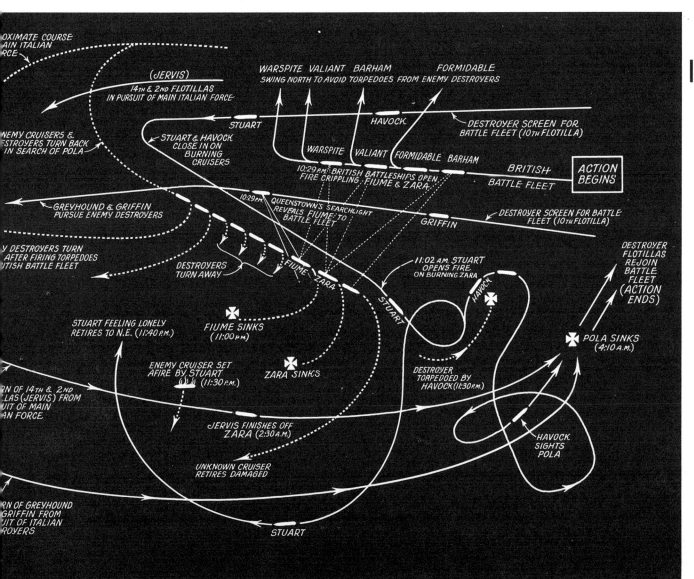

APPROXIMATE COURSE
MAIN ITALIAN
FORCE

(JERVIS)
14TH & 2ND FLOTILLAS
IN PURSUIT OF MAIN ITALIAN FORCE

WARSPITE VALIANT BARHAM   FORMIDABLE
SWING NORTH TO AVOID TORPEDOES FROM ENEMY DESTROYERS

ENEMY CRUISERS &
DESTROYERS TURN BACK
IN SEARCH OF POLA

STUART & HAVOCK
CLOSE IN ON
BURNING
CRUISERS

STUART

HAVOCK

DESTROYER SCREEN FOR
BATTLE FLEET (10TH FLOTILLA)

WARSPITE VALIANT FORMIDABLE BARHAM

10:29 P.M. BRITISH BATTLESHIPS OPEN
FIRE CRIPPLING FIUME & ZARA

BRITISH
BATTLE FLEET

ACTION
BEGINS

GREYHOUND & GRIFFIN
PURSUE ENEMY DESTROYERS

10:29 P.M.
QUEENSTOWN'S SEARCHLIGHT
REVEALS FIUME TO
BATTLE FLEET

GRIFFIN

DESTROYER SCREEN FOR BATTLE
FLEET (10TH FLOTILLA)

Y DESTROYERS TURN
AFTER FIRING TORPEDOES
RITISH BATTLE FLEET

DESTROYERS
TURN AWAY

FIUME ZARA

11:02 A.M. STUART
OPENS FIRE
ON BURNING ZARA

STUART

HAVOCK

DESTROYER
FLOTILLAS
REJOIN
BATTLE
FLEET
(ACTION
ENDS)

STUART FEELING LONELY
RETIRES TO N.E. (11:40 P.M.)

FIUME SINKS
(11:00 P.M.)

POLA SINKS
(4:10 A.M.)

ENEMY CRUISER SET
AFIRE BY STUART
(11:30 P.M.)

ZARA SINKS

DESTROYER
TORPEDOED BY
HAVOCK (11:30 P.M.)

RN OF 14TH & 2ND
LAS (JERVIS) FROM
UIT OF MAIN
AN FORCE

JERVIS FINISHES OFF
ZARA (2:30 A.M.)

HAVOCK
SIGHTS
POLA

UNKNOWN CRUISER
RETIRES DAMAGED

RN OF GREYHOUND
GRIFFIN FROM
UIT OF ITALIAN
ROYERS

STUART

the enemy cruisers then opened fire, beyond the range of the British cruiser's guns, but turned away when attacked from the air.

When the force first was contacted, *Formidable* sent away a striking force of Albacores, the faster plane that had replaced the Swordfish as the torpedo carrier and dive bomber of the Fleet Air Arm. They came up just as the Italians were engaging Admiral Pridham-Wippell's light forces. They dived to the attack, and one scored a hit on *Vittorio Veneto,* which reduced her speed. Two hours later a second striking force from *Formidable,* armed with torpedoes instead of bombs, attacked and scored one or two torpedo hits. That further reduced her speed to an estimated thirteen knots. There was hope now that the British battleships, speeding up from the southeast, could overtake her before she could get back to a safe port. In the meanwhile a second force of enemy cruisers and destroyers was discovered to the northward of the main body. They appeared to be on a course to join up.

No commander cares to fight a night action if he can engage by daylight, but Admiral Cunningham knew there would be no hope of catching the Italians the next morning. He ordered Admiral Pridham-Wippell to go ahead with his light forces to harass the already battered enemy force. Then he ordered another attack by *Formidable's* aircraft at dusk in the hope of further slowing the enemy, and pushed on himself with all speed to come up with the Italian ships during the hours of darkness. The *Formidable's* third striking force, which was joined from Malta by three of the planes from *Illustrious'* squadrons that had been put ashore when she left for the States, attacked the fleeing Italian ships at dusk and hit the heavy cruiser *Pola,* which slowed and began to fall behind.

After the dusk attack by planes, the main enemy force turned to the southwest, away from the track of the oncoming British fleet, but sent three cruisers and several destroyers back to find the damaged *Pola.* At 10:30 P.M., they ran into the British battle line, which was steaming with *Warspite* in the lead, followed by *Valiant, Formidable,* and *Barham.*

The Italian ships, their guns trained fore and aft, still seemed unaware of the presence of the British ships as the destroyer *Queenstown* at the Admiral's orders, illuminated them with her searchlight. *Warspite* and *Valiant* opened on the second cruiser with their fifteen-inch guns at the almost point-blank range of four thousand yards. She was the ten-thousand-ton, eight-inch gun

Belfast and two other cruisers in action off Crete.

cruiser *Fiume.* Both broadsides hit her. She sank in half an hour.

Barham opened fire on the leading ship, which either was a small cruiser or a large destroyer, and also scored. The Italian ship turned away, on fire, and was not seen again. Two up, two down.

With the two leading ships so neatly disposed of, all three British battleships, with *Formidable* among them as an interested onlooker, centered their fire on the third enemy vessel, the heavy cruiser *Zara,* onto which the *Queenstown* had shifted her light and which she also was illuminating with star shells. In a matter of minutes, *Zara* was hit by some fifteen to twenty fifteen-inch shells. The destroyer *Jervis* found her later in the night dead in the water and burning and sank her with a torpedo.

Before the surprise meeting with the enemy cruisers, Admiral Cunningham had sent eight of the twelve destroyers with him ahead to find and attack the main enemy force. Immediately after the brisk action with the Italian cruisers, he turned his battle line away to the northward and sent his remaining four destroyers on to join their fellows. In several wild scrambles, the British tin cans finished off the two crippled cruisers still afloat, *Pola* and *Zara,* engaging Italian destroyers and cruisers in the process. At dawn, all twelve of them steamed back to join the battle fleet. After the firing he had witnessed off on the horizon, the Commander in Chief hardly could believe his ears when one of his staff reported: "All twelve there, sir."

The Battle of Cape Matapan is not one of the great surface battles either of this war or of previous ones — three Italian cruisers and two destroyers sunk and others damaged. But it apparently was the clinching argument that determined the decision of the Italian admirals not to challenge again with surface ships Britain's Mediterranean Fleet, not even when it was reduced to a cruiser-destroyer level by losses, the diversion of some of its strength to the Far East, and the sinking of *Barham* by a submarine on November 23, 1941. Ten days after *Barham*, *Ark Royal* of Force H met a similar fate while steaming toward Gibraltar after a convoy operation.

The Italian fleet spent most of the rest of the war in harbor, under intermittent air attack. When it steamed out to surrender in 1943, German bombers also attacked it and sank its latest addition, the battleship *Roma*. Six other battleships, including the still unrepaired *Conte de Cavour* and most of the submarines and destroyers, meekly surrendered.

Force H, based on Gibraltar, had as equally rough a time as did the Mediterranean Fleet against the Italian and German aircraft, but it also had the pleasure of one of the most audacious attacks of the early days of the war. On February 8-9, 1941, it steamed into the Ligurian Sea to bombard at dawn on the ninth the big Italian seaport of Genoa. *Renown* and *Malaya*, the two capital ships of the force involved, poured twenty rounds each into the port area, knocking out electric works, docks, and ships. It went in and out without suffering any major losses from air attack.

It was not in convoy or in fleet actions, however, that the British forces in the Mediterranean suffered their worst days, but in support of land operations through Egypt and Libya, and in Greece and Crete. One of the best days of this type of land support was January 3, 1941, when three battleships and *Illustrious'* planes with shell and bomb helped the Army of the Nile take Bardia and forty-five-thousand Italian prisoners with an inferior land force. One of the worst periods was that from May 21 to June 9 during the evacuation from Crete, when it suffered the loss of two cruisers and six destroyers under blistering air attacks. Ships lost during that period were the cruisers *Gloucester* and *Fiji*, and the destroyers *Juno*, *Greyhound*, *Kelly*, *Kashmir*, *Imperial*, and *Hereward*. Fully as important to naval operations was crippling damage sustained by the carrier *Formidable*, the battleship *Warspite*, the cruisers *Dido* and *Orion*, and many others of Admiral Cunningham's ships. The four named all had to make the long trip around Africa to the United States to be repaired. It was fortunate during that period, as well as many others, that the British had a timid naval adversary in the Mediterranean.

The trouncing the British fleet assimilated off Crete, from an estimated five hundred attacking German and Italian planes, has been hailed as a

Hit by three torpedoes at close range, Barham explodes in four minutes.

victory of air power over sea power. It was something less than that. As the noted British naval writer, Bartimeus, said in his official story of the eastern Mediterranean campaign, *East of Malta, West of Suez*, off Crete the British Mediterranean Fleet was "naked under heaven." Many of the hits on the British ships were made while they were almost stopped in rescue attempts or engaged in taking off men from the beaches. The fleet did carry out its mission, evacuating sixteen thousand men from an impossible position where they had been placed against Admiral Cunningham's recommendations. He had warned the Admiralty that Crete could not be held.

Japan's attack in Asia did nothing to ease the task of the Mediterranean Fleet. Some units had to be shifted to the Indian Ocean, where the aircraft carrier *Hermes* and the cruisers *Cornwall, Dorsetshire,* and *Naiad* were lost in battle with a Japanese carrier force off Ceylon. But with the landing of the United States Army in North Africa on November 8, 1942, the tide definitely turned. Even before that the United States aircraft carrier *Wasp* had joined up with Force H to take ships and planes to Malta.

In the spring and summer of 1943, the German and Italian armies again were chased back from Egypt and this time completely out of North Africa. Then came the Sicily landings, in which two thousand craft — most of the smaller amphibious vessels being American — were used, the invasion of Italy at Salerno and Anzio, and finally the landings in southern France.

With the invasion of Italy, the Italian fleet surrendered. Except for a few German submarines still operating in those waters, but not for long, the Mediterranean sea campaign was over.

The Italian fleet that sailed out to surrender to the Allies on September 3, 1943, consisted of six battleships: the new *Roma* (completed since the beginning of the war and which never saw action until she was attacked by her erstwhile ally, the *Luftwaffe*), the *Italia,* (ex-*Littorio*), *Vittorio Veneto, Andrea Doria, Caio Duilio,* and *Giulio Cesare.* Also surrendered with the battleships were nine cruisers, eleven destroyers, and many smaller craft. The uncompleted battleship *Impero,* a few cruisers and destroyers remained in German hands until the German surrender in May, 1945. They were several times attacked in port by Allied bombers. The Germans never manned them or attempted to send them to sea.

By June 10, 1945, the fifth anniversary of Italy's declaration of war, the invincible armada Mussolini had boasted of no longer existed. Its whole career had been one of frustration. It had failed to strike a single telling blow. The British Mediterranean Fleet sailed then to join the United States fleet in the Pacific and in the Indian Ocean to help fashion the victory over Japan.

A Navy ceases to exist—the Italian Fleet surrenders, September 3, 1943.

PEARL HARBOR

At dawn on December 7, 1941, the major components of the Pacific Fleet of the world's second greatest sea power lay peacefully alongside the docks or at anchor in Pearl Harbor, seven miles from Honolulu on Oahu, the Hawaiian Islands. There were eight battleships there, seven cruisers, twenty-five destroyers, five submarines, a hospital ship, and various other fleet tenders, supply vessels, and smaller ships.

By 10 A.M. the same day, five of the eight battleships were sunk or sinking, the other three damaged. Sunk also were the target and anti-aircraft ship *Utah* and the mine layer *Oglala*. Three destroyers, all in dry dock, the *Cassin*, *Downes*, and *Shaw*, were twisted by bombs and internal explosions and blackened by fire. *Shaw* was minus her bow; her forward magazine had exploded. The floating dry dock in which *Shaw* was berthed rested on the bottom. Damaged were the light cruisers *Honolulu*, *Helena*, and *Raleigh*,

Japan warms up for the thrust.

the seaplane tender *Curtiss,* and the repair ship *Vestal.* Dead or missing were 3,077 Navy and Marine officers and men. Eight hundred and seventy-six were wounded. One hundred and seventy-seven of the 475 Army and Navy planes on the island were destroyed, and 70 more were damaged.

By whatever yardstick you care to measure it, in less than four hours the United States had become a third-rate sea power instead of second in the world. Japan, the attacker, now was second. With the beating the British fleet had been taking, and was to take, Nippon was close to first place.

The attack was made by fleet aircraft of the Imperial Japanese Navy, operating from six Japanese carriers — *Kaga, Akagi, Soryu,* and *Hiryu* — all of which were sunk in the Battle of Midway six months later — *Shokaku,* and *Zuikaku.* They were escorted by the battleships *Hiei* and *Kirishima,* the heavy cruisers *Tore* and *Chihuma,* the light cruiser *Nagara,* and twenty destroyers. The Japanese were expecting to lose half of their ships and most of their planes in the attack. The total loss was twenty-nine planes.

The Japanese, who had a much better weather forecasting service than did our Navy at the start of the war, had taken full advantage of the thick weather that generally prevails over the North Pacific between the Hawaiian Archipelago (Hawaii to Midway) and the Aleutians. They had followed a cold front down from the north to within 230 miles of Pearl Harbor. They launched the first wave of 190 planes of the attack force from there at dawn. A second wave of 170 planes took off an hour later. Three hundred and thirty-one of the 360 attacking planes safely returned to their carriers.

The attack operation had been put into effect weeks before December 7, while Ambassador Nomura and Special Envoy Kurusu still were consulting with Secretary of State Hull in Washington on a formula to resolve difficulties between the two countries, difficulties that had been precipitated by Japan's war of aggression in the Far East. The attack force had sailed from Salki training center November 17, rendezvoused at Tankan Bay, in the Kuriles, and sortied from there on November 26 for the attack. Japanese submarine squadrons were deployed off our West Coast ports and on the steamer lanes to Honolulu and the South Pacific.

No United States air operation has been better executed than was the attack by the Japanese

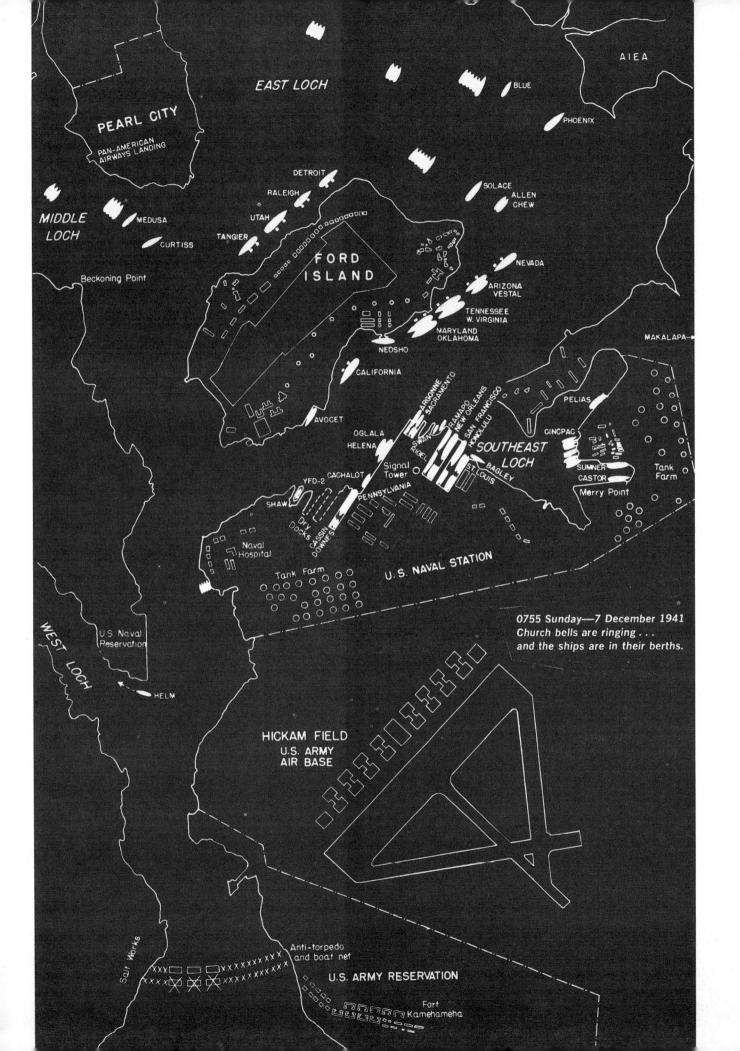

fliers. First came the fighter planes, flying low and fast, to strafe the big PBY seaplanes in the anchorage and on the ramps at Kaneohe Naval Air Station, on the north side of Oahu Island, directly across the mountains from Pearl Harbor. Other fighter groups attacked other airfields on the island — Wheeler Field, an Army fighter base near Schofield Barracks; Bellows Field, not far from Kaneohe; Ewa Field, the Marine air base near Pearl Harbor; and finally Ford Island, the principal Navy air base in Pearl Harbor, and Hickam Field, the principal Army air base, which was

less than a mile away. Their task was to strafe and disable any planes standing on the aprons ready to take off. These fighters also carried small bombs, which they dropped on hangars, machine shops, and on the United States planes themselves. After the fighters came the torpedo planes and dive bombers to attack our battleships and, later in the morning, other planes to drop armor-piercing bombs.

The exact times of attack are not known and probably never will be, within minutes. No one on the American side had been assigned to keep such

Bombs are dropped . . .

180

and torpedoes are launched . . .

and all hell breaks loose.

a log that morning. It is possible, from conflicting statements, to arrive at this approximation: Kaneohe, about 7:40 A.M.; Bellows Field, approximately the same time; Wheeler Field, 7:40 to 7:50; Hickam Field and Ford Island, 7:50 to 7:55; attack on the battleships, 7:50 to 7:55. A Hawaiian worker at Kaneohe Air Station said that when the planes began attacking that base, he ran to a nearby telephone and attempted to warn Hickam Field. The Army operator at the other end of the wire refused to believe his excited warning and hung up on him. It appears obvious that Hickam Field was not then under attack. The time lag was so short, however, that even had the worker been believed, there probably would have been insufficient time to alert the field. Had two earlier warnings been taken seriously, however, the disaster would not have been so great. The first alarm came from the destroyer *Ward*.

One string of the Japanese bow that morning was a squadron of three two-man submarines, small cigar-shaped submersibles of about forty-five tons weight, driven by electric motors and with two torpedo tubes. What is believed to have been one of these was seen attempting to enter Pearl Harbor at six thirty that morning. As per orders under which the fleet had been operating for some weeks, it was attacked by the destroyer *Ward* and probably destroyed. The latter fact is not important. What is important is that *Ward's* captain, Lieutenant William W. Outerbridge, sent to Pacific Fleet Headquarters at 6:51 A.M., an hour before the enemy planes arrived over Pearl Harbor, the following message: "We have dropped depth charges on sub operating in defensive area." Two minutes later he amplified the previous message. When no answer had come after several minutes, he queried for verification that it had been received and was given an affirmative. At 7:12 A.M., his messages finally reached the duty officer at Fleet Headquarters, who transmitted it to the Chief of Staff. Verification was requested, but no further action was taken.

Half an hour before the enemy attack would have been too late adequately to prepare a defense, but much could have been done. Watertight integrity could have been established on the battleships. The crews could have been alerted. Fighter planes could have been sent up. The two carrier task forces at sea, the *Enterprise* and *Lexington* groups, could have been notified. All these measures would not have prevented the attack, but they would have mitigated its effect.

Ward's attack, first by gunfire and then by depth charges, means, of course, that the United States actually fired the first shot of the war.

181

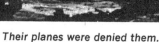
Their planes were denied them.

A second and even more revealing warning also was given before the attack that morning. Private Joseph Lockard, on duty at a newly-installed Army radar station on the north shore of Oahu, saw at 7:02 A.M. on the scope of his detection set a flight of airplanes some one hundred miles north and east. He was not supposed to be on duty but had remained to practice. He reported this intelligence to the Army Air Information Service. He was told that Navy planes from *Enterprise* were expected in from the north. The Duty Officer to whom he had made his report told him to forget about it. Thus both the Navy and the Army had advance warning of the attack. Neither acted on the information. Lockard was given the Distinguished Service Medal, promoted to sergeant, and later became an officer. Like Admiral Cunningham during the dark days in the Mediterranean, who, when he was informed of the award of a British honor, said he would prefer two squadrons of fighter planes, twenty-year-old Private Lockard probably would have preferred that his alarm had been heeded. He still would have been a hero, and part of the damage, at least, of Pearl Harbor would have been averted.

The only effective air resistance offered to the Japanese attack was by a flight of four outmoded P-36 Army fighter planes that took off from Wheeler Field after the first attack, and two new P-40's that were among eight fighter planes that had been left the night before on a small Army field at Haliawa, which was not attacked by the Japanese. Among them they were credited with shooting down eight to ten planes. Only one of the six American pilots was killed. The remaining eighteen to twenty Japanese planes that were shot down fell to anti-aircraft fire from ship and shore. Considering the damage done, the attack was no less economical for the Japanese than was that of the British on the Italian fleet at Taranto. The latter attack, however, was made during a state of

war. The Japanese profited greatly by surprise. As at Port Arthur twenty seven years before against the Russians, the Japanese began their war before declaring their intentions.

The principal damage to the United States vessels was done by a strictly naval weapon, the plane-borne torpedo. *Arizona* already was hit by torpedoes and settling before the bomb from one of the planes flying horizontally went down her stack. The other four battleships that were sunk — *Oklahoma, Nevada, California,* and *West Virginia* — and *Utah* and *Oglala,* all were victims of torpedoes, the latter ship as sort of an enemy dividend on the torpedo that exploded against *Helena,* with which she was moored. The explosion opened her seams. The damage to *Raleigh* also was done by a torpedo. The torpedoes were especially prepared for the job, as were those of the British at Taranto. They had fins to keep them from sounding and sticking

Cassin and **Downes** are destroyed—**Pennsylvania** survives.

182

Phoenix slips out to sea.

California settles in the mud.

in the mud of the shallow harbor. They were set to explode after only a short run, and they carried extra large warheads, so as to do the maximum damage.

It was a beautiful target that was provided for the enemy. Seven of the eight battleships in Pearl Harbor were moored in a row, to permanent platforms set atop piles along the east side of Ford Island. It was their customary spot. The sailors called it "Battleship Row." The *Raleigh* and *Utah* were similarly berthed on the other side of Ford Island, in the areas where the carriers would have been had they been in the harbor instead of at sea on December 7. With her boarded-over decks, *Utah* apparently was mistaken for a carrier.

Much unjustified criticism has been made of that type of berthing. It is difficult to see how they could have been berthed otherwise in the restricted harbor area. A legitimate criticism is that they

Nevada's fires are put out—once repaired, she would later pound Nazi batteries at Normandy.

were not protected by torpedo nets, which would have been a relatively simple precaution to have taken. They might have been back in action long before they were had that been done, or had their watertight doors been closed so the torpdo hits would not have flooded them. The two battleships that were inboard in the line, *Tennessee* and *Maryland,* were little hurt. *West Virginia* and *Oklahoma* protected them from the torpedoes as a net would have protected all the ships. *Pennsylvania,* the eighth ship of the line, was in a dry dock and escaped major damage. All but *Arizona* lived to fight another day.

The airplanes on the various Army fields all were bunched so they could be guarded closely by only a few men. The Army was more fearful of sabotage by some of the 150,000 aliens and first-generation Japanese in the islands than they were of air attack. Bunched, the planes made an easy target for the strafing, bombing enemy planes.

Through their extensive espionage organization in the Hawaiian Islands, the Japanese were aware of all these dispositions of United States forces and the defensive weaknesses. They were aware, too, that there was little long-range air patrol being carried out by the Navy, which, under a prewar division of responsibility between the two services, assumed the duty of reconnaissance and protection right up to the shorelines of Hawaii. On the morning in question, the Navy had only three planes in the air off Oahu. They were engaged in a drill with submarines south of the island.

The enemy probably was aware too that the Navy was contemptuous of his strength and particularly of the possibility that he might attack Pearl Harbor. The report made by the Presidential Investigation Commission headed by Justice Owen J. Roberts said that Captain C. H. (now Rear Admiral) McMorris, war plans officer on the staff of Admiral Husband F. Kimmel, then Commander

183

in Chief of the Pacific Fleet, only a few days before the attack, discounted such a possibility at a conference among Navy and Army officers, including Lieutenant General Walter C. Short, commander of the Hawaiian Department. This despite the fact that in the Navy's own war games the Islands had been "attacked" successfully on much the same pattern as that used by the Japanese.

During the twelve months preceding December 7, and especially during the last few weeks, there had been a hurried building up of American forces and construction of bases. *Enterprise* was returning on December 7, as a matter of fact, from a mission of ferrying twelve Marine fighter planes — the then new Grumman Wildcats — to Wake Island. New anti-aircraft defenses were under construction on Oahu and other of our island bases. The radar set on which Private Lockard detected the approach of the Japanese striking force had only recently been taken to the Islands and installed. All physical precautions are futile, however, unless there is at the same time a mental alertness on the part of the high command. One of the most damning criticisms of the Roberts Report was that that attribute was lacking in our Navy and Army commanders on Oahu.

The strategy of the Japanese attack is obvious. It was to immobilize our Pacfic Fleet and lift the danger of attack from the flank as they moved south on Hong Kong, the Philippines, Singapore, and the Dutch East Indies. Captain Y. Watanabe, gunnery officer on the staff of Admiral Yamamoto, explained the Japanese strategy to interrogators after the war thus: "In Japanese tactics, we are told when we have two enemies, one in front and one in back, first we must cut in front by sword. Only cut and not kill, but make it hard. Then we attack the back enemy and kill him. Then we come back to the front enemy and kill him. This time we took that tactic, having no aim to capture Pearl Harbor but just to cripple it. We might have returned to capture later."

Had the three aircraft carriers assigned to the Pacific Fleet — *Saratoga* (which was on the West Coast), the old *Lexington*, and *Enterprise* — been in Pearl Harbor that morning, and it had been planned that *Enterprise* would be there, the attack would have been much more effective than it was. There is no reason to believe they would have escaped the fate of the battleships.

The Japanese tactic of "cut but not kill" did not work in this case. The killing stroke should have been used. Only two United States infantry divisions were on Oahu that morning. Deprived of air support, those could not have held out long against the strength the Japanese could have thrown against the island. Even the Army bombers that were flown in quickly to take the place of those destroyed and the planes of the Navy's three aircraft carriers hardly could have coped with the great naval air strength the Japanese could have massed with the fifteen large carriers and smaller ones they had then.

In centering their attack on the battleships and in failing to storm the islands, the Japanese gave the United States the time it needed to gather and deploy its naval and air forces. When they attempted to seize Midway six months later, they suffered a crushing defeat.

Pearl Harbor was the worst defeat ever suffered by the United States. But it was a defeat suffered largely because of Japanese treachery, because of complacence and the hardening of the professional naval and military arteries of which David Lloyd George spoke in damning the British Admiralty in World War I. The United States had both sea and air power, but they were not coordinated as they were later.

In the long view, Pearl Harbor was a victory. It jolted Navy and Army commanders out of a complacency that might have led to more serious results even than Pearl Harbor had it continued. It impressed all doubters with the efficiency of the enemy who had attacked. More importantly, it welded together the United States far better than anything else could have done. The men who died there did not die in vain. Their death made of the then forty eight states truly a united nation.

California sails to fight again.

Japan leaves a relic—forty-five-ton midget.

Hermes goes down in the Bay of Bengal.

EARLY RAIDS IN THE PACIFIC

The attack on Pearl Harbor touched off the bloodiest and most merciless war ever waged in the world's oceans. On that first day, the United States Navy lost more men than in all its previous naval history. In three and two-thirds years, our losses of combatant vessels totaled 350 ships, or more than the 338 we had in commission when Japan attacked. Japan, over the same period, lost almost all her navy.

The first strictly offensive blow of retaliation by the Pacific Fleet was almost two months in coming. It was in the Marshall and Gilbert Islands that the first installment was collected on the debt the Japanese incurred at Pearl Harbor.

Vice Admiral (later Fleet Admiral) William F. Halsey, Jr., had covered the movement of a convoy to Samoa in mid-January. On his way back to Pearl Harbor, he was ordered to make an attack on the Marshall Islands, the Central Pacific string of former German coral atolls over which Japan had been given a mandate by the League of Nations. It was part of the loot that had been secretly promised her by Great Britain as a price for her entry on the Allied side in World War I.

Japan had been fortifying the islands for many years. But no one knew just how good a job had been done. Admiral Halsey went in to find out and to blunt the spear aimed at the lifeline from Honolulu and the States to the South Pacific and Australia.

It was a two-barreled operation. Halsey, with his one carrier, *Enterprise*, the heavy cruisers *Chester, Northampton,* and *Salt Lake City,* and six destroyers, was ordered to work over three of the Marshall group. Rear Admiral (later Vice Admiral) Frank Jack Fletcher, in the carrier *Yorktown* (which had just come out to replace *Saratoga,* torpedoed on January 13 by a Japanese submarine while en route to Pearl Harbor from delivering more planes at Midway), was to attack Mili, Jaluit, and Makin. Jaluit and Mili are in the southern Marshalls. Makin is in the British Gilberts, which the Japanese had seized without opposition at the beginning of the war. With *Yorktown* were the cruisers *Louisville* and *St. Louis* and four destroyers.

The two groups of United States ships were designated as "task forces," a comparatively new word in naval terminology. The two that were deployed off the Gilberts and Marshalls the morning of January 31, 1942, contained two-thirds of the carrier strength of the Navy in the Pacific. They were, in fact, the "Pacific Fleet," as such small task forces were being described in those days. In the latter days of the war the major task forces — Task Force 58 and Task Force 38 — were in reality full fleets.

The raid was planned Pearl Harbor style, although in somewhat less force, and with the added fillip of a shore bombardment of two of the Marshall atolls by three of the cruisers and three of the destroyers that were with Halsey. They were to close to gun range after *Enterprise* fliers had taken care of the air opposition.

Like the attack of the Japanese on Pearl Harbor, the attack of the American fliers on the Marshalls caught the enemy completely by surprise. Only at Maloelap was there any slip-up. The major air opposition was found there — thirty two-motored bombers and twelve fighters. Only six American fighters, each carrying one hundred-pound bombs in addition to their machine guns, were sent

186

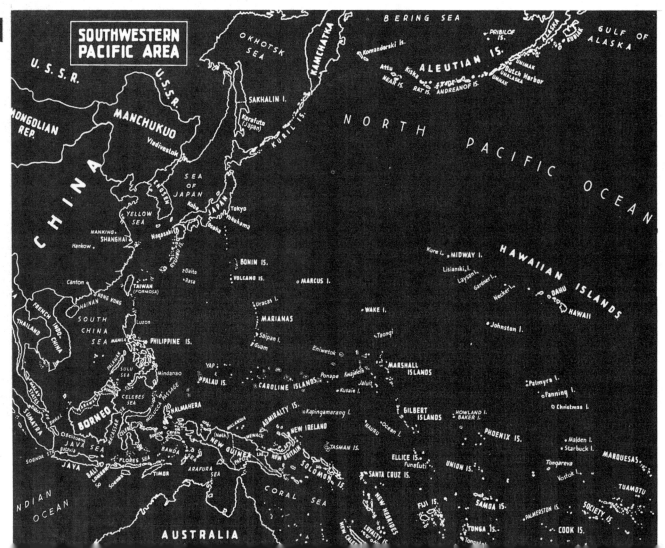

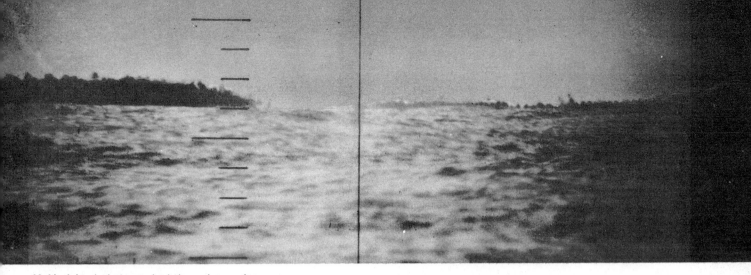

Makin Island photographed through a periscope.

there. The task was too big for them. Most of the enemy planes escaped with little damage from the first air attack. These gave the cruiser *Chester* an uneasy hour of dodging one thousand-pound and one hundred-pound bombs. Fortunately she escaped all but one hit, by a one hundred-pound bomb dropped by a Japanese fighter. Eight men were killed and thirty-four wounded. Several of the casualties were *Chester's* Negro mess attendants, who were grouped near the wardroom, near where the bomb landed.

The biggest group of ships was found in Kwajalein lagoon — a magnificent anchorage the United States fleet later used to good advantage when the atoll was taken in February, 1944 — and it was there Admiral Halsey centered his principal

Enterprise's brood reloads.

air attack. The first wave carried only bombs. When the fat target of one cruiser, a twenty-thousand-ton liner identified as the *Yawata* class and converted as a plane carrier, three fleet oilers, a mother ship, five submarines, and several supply vessels was reported, a group of torpedo planes was sent from *Enterprise*. The fliers reported they had sunk the liner, the cruiser, the three oilers, at least two of the submarines, and the submarine tender. The Japanese, in postwar questioning, said none was sunk. The fact probably was somewhere in between.

In the lagoon at Wotje, eight supply vessels, ranging from medium to small, were found. All but one were sunk. The lone survivor was hit, and it was beached by the Japanese.

187

The *Yorktown* task force ran into bad weather and then found little at which to shoot. At Jaluit were found only two medium-sized supply ships, one of which was hit by a bomb and set afire. Both ships and shore installations were strafed. A seaplane tender with two four-motored Kawanishis nesting nearby was found at Makin. All three were destroyed. At Mili nothing was found except a strip of land from which the coconut palms had been removed and which may have been in process of transformation into an airfield.

The cost to the two task groups was the damage to *Chester* and fourteen planes lost, one in an accident at take-off. Eight of the losses were due to the bad weather over the *Yorktown* group and not to enemy opposition.

Although the enemy's ship losses were not inconsiderable, the principal value of the raid was to fleet morale. Our fliers learned that the Japanese had faster, more maneuverable planes, but that they could outfly and outfight the Japanese pilots. They also learned that their slower planes were far sturdier than those of the enemy, that they had a chance of getting home even when their

A cruiser's guns soften up Wake.

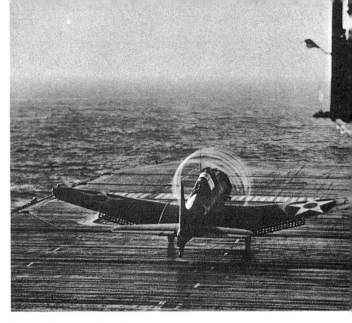

A propeller cuts the air . . .

plane was badly shot up. Above all, the raid was something for the men of the fleet to cheer about. It was action. And that was what they wanted.

Two more raids of a similar nature were made, and another was attempted during the following two months, all of them equally as successful as was the first. On February 24, Halsey led his *Enterprise* task group, with *Northampton* and *Salt Lake City* as escort, against Wake Island in a combined plane and ship attack. Then, on March 4, he steamed to within less than one thousand miles of Tokyo, to the Japanese listening post and radio-direction-finding station island of Marcus, and sent in a hit-and-run, one-shot air attack. One dive bomber was lost at Wake and one at Marcus.

Four days before the Wake attack, Vice Admiral Wilson Brown, later to serve as President

Roosevelt's naval aide, started in on the carrier *Lexington* to hit Rabaul on New Britain Island. The force was detected by the Japanese and attacked by eighteen two-engined enemy bombers from Bougainville. It was during this attack that the late Lieutenant Commander Edward M. (Butch) O'Hare, then a junior grade lieutenant, tackled nine enemy bombers while alone, shot down five of them, and damaged a sixth. None of the American ships were damaged in the Japanese plane attack. But with the element of surprise lost, Admiral Brown turned back from his projected assault on Rabaul.

When *Lexington* was joined by *Yorktown* a few days later, Admiral Brown steamed to the south of New Guinea and sent a plane attack against Salamaua and Lae — on the north coast of

and a Dauntless, with a thousand pounds of bombs under its belly, waits its turn at Wake.

An Avenger wheels to the attack on burning Marcus Island.

the big island. In upsetting Japanese plans, this raid was of considerably more importance than the more widely publicized hit-and-run attack of Halsey's task force on the Marshalls and Gilberts, Wake and Marcus.

Admiral Brown was escorted by the heavy cruisers *Minneapolis, Indianapolis, Pensacola, San Francisco,* and *Louisville,* and two squadrons of destroyers. He took his two carriers in close to the shore in the Gulf of Papua, on which lay the only remaining Allied base on the island, Port Moresby. Shortly after dawn on March 10, an attack group of 103 planes was launched from the two United States carriers. They flew through a seventy-five-hundred-foot-high pass in the sixteen-thousand-foot-high Owen Stanley Range of mountains to

Heavy cruisers **Indianapolis** and . . .

189

San Francisco *covered for the devastating air strikes at Salamau and Lae.*

swoop down on the Japanese unaware. It was a pass that was relatively free from fog during the morning hours, the Navy fliers had learned. It was information the Japanese apparently did not have. At least they had no plane guard on their end of the pass.

Only three Japanese float fighters rose to contest the issue with the Americans. They were shot down. Anti-aircraft guns were unmanned until after the first attack wave was in. Five transports of seven found in the Lae-Salamaua bight, one light cruiser, one destroyer, and two heavy cruisers were either sunk or so badly damaged they had to be beached. The other two transports in the harbor and two others of a convoy that was just coming in to the anchorage were hit and badly damaged. One United States dive bomber was lost.

Most of the enemy shipping had just arrived. Some of the supplies they carried had not yet been unloaded. A conservative estimate was that it upset the Japanese timetable on New Guinea by three to six months. It gave General MacArthur the time he desperately needed to reinforce Port Moresby and to build it up as the base from which he struck in August against the Japanese on the north shore of the islands. The air wing of sea power truthfully can be said to have made possible, or at least made less difficult, the Army's subsequent attack. The carrier again had proved its versatility. Since the Japanese were doing a daily reconnaissance of Port Moresby at that time, it would have been impossible to have massed as many as 103 attack planes there without the enemy's knowledge. The carriers were able to steam in to position during the night and send in an attack with no forewarning to the enemy.

In Far Eastern waters during these early months of the war, the picture was bleak. There the Japanese had such superiority at sea and in the air that the Allied ships of Britain, the United States, and the Netherlands were able to present only token resistance to the enemy advance — especially after the loss on the third day of the war of the British battleship *Prince of Wales* and the battle cruiser *Repulse*.

The two British warships, the thirty-five-thousand-ton *Prince of Wales*, the newest and best of the British battleships, had arrived at Singapore only a short time before. When word came the afternoon of December 8 (December 7, Honolulu time) that the Japanese were landing at Kota Bharu and Singora, halfway up the Malay Peninsula, Admiral Sir Tom (Tom Thumb) Phillips sortied from Singapore with his two capital ships, escorted by four destroyers, to attack the Japanese transports off Singora. Steaming northward under low clouds, the force escaped detection until the afternoon of December 9, when three Japanese reconnaissance aircraft sighted them.

As soon as he was sure his position was known to the enemy, Admiral Phillips turned back south, intending to return to Singapore. He considered the risk of an attack at Singora without air protection as being too great. At about midnight, however, he received an erroneous report of a new Japanese landing at Kuantan, far south of Kota Bharu. This was not far west of his course for Singapore, so he altered his course to investigate, setting speed to arrive off Kuantan shortly after dawn.

As planned, the force made its landfall at dawn. But it found no Japanese force there. Admiral Phillips then turned back to investigate a small convoy of junks he had passed on his way in. It was from them the word of his presence probably was flashed. At 11:18 A.M. the first wave of Japanese planes struck. They were land bombers and made a conventional horizontal attack from twelve thousand feet. The *Repulse* received one topside hit that did little damage. But then came the torpedo bombers. *Prince of Wales* took one hit with the first wave. At twelve twenty, under new and heavy attack, *Prince of Wales* took three more torpedo hits and the *Repulse* one. Three minutes later, *Repulse* was hit by four more torpedoes, and at twelve thirty-three she heeled over and sank.

Admiral Phillips continued to fight from his stricken flagship, but she now was a sitting duck for the horizontal bombers, who scored one damaging hit amidships and several near-misses before she too capsized from the weight of water taken aboard through the holes in her skin made by the torpedoes. That was at 1:20 P.M. In a two-hour fight, during which Japanese plane losses were no more than half a dozen, two of the world's finest warships had been destroyed by plane-borne torpedoes and bombs.

Prince of Wales and *Repulse* off Malaya—doomed targets for Japanese bombers.

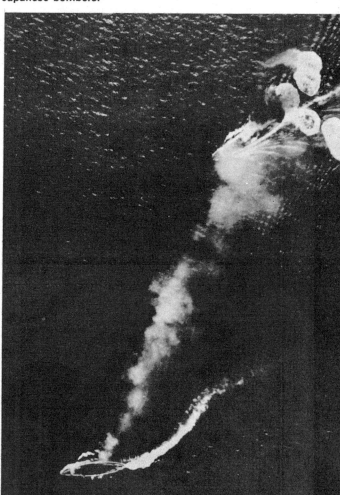

190

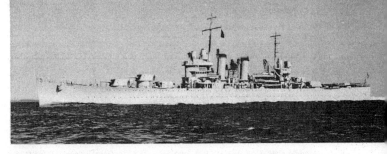

Workhorse *Boise* fought all over the map—the Pacific, Atlantic, Mediterranean, and back to the Pacific.

Air-power protagonists hailed the sinking of the two ships as a complete vindication of their claims. It was something less than that. Had *Prince of Wales* and *Repulse* been with an aircraft carrier, or had they been given air cover from shore bases, the attack of the Japanese planes could have been much less disastrous. As it was, the enemy's torpedo squadrons were able to make their runs against the opposition only of anti-aircraft fire, which at that time was notoriously ineffective. The horizontal bombers faced only the same hazard.

Admiral Phillips has been accused of professional blindness in leading his task force into such a situation. He was a braver and more astute naval leader than that. General MacArthur has revealed that, in a telephone conversation with Admiral Phillips from Manila shortly before the latter sailed for Singora, the British naval leader expressed himself as well aware of the odds against him. He knew the gamble he was taking. Because of the need of action to stop the Japanese at sea before they could get large numbers of men ashore in Malaya, he took a magnificent chance. The weather, which protected him the first afternoon and most of the next day, cleared long enough to reveal his position to patrolling enemy aircraft. The erroneous report of the landing at Kuantan led him to change his plans for a quick return to Singapore. The enemy junks sighting him completed the picture. Without air protection, he was, of course, doomed. He gambled. He lost. Under different circumstances of chance and weather he might have won.

Destruction of the two British battleships (the thirty-two-thousand-ton *Repulse* was older but fully as powerful a vessel as *Prince of Wales*) was a staggering blow to Allied hopes. There was left to resist the Japanese advance only the British heavy cruiser *Exeter*, the United States heavy cruiser *Houston*, the two United States light cruisers *Boise* and *Marblehead* (the latter in the Far East purely by accident), the Dutch light cruisers *de Ruyter*, *Java*, and *Tromp*, a few Australian, Netherlands, and United States destroyers, a few squadrons of submarines, and a diminishing land-based air force. Only delaying actions were possible against a vastly superior and balanced fleet, strongly supported by carrier-borne and land-based air power.

The very islands lent themselves ideally to Japanese strategy, which was to advance only in short sea hauls behind overpowering air bombing and reconnaissance. Even when their transport trains were sighted, there generally was little time for the outnumbered Allied surface vessels to intercept them before they had accomplished their mission of putting a landing force ashore. One of two such interception attempts that succeeded was that off Balikpapan, Borneo, on January 24, 1942.

Late in November, 1941, when it became obvious that war with Japan was imminent and inevitable, Admiral Thomas C. Hart had ordered his small Asiatic Fleet out of Manila Bay, sending it south to the Netherlands Indies. It was really a "fleet" only because the Navy officially called it that. It was hardly even a squadron, with only one heavy cruiser, two light cruisers, and twelve destroyers. Most of the tin cans were ancients of 1917 lineage. Until the night of January 24, they had no contact with enemy surface vessels. Their principal tasks had been the escort of vessels south from Manila Bay and the movement of reinforcements and supply vessels to Singapore, Sumatra, and Java.

As originally planned, when word came of the movement south toward Balikpapan of a large Japanese convoy, the light cruisers *Boise* and *Marblehead* and the four destroyers *John D. Ford*, *Pope*, *Parrott*, and *Paul Jones* sailed to make the attack. En route to the rendezvous, the *Boise* strained her bottom plates against an uncharted pinnacle and *Marblehead* developed engine trouble. The four destroyers went in alone.

Reduction in the size of the force may have been an element in the success of the attack. The four low-silhouette destroyers steamed through the Japanese destroyer screen without detection. They made one run through the enemy transports firing torpedoes. Then, when their forty-eight torpedoes were exhausted, they opened up with their deck guns. In the confusion of the action, no accurate count of enemy ships destroyed was made by Commander P. H. Talbot, the commodore of the little force. A Netherlands submarine commander,

191

Dutch light cruiser **Tromp.**

who was running at periscope depth to watch the show, said he saw thirteen enemy ships go down, one of them a destroyer. (After the war, the Japanese gave the toll as only two transports sunk but several others damaged.) The four United States destroyers steamed safely back out through the disorganized enemy screen with only four casualties — one dead, three wounded — the result of a shell hit on *John D. Ford*.

One more such raid was to be made before the Battle of the Java Sea, and the wave of conquest rolling south from Japan, made further resistance impossible, and the Indies were abandoned. On February 19, a combined United States–Netherlands attack was made on another Japanese convoy in Badung Strait off Bali. The results were not as satisfactory as those of the Macassar Strait strike. The Netherlands destroyer *Piet Hein* was lost, the Netherlands light cruiser *Tromp* and the United States destroyer *Stewart* both were put out of action by Japanese gunfire and later were lost to Japanese bombers while in Javanese ports for repairs. How many enemy vessels were sunk was not known. Several were damaged. This time there was no friendly submarine within eye range to keep a box score.

Matters were becoming more desperate every day, however, for the diminishing Allied naval forces. On February 4, *Houston* had been hit by a bomb, killing forty-eight men and putting her after turret out of action, and *Marblehead* had been so disabled by two bomb hits and a near-miss she had to start for Tjilatjap, on the south coast of Java, to make emergency repairs. Before these were completed, the Battle of the Java Sea had been lost, and she started the long voyage home to the States.

The crippling of *Marblehead* and the loss of the use of the after turret of *Houston* was a discouraging blow just at a time when the outlook had brightened somewhat. Air attacks on Singapore had become so heavy late in January that convoys to Malaya had been discontinued, freeing several British vessels for operations with the United States–Netherlands force. Rear Admiral Karel W.·F. M. Doorman of the Royal Netherlands Navy had been placed in tactical command. Built around the *Houston*, the force was strong enough to do considerable damage to the Japanese if it could escape air attack and too close air surveillance. An attempt was being made at the same time to build up fighter plane strength ashore so better air protection could be given over Javanese ports, on which the naval forces depended so greatly; a fleet is only as strong as its base. The aircraft

Gallant **Langley**, *forerunner of the carrier, will be sunk by aerial action.*

tender *Langley* (our first carrier, long since converted) was en route from Australia to Tjilatjap in company of the oiler *Pecos* with thirty-two P-40 Army fighter planes on her deck on February 27 when she was found by Japanese planes and sunk. *Pecos*, with *Langley* survivors, was sunk the following day. The British aircraft tender *Seawitch*, with twenty-seven assembled fighters aboard, made port safely, but by then it was too late. The Battle of the Java Sea had been fought and lost. It hardly could have had any other result.

By mid-February, the Japanese had taken Singapore. They were well established on Sumatra and Bali. Java was the last barrier between them and Australia. On February 25, the enemy began a movement south in strength. Admiral Doorman and his crippled striking force, consisting of the American *Houston*, the British *Exeter* and *Perth*, the Netherlands light cruisers *De Ruyter* and *Java*, two Netherlands destroyers, three British destroyers, and the four old American four-stackers, *J. D. Edwards*, *Alden*, *Ford*, and *Paul Jones*, went out to try and stop them.

Moving south toward Java were no less than five enemy transport trains of some 150 ships, protected by fifteen to twenty cruisers, heavy and light, and several squadrons of destroyers. The transports and supply ships were fat targets if the Allied naval force could get to them. On February 26, Admiral Doorman led his little force to sea from Surabaja to make the attempt. He first swept to the eastward, but early on the morning of February 27, on receipt of a reconnaissance report placing the main enemy convoys to westward, he turned back to intercept them. Two hours after dawn, his force was sighted by enemy planes. Despite this, he continued on, but without finding the enemy ships. Then, needing fuel and with his men near exhaustion from almost continuous battle quarters for days, he turned back to Surabaja to refuel and await further reconnaissance reports.

By midafternoon two enemy transport trains had been located within striking distance, and

De Ruyter *went down with Doorman's flag in the Java Sea.*

Java *lost her fight along with* **De Ruyter.**

again the Allied force put to sea. Admiral Doorman led in *De Ruyter*, followed by *Exeter, Houston, Perth,* and *Java,* in that order. Ahead and on the flanks were the nine destroyers.

The force had hardly cleared the mine fields when the leading destroyers reported contact with an enemy force of cruisers and destroyers. Action was opened shortly after four o'clock at a range of about thirty thousand yards, but the two forces were on converging courses and the range was closed rapidly.

For the first fifteen minutes of the action, neither side apparently scored any hits, although closely-bunched salvos were sending up columns of

spray around the leading Allied vessels. The first hit apparently was scored on a Japanese heavy cruiser, by either *Houston* or *Exeter,* the only two Allied vessels mounting eight-inch rifles. The accurate Allied fire must have had the Japanese commander worried, for soon after this first hit one of the Japanese destroyer squadrons launched a torpedo attack. Enemy submarines also are believed to have been in the area and firing at the Allied vessels.

The odds were so heavy against the Allied force, the battle could have had but one outcome. *De Ruyter, Houston,* and *Exeter* all received shell hits during the first hour of intermittent action,

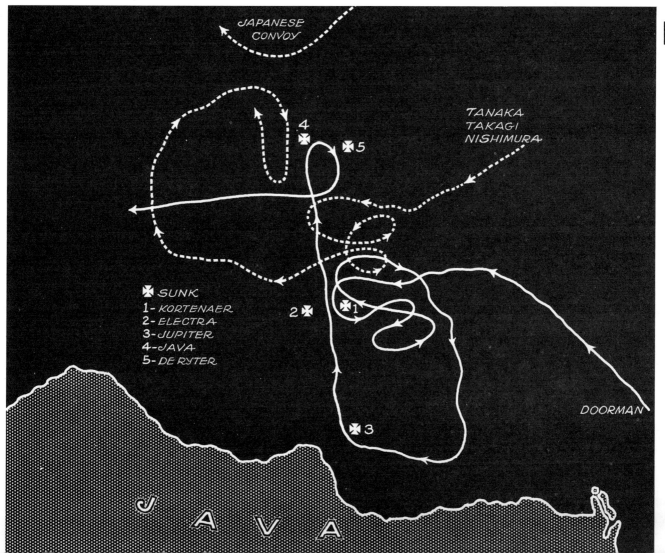

and the Netherlands destroyer *Kortenaer* was sunk by a torpedo. The shell hit on *Exeter* had slowed her considerably, and the Allied force fell into confusion as enemy cruisers and destroyers closed in from the north and the west. In attempting to cover the crippled *Exeter* from a torpedo attack, the British destroyer *Electra* was sunk.

Undaunted by his heavy losses, Admiral Doorman re-formed his column and turned back north to renew the engagement. At the same time he ordered the American destroyer squadron to make a torpedo attack on the Japanese cruiser line. When this attack was launched, the Japanese turned away. In the meantime, contact had been lost between the American destroyers and Admiral Doorman, and since all their torpedoes were exhausted and their fuel was low, they decided to return to Surabaja, where the *Exeter* and the remaining Netherlands destroyer had preceded them.

With the two remaining British destroyers, *Encounter* and *Jupiter*, as anti-submarine guard, Admiral Doorman led his little cruiser line, now reduced to *De Ruyter, Java, Houston,* and *Perth,* to the westward toward the last reported position of the main Japanese transport train. At 9:25 P.M., *Jupiter* was hit by a torpedo and sunk, and at 11:15 P.M. *Java* and then *De Ruyter* suffered like disaster. Admiral Doorman went down with his flagship.

194

Houston and *Perth,* the only surviving ships, since *Encounter* had been ordered back to Surabaja with 113 survivors from *Kortenaer,* which she had accidentally found as the force steamed through the area of the afternoon engagement, turned westward toward Tandjungpriok. From there, the next evening *Houston* attempted to escape through Sunda Strait to Australia, but was intercepted by the heavy cruisers *Mogami* and *Mikuma*, and was sunk near the Duizend Islands. Survivors of *Houston* were freed from a prison camp in Thailand after the end of the war.

The crippled *Exeter*, the British destroyer *Encounter*, and the American destroyer *Pope* also were ordered to Australia via Sunda Strait. Like *Houston, Perth,* and the Dutch destroyer *Evertsen,* they also were intercepted by enemy cruisers and sunk. The only ships of the little Allied force to escape were the other four American destroyers. They steamed out of Surabaja the night of February 28 and ran safely through Bali Strait past a Japanese destroyer guard of three ships that opened fire on them but scored no hits. Four days later they reached Australia. The Japanese, it was learned after the war, lost no combatant ships in the encounter. *Houston* sank two transports before going down.

The Far Eastern naval campaign of the first three months of the war had been one of the most disastrous in naval history. Except for the four United States destroyers, all Allied ships in the area were lost. At the same time it was one of the most courageous losing series of battles ever fought. With their lives the men of the Allied ships bought the time needed to build up the defenses of Australia and save that continent from the fate of Southeast Asia and the Indies.

With the Indies subdued and the straits opened to the south and west, the Japanese pressed on into the Indian Ocean and the Bay of Bengal. There, on March 30, enemy carrier planes sank the British light cruiser *Naiad*. Ten days later they destroyed with dive bombers the British heavy cruisers *Dorsetshire* and *Cornwall*, and on April 10 they caught and sank the old British aircraft

Exeter starts her death roll . . .

and Pope is blown out of the water.

The end of **Dorsetshire.**

carrier *Hermes,* which had fought so valiantly in the Mediterranean. She had been in the Far East only a few months.

By May 1, 1942, the Japanese had won their empire. They were masters of all of the western Pacific and the Indian Ocean. All they had to do was hold it.

One of the principal reasons the Japanese found the empire they had won so difficult to hold and to exploit was the Pacific Fleet submarines. Waging unrestricted warfare against the Japanese bridge of ships from the empire to China and the islands of the South Seas, American submarines had almost cut the bridge before land-based aircraft from China and the Philippines, and the car-

rier fliers, got close enough to join the battle and sever the last girders.

After war's end, interrogation of the Japanese Navy's surviving high commanders brought more eloquent testimony than any the submarine people themselves had given as to the efficacy of the United States submarines, their captains, and their crews. It was an efficiency that was surprising to the Japanese. Vice Admiral Miwa, who commanded Japan's submarines during most of the war, said that most of the American submarines and the American techniques, were superior to those of Japan. Discussing the sinking of the battleship *Kongo,* which was torpedoed by *Sealion* on November 21, 1944, as she was attempting to retreat from

the Battle of Samar to Japanese home waters, Admiral Miwa said:

As commander of the Sixth Fleet (submarines), I discussed this operation by the American submarine with my officers, saying it should be an example to our own forces of a brave, skillful operation. . . . I expected that your submarine crews would all be on the same level with Japanese crews and likewise the devices of the submarines; but they were superior to the Japanese.

The statistics of the sinking of Japanese warships and of merchant vessels, as compiled from both United States Navy Department and Japanese Admiralty records, show what a part the American undersea boats played in the war. Of the 611 naval vessels the Japanese lost during the war, American submarines sank 201. In this bag were one battleship, eight aircraft carriers, fifteen cruisers, forty-two destroyers, one hundred lesser warships, and even twenty-eight Japanese submarines. Of 2,117 Japanese merchant vessels lost from all causes during the war, United States submarines sent down 1,113. Following is the complete box score:

JAPANESE MARITIME LOSSES

Sinking Agent	Naval Vessels		Merchant Vessels	
	No.	Tonnage	No.	Tonnage
Submarines	201	540,192	1,113	4,779,902
Carrier-based Aircraft	161	711,236	359	1,390,241
Land-based Aircraft	81	75,657	328	858,385
Mines	19	17,995	247	591,660
Surface Craft	112	277,817	11	43,349
Miscellaneous	37	199,403	59	250,321
TOTAL	611	1,822,210	2,117	7,913,858

American submarines were no less successful in evading Japanese anti-submarine measures as they were in sinking enemy vessels. Forty-eight were lost on Pacific war patrols. But this is 23 less than the number of American destroyers lost in the war and contrasts with 130 Japanese submarines destroyed by Allied forces in the Pacific, 85 Italian submarines, on limited Mediterranean operations, and 781 German.

Enemy ship sinkings were only a part of submarine duties. They scouted ahead when the fleet went to sea; they laid mines in enemy waters; they rescued American fliers (504 of them); they landed Carlson's Second Marine Raiders at Makin, a Ranger battalion on Attu, and a demolition party on Honshu; they scouted shore lines for landings, and took innumerable periscope photographs of invasion terrain. Submarines evacuated Francis B. Sayre, the High Commissioner to the Philippines, from Corregidor, and also took off "the Rock" several million dollars in gold bars.

The United States was as weak in submarines as in most other fleet units when the Japanese attacked at Pearl Harbor. The total in commission at that time was only a few over a hundred, less than half of which were on fleet duty. Of these, twenty-nine were attached to the Asiatic Fleet. First blood was drawn by one of these, *Swordfish*, which sank the eight thousand-ton Japanese freighter *Atsutasan Maru*, off Hainan Island in the South China Sea on December 14, 1941.

In those early days of the war, scouting was the number one objective. It was more important to the American Navy command to have information on enemy fleet movements than it was to send down enemy shipping. Sinkings by United States submarines the first full year of the war totaled 134 ships of 580,390 tons. This total rose to 284

Through the periscope—a Japanese freighter and . . .

ships of 1,341,968 tons in 1943, as additional 1,500-ton submarines, equipped with radar and the newest sonic devices, began to come out of American shipyards. Submarine warfare reached its peak of efficiency in 1944 when, with numbers so increased that they could hunt in packs instead of singly, Pacific Fleet units sent down 492 Japanese ships aggregating 2,387,780 tons.

It was during 1944 when most of the sinking of combatant Japanese ships occurred. Two of the more important of these sinkings — within a period of three weeks — were of two brand-new Japanese aircraft carriers, the *Shinano* and *Unryu*. The *Shinano* was the largest aircraft carrier ever built, constructed on a battleship hull rated at sixty-nine thousand tons. *Archerfish* sank her on November 29, 1944, while she was on her trial run outside Tokyo Bay. Twenty days later, *Redfish* intercepted *Unryu* in the East China Sea en route south to aid in the Philippines campaign, and sent her down with two torpedoes. A similar damaging blow had been delivered on June 19, 1944, during the Saipan campaign, when *Albacore* and *Cavalla* intercepted the Japanese fleet steaming east from the Philippines to attempt to disrupt the Mariana invasion and sent down the aircraft carriers *Shokaku* and *Taiho*. No one can say, of course, how the course of events in the Marianas and the Philippines might have been changed had those four carriers not been sunk when they were. But had they and their air groups stayed in the fight, both campaigns would have been made much more difficult.

In addition to sinkings, American submarines damaged many major Japanese vessels and kept them out of action for months. Both *Musashi* and *Yamato*, the world's two greatest battleships, were so hit and laid up for considerable periods before finally being sunk by carrier fliers. It has been estimated that from the middle of 1943 to the end of the war at least one major Japanese ship — battleship, carrier, or heavy cruiser — was immobilized in Japanese shipyards for repairs because of American submarine attacks.

One of the hardest earned of the figures in the American submariners' box score was that of forty-two enemy destroyers, the most potent submarine killers. Many of them were bagged in the spring and summer of 1944 when orders went out to make Japanese destroyers the number one target. One of the best of the destroyer destroyers was Commander Sam Dealey, who, with his submarine *Harder*, sank five destroyers in five days in the Sulu Sea. Two of these were destroyed by what the submariners call "down-the-throat" shots. That technique was to attract the attention of the enemy, wait until he was within twelve hundred yards, and then fire a spread directly at him or "down his throat." It was a deadly game, of course. If it didn't work, the submarine seldom had a chance to fire a second spread. *Harder* was lost with all hands in what probably was just such an attack a few months after the successful five-for-five foray.

Although statistically submarine duty was no more hazardous for American sailors in the Pacific than several other branches of service, submarine warfare placed a greater strain continuously on its people than did any other method of naval warfare. The average length of patrol was sixty days. Most of those were spent in enemy waters. Identification was difficult from the air, and in going to and from patrol, submarines had to be watchful against attacks by American fliers as well as from Japanese pilots. Several actually were attacked, but so far as is known, none were sunk by their own fellows.

a Japanese destroyer.

In the early days of the war, the old submarines were always dark and cold. New insulation and air conditioning later made life much more bearable. It was still a grim existence, however, and when a submarine came back from patrol, her crews were given the best there was available in the way of accommodations and recreation. Afloat they ate a carefully considered diet to make up for sixty days of no sunlight.

The typical American submarine was one of about fifteen hundred tons displacement, the size of a prewar destroyer. She was three hundred feet long, had a top speed of twenty knots on the surface, and carried a crew of one hundred officers and men. She had six forward torpedo tubes, which could be fired in salvo, and four aft. Her total torpedo capacity was twenty-four. Torpedoes were of two types: a steam torpedo that could make forty-five knots (about fifty-one miles an hour) but which left a wake, and an electric torpedo that left little wake but the speed of which was only thirty knots.

German submarines, and some Japanese, were more highly developed at the start of the war than were the American submarines. Some of the largest Japanese submarines had a deck hangar for four airplanes, which were launched by catapult.

It seems only justice that the weapon of naval warfare which had been developed as an attack ship in 1776 by an American, Bushnell, was used so effectively by the United States Navy in fighting its greatest naval war. Sergeant Ezra Lee actually navigated Bushnell's little one-man submersible against the bottom of the British frigate *Eagle* in New York harbor, but he was unable to complete his mission of destruction because *Eagle's* bottom was covered with copper, which made it impossible for him to attach to it with a wood screw the one hundred-pound case of powder that was his "torpedo." The first really successful powered submarine was built in the United States by John Holland, a naturalized Irishman, in 1877. It was the United States Navy's SS-1. Her dimensions — fifty-three feet in length, a ten-foot beam and seventy-ton displacement — were only a little larger than the two-man submarines that were used successfully by the Japanese in their attack on Pearl Harbor. The Holland submarine was the prototype for the first British Navy submarines. Simon Lake, another American submarine builder, contributed basic ideas that are incorporated in the submarines of today.

As the submarine leaders themselves point out, the submarine was only one member of a team that helped win the war against Japan. But it was a very important member.

Aboard without his papers—but not for long.

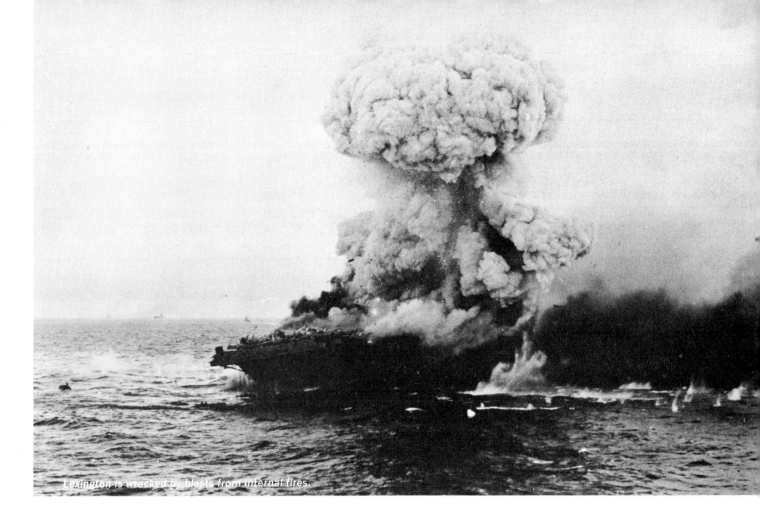

Lexington is wrecked by blasts from internal fires.

THE CORAL SEA AND MIDWAY

CHAPTER 17

From Salamis in 480 B.C., until May 7 and 8, 1942, all the great naval battles of history had been fought between fleets operating against each other on the surface of the sea. At Taranto and Pearl Harbor, fleets in port had been destroyed by aircraft operating from carriers at sea. In the Coral Sea in the South Pacific was fought the first great sea battle in which the opposing forces never came within gun range, in which the only contact was by air. It is a date to remember. The Battle of the Coral Sea opened a new phase of naval warfare.

In the three months to May 1, 1942, after the Allied Far Eastern Naval forces had been hunted down and destroyed, the Japanese had continued to move on south and east. In March they landed large forces at Salamaua and Lae, on New Guinea's north coast, and occupied the islands of Buka and Bougainville in the Upper Solomons. On May 1, they moved on down the Solomons chain to Tulagi (on Florida Island) and Guadalcanal.

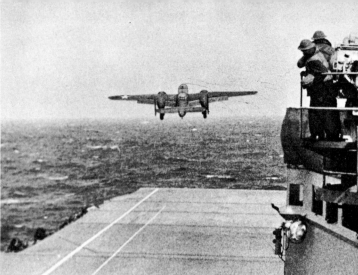

*One of Doolittle's B-25's starts along **Hornet's** flight deck . . .*   *and takes off for Tokyo and points east.*

The Allied position was critical. General Mac-Arthur in Australia had less than five hundred airplanes. The Pacific Fleet, although strengthened by the addition of the carrier *Hornet* and a few destroyers, still was far from a match for the Japanese fleet. Many island bases were in process of construction but were only thinly held. On New Caledonia, for instance, two airfields had been built, but the two-hundred-mile-long French island was garrisoned only by one division of American troops, named the Americal.

The outnumbered United States Pacific Fleet had to protect a seven-thousand-mile-long line from the Aleutians to Australia. It would have been a hopeless task but for one great advantage. We held the key to the Japanese code. Actual operations plans, of course, seldom are transmitted by radio. Within limits, however, it was possible for our commanders to make an informed guess as to

where the Japanese would strike next, by intercepting messages on ship movements and plotting where the Japanese were building up strength. In the spring of 1942 it appeared certain they planned to wipe out the Allied finger-tip hold on New Guinea, at Port Moresby, and perhaps move on down to the New Hebrides or New Caledonia.

After the Salamaua-Lae raid of March 10, the task force built around the *Lexington* and *Yorktown* had continued to operate in the South Pacific. After the Doolittle raid on Tokyo on April 18, *Enterprise* and *Hornet* also started south, escorting a transport train of Marines to Efate in the New Hebrides.

The United States fliers were the first to strike. On May 4, Rear Admiral Frank Jack Fletcher took *Yorktown* in to within one hundred miles of the Solomons and sent in her fliers to attack the eighteen Japanese vessels at Tulagi that

Shoho takes a clean torpedo hit amidships.

had brought down the occupying force four days previously. With the loss of one plane, the entire Japanese force was destroyed.

The following day, *Yorktown* joined up with *Lexington*, on which Rear Admiral (later Vice Admiral) Aubrey W. Fitch had replaced Admiral Brown, and the two steamed northwestward to intercept the Japanese invasion force off the eastern end of the Louisiade Archipelago, the small group of islands to the southeastward of New Guinea. Early on the morning of May 7, a scout plane from *Lexington* sighted one enemy task force led by the aircraft carrier *Shoho*. An attack group was launched and in a furious strike hit the enemy carrier with at least nine torpedoes and eight to ten one-thousand-pound bombs, sinking her. Planes from *Shoho* and two other Japanese carriers sought vainly for the American carriers but failed to find them. They found instead the fleet oiler *Neosho* and her escorting destroyer *Sims*, which had just refueled the United States force. *Sims* was sunk immediately. *Neosho* was badly hit, but her empty, watertight fuel-oil tanks kept her afloat for four days. Half of her crew, but only fourteen survivors of *Sims*, were picked up by American destroyers.

The next morning the two carrier forces located each other at about the same time and launched attack groups. While the United States fliers were attacking and heavily damaging the Japanese carrier *Shokaku*, an estimated 105 enemy planes attacked *Lexington* and *Yorktown*. The old *Lexington*, the converted battle cruiser, took at least two and perhaps five torpedo hits and five bomb hits. *Yorktown* escaped with only one bomb hit, and that in a spot where it did not disable her. After the attack, *Lexington's* fires were extinguished or localized. But as she was steaming out of the area at twenty knots, she was wracked by several explosions that set new and big fires. At sunset she had to be abandoned and sunk by torpedoes from her own destroyer escort. It is surmised that the pounding she had taken had opened some of her gasoline lines and that a spark had ignited the gases.

There was one incident of that day — small in the scheme of battles, but unforgettably poignant to all those who participated in or heard of it,

Shokaku *turns desperately but fails to elude the bombs.*

A Japanese torpedo plane gets through **Lexington's** *AA screen to drop her tin fish.*

which illustrates the terrific strain of three-hundred-mile-an-hour warfare — the loss of Commander William B. Ault, of the *Lexington* Air Group. Commander Ault had led the attack on *Shokaku* and had delivered on her deck one of the three one-thousand-pound bombs that hit her and put her out of action for two months. He was wounded in the attack and became lost attempting to find his way back to the American task force.

202 | For over an hour, while *Lexington* was burning, Commander Ault sought aid, over his voice radio, in finding his way home. Some of his messages were relayed by other fliers, who could hear him when *Yorktown's* Search and Attack Director could not. He apparently was over the horizon from the force, because he could not be located on the radar screen and finally he was told he had better head for the nearest land. The Commander answered that his best guess was that the nearest land was two hundred miles away, and he had gas only for twenty minutes, which would take him only a fraction of the distance. The answer came back that the ship was sorry, but nothing could be done for him. "You're on your own," he was told.

That meant ditching his crippled plane in the water, far from land and with little hope of rescue even if he was successful in making a crash landing.

"O.K.," he was heard to answer. "So long, people. Remember, we got a thousand-pound-bomb hit on that flattop."

Nothing more was heard of him. The Navy Department carried him on its list of "Missing in Action" for several months. Then they scratched him even off that list.

Battle of the Coral Sea, May 8, 1942.

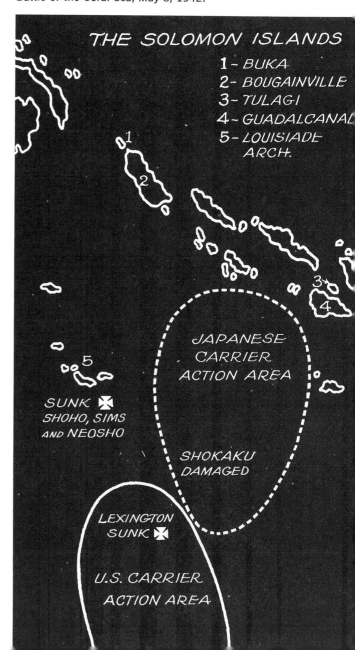

THE SOLOMON ISLANDS

1 - BUKA
2 - BOUGAINVILLE
3 - TULAGI
4 - GUADALCANAL
5 - LOUISIADE ARCH.

JAPANESE CARRIER ACTION AREA

SHOKAKU DAMAGED

SUNK ✠ SHOHO, SIMS AND NEOSHO

LEXINGTON SUNK ✠

U.S. CARRIER ACTION AREA

In ships lost in the Coral Sea, the score was in favor of the Japanese — three ships to one. But several of Japan's ships were damaged, and more importantly, the enemy abandoned the attempt to move south. His timidity at a time when he had overwhelming superiority cost him heavily. He never got another chance.

The enemy's advance in the south was timed within a month of a far more ambitious venture, the seizure of Midway Atoll, twelve hundred miles west of Pearl Harbor, and of bases in the Aleutians. Intercepted messages indicated it was to be a major effort, and that to stop it would require every ship and plane the United States had. The damaged *Yorktown*, after a short stop at Tongatabu to make emergency repairs, headed north. *Enterprise* and *Hornet* and their escorts also were ordered back. This force, under Admiral Halsey, had been too far to the eastward to take part in the Coral Sea fight. An enemy reconnaissance plane had spotted them one afternoon, however, and it appeared probable that enemy intelligence placed all three United States carriers in the Pacific far to the south of where they would be needed. The enemy's smugness off Midway, in launching his attack on June 4, before making a search to the east, where the United States carriers were, indicates he had no thought that they would be within three thousand miles of his force.

In striking at Midway and the Aleutians on June 4, the Japanese were attempting an attack that would have been successful six months before had they properly evaluated the known weaknesses of the United States in the Pacific.

This time planning landings at Midway and in the Aleutians, the Japanese sortied in full force, under command of Admiral Yamamoto, Commander in Chief of the Imperial Japanese Fleet. In his force, spread over the North Pacific from Midway to the Aleutians, were eleven battleships, eight aircraft carriers (one of which was not oper-

Midway and the kill—two Dauntlesses peel off to finish a burning ship.

ative but was being used as a plane ferry), ten heavy cruisers, eight light cruisers, sixteen transports, plus tenders, oilers, supply ships, and sixty-two destroyers. They were divided into the following task groups:

MIDWAY ATTACK FORCE

Battleships:	*Haruna, Kirishima*
Carriers:	*Akagi, Kaga, Hiryu, Soryu*
Heavy Cruisers:	*Tone, Chikuma*
Light Cruisers:	*Nagara*
Others:	16 destroyers, 3 fleet oilers, 6 supply ships

MIDWAY BOMBARDMENT-OCCUPATION FORCE

Battleships:	*Kongo, Hiei*
Heavy Cruisers:	*Atago, Chokai, Kumano, Suzuya, Mikuma, Mogami*
Carriers:	*Chitose* (plane ferry)
Light Cruisers:	*Naka, Jintsu*
Others:	33 destroyers, 16 transports, 4 supply ships, 1 seaplane tender, 1 subchaser, 2 patrol boats, 1 mine sweeper

ALEUTIAN ATTACK FORCE

Carriers:	*Ryujo, Junyo*
Heavy Cruisers:	*Takao, Maya*
Others:	3 destroyers, 1 fleet oiler, 22 submarines

ALEUTIAN LANDING FORCE

Light Cruisers:	*Kiso, Tama, Abukuma*
Others:	6 destroyers, 1 mine layer, 2 oilers, 1 submarine tender, 3 transports, 2 seaplane tenders, 2 supply ships

MAIN BODY (Admiral Yamamoto)

Battleships:	*Yamato, Matsu, Nagato, Ise, Huyga, Fuso, Yamashiro*
Carriers:	*Zuiho*
Light Cruisers:	*Katagami, Oi Sendai*
Others:	4 destroyers, 4 fleet oilers

(*Ise, Huyga, Fuso, Yamashiro, Zuiho, Katagami, Oi Sendai,* three destroyers, and two of the oilers were detached just before the battle and sent north to intercept any United States forces attempting to move between the Aleutians and Midway. They rejoined Main Body on June 5 for the retirement.)

Against this Combined Fleet of Japan, the United States deployed the following forces (not counting the old battleships that steamed out of West Coast ports so the Japanese wouldn't know where they were, but which never got within three thousand miles of the action):

MIDWAY DEFENSE FORCE

Aircraft Carriers: *Yorktown, Enterprise, Hornet*
Heavy Cruisers: *Astoria, Portland, Vincennes, New Orleans, Minneapolis, Northampton, Pensacola*
Light Cruisers: *Atlanta*
Destroyers (14): *Hammann, Morris, Russell, Anderson, Hughes, Balch, Benham, Phelps, Worden, Aylwin, Monaghan, Ellet, Maury, Conyngham*
Submarines (25): *Cachlot, Cuttlefish, Dolphin, Drum, Finback, Flying Fish, Gato, Grayling, Greenling, Grenadier, Grouper, Growler, Gudgeon, Narwhal, Nautilus, Pike, Plunger, Pollack, Pompano, Porpoise, Tambor, Tarpon, Trigger, Trout, Tuna*

ALEUTIAN DEFENSE FORCE

Heavy Cruisers: *Indianapolis, Louisville*
Light Cruisers: *Honolulu, St. Louis, Nashville*
Others: 4 destroyers, 1 fleet oiler, numerous mine sweepers, auxiliaries

The Japanese transport train, whose commander probably had not expected to be sighted

seven hundred miles from Midway, as he was on June 3, steamed in boldly from the west. The carrier force used the same approach as that for the attack on Pearl Harbor, that is, through the North Pacific, where there are no island bases for thirteen hundred miles between Midway and Kiska, and where the weather uniformly is foggy or stormy. In his eagerness to effect a surprise on the island garrison, Vice Admiral Chuchi Nagumo, who had directed the Pearl Harbor attack, launched his air groups at dawn from two hundred miles north of Midway without first making a search for any United States naval force.

Because of the excellent reconnaissance of two Navy search planes, commanded by Ensign Howard D. Ady of San Antonio, Texas, and Lieutenant William A. Chase of Altoona, Pennsylvania, the Japanese failed even of a surprise at Midway. Ady sighted the enemy carrier force just after it had launched its attack groups. Lieutenant Chase saw the attack groups flying in. Each gave the alarm in plain voice. They were heard both at Midway and on the United States carriers, which were 250 miles to the northeast of the Japanese position, a position toward which they had steamed the day before

Kaga's perfect circle will not save her.

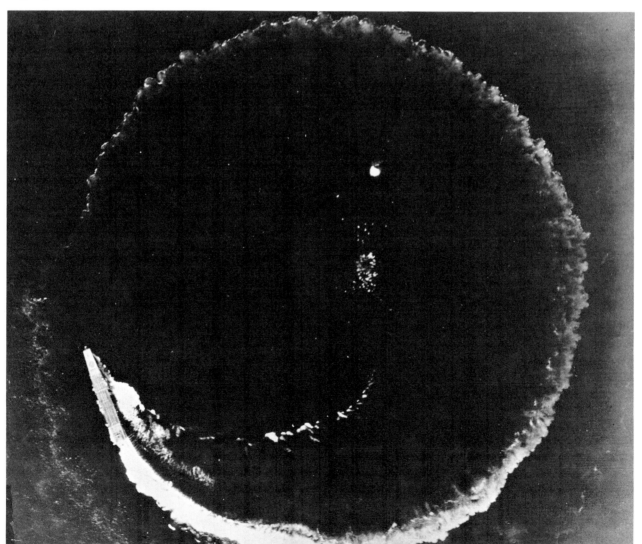

Quite useless—a Mogami class cruiser wallows dead in the water.

on word of the sighting of the enemy transport train.

Unlike December 7, on June 4 the Japanese found the United States air and naval forces waiting for them. On word of the incoming attack, every plane that could fly was sent into the air from Midway. These were twenty-seven dive bombers, six new Grumman Avenger torpedo planes, four B-26 Army medium bombers armed with torpedoes, sixteen B-17 Army bombers, and twenty-seven Navy fighters, most of them the outmoded Brewster Buffaloes. Because the fighter planes were needed for the defense of the island, the American attack groups had to carry out their mission without fighter protection. In that first attack, five of the torpedo planes, half of the dive bombers, and two of the B-26's failed to come back. They heavily damaged and set afire the carrier *Kaga* and an unidentified cruiser. It was during this attack that Major Lofton Henderson of the Marines dived his disabled plane into *Kaga,* proving that Americans, too, knew how to die if the need for such a sacrifice was great enough. Knowing the strength of the Midway forces, which was far too slight to do the job that had to be done, Henderson must have thought the need was great.

When word was received on the American carriers of the sighting of the Japanese striking force, they headed toward the enemy at full speed. At about 175 miles, *Enterprise* and *Hornet*

launched their planes. An hour later, *Yorktown* sent out her attack groups.

The *Enterprise* and *Hornet* groups, expecting the Japanese carriers to proceed toward Midway, set their course to intercept them. They failed to find them on the first cast. (After launching their attack groups, the enemy carriers had turned to the northeast, apparently with the intention of running back toward the fog bank that had covered their approach one hundred miles to the north.) The leaders of the two American flights, believing they had come in astern of the Japanese carriers, flew great circles toward Midway and, after failing to find their targets, finally landed there to refuel.

Two of the leaders of the *Yorktown* squadrons — Commander Jack Waldron of Torpedo Eight and Lieutenant Commander McClusky of Bombing Eight — made the right guess on what the Japanese carriers had done. They searched to the north. Waldron sighted the burning *Kaga* and a cruiser at eleven fifteen. His fifteen planes were running short of fuel. After sending in his contact report, he asked for orders. "Attack at once," he was told. He attacked. Jumped by fighters miles out, of the fifteen planes and thirty men, only Ensign George H. (Tex) Gay Jr., of Houston, Texas, survived. He crash-landed at sea and spent the rest of the afternoon, the night, and the next day in the water awaiting rescue. He saw the remaining two car-

Direct bomb hit on **Yorktown**.

Helpless **Yorktown** *will be the victim, some days later, of an enemy submarine.*

206

riers of the three leaders attacked and set on fire. He believes he got a hit on *Akagi* just before the Zeroes shot him down.

With the Japanese striking force relocated, *Enterprise* and *Hornet* planes, having refueled at Midway, flew out to attack them. By midafternoon *Soryu, Akagi,* and *Kaga* all had been hit so heavily they were being abandoned by their crews. None survived the night. *Kaga* was helped on her way to Davy Jones's locker by a spread of torpedoes from one of her escorting destroyers when it was apparent she could not be saved. *Soryu* floated for several hours. She finally was sunk by torpedoes from the United States submarine *Nautilus,* one of twenty-five that had formed a scouting line ahead of our carriers, but which failed otherwise to make contact with the enemy fleet.

When our fliers first attacked, no group picked *Hiryu* as its target. At one o'clock, she received word — from a search plane that was shot down but not before it had gotten away its contact report — that the Japanese had United States carriers to deal with as well as the Midway planes, a fact that already had become painfully evident to

Admiral Nagumo with the ferocious attack on his striking force. *Hiryu* launched an attack group of eighteen dive bombers and six fighters.

Since early morning, the three United States carriers had been operating on a broad front hull down from each other, with *Yorktown* on the northern flank. It was she *Hiryu's* dive bombers found. Radar picked up the enemy planes some fifty miles away, and fighters were sent out to intercept them. Eleven of the eighteen bombers were shot down, but the other seven — this was Japan's first air team, as can well be imagined — got through to dropping distance. Three of them hit *Yorktown* with their bombs. The most damaging hit was one that went down one of her elevators and exploded below decks, rupturing her main steam line.

Damage control had improved somewhat since the Coral Sea a month before, and by 5 P.M. (the dive-bomber attack started at 2 P.M. and lasted twenty minutes), *Yorktown's* men had her flight deck patched and her fires under control. Then came the torpedo planes, also from *Hiryu.* Again the American fighter patrol was waiting, but it wasn't big enough. Two of the torpedo planes got through, and each drove home his lethal tin fish against the side of the big American carrier, which, because of her previous damage, was not able to make within twelve knots of her best speed. She began to heel over. Afraid his men would be trapped aboard, Captain (later Rear Admiral) Eliott Buckmaster ordered her abandoned. Admiral Fletcher, who had his flag in her when the dive bombers hit, had shifted with his staff to *Astoria* by small boat because *Yorktown's* radio had been destroyed. *Yorktown* survived the day but was sunk by an enemy submarine several days later.

Hiryu's attack on *Yorktown* cost her her life. A *Yorktown* scout bomber had sighted *Hiryu* fifteen minutes before her planes attacked his own ship. A striking force of dive bombers from *Enterprise* and *Hornet* caught the remaining enemy carrier at dusk and damaged her so heavily she sank during the night. This was not known for several days, however, until thirty-five survivors of her crew were sighted in a lifeboat by a patrol plane and taken prisoner by the crew of an American destroyer.

The initial cost in United States ships, planes, and men had been large: the *Yorktown*, 500 men, 150 planes; but the blow to the enemy was far more costly: four of his carriers and their air groups destroyed, one cruiser and one destroyer sunk, and damage to several other vessels. Admiral Yamamoto, his air power gone, gave the signal at ten o'clock that night to abandon the attempt to take Midway.

Fifteen hundred miles to the north, the secondary phase of the Japanese plan to close the North Pacific avenue of attack against Nippon was more successful.

Twelve planes from *Ryujo* attacked the United States naval base at Dutch Harbor on June 3, and thirty-two planes from both Japanese carriers made a second attack the next day. Some shore installations were destroyed and several men killed, but no seaworthy ships were sunk. Army fighter planes from a recently established strip on Umnak Island intercepted the second day's attack and shot down two Japanese fighters and two dive bombers. United States Army and Navy search planes discovered the Japanese forces in the fogs but failed to hit them either with bombs or torpedoes.

The original Japanese plan, according to Captain Taisuke Ito, an air officer on the staff of the Commander of the Second Japanese Fleet at Paramushiro, in the Kuriles, was to occupy Adak — which later became the main United States base in the Aleutians — Kiska, and Attu. After the disaster at Midway, however, it was decided only to make the Attu and Kiska landings, which were carried out.

There never was a Japanese intention, as was believed for many months in the United States, to attempt to take Dutch Harbor, or to attack either Alaska or the United States mainland. If the Midway operation had been successful, Captain Ito and other Japanese officers who participated in the planning said, Japan would have had a base, along with the Aleutians, from which patrol could be maintained across the thirteen hundred miles of

Hammann, *trying to help* **Yorktown,** *takes a torpedo and vanishes in a few minutes.*

Battle of Midway, June 4, 1942.

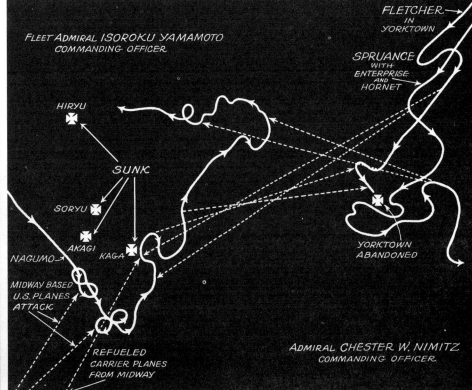

FLETCHER → IN YORKTOWN

SPRUANCE WITH ENTERPRISE AND HORNET

Fleet Admiral ISOROKU YAMAMOTO COMMANDING OFFICER

HIRYU

SUNK

SORYU

AKAGI

KAGA

NAGUMO

YORKTOWN ABANDONED

MIDWAY BASED U.S. PLANES ATTACK

REFUELED CARRIER PLANES FROM MIDWAY

ADMIRAL CHESTER W. NIMITZ COMMANDING OFFICER

North Pacific that stretch between Midway and Kiska. That would close the door to attack from that direction against the home islands. That was the basic reason for the all-out attempt of June, 1942.

The Japanese held their positions in the Aleutians for almost a year. They were driven out of Attu in May, 1943, and they evacuated Kiska in the face of United States invasion under Navy command in July, slipping in a cruiser-destroyer force through the fog that shrouds the Aleutians chain ten months out of the year to take off the 5,100 men who had spent an uncomfortable fourteen months on that bleak island under intermittent United States plane and ship bombardment.

The Japanese Navy deployed strong forces in North Pacific waters in the summer of 1942, expecting a quicker United States attempt to retake the islands. At one time they had a force built around four carriers lying south of the Aleutians. But when the United States made no move quickly to build up an attack group, all the combatant vessels, except the cruiser and destroyer divisions that made up the Fifth Fleet at Paramushiro, were withdrawn for more important duties five thousand miles to the south, in the Solomons.

United States planes and submarines inflicted constant attrition on what light forces and supply trains the Japanese kept in northern waters, and on March 26, 1943, a United States task force consisting of the heavy cruiser *Salt Lake City*, the light cruiser *Richmond*, and four United States destroyers—*Bailey, Coghlan, Dale,* and *Monaghan* — outfought a Japanese force of the heavy cruisers *Nachi* and *Maya*, the light cruisers *Tama* and *Abukuma*, and six destroyers, which were escorting two large supply ships to Attu, and turned them back to Paramushiro. It was the last convoy the Japanese attempted to send in. After that, what little supplies were received at Attu and Kiska arrived by submarine. In the Battle of the Komandorskies, as it has been called because it took place just to the eastward of the Soviet islands of that name in the Bering Sea, no ships were sunk

on either side. The *Salt Lake City* and the destroyer *Bailey* both were hit by Japanese shells, and the Japanese *Nachi* and *Tama* suffered considerable damage and casualties from American shell hits. It was a moral victory, however, for the outgunned American force, and wrote a death warrant for the 2,300-man Japanese garrison on Attu, all but thirty of whom were killed in the American invasion two months later. The thirty were taken prisoner.

The Battle of Midway was a victory of intelligence, more than of ships and of men. The breaking of the Japanese code by United States Naval Intelligence enabled our commanders to know what were the Japanese intentions, and what was their strength. That was the extra weapon that enabled a numerically inferior force to defeat the Japanese Combined Fleets.

Midway was not the decisive naval battle of the war. But it was an important one. Japanese naval commanders showed an increasingly confused attitude after Midway. In the mind of everyone, as he set out on a mission, must have been the memory of that battle. At Coral Sea and Midway, the Imperial Japanese Navy met its first setbacks. Its commanders lost their belief that everything they tried would work beyond all expectations — as the attack on Pearl Harbor had. Correspondingly, the morale of the still outnumbered United States naval forces rose. After Midway, it was a matter of time — but also of many bloody battles.

In the long view of naval history, the two great carrier battles of May–June, 1942, established the airplane carrier as the capital ship of World War II. She and not the battleship was the key to the war at sea. United States naval aviation had come into its own. It had been a long, hard struggle from the pioneer days of 1910-11-12, but recognition finally was universal. The danger for tomorrow could be that the air admirals should prove themselves as unresponsive to new ideas as were the battleship admirals in the 1920's and 1930's. The science of naval warfare is not and never can be static.

*Behind her destroyer smoke screen, **Salt Lake City** fights against heavy odds.*

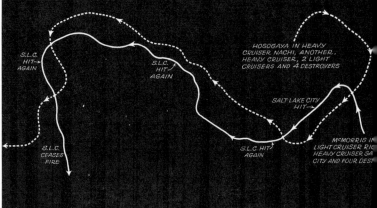

BATTLE FOR A FOOTHOLD 1942-1943

The invasion had gone much better than expected. The reinforced First Marine Division had landed on Guadalcanal, on Tulagi, and on the small islands of Tulagi Harbor, in the Lower Solomons, early in the morning of August 7, 1942. Planes from the three American carriers of the covering force had taken immediate command of the air. The surprise had been complete. Opposition ashore had been overestimated. Only on Tulagi, Gavatu and Tanambogo — the latter two being small islands in Tulagi Harbor — had there been any real fighting. The assault groups on Guadalcanal had marched, with only sniper opposition, to seize control of the almost-completed airfield within a few hours of landing.

The invasion force was the largest Allied naval group mustered in the Pacific since the start of the war. Gathered there were three of the four United States aircraft carriers left in the Pacific — *Saratoga*, *Enterprise*, and *Wasp*, which had just returned from the Mediterranean. There too was one of America's newest battleships, the thirty-five-thousand-ton, sixteen-inch-gunned *North Carolina.* The three carriers and their escorts of *North Carolina,* five heavy cruisers, one light cruiser, and sixteen destroyers, made up the covering force. It was under the command of Vice Admiral Frank Jack Fletcher. With the twenty-three transports and supply vessels, carrying 19,500 Marines and combat supplies for sixty days, was a bombardment force of four heavy and one light American cruisers, two heavy and one light Australian cruisers, and twenty destroyers. Rear Admiral Richmond Kelly Turner, former Chief of War Plans in the Navy Department in Washington, was commander of this force, with Rear Admiral V. A. C. Crutchley, of the British Royal Navy, as second in command. Major General (later General) Alexander Archer Vandegrift was in command of the Marines. Five fleet oilers were in South Pacific ports or at sea, ready to refuel the force.

Two months of hurried preparation had preceded the arrival of this fleet of seventy-six combatant ships and transports off the Lower Solomons that August 7. *Saratoga* and *Enterprise* and about half the cruisers and destroyers had left Pearl Harbor on July 7. *Wasp* and *North Carolina,* the *Vincennes,* and several destroyers had left the Canal Zone about the same time. Seven of the transports had sailed from San Diego in early July. Twelve transports sailed from Wellington, New Zealand, where the First Division had been training. Four small attack transports, refitted from old four-stack destroyers, had sailed from Nouméa, New Caledonia, with Marine Raider units. Admiral Crutchley's force of four cruisers and nine destroyers had come up from Brisbane. The rendezvous had taken place south of the Fijis, from where, on July 31, the combined force had set course for Guadalcanal and Tulagi.

Tension was high in the fleet, as the force cleared the New Hebrides — where bases had been established at Efate and on the northern island of Espiritu Santo, to support the Solomons opera-

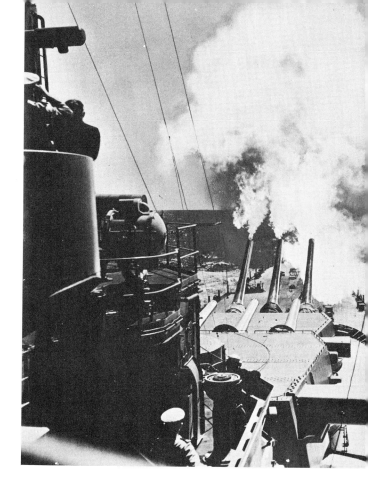

North Carolina *fires her number one turret.*

tion — and headed north through the Coral Sea, walking the chalk line of the 159th longitude near the dividing line that separated the South Pacific Ocean Area, which was under Vice Admiral Robert L. Ghormley, from the Southwest Pacific Area, which was under over-all command of General Douglas MacArthur. Bombers of MacArthur's command had been making small raids on the Upper Solomons and on the Japanese base of Rabaul, and B-17's of the Army's Seventh Air Force had been raiding Guadalcanal from the New Hebrides. None of the raids had been in strength, however, seldom more than five or six planes. That was about all that could be put in the air for a strike at that time.

Saratoga, *attached to Admiral Fletcher's Command.*

Despite Japanese aerial reconnaissance over the Coral Sea, the American-Australian force sailed in to the attack without being detected. Some of the lack of opposition on the beaches was because the Japanese on Guadalcanal and Tulagi, not having been warned of the approach, thought the arrival of the carrier planes signaled only another raid. They had taken to their dugouts to sit it out. The Marines were ashore before the Japanese knew they were there.

At one minute past midnight, August 8–9, which, in combat phraseology, was "D-plus-2 Day," the first American invasion in the Pacific was an unqualified success. Japanese land-based bombers had come down from Rabaul, Buin, and Faisi to the attack on both August 7 and 8, but had had little success. The transport *George F. Elliott* had been set afire by bombing attack and then sunk, and one destroyer, *Jarvis*, had been seriously damaged and later lost en route to Nouméa. But the carrier force had not even been found or attacked.

But the situation was ripe for disaster. The days of tension en route to the assault and forty-eight hours of almost constant duty aboard the ships in the fleet, especially the cruisers and destroyers that had done the bombardment and now were screening the half-unloaded transports from surface attack, had left the crews exhausted. The unexpected ease of the invasion and the failure of the Japanese either to detect the force or to marshal a sizable air or surface strike in thirty-six hours also had left the command self-confident.

Early in the afternoon of August 8, an American search plane saw a Japanese force of cruisers and destroyers two hundred miles away up The Slot — the broad sound that separates the parallel rows of islands that make up the Solomons — but the American command expected them to put in for the night at Rekata Bay, a Japanese anchorage on the north side of Santa Isabel Island. No air strike was sent against them — the American carrier pilots still being busy supporting the Marines ashore — nor were any unusual precautions taken

to intercept them or guard against a night attack by them on Admiral Crutchley's surface forces.

The Japanese force was composed of five heavy cruisers: *Chokai, Aoba, Furutaka, Kinugara,* and *Kako;* two light cruisers: *Tenryu* and *Tatsuta;* and two destroyers.

Deployed on either side of Savo Island, which sits like a sentinel almost exactly halfway between the western tips of Guadalcanal and Florida Islands, were five heavy cruisers of the American-Australian close-support force, and six United States destroyers. In the passage south of Savo were the Australian *Canberra* and the American heavy cruiser *Chicago,* with the destroyers *Patterson* and *Bagley.* To the north of Savo were the American heavy cruisers *Vincennes, Quincy,* and *Astoria,* and the destroyers *Helm* and *Wilson.* West of Savo, presumably guarding against just such an attack as was made, were the United States destroyers *Ralph Talbot* and *Blue.*

The screening force was without a flag commander. Admiral Crutchley, aboard his flagship *Australia,* had steamed over to the transport area to attend a conference called by Admiral Turner. Admiral Fletcher, aboard *Saratoga,* had reported to Admiral Ghormley, the Area Commander, that he had lost twenty-one fighter planes, and that he needed fuel. He asked permission to retire to his fueling rendezvous, to give his fliers a rest, and to secure fighter reinforcement. Admiral Ghormley acceded to the request. When he heard of this plan, Admiral Turner decided he could not keep his transports in the area without air protection — it would be over a week before Henderson Field, on Guadalcanal, was to become operable — and he laid plans to withdraw them the next day, whether or not they were unloaded of supplies, which many of them were not. While the decision was being discussed, the Japanese struck.

The Japanese force was under the command of Rear Admiral Mikawa. He had his flag in the heavy cruiser *Chokai,* which led the column, with the light cruisers and the two destroyers bringing up the rear, the customary Japanese formation for

Astoria, which was to meet her end at night.

a night attack. His orders were to find and destroy the enemy naval forces off Guadalcanal and Tulagi. As they steamed down the dark channel between New Georgia and Santa Isabel Islands, a plane was launched from *Chokai* to reconnoiter the American position. It hovered over the area of Savo for almost an hour, relaying exact information to Admiral Mikawa as to the Allied ship disposition. This is what the Japanese pilot saw: the two American picket destroyers steaming slowly back and forth across the two passages past Savo; the two cruiser groups sailing squares in the passages at only ten knots (they also were running short of fuel) and the transports bunched off Tulagi. Admiral Mikawa steamed in at twenty-five knots, heading for the southern passage.

As the Japanese force passed between the two screening American destroyers, all guns were trained out, in the expectation they would be seen. There was no sign from either, although the Japanese force steamed across the wake of *Blue* at a distance estimated as no greater than five hundred yards. On even the darkest night, a moving ship should be seen at that distance. Ahead the Japanese saw the silhouettes of *Chicago* and *Canberra* against the eastern sky. They bored in to point-blank attack.

At 1:46 A.M. the Japanese opened fire with both deck guns and torpedoes (Japanese heavy, as well as light cruisers, carry torpedo tubes, which United States heavy cruisers do not). *Canberra* was hit by both eight-inch and five-inch shells and several torpedoes and was put out of action, to be scuttled the next morning. *Chicago* lost part of her bow with a torpedo hit and also took shell fire aboard. Her effort to illuminate the enemy force with star shells was unsuccessful. Only six of forty-four that were fired successfully exploded.

Admiral Mikawa did not wait to assess the damage, but swung left, still at twenty-five knots, to engage the northern force. In the turn, he led his heavy cruisers to the west of the American cruiser line, while his two light cruisers passed to the east. *Vincennes*, *Quincy*, and *Astoria* were caught between two divisions of enemy ships at a range of two thousand yards. In a matter of seconds, all three United States cruisers were afire from shell and torpedo hits. Only *Astoria*, last in line, was able to get away a salvo before she was struck. *Quincy* and *Vincennes* sank within minutes. *Astoria* burned all night and sank at noon on August 9.

In an engagement that lasted only a little over half an hour, from first torpedo spread to last gun salvo, Admiral Mikawa's force had fatally hurt

Canberra, too damaged to fight, about to be scuttled.

four Allied heavy cruisers and put another out of action for months, and with only inconsequential damage to his own ships — slight shell damage and a dozen men killed. Between his still battleworthy force and the transports off Tulagi there stood only one heavy Australian cruiser and a few United States destroyers. He milled around outside Savo for a time, trying to make up his mind. Then, not sure of the damage he had done and fearful of being within range of air attack at dawn — he did not know, of course, that Admiral Fletcher was steaming south at twenty knots with the only United States planes capable of doing his ships any damage — Admiral Mikawa decided to call it a night. He set course for home, which was Rabaul for the light cruisers and Kavieng, New Ireland, for the heavies. As the Japanese heavy cruisers were entering Kavieng Harbor the next day, the old United States submarine S-44 hit and sank the *Kako* with a spread of torpedoes.

But for Admiral Mikawa's timidity (the Japanese commanders, like some of the Allied countries, often showed strange contradictions in their decisions) that night could have been catastrophic for the first Allied invasion attempt. Had he shown the same dogged obedience to orders that other Japanese commanders later displayed, and had he gone on to attack the transports, Guadalcanal and Tulagi might have been lost and the victory over Japan set back by months, if not a year or more. For it was the same transports Mikawa did not attack that night aboard which reinforcements finally were sent to the Marines on Guadalcanal. Some of them continued to be used all through the war. In August, 1942, they were the only transports available in the South Pacific.

As it was, the engagement of August 9, 1942, which is called "The First Battle of Savo," was the worst licking the United States ever took. The carelessness there was far less excusable than that at Pearl Harbor. For our commanders had warning of the approach of the force and did not even alert our ships. The captain of one United States

cruiser did not put it in his night orders that Admiral Mikawa's force had been sighted in the afternoon and that extra precautions should be taken, which was typical of the practice on most United States ships at that time — to keep all information away from the men of the ship who also had to do the fighting and the dying. It was not until the final stages of the war that it became practice to thoroughly brief all hands on the task and the dangers ahead and then keep them informed of changing conditions.

"The fact must be faced," said Admiral Crutchley, in his report, "that we had an adequate force placed for the very purpose of repelling surface attack and when the surface attack was made it destroyed our force."

The disaster to the Allied cruisers off Savo, and withdrawal of the United States transports and carriers, found the Japanese Navy unprepared to take advantage of the victory its small cruiser force had won. Most of the Japanese Navy, and especially the carriers they had left after Midway, still were in the North Pacific deploying against an expected United States reaction to the seizure of Kiska and Attu, or in home island waters where the Japanese commanders were still suffering mental paralysis from the shock of Midway.

When the Japanese did react, however, it was in heavy force, much greater than the United States Pacific Fleet could deploy against them. In addition to the Eighth Fleet, composed of cruisers, which was based on Rabaul and Kavieng, and which had made the night attack August 8–9, units of the Second and Third Fleets were sent south from the home islands to join the battle.

Until Midway, the Japanese fleets had been organized by ship category. First Fleet was composed of carriers and escorts, Second Fleet was composed of battleships and destroyers. Third, Fifth, and Eighth Fleets were composed of cruisers. After Midway, it was planned to build the major fleets around carriers, with battleships and/or cruisers and destroyers with each carrier division. It was the balanced-task-force idea that already had been put into practice, because of necessity, in the Pacific Fleet when all but one of the United States battleships in the Pacific were sunk or put out of action at Pearl Harbor.

213

The Japanese Second and Third Fleet units left the Inland Sea on August 16 for Truk. As they neared Truk on the twentieth to refuel and take on provisions, word was received that the United States carrier force that had covered the Guadalcanal landings was still in that area. The call at Truk was canceled, and the two fleet units, which the Japanese called "Mobile Force," headed on south. Their mission was twofold. First it was to intercept and destroy the American naval forces if found. Second, it was to protect a transport train of their own that was taking reinforcements to Guadalcanal.

The Japanese force consisted of the carriers *Shokaku*, *Zuikaku*, and *Ryujo*, the battleships *Kirishima* and *Hiei*, the heavy cruisers *Suzuya*, *Ku-*

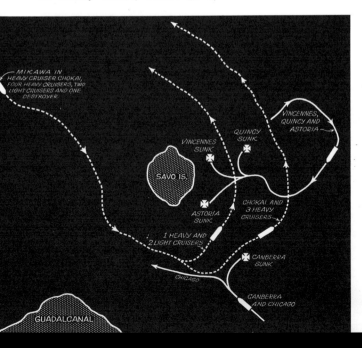

mano, *Tone*, and *Chikuma*, the light cruiser *Jintsu* and fourteen destroyers. They were divided into four groups: the two large carriers and battleships together; *Ruyjo*, *Tone*, and two destroyers some distance away; the other three heavy cruisers and eight destroyers as a scouting line; and *Jintsu* and four destroyers escorting the four transports, which had set out from Truk for Guadalcanal.

The United States carrier group that had covered the original Guadalcanal landings (minus the four cruisers that had been sunk, *Chicago*, which had been sent back to base for repairs, and several destroyers detached for other duties) was still in the Guadalcanal area awaiting developments.

South of the Solomons, Admiral Fletcher also had received word of the approach of the Japanese carriers. Believing he had time to refuel at least part of his forces, he sent *Wasp* and her escorts back to meet the oilers. Then, on August 22, came a contact report that the Japanese force was south of Truk and heading for Guadalcanal. With *Saratoga*, *Enterprise*, and escorts, Fletcher turned north. By morning he was northeast of Malaita, near Stewart Island. At noon a patrol plane winging on search some three hundred miles north of Guadalcanal sighted *Ruyjo* and her escorts, and in midafternoon an *Enterprise* search pair found *Shokaku* and *Zuikaku* to the east of *Ryujo*.

The Japanese also had their search planes out. Shortly after noon, the American task force was discovered by a Japanese search plane that winged within ten miles of the force before it was shot down. It was the familiar pattern, both carrier forces discovering each other at about the same time.

Ryujo, with most of her planes away on a strike at Guadalcanal, or on searches, fell easy victim to the attacking United States fliers. Hit by at least ten bombs and half as many torpedoes, she quickly blew up and sank, as had the *Shoho* south of the Solomons three and one-half months before. *Shokaku* and *Zuikaku* never were found by the American attack group that was sent at them. The two search planes attacked but achieved only near-misses on *Shokaku*, and no damage. The heavy cruiser *Chikuma*, however, was hit with a one-thousand-pound bomb, and several destroyers in all three forces were strafed.

While all this was going on over the horizon, the United States carrier force also came under heavy attack. The Japanese fliers concentrated on *Enterprise*. (*Saratoga* was operating some distance away as was customary). Despite interception by fighter planes and a heavy anti-aircraft barrage put up by *Enterprise*, *North Carolina*, and their escorts, three bomb hits were scored on *En-*

214

The flight deck of Enterprise is hit.

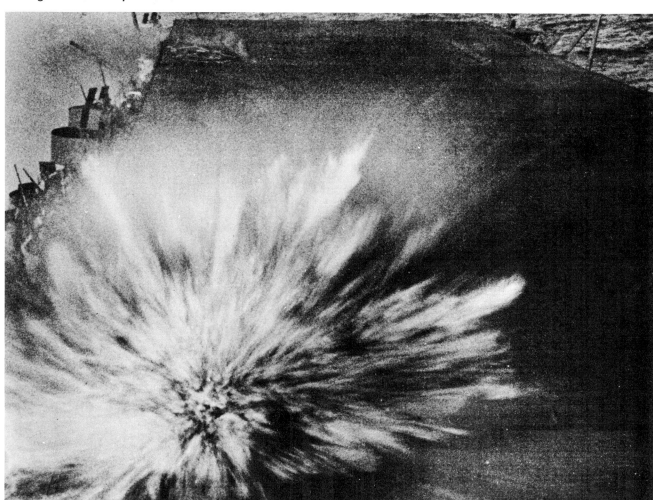

Wasp, struck by three torpedoes, must be destroyed later.

terprise and several near-misses on her and on *North Carolina*. Despite her wounds, *Enterprise* was able to repair the damage and to limp back to Pearl Harbor for repairs. The air score for the day was ninety Japanese planes shot down to twenty American planes lost. The Japanese air losses were so heavy that their two remaining carriers turned back toward Truk, fearing another air fight with their depleted force.

The next morning, August 24, Marine and Navy dive bombers from Guadalcanal found the transport force the Japanese carriers were supposed to be covering, attacked, and set afire the largest transport, *Kinryu Maru,* and hit *Jintsu* with a bomb which necessitated her return to Japan for repair. Later in the day, while the destroyer *Matsuki* was standing by *Kinryu Maru* to take off her survivors and sink her, a small force of B-17's from Espiritu Santo attacked and hit and sank her, too. The rest of the Japanese transports were diverted to the Shortland Islands. The first large-scale attempt to reinforce Guadalcanal had failed.

The Japanese, belatedly recognizing the importance of Guadalcanal and Tulagi, returned to the attack, and to the reinforcement of their land forces on Guadalcanal. All through September, October, and November they poured, or attempted to pour, men and supplies into the area — by transport, by cruisers, and on the decks of destroyers. All available submarines, surface, and air forces in the South Pacific were thrown into the fight, and for those three months it was touch and go whether Guadalcanal and Tulagi could be held.

Faced with superior surface and air forces, the United States Navy went, for a time, purely on the defensive. Cruising back and forth between Espiritu Santo and the Solomons, in seas alive with Japanese submarines, the inevitable finally occurred. On August 31, *Saratoga* was hit by a torpedo and sent limping back to Pearl Harbor, and on September 15, *Wasp* was sunk, and *North Carolina* and the destroyer *O'Brien* were hit by torpedoes from two Japanese submarines. At United States naval headquarters in Nouméa the atmosphere was one of near panic.

Those were the darkest days of the war in the South Pacific. On Guadalcanal, the Marines went without reinforcements or supplies (except what could be taken in by destroyers and submarines) until September 18, while the Japanese surface groups steamed in every few days to bombard Marine positions and especially newly-completed Henderson Field on Guadalcanal. The only break in this routine was on October 11, when a surface force of heavy and light cruisers and destroyers, under Rear Admiral Norman Scott, later to be killed, intercepted a Japanese force off Cape Esperance, Guadalcanal, and sank one Japanese heavy cruiser and one destroyer, with the loss of one United States destroyer, *Duncan,* and damage to the light cruiser *Boise* and the heavy cruiser *Salt Lake City.*

In mid-October, Vice Admiral Halsey, who had missed Midway because of illness and who had been back in the States getting medical treatment, relieved Vice Admiral Ghormley as Commander in the South Pacific, and things began to change.

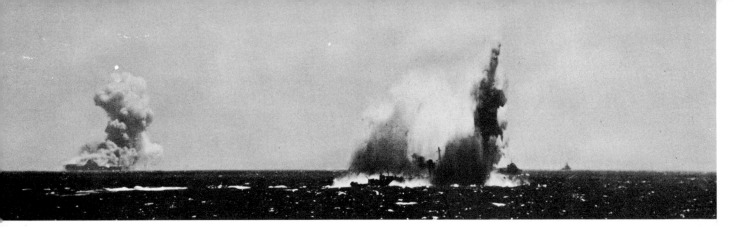

O'Brien is another submarine victim while **Wasp** burns.

Admiral Halsey knew that in sea warfare nothing pays off so heavily as audacity. He had proved it in the Marshall-Gilbert raids and the Wake-Marcus raids of the preceding February and March.

"Take off the neckties," was Halsey's first order. (There was still a good deal of spit and polish in the Fleet.) His second was "strike x repeat x strike." Outnumbered or not, the ships of the Pacific Fleet were going to go in and start hitting, not cruise around waiting to be torpedoed. Halsey knew the risks. "You can't make an omelet without breaking eggs," he told correspondents on his first survey flight through his new command in November, 1942. He also knew that you never won a naval war waiting for the other fellow to come to you. If you did, you fought it on his terms, not on your terms.

216

The Battle for Guadalcanal was building up to a climax when Admiral Halsey took command. With almost uncontested control of the sea in the immediate area, and with air superiority, the Japanese were able to build up their ground forces on Guadalcanal to a point where they had numerical superiority, or close to it. The all-out attack was set for late October. On October 25, *Hornet* and *Enterprise*, which had been rushed back from Pearl Harbor after her repairs, drove north to engage the vastly superior Japanese force. The battleship *South Dakota*, which had strained her bottom plates on an uncharted pinnacle just outside the harbor of Tongatabu in early September, had joined up with the carriers in place of *North Carolina*. But it was a small force compared to that the Japanese sent down, which was as follows:

Carriers — *Shokaku, Zuikaku, Zuiho,* and *Junyo;* battleships — *Kongo, Haruna, Hiei,* and *Kirishima;* ten heavy cruisers; two light cruisers; twenty-four destroyers.

The battle, fought off the Santa Cruz islands to the northeast of Guadalcanal, followed the pattern of the previous carrier engagements. Each group located the other about the same time. The air striking forces passed each other en route. On the American side, *Hornet* was so badly hit she had to be abandoned and sunk when the Japanese advance force of battleships and cruisers approached her near dusk. *Enterprise* again was hit by three bombs, but not put out of action, and *South Dakota*, the light cruiser *San Juan*, and the destroyer *Smith* all suffered damage. Seventy-four pilots and crewmen were lost.

Although the Japanese lost no ships, *Shokaku* and *Zuiho* were both hit, the former so badly she needed four months in the home island for repairs, and so were some of the cruisers and destroyers. They lost also, what was more important, over one hundred planes and trained pilots and air crews. And again the Japanese admirals showed a lack of daring that lost them their opportunity to drive in for a surface fight.

Captain Kikunori Kijima, who was aboard *Chikuma* as Chief of Staff of Cruiser Division Six, told United States questioners after the war that the Battle of Santa Cruz and the failure of the land

South Dakota *defends herself against torpedo attack.*

Hornet battles three attackers.

Enterprise speeds past a crashing enemy.

A damaged *Chikuma* class cruiser runs for home from *Santa Cruz.*

attack to break through at the same time was the turning point of the Solomon campaign. United States air and land reinforcements continued to go in. Japanese reinforcements dropped away to a trickle.

The final clinchers came the nights of November 12–13 and November 14–15, when first the United States cruiser force, led by Rear Admiral Daniel J. Callaghan and Rear Admiral Norman Scott (both of whom were killed) slugged it out with the *Hiei* and *Kirishima*, sinking — with the aid of planes the next day — *Hiei*, and then the battleships *South Dakota* and *Washington* polished off *Kirishima* in the second engagement. In the second battle, the new and superior radar equipment of the new American battleships decided the issue, *Washington* having *Kirishima* out of action before the Japanese had even seen her.

Equally as important as these surface-ship actions was the destruction, by Navy and Marine fliers from Guadalcanal, on November 14 and 15 of an entire train of eleven transports, aboard which was a division of reinforcements. It was to cover their approach that the Japanese had sent out the battleships. Seven of the transports were sunk the fourteenth. The other four managed to reach the island in a damaged condition and beach themselves. But they were able to put ashore only fifteen hundred troops. And those were so shocked by their ordeal, they added little to the shore defenses.

As Admiral Halsey had predicted, the cost had been high — the *Hornet*, the light cruisers *Atlanta* and *Juneau* and seven destroyers sunk, and other ships damaged. But the omelet made was a very satisfying one: control of the sea as well as the air.

The Japanese only made one more attempt at large-scale reinforcement. They sent in a destroyer force the night of November 30. They were intercepted off Tassafaronga by a force of four United States heavy cruisers, one light cruiser, and seven destroyers under command of Rear Admiral Carleton Wright. In the melee one Japanese destroyer was sunk, but the United States lost the heavy cruiser *Northampton*, both *New Orleans* and *Minneapolis* had their bows blown off by torpedoes, and

217

Atlanta had to be scuttled off Guadalcanal.

Minneapolis, *minus her bow, makes for Pearl Harbor and repairs.*

Pensacola was badly damaged. So it was hardly an American victory. However, the reinforcements were not landed.

In January, the Japanese gave up the fight for Guadalcanal and evacuated all the officers and some of the men in a night maneuver by twenty destroyers. The Japanese radio at the time officially admitted 16,500 men lost in the land fighting alone. The total was believed to be nearer 30,000. At sea, Japanese losses in men were not so high, but they were highly trained men who were lost. And what is even more important, the morale of the Japanese Navy was so shaken that it never rebounded. The Japanese Navy dropped back on the defensive, and suffered the fate of all navies which do that.

Island by island, the Marines and Army moved up the Solomon chain under naval protection through 1943, until they had Rabaul in fighter-plane range from Bougainville. That was the end of Japanese naval and air resistance in the South Pacific.

Long before the Bougainville beachhead was established, most of the United States major naval vessels had been withdrawn to the Central and North Pacific, where they covered the Attu campaign and the reoccupation of Kiska and started the long cruise through the Marshalls, the Carolines, and the Marianas to the Philippines, Iwo Jima, and the Japanese home islands.

Once control of the seas was attained, the issue of island warfare never was in doubt.

The deadly battle for the islands goes on.

218

WAR IN THE ATLANTIC 1941-1943

CHAPTER 19

The bombs falling on Pearl Harbor on December 7, 1941, must have sounded like the clap of thunder heralding doomsday to many Americans. To the British and their Allies fighting the Axis in the seas around Europe and the air above, it was the most hopeful sound since Hitler had struck at Poland two years and three months before. The Pacific was relatively remote to them. What was happening in the North Sea, the North Atlantic, and the Mediterranean was their immediate and vital concern. They knew that the attack at Pearl Harbor meant United States entry as a full combatant in the war against Germany and Italy. That meant that at long last there was hope of winning the war. They could hold on now with new resolve while America got ready.

The outlook at sea was black at the end of 1941. New construction in Britain and the United States was not keeping pace with ship sinkings. Britain's naval forces were growing weaker each

Targets of the wolf pack—supplies must continue in an end-less flow.

day, while the Axis submarine fleets were increasing in size and in effectiveness. As in the winter of 1916–1917, England, "that fortress built by Nature for herself," was in danger of being starved out, while Germany and Italy, with most of Europe in their control — which was not the situation with Germany and Austria-Hungary in World War I — were largely self-sufficient.

The first task of the United States in the Atlantic was to help Britain meet and conquer the submarine menace. That had to precede any Allied attack on the Axis land position in Europe and North Africa. On the success or failure of that depended the success or failure of the air war too. The big bombers could be flown across the ocean. But not the fuel to keep them flying. And not in sufficient quantities the bombs that they must drop. In World War II, that job of supply still was the task of the surface ship.

Conditions got worse before they got better. With a full-scale naval war going on in the Pacific, the Atlantic Fleet was on short rations of ships, men, and planes. Nazi submarines penetrated to within sight of America's great harbors on the Axis declarations of war on December 8 and sank shipping in sight of boardwalk strollers at Atlantic City and all up and down the Atlantic Coast. The year 1942 was the worst of the war for submarine sinkings, with the tonnage of 8,245,000 sunk almost twice as great as 1940 and 1941, when the figures were, respectively, 4,407,000 and 4,398,000. The chart on sinkings of German submarines began to rise, however, from nine in 1939, twenty-two in 1940, and thirty-five in 1941, to eighty-five in 1942. And, just as importantly, both United States and British ship-construction figures went up, those of the United States by almost 400 per cent. The gain-loss figure at the end of 1942 still

was minus 1,063,000 tons, but that was less than half the figure of net loss in 1941 and a third that of 1940. Construction in United States shipyards rose from 1,169,000 tons in 1941 to 5,339,000 tons in 1942.

The United States entry was not an abrupt transition from peace to war. The Navy had been waging "a shooting war" against the submarines as far east as Iceland for several months, to which point it had been escorting American ships with war materials for Britain. One destroyer, *Reuben James,* had been sunk on this duty and another, U.S.S. *Kearney,* hit by a torpedo. At Iceland, the convoys were turned over to the British Navy. The United States Neutrality Act also had been modified to void the "cash and carry" provision for belligerents. The first few months of declared war, however, were trying ones. United States shipping that had moved heretofore in coastwise trade without fear of attack found itself a prime target. Axis submarines lay submerged off the United States East Coast during the daylight hours, then surfaced at night to attack single ships moving close inshore. American coastal cities were browned out to lessen the sky glare, against which the coastal vessels were so starkly silhouetted.

Until American shipyards could catch up with the need to provide the anti-submarine escort vessels, many makeshifts were put into effect. Civilian aviators pooled their skills and their little pleasure planes to set up a coastal air patrol. Thousands of small-boat skippers were recruited with their frail craft to do day-and-night surface patrol of inshore sea lanes. Neither of these groups could take action against submarines, but they could and did report them. And the sound of their engines and the beat of their propellers on Axis eardrums served to make the submarine crews wary.

In the spring of 1943, the anti-submarine campaign was in full swing. A "Tenth Fleet" had been organized in the Navy Department at Washington to correlate all anti-submarine work. Escort carriers — some of which already had been built for Britain and had gone into action — were being turned out like automobiles in Detroit. The destroyer escort, a cheaply built anti-submarine ship of slow speed but long range, had been evolved, and they were sliding off the ways in increasing numbers. The blimp fleet had been augmented. New methods of detection had been perfected, including plane radar searches, which made it possible to detect submarines on the surface at night, and the magno-detector, which would record the presence of the undersea boats fathoms down, and which was being used by planes. It eventually effectively sealed the Gibraltar entrance to the Mediterranean. The rate of German submarine sinkings rose to twelve a week and held fairly constant there for the rest of the war. Convoys moved to and from Britain, and later North Africa and the Continent, on regular schedules and with few attacks.

Many submarine packs were hunted down by countering packs of escort carriers and destroyer escorts, and were kept so busy defending themselves they didn't even see a convoy. In one such brush near the end of the war, a task force of four escort carriers and seventy-five destroyers and destroyer escorts picked up one of these packs off Iceland and pursued it for several weeks, sinking eight of the twelve in the original flotilla before it ever reached the congested steamer lanes of the North Atlantic Coast. Submarine sinkings dropped to 3,611,000 tons in 1943, to 1,422,000 in 1944, and to 458,000 tons in the four months of 1945 before Germany surrendered. Troop convoys were given special protection and a better record for transport of United States soldiers was achieved than in 1917–1918. Of the 4,453,061 United States soldiers transported overseas by ships, only 3,604 were lost in sinkings.

The British anti-submarine forces did the major work of defeating the German and Italian submarine fleets. An Allied evaluation after the war credited the British with 640 of the 781 "kills" in the North Atlantic and North Sea, to 141 for United States forces.

Just as all phases of the war at sea in World War II were on a greater scale than in World War I, so was that by, and against, the submarine. In 1917, the first year of unrestricted warfare by the Germans, the toll of Allied shipping was 5,639,000 tons, and for the ten months of 1918, 2,562,000

Answer to the wolf pack—American destroyer escort and escort carrier—British and Canadian corvette and frigate.

Depth attack . . .

again attack . . .

and again attack.

American Coast Guard cutter **Eastwind** liquidates a German radio weather station on Greenland.

Safe arrival—a destroyer mothers her charges to port.

tons. The total from 1914 to 1918 was 11,018,805 tons. For 1939–1945, the comparable figure was 23,351,000. The figures on submarine sinkings show an even greater total for World War II — 781 for Germany from 1939 through April, 1945, against 178 in the four years of the first world conflict.

Grim as was the battle in the North Atlantic against the submarine, there was one convoy run that made the North Atlantic seem like a pleasure cruise. That was the route from Iceland through the Arctic Ocean past Norway and Finland to Murmansk, Soviet Russia's northernmost European port. Except for the Pacific route from the United States West Coast to Vladivostok, it was the only sea lane open between Soviet Russia and her allies. What made it such a hell run was that for almost its entire length it was within reach of German land-based aircraft. The restricted waters also made it a prime arena for German submarines. And always in the background was the menace of the surviving German surface ships, anchored in the Norwegian fjords, which made it necessary to screen each convoy with Allied war vessels capable of slugging it out with *Tirpitz*, *Scharnhorst,* and the other Nazi men-of-war.

It was the Murmansk run that made the setting for the last dramatic big-gun action of the

Scharnhorst—her last gamble—a British convoy.

Battle for Europe. On the day after Christmas, 1943, H.M.S. *Duke of York,* four British cruisers, and eight British destroyers cornered the last remaining undamaged German pocket battleship, *Scharnhorst,* and sank her off North Cape, Norway, the most northerly point of Europe. She had attempted to intercept a large Murmansk convoy.

Scharnhorst had been inactive since she had escaped from Brest, France, with *Gneisenau* on February 12, 1942. In late 1943 she was the only one of the five former German battleships still battleworthy. *Graf Spee* and *Bismarck* had been sunk. *Gneisenau* was at Gdynia, Poland, bomb-battered and unable to put to sea, and *Tirpitz* was in Tromsoe Fjord, neither seaworthy nor battleworthy. On September 22, 1943, three midget British submarines had penetrated Kaa Fjord and hurt her so badly she never saw action again. British bombers gave her the *coup de grâce* in December, 1944, when they found her in Tromsoe, hit her with twelve-thousand-pound bombs, and turned her over.

Scharnhorst was still very much a fighting ship when she put to sea on Christmas Day to try her luck against the convoy. She flew the flag of Rear Admiral Bey, an old destroyer man. Bey knew she would be outnumbered, perhaps outgunned. The weather was on her side, though, with hardly any daylight in those northern latitudes at that time of the year. And the prize was worth the risk. *Scharnhorst,* with her nine 11-inch guns, twelve 5.9's, and fourteen 4.1's could do more damage among a convoy of merchantmen in an hour than could a pack of submarines or half a hundred planes. With her high speed of twenty-nine knots, she stood a good chance of being able to outrun any British battleship she might meet, and her armament and armor was sufficient to beat off any

British cruisers. She was unescorted. In the murky seeing her men would have the advantage of knowing that any ship they sighted was an enemy.

The British Home Fleet had been expecting and awaiting just such a move. With the convoy for Murmansk off North Cape on December 26, were the usual destroyers — to counter submarine attack—and the three cruisers, *Norfolk, Belfast,* and *Sheffield.* Norfolk carried eight-inch, the other two were armed with six-inch guns. Two hundred miles to the southwest was the covering force — *Duke of York,* the light cruiser *Jamaica,* and four destroyers.

Everything worked out as the two Admiralties had planned it. *Scharnhorst* intercepted the convoy; *York* intercepted *Scharnhorst.* Official British Admiralty records put the battle in six phases.

Phase 1: Through the Arctic mists, at 9:35 A.M., December 26, 1943, the sweeping radar beams from H.M.S. *Belfast,* flag of Rear Admiral Burnett, picked out *Scharnhorst* on a collision course. The three British cruisers were south of the merchant vessels, guarding against just such an attack. They flung themselves at the big German vessel, twice their size, first illuminating her with star shells — necessary even at that time in the morning — and then opening fire with their main batteries. There was a British hit on the first salvo, and *Scharnhorst* turned sharply away and faded into the mist.

Bey went down with his ship ten hours and ten minutes later, so no one knows what were his reasons. A good one would be that he chose not to risk crippling damage in a fight with the torpedo-carrying cruisers while there was a chance he could run around them and get in among the unarmed merchant ships.

It was now a guessing game. And Admiral Burnett outguessed Admiral Bey. When the latter turned back toward the convoy, at 12:30 P.M., after a run at full speed to get athwart its course, he found the three British cruisers again across his path. Again he turned away, with *Belfast, Norfolk* and *Sheffield* in close pursuit. That was Phase 2.

Long before Phase 2 began, *Duke of York* was on her way. When the electrifying message flashed out from *Belfast* at 9:30 A.M. that she had sighted and was engaging *Scharnhorst,* Sir Bruce Fraser, Commander in Chief, British Home Fleet, wearing his flag in the *Duke,* turned on an intercepting course to put his force between *Scharnhorst* and her Norwegian bases. As the cruisers, keeping perilous contact with *Scharnhorst,* sent out frequent messages, *Duke of York* closed in. On the big chart of flag plot, the lines began to converge on Point X. At 4:15 P.M., while the cruisers still could not see *Duke* and did not know where she was, they received the message from Admiral Fraser to illuminate the enemy with star shells. The trap had

Duke of York opens fire.

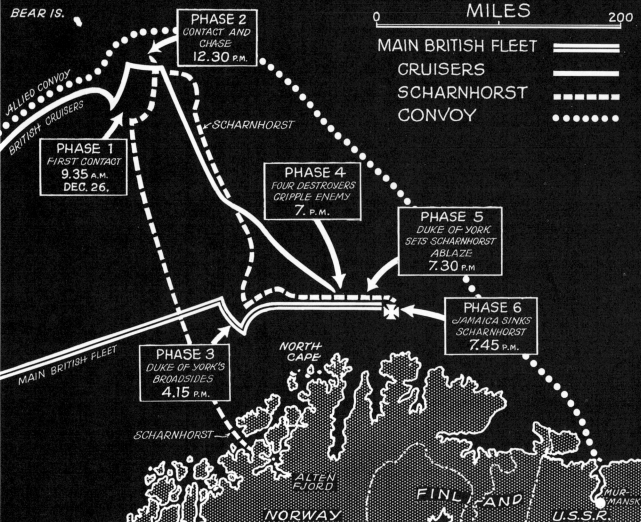

Scharnhorst, *attempting a convoy raid, is lured into the trap.*

been sprung. Phase 3 of the battle had begun.

Sharply illumined by the great light burning under the parachute that had burst out of the cruiser's star shell, *Scharnhorst* stood sharply etched against the dark winter sky for *Duke of York's* gunners. The first salvo of fourteen-inch shells was a straddle. The second salvo scored a hit. *Scharnhorst* again turned away and, using her superior speed, began to draw away from the British ships — all but the destroyers.

Phase 4 began at 7 P.M. with a destroyer attack from ahead by the four destroyers that had accompanied *Duke of York* — *Savage, Saumarez, Scorpion,* and the Norwegian *Stord*. As *Scharnhorst* had drawn away from the battleship, they had sped up on either side of her, but out of range of her eleven-inch guns and after almost three hours had won their attack position. Two on each side, they drove in to launch their torpedoes, firing from only two thousand yards — almost point-blank range for a torpedo attack. Several hit. Out of the hail of fire from *Scharnhorst's* batteries,

only *Saumarez* sustained a hit, and it was not damaging. The German battleship slowed to twenty knots.

The destroyers had done their work, slowed the enemy for the kill. At 7:30 P.M., *Duke of York* opened Phase 5 as she came within range and opened fire with all her guns. In minutes, *Scharnhorst* had taken several hits and was ablaze. By now, too, the three British cruisers that had been trailing her since twelve-thirty were in the melee, and four destroyers from the convoy escort had joined up. It was pitch-black by now, and it was difficult for the British ships to keep out of each other's way. Sir Bruce had the answer. "Clear the area of the target," he commanded, "except for those ships with torpedoes. One destroyer illuminate with searchlight." A thin pencil of light shot out from one of the destroyers, to silhouette the burning German vessel. Then *Jamaica,* maneuvering as at practice, got into position and fired a full broadside of torpedoes. At 7:45 P.M. *Scharnhorst* turned over and sank. Phase 6 was ended. Only a handful of *Scharnhorst's* more than one thousand men survived, to be pulled from the ice-cold waters by the British destroyer men.

There was fighting still to be done in the North Sea, in the English Channel, in the North Atlantic, and in the Mediterranean. But the last major surface menace to the convoys and to Allied operations had been removed. With the surrender of the Italian fleet and the scuttling of the battered survivors of the French fleet in Toulon the next summer, all major British ships were free to sail to join the United States fleet in the Pacific. *Duke of York* took part in the Okinawa campaign and was on hand for the Japanese surrender.

The submarine war, and the war at sea against the German airplanes, went on until the fall of Berlin and the German surrender. But from 1943 on it was a winning one. As in 1914–1918, Germany had been taught again the lesson of history, that the country which controls the seas rules the world. In World War II (1939–1945), sea power was the key to victory, in the Atlantic as in the Pacific.

Jamaica will finish *Scharnhorst* with torpedoes.

227

British midget submarine — three of her type severely damaged Tirpitz *in a Norwegian fjord.*

Tirpitz—sister to *Bismarck*.

The Royal Air Force visits *Tirpitz* . . .

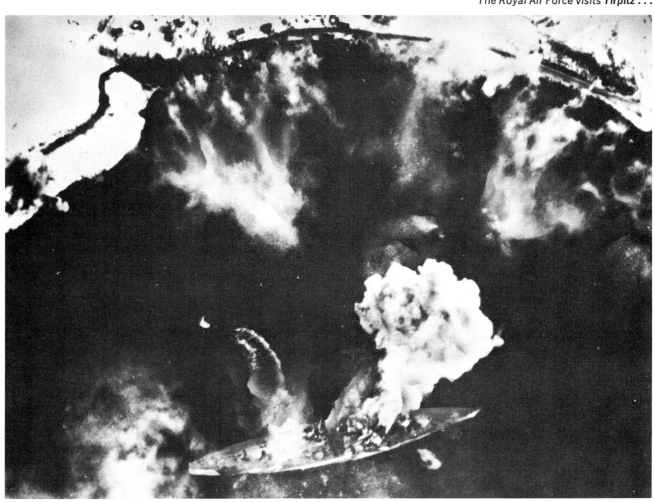

and she becomes a capsized hulk in Tromsoe Fjord.

Richelieu's main batteries open fire — all eight fifteen-inch rifles are located forward.

NORTH AFRICAN LANDINGS - 1943

From Casco Bay, Maine, from Hampton Roads, Virginia, from Hamilton Harbor at Bermuda, from Liverpool, Belfast, and other British and North Ireland ports, blue-gray United States and British battleships, aircraft carriers, destroyers, cutters, transports, and supply ships began to put to sea in late October and early November of 1942. Their destinations all were the same — the French-held north and northwest coasts of Africa. The greatest amphibious assault ever planned up to that time — an attack on a continent — was underway.

No one was ready. The United States Navy already was heavily committed in the Solomons, in the South Pacific, where the battle on Guadalcanal was going none too well. The United States had been in the war less than a year. Its great ship-building capacity was not yet being fully realized. Submarine sinkings still were running well ahead of replacements. Diplomatic as well as military

CHAPTER 20

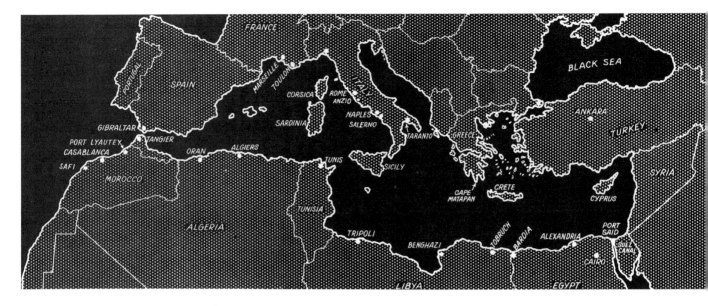

considerations dictated, however, that some action be taken by the Western Allies against Hitler beyond that of air raids, which, at that time, still were only in small force.

Two possibilities were an amphibious and airborne attack across the Channel against Nazi-held northern France and the Low Countries, or against Europe's "soft underbelly" — Italy and the Balkans. Hitler had attacked Soviet Russia in June of 1941, and the Russians since had been demanding the setting up of a Second Front, which the United States and Britain desired as much as did Stalin, but which they felt themselves unable to accomplish on the scale that was needed. The situation in Russia, with the German armies holding Stalingrad and Leningrad under siege, and still in sight of Moscow, was critical. If an attack from the West was delayed too long, there was the possibility that Soviet Russia might be knocked out of the war.

Despite the slender resources available, the United States Joint Chiefs of Staff favored an attack on northern France. Prime Minister Winston Churchill and his military advisors were insistent on an attack from the south instead. They believed it had a much greater chance of success. Hitler never had been able to secure the full collaboration of the French, despite the efforts of Pierre Laval and Admiral Darlan, thus leaving southern France and northern Africa still largely in friendly French hands, with the possibility of only token resistance. The attack across the Channel would be a direct engagement with the German Army, Air Force, and Navy.

The decision finally was reached to make the first move against North Africa to secure bases for an attack on Italy. The United States had continued to retain diplomatic relations with Marshal Pétain's Vichy government, and there was believed to be a fair chance that if the Allied invasion of North Africa was in sufficient force to give fair assurance of success, the co-operation of many French commanders there might be expected. General Weygand, the former French Chief of Staff and North African Commander, was reported to have said: "If the English come with twenty divisions, I will embrace them; if they come with four, I will fight." The diplomatic wheels immediately were set in motion, through the United States diplomatic staff in Vichy and State Department representatives in North Africa, who were headed by Robert Murphy, Counselor of the American Embassy. Mr. Murphy had been sent to Algiers by President Roosevelt as early as 1940 to encourage the French leaders there to resist any German attempts to take over that area. The military plan drafting began both in London, where General Eisenhower and Admiral Stark were the top United States Army and Navy commanders, respectively, and in Washington.

The strategic plan for the operation — which was given the code name of "Torch" — was to seize the northwest Atlantic coastal ports of French Morocco, particularly Casablanca, and the Algerian ports of Oran and Algiers on the Mediterranean. Since neither the United States nor Britain had either the men or the ships to mount such an operation alone, it had to be planned as a joint operation, which added to the difficulty.

It finally was decided to entrust the action to three separate task forces. Seizure of the Moroccan Atlantic coastal ports was to be carried out by an all-American naval and military force. The attack, or occupation, of Oran, was to be made by a joint United States–British force, the United States Army furnishing the landing force and the British the naval escort. The seizure of Algiers and that part of the Algerian coast was to be done by another joint United States–British force, with the landing force part British Army and part United States Army and the naval escort wholly British. The forces were designated, in order, as Western Task Force, Center Task Force, and Eastern Task Force. In addition, Britain's famed Force H, the British Navy task group based on Gibraltar that had fought so valiantly to maintain control of the western Mediterranean since 1939, was to cover the Mediterranean operations, guarding against any sortie by either the remnants of the French fleet at Oran, Algiers, and Toulon, or the battered Italian fleet from its Mediterranean and Adriatic bases.

Amphibious operations still were in a formative stage when the planning for Operation Torch was begun. But the main outlines — which held until war's end — were that the Navy was in overall command during the passage from base to target and until the Army was securely set up ashore. Then the Army commander was supreme and could call on the Navy for fire support — from gun or plane — for reinforcement, and for quick supply. That seems so logical a division of authority — each specialist doing the job for which he had the

training and the knowledge — that it would seem there could be no questioning of it. Many Army officers did question it, however. When things went wrong in the Algiers operation, Major General Charles W. Ryder, the Army commander, officially recommended that in future operations the Army take command as soon as the men were put into the boats, and that the boat crews be Army personnel, not Navy personnel. Admiral Sir Andrew Cunningham, over-all commander of the Mediterranean operations, made the fitting reply to that: "This (Ryder's proposal) is not the real answer," he wrote. "The solution is that, whatever uniform the crews wear, they must be trained seamen with special practice in the technique of landing operations, and in close touch with the requirements of the troops they have to land and maintain." General Ryder had confused theory with practice. The theory was sound, as was proved many times later. It was lack of practice and experience that caused the trouble at Algiers. The Navy was no more to blame for that than was the Army.

Torch was a ship-to-shore operation, as distinguished from a shore-to-shore movement, such as was largely the assault on the Normandy beaches a year and a half later. In a ship-to-shore assault, the assault forces are taken by large transport from their base to a point off a hostile shore. They then man the small boats in which they make the attack. In a shore-to-shore operation, the assault troops enter their attack craft at the base and

Destination North Africa.

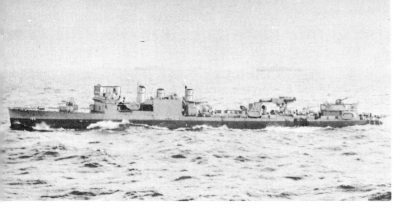

Old veteran of '19 — destroyer **Bernadou** patrols off North Africa.

are carried in them direct to the target beach.

Since all ship-to-shore operations are essentially the same, differing only in detail, an examination of that phase of Operation Torch carried out by the all-American Western Task Force will give a good over-all picture of all similar amphibious assaults, even though it was the smallest of the three forces engaged in Operation Torch — a lift of thirty-seven thousand troops against thirty-nine thousand for the Center Group and eighty-three thousand for the Eastern Group, which attacked the Algiers area.

The objective of the Western Task Force was to attack and seize control of the French Moroccan coast from Port Lyautey, the northernmost port, to Safi, 250 miles to the south. Casablanca, the main target, lay about a third of the way south from Fort Lyautey. Frontal assaults were not planned. Attacks were to be made across flanking beaches, and then envelopment. The hope, partly realized, was that French resistance would be only token, so that the harbors could be taken little damaged and immediately put to use.

Rear Admiral (later Vice Admiral) Henry K. Hewitt, USN, Commander Amphibious Force Atlantic Fleet, was put in command of the Western

Task Force. Major General (later General) George F. Patton, Jr., was in charge of the thirty-seven thousand Army troops. Admiral Hewitt was in full charge of the operation until General Patton was firmly ashore with all his troops.

The United States naval forces engaged were divided into two main categories: Covering Group and Attack Group. The latter was further divided into Air Group, Fire Support Group, and Transport Group.

The Covering Group of Western Task Force was composed of the new thirty-five-thousand-ton, sixteen-inch-gunned battleship *Massachusetts*, the eight-inch-gunned heavy cruisers *Wichita* and *Tuscaloosa*, and four destroyers. Their principal task was to guard against interception by an enemy surface group of which the most powerful was that at Dakar, the French battleship *Richelieu*, three cruisers, and destroyers. The Covering Group served the same tactical purpose as Force H in the Mediterranean. If conditions permitted, they also could furnish fire support for land operations. As it worked out, that is what they did, since no major German, Italian, or French naval units attempted to interfere with the landings. Rear Admiral Robert C. Giffen was in charge of the Covering Group, flying his flag in *Massachusetts*.

The Attack Group was divided into three sections. One attacked the Port Lyautey region. It was called the Northern Attack Group. A second attacked the Casablanca area. It was called Center Attack Group. A third attacked the Safi area. It was called Southern Attack Group.

The Northern Group of Western Task Force was made up as follows: Transport Group (transports and supply ships) — *Henry T. Allen, John Penn, George Clymer, Susan B. Anthony, Electra,*

A salvo from **Jean Bart** overshoots an American cruiser off Casablanca.

Augusta fires a full eight-inch salvo at shore batteries.

Algorab, Florence Nightingale, and *Anne Arundel;* Fire Support Group — the old battleship *Texas* and the light cruiser *Savannah;* Air Group — the converted carriers *Sangamon* and *Chenango.* With each group were screening destroyers, and with the force a fleet oiler, two mine sweepers, and a small aircraft tender, *Barnegat.* The destroyers were *Roe, Livermore, Kearny, Ericsson, Parker, Hambleton,* and *Macomb.* The submarine *Shad* served as a guide to lead the force in to the debarking area.

The Center Attack Group was made up of: Transport Group — *Leonard Wood, Thomas Jefferson, Charles Carroll, Joseph T. Dickman, William P. Biddle, Joseph Hewes, Tasker H. Bliss, Edward Rutledge, Hugh L. Scott, Ancon, Elizabeth C. Stanton, Thurston, Procyon, Oberon,* and *Arcturus;* Fire Support Group — the heavy cruiser *Augusta* and the light cruiser *Brooklyn;* Air Group — the carrier *Ranger* and the converted carrier *Suwanee.* Screening the various groups were the light cruiser *Cleveland* and the destroyers *Wilkes, Swanson, Ludlow, Murphy, Bristol, Woolsey, Edison, Tillman, Boyle, Rowan, Ellyson, Forrest, Fitch, Corry,* and *Hobson.* The submarines *Gunnel* and *Herring* acted as guides for the Center Attack Group. Also along were three mine sweepers, three mine layers, and the fleet oiler *Winooski.*

The Southern Attack Group was composed of the following: Transport Group — *Harris, Calvert, Titania, Dorothea, Lyon,* and *Lakehurst;* Fire Support Group — the old battleship *New York* and the light cruiser *Philadelphia;* Air Group — the converted carrier *Santee.* Screening the various units were the destroyers *Mervine, Knight, Beatty, Cowie, Quick, Doran, Cole Bernadou, Rodman,* and *Emmons.* The submarine *Barb* was the beacon ship

French cruisers came out to intercept but . . .

for the Southern Force. Also in attendance were two mine sweepers and a mine layer, the fleet oilers *Housatonic* and *Merrimack,* and a fleet tug.

The 105 vessels of the Western Task Group sailed over a period of a week from four different harbors. The five beacon submarines rendezvoused at New London, Connecticut, and took their departure from Montauk Point, Long Island, on October 19 and 20. The transports of the Northern and Southern Groups left Hampton Roads on October 23 and headed southwesterly. The transports of the Southern Group left the next day and headed northeasterly, as though bound for Britain. The Covering Group, led by *Massachusetts,* left Casco Bay (Portland), Maine, also on the twenty-fourth. A day later the Air Force Groups, under command of Rear Admiral Ernest D. McWhorter, left Bermuda, where they had been training for several days.

233

On October 26, the transport groups rendezvoused with Admiral Giffen's Covering Force north of Bermuda, and on October 28, the carriers joined up several hundred miles to eastward. They proceeded toward Morocco together, twice refueling from the accompanying fleet oilers, until the

are turned back by American guns.

British sea and air power join the assault.

 night of November 6, when the Southern Group broke off and headed southeasterly for Safi, and the other two continued on toward Casablanca and Port Lyautey.

The bare recital of the start of Operation Torch makes it sound much more simple than it was. Even before the decision had been made at London on July 25, that North Africa should be the first target for the United States–British attack in the European theater of war, Admiral Hewitt and his staff had begun preliminary planning. Old coastal surveys were brought up-to-date through French sources, through aerial photographs, through submarine reconnaissance. Tides and weather records were studied. Then, as D-Day approached, accurate, up-to-the-minute weather reports were compiled and transmitted to the force commanders. Training for amphibious operations was carried on as intensively as was possible with available men and weapons.

Operation Torch was made with transports and landing craft that were crude by the yardstick of later attacks. Only the smaller landing craft, such as were used by the Marines at Guadalcanal — LCP's, LCP(R)'s and LCV's — were available in November, 1942. The LST's, the LCI's, the amphibious tractors and the amphibious tanks and jeeps, which were to play so important a part in later Pacific operations, still were to come. Some of them were only in the drafting-board stage

when the landings were begun at Port Lyautey, Fedala, near Casablanca, and Safi, in the early morning hours of November 8, 1942.

Despite the diplomatic negotiations with the French, culminating in the submarine visit of Major General Mark Clark to some French leaders in Algeria, the attack came as a surprise to most of the French commanders, few of whom had been a party to the negotiations or had known of them, and particularly to the Germans and Italians. Mussolini's son-in-law, Count Ciano, wrote in his diary that the Axis leaders had no prior knowledge of the U.S. Western Task Force, or its target, and they believed the two groups that attacked Algeria — which ships had been sighted when they passed through the Strait of Gibraltar — were only a convoy to Malta. The failure to take the French more completely into confidence caused much unnecessary fighting, especially at Casablanca. But surprise was considered a more important factor.

Despite the expressed pre-sailing pessimism of General Patton, who was quoted as saying that the Navy had never in its history "landed an army at the planned time and place," the attack by the Western Task Group was begun almost on schedule. Each of the three task groups was at its assigned area off the Moroccan coast within minutes of the hour decided on weeks before. Where there were breakdowns, they were between ship and shore. Most of them were because of insufficient

234

Aftermath—immobilized French units in Casablanca Harbor.

also on shore batteries, air fields, and on enemy ships. Forty-four of 172 Navy planes engaged were lost, but some of these losses were operational. Most of the personnel in the planes lost were rescued, or were released from imprisonment after French capitulation.

The only naval surface resistance came from the French naval forces at Casablanca, where was moored the uncompleted French battleship, *Jean Bart*. Unable to steam, she fired her four fifteen-inch guns as a fixed battery until she was put out of action by plane attacks and by five hits from *Massachusetts'* sixteen-inch guns. The Covering Group had taken on the task of silencing *Jean Bart* and shore batteries. When French Admiral Micheler, who fought his small forces well, sent two destroyer leaders, *Miland* and *Albatross* (twenty-five hundred tons, five 5½-inch guns, four torpedo tubes), and the five destroyers *L'Alcyon, Brestois, Boulonnais, Fougueux,* and *Frondeur* (fourteen hundred tons, four 5.1-inch guns, four torpedo tubes) out to attack the transports, it was the Center Force's Support Group that intercepted and drove them back. These were the cruisers *Augusta* and *Brooklyn* and the destroyers *Wilkes* and *Swanson.* The destroyer *Ludlow*, one of the immediate transport guard, also participated.

The French destroyers, eight French submarines, the light cruiser *Prikauguet*, and three French corvettes made a second sortie the afternoon of the eighth, and again on November 9, before Admiral Micheler finally received orders from Algiers to halt the fighting. *Jean Bart* also got her guns back into action, but was bombed into silence by Navy planes. Under the fire of *Augusta, Brooklyn,* and also Admiral Giffen's Covering Force, and through bombing and strafing American Navy planes, the French lost all eight submarines and four destroyers. Every other French ship was damaged. The only damage done to American ships were single-shell hits on *Massachusetts, Brooklyn, Wichita,* and *Ludlow.* That on *Massachusetts* came from a shore battery. None was serious; no one was killed.

On November 11 — the twenty-fourth anniversary of the Armistice ending World War I — everything was well in hand off the Moroccan

training and the natural hazards of landing in darkness on a hostile shore. The support and covering forces kept all French naval units away from the transports, despite several well-planned sorties by the destroyer groups at Casablanca, and gave accurate and continuing fire support to the troops ashore. It could have been more effective had there not been the uncertainty as to French reaction and an expressed command desire to do as little damage as possible, especially to inhabited areas. This paid off well in French good will after resistance was overcome or suspended, but it didn't make for the most efficient attack.

Navy air played its important part, even though the carrier fliers, like the small-boat men, had had little time for training and were participating in their first combat landing operation. French fighter planes strafed the beaches, but there was no interference with the cruiser and battleship planes spotting fire for their ships, and no transports were hit by bombs. The American planes made effective bombing and strafing attacks

Dutch ships continue the transport of troops and supplies.

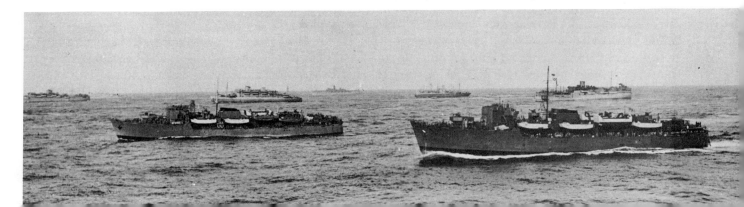

*Powerful silhouette—**Valiant, Nelson, Rodney,** and **Warspite** ready for Sicily.*

coast. French resistance had ceased, and French co-operation begun. Casablanca Harbor lay open to the American transports, which had been lying in the open sea off Safi, Fedala, and Port Lyautey since the early morning hours of November 8. Admiral Hewitt, however, made the decision to keep the harbor clear for a fast convoy that was due in on November 13, and declined requests of the transport command to move inside. It proved a costly decision. Three German submarines, which had been steaming toward the scene for three days, arrived the night of November 11 and the next day. Despite determined efforts of the destroyer guard and anti-submarine plane patrols, they succeeded in penetrating the screen and torpedoing the transports *J. Hewes, Tasker Bliss, Edward Rutledge,* and *Hugh L. Scott,* the tanker *Winooski,* and the destroyer *Hamilton.* The transports all were sunk. The other two American ships were salvaged. The cargo ship *Electra* of the Northern Group was torpedoed November 15, while proceeding to Casablanca, but she was beached and later salvaged. Had Admiral Hewitt made the other decision, the Morocco expedition might have been carried through without loss of a single ship.

The expedition against Algeria went no less successfully, although there naval losses were much higher. Axis submarine reaction was quicker, and the German and Italian Air Force had Oran and Algiers in range. Eight transports, three destroyers, an escort carrier, two cutters, a sloop, a mine sweeper, an anti-aircraft cruiser, a corvette, a collier, and an ammunition ship fell to Axis submarines or planes. All but one of these losses — the transport *Leedstown* — were British.

The successful conclusion of an assault is for the Navy, as well as for the Army, only the end of the beginning. Then starts the hard, grinding work of harbor clearance and repair, base building, and always, the convoying of men and supplies from rear base to fighting line. For the African invasion, the United States was rear base, a rear base over three thousand miles away. Every shell, every landing mat, every gallon of gasoline and oil, and almost every pound of food that was needed by our forces in North Africa was carried there across the North Atlantic by Navy-guarded convoys.

Caught between the British forces driving in from the east and the American and British forces driving from the west, the Italian and German armies finally were pinned in the Tunisian peninsula by early May, and on May 12, General Dwight D. Eisenhower, Allied Commander, announced that Africa was "secure."

Long before the remnants of the two enemy armies surrendered at Bizerte, plans were laid to get the ships and wheels moving for the next advance, to Sicily. The landing craft that were not yet ready in November — the LST's, LCI's, LCT's and DUKW's — were rolling off the assembly lines in the States by the score in early 1943, thence making the long voyage to the Mediterranean. The LST's and LCI's made the twenty-day trip under their own power. The LCT's and the DUKW's made it perched on top of the LST's, or on their tank decks.

By July 1, everything was in readiness for Operation Husky — the attack on Sicily. Every North African harbor was jammed with Allied ships, from battleships down to LCT's. On July 6, the great flotilla of 2,500 ships and 250,000 men got underway for the first assault on what Winston Churchill had called the "soft underbelly of Europe." It was soft only relatively.

The attack on Sicily was largely a shore-to-shore operation. One assault force had come from England in large transports, but the bulk of the attack transports were the actual landing craft, which steamed directly into the beaches — or as close as they could get in shallow water — and put their loads of men and tanks and guns directly on the shore instead of into small boats for the last leg, as was necessary in a ship-to-shore assault such as that on the North African beaches.

Sicily was, in its essentials, a repeat performance of Casablanca and Fedala and Oran. And a preview on a small scale of the assault a year later on Normandy. Again the British and United States naval forces landed the troops on schedule. Again there were mistakes, but only small ones. Again the combatant ships were called on to furnish the artillery support for the advancing infantry against enemy strong points, tank columns, and troop concentrations. Again they delivered. In a month Sicily was secured. Then came Italy.

Two of the bloodiest beachheads of the European war were those of Salerno and Anzio, where the two Italian landings were made. At each beach the supporting naval vessels had to stay and slug it out with enemy shore batteries and enemy aviation. In each case they did. In testimony at his war-crimes trial in Nuremberg after the war, Field Marshal Kesselring, the German Commander in the Italian campaign, said that it was the Anzio operation that broke the back of his defense. It drove a wedge against his southward supply line to Cassino. In attempting to drive its beachhead defenders back into the sea, he exhausted his reserves. Naval fire support, especially at Anzio, was a decisive factor in the success of each operation. The Anzio naval force, under the command of Rear Admiral Frank J. Lowry, made the coastal roads above and below Anzio unusable by the Germans during daylight and sealed the fate of the enemy armies below Rome.

With the surrender of the Italian fleet in September, 1943, the Mediterranean became, in effect, an Allied lake. A few German submarines still operated out of French ports, and there was still a considerable concentration of French naval vessels at Toulon. This threat also was ended the following summer, when the landings in southern France were made and Allied naval activities in European waters, except for convoy and supply, shifted to the English Channel, the North Sea, and the Rhine.

Warspite's guns hammer Sicily installations.

A burning landing craft lights up a transport off Salerno.

238

NORMANDY AND SOUTHERN FRANCE

The successful landings in North Africa in November, 1942, and the United States triumph on Guadalcanal marked, as Sir Winston Churchill said, "the end of the beginning" of the Allied march toward victory over the Axis Powers and Japan.

At six thirty the morning of June 6, 1944, the first waves of British and American troops began wading ashore on sixty miles of beach of Normandy Province of northern France to commence the "beginning of the end" of the war in Europe.

In an order of the day on June 5 to the Allied naval forces under his command, Admiral Sir Bertram Ramsay, the Supreme Naval Commander, called it "the greatest amphibious operation in history."

The famed Spanish Armada of 1588 totaled only 130 ships. It would have been lost in the great fleet that sailed from England on that June day of 1944 for the Far Shore, as the Normandy beaches were called. There were 2,727 ships and

Dangerous work—Nazi mines laid in the ship channels are exploded by minesweepers.

small craft engaged on the first day alone. They ranged from battleships to PT boats. From the air it must have seemed that a determined man could have walked dry-footed from Plymouth on the English shore to the French coast.

Years later it still seems incredible that such an array of ships of all sizes and shapes could have sortied from ports only a nautical stone's throw from the German-held beaches and that most of them could have arrived at their assigned positions off the French shore without a single hostile shot being fired at them. It was not until 5 A.M. (broad daylight in those latitudes) that German shore batteries opened on two American destroyers that were in the vanguard.

By that hour, channels had been swept for the invading transports, small craft and fire support ships and underwater demolition teams already were at work inshore dismantling mines and blowing up the elaborate system of obstacles the Germans had erected along the beach.

This tactical surprise was a major factor in the success of Operation Neptune-Overlord, the code name given this historic invasion of Hitler's Fortress Europe. The name Neptune, which was not as well publicized as that of Overlord, referred to the naval phases.

Plans for Neptune-Overlord had been in the making for over a year. The active phase began in March, 1943, when a Combined Planning Staff headed by a British officer, Lieutenant General Sir Frederick E. Morgan, was set up in London. It went into high gear when General of the Army Dwight D. Eisenhower, then wearing only four stars, was named as Supreme Commander by President Franklin D. Roosevelt. That was Christmas Eve, 1943.

The Supreme Naval Commander under General Eisenhower, Admiral Ramsay of the Royal Navy, had come out of retirement at the beginning of World War II to head the Dover Patrol and win his place in history as the organizer of the Dunkirk evacuation.

The bulk of the naval forces assigned were British and American. But also included were Canadian, French, and Dutch cruisers, destroyers, and gunboats. Heading the United States contingent were the old battleships *Arkansas*, *Nevada*, and *Texas*. *Nevada* had been sunk at Pearl Harbor on December 7, 1941, but had been raised to fight valiantly in several amphibious operations. Normandy, and the following Cherbourg bombardments, marked her finest hours of the war. The other major American ships involved were the

Thirty months from the mud floor of Pearl Harbor, **Nevada**
opens fire on the enemy guns . . .

as the shore batteries' answers splash in near misses.

heavy cruisers *Augusta*, *Quincy*, and *Tuscaloosa*.

Some of these did not arrive in British waters until a few weeks before D-Day. Washington had thought the British capable of furnishing fire support for all the Normandy landings. But the British still were fearful of a breakout of remaining German ships from Norwegian or German ports and insisted on keeping strong forces on guard in the North Sea against that possibility.

The ranking American naval officer was Alan G. Kirk, then a rear admiral who was to go on from a distinguished naval career to a postwar one in diplomacy. He was in charge of Western Naval Task Force, which covered the American landings on Omaha and Utah beaches and aided in the capture of Cherbourg. Admiral Kirk flew his flag in *Augusta*. (No American naval forces were in the assault and support groups for the British landings to eastward.) Under Admiral Kirk in charge of various Allied naval assault or bombardment groups were Rear Admirals Don P. Moon, Morton L. Deyo, John L. Hall, and C. F. Bryant.

Admiral Kirk had been Naval Attaché in London at the outbreak of the war and was familiar with many British Navy personalities and with British methods and nomenclature. He took up his post in November, 1943. The invasion had been set for the spring or early summer of 1944 at the Quebec Conference the previous August.

Planning for the invasion began to get up a full head of steam with the arrival of General Eisenhower in England on January 14. General Eisenhower, in his early thinking about the invasion of Europe, envisioned a simultaneous assault from the north and from the south. He also favored a five-division front for the northern landing instead of the three-division front that had been agreed on at the Quebec conference the previous August. When it finally was agreed that there were not enough assault craft and covering ships available for both attacks, General Eisenhower reluctantly agreed to a postponement until August 15 for the assault in Southern France. All efforts then centered on Normandy.

The Germans were not unaware of what was being planned. Long before the spring of 1944, Hitler had ordered a defense built along the French and Belgian coasts, and in November, 1943, he placed his best-known general, Field Marshal Erwin Rommel, the former leader in North Africa, as tactical commander of the beach defense forces in the event of attack.

Directly across the Channel from England, the most elaborate beach fortifications were placed. Guns up to 210 mm. were spotted strategically to cover the landing beaches from the Pas-de-Calais opposite Dover on the east to the Contentin Peninsula and the vital port of Cherbourg to the southwest. In the German command in early June were fifty-eight divisions.

At sea, the Germans had no such defensive array. Under Admiral Krancke in the Bay of Biscay and the French Channel ports were only three destroyers, five large torpedo boats, thirty E Boats, similar to Allied PT's, and thirty-six submarines. They did little to slow the invasion. Their most effective effort was an attack on a practice deployment the night of April 27–28 when they got undetected among the American landing craft and sank two LST's with a loss of 638 men, more than the losses at Utah Beach on D-Day.

The British and American air forces also had practically driven the German *Luftwaffe* from the skies over France by early 1944. So the assault depended on how well air and naval bombardment could neutralize the beach defenses and how fast the navy could put the men ashore to establish a beachhead and then break out of it. One of the major tasks of the Allied air forces that was done superbly was to so bomb rail and road lines leading

Floating breakwater sections are brought into place.

Air bombardment pounds supply areas . . .

243

and batters enemy communications.

To drop behind the lines—British paratroopers board their plane.

into the Valley of the Seine that many essential supplies needed for the defense never reached the Germans.

The American buildup in England had been going ahead rapidly, both as to men and to equipment. At the time of the attack, it was estimated there were 1,100,000 American soldiers, 425,000 airmen, and 125,000 sailors based in or on the British Islands. Most of them played a part, directly or indirectly, in the assault on Fortress Europe.

In landing craft, the United States also made the major contribution, furnishing, in fact, all of the largest craft used in the attack, the Landing Ship, Tank (LST). Every other area of combat, in the Pacific and in the Mediterranean, was stripped to a bare minimum to build up Operation Neptune-Overlord. Which was, of course, necessary. This was a major effort against a prepared, resolute foe. The effort proved to be none too great.

As D-Day neared, all disagreement among the British and American leaders faded. Even Winston Churchill, who had opposed any movement across the Channel until Germany was much nearer collapse than she was in the early days of 1944, began to view the prospects with enthusiasm.

The plans as finally agreed on were for a landing of five divisions — three British, two American — on a fifty-mile front from the mouth of the Orne River to a point halfway up the Contentin Penin-

sula. Two airborne divisions were to drop behind the American beach areas and one behind the British in the night hours before the daylight landings, to seize strategic crossroads and bar reinforcements by the Germans of the beach defenses.

The final great decisions — the day and the hour — were set on May 1. D-Day was to be between June 4 and 8. H-Hour was to be at sunrise or thereabouts, a few hours after low water so the landing craft would go in on a rising tide. (The tides ranged from eighteen feet to twenty-five along the Normandy beaches.) There also had to be enough moonlight earlier to enable the paratroopers to distinguish targets in their areas. The period early in June and one in mid-June were the only two that met those conditions. Early in May, Admiral Ramsay advised General Eisenhower that either June 5 or June 6 would be acceptable, and June 5 was named. Two twenty-four-hour postponements would be possible, but no more.

One thing always is certain in the English Channel. In any month there will be at least one first-class storm. On June 4, with many ships already on the move, a typical northwester was blowing. Conditions looked hopeless. And they were for an assault on June 5. A postponement was ordered. Captain J. M. Stagg, the Royal Air Force meteorologist on Eisenhower's staff, predicted a diminution of the wind and rain for June 6, and

The assault on the beaches of France begins.

The naval shelling continues—**Arkansas'** guns go into action.

twenty-four hours before H-Hour, General Eisenhower gave the word. "O.K. Let's go," was the way he was reported to have phrased it.

The turn in the weather so accurately forecast by Captain Stagg was not foreseen by the Germans, since they had no accurate information as to conditions in the North Atlantic. They thought conditions were so forbidding the landings would not be attempted. This was an important factor in the surprise. The Germans were resting in their tents on D-Day and were slow to react. The landings might have been much more bloody than they were.

Hitler also had invoked his mystic sense, which sometimes had worked well but this time did not, to decide that the Pas-de-Calais area was the main Allied target. He ordered the defense concentrated there. It was days before the landings to westward were read by the Germans as anything but a diversion. Dummy camps in East Anglia, in southeastern England, and pretended invasion activity there, helped delude the Germans.

Many vessels of the great armada of almost three thousand craft already were under way when Eisenhower gave the signal to attack. All they had to do was to keep on going. This was true of the American bombardment force headed by the old battleships *Arkansas*, *Nevada*, and *Texas* and the

three new heavy cruisers *Augusta*, *Quincy*, and *Tuscaloosa*. They had been basing on Belfast Lock, in Northern Ireland. They were in the Irish Sea headed south when the first twenty-four-hour postponement came and merely countermarched during the night until the new order came early the morning of the fifth. Then they turned again for France.

In the van of the vast Allied array were the mine sweepers. They had one of the hardest and most hazardous tasks of the fleet. Of relatively small size, lightly armed and lightly armored, they were in constant danger of being blown to kingdom come by the mines they were attempting to sweep and explode. The first shot at Utah Beach was fired shortly after 5 A.M. at them by German shore batteries. The British cruiser *Black Prince* answered, and in a few minutes the whole beach was aflame. Targets had been selected before the bombardment forces sailed, based on aerial reconnaissance maps. Ship fire also was depended on to breach the sea walls, explode mine fields along the beaches, keep the emplaced German guns so busy they would not have time to concentrate on the small boats landing the men along the beaches, and hold the German defenders in their bunkers to the last moment.

Unlike some of the landings in the Pacific and those in North Africa in late 1942, the naval phase

American paratroopers are hauled aloft in a glider.

Men and materiel pour onto the beaches . . .

and still they come . . . |247

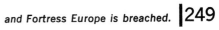

and Fortress Europe is breached. |249

Sunken ships form a breakwater and also function as mooring spots for small craft.

of the Normandy beachheads was largely ship against shore, with little worry about naval or air attack. Of the five American ships lost, only one, *Meredith,* a destroyer, was an air victim. She was hit by a glide bomb in a night aerial attack. Another destroyer, *Glennon,* was damaged in part by gunfire. But she first had been stopped by a mine. A third destroyer, *Corry,* a destroyer escort, the *Rich,* and the transport *Susan B. Anthony* all fell victims to mines.

There is not space in a brief history to tell in detail all the naval phases of Normandy. The Allied ships did put the men ashore, did cover the landings creditably, and did keep the men and the supplies pouring in. A storm on the nineteenth and twentieth of June destroyed the artificial harbors formed by sunken ships, caissons, and floating docks off the American beaches. But by that time, so much equipment was ashore and so many men that the security of the beachhead was not seriously imperiled.

Commanders on both sides, German as well as American and British, praised the accuracy of naval gunfire and the fortude with which the attacks were made during the first three anxious days before the Army artillery was ashore in suffi-

250

Landing craft takes supplies off a sunken Liberty ship.

Invasion of Southern France—landing ship tanks (LSTs) are loaded with materiel at an Italian port.

Quincy's *rifles fire at Nazi shore guns.*

cient number. Some of the American destroyers dared shoal water on D-Day to deal with German defenses in critical areas.

Field Marshal Gerd von Runstedt, supreme German commander in the west, credited naval fire with having been a decisive factor in preventing effective counterattack during the first few critical days. Other German commanders were no less impressed. With no previous experience they hardly could foresee naval fire accuracy, nor could they credit its efficacy.

When the storm of June 19–20 swept away the artificial harbor, or "mulberry" as it was called, off the American beaches, the need to secure the port of Cherbourg became urgent. The Contentin Peninsula had been sealed off by elements of the VII Corps, led by Major General J. Lawton (Lightning Joe) Collins, by June 18. Four days later, the American forces, swollen to six divisions and combined with other attack groups, began the advance to clear the peninsula of its garrison of forty thousand Germans and open Cherbourg to Allied shipping.

*Old cruiser **Omaha** convoying off Southern France.*

Allied naval support had been offered to General Collins. But Lightning Joe, like many of his contemporaries, could not believe even after D-Day at Utah Beach that naval fire could be as accurate as it was. He also may have thought that the Army had no need to share honors on this operation. Lieutenant General (later General of the Army) Omar N. Bradley, then head of the First Army in over-all command ashore, was not so touchy. On June 20, he asked Admiral Ramsay for fire support against some of the protected big guns defending Cherbourg. They ranged from 150 mm.'s up to one battery of 280's.

Unfortunately, the storm had scattered the bombardment ships through several Channel ports,

and they could not be reassembled for their shoot until June 25. On that day, in calm seas, the entire western bombardment forces, led by the three American battleships, pounded German shore batteries. It was not the best shoot ever made, but General Collins admitted its helpfulness in silencing some guns and in helping break German morale. The next day the German command surrendered.

With Cherbourg secured, Admiral Kirk's Western Naval Task Force was dissolved on July 10, and most of the naval ships engaged in the Channel steamed for the Mediterranean to take part in the long-delayed amphibious attack on Southern France. This had been named Anvil when

253

Quincy is almost hit by accurate German shore fire as . . .

Augusta, *laying a smoke screen, is just missed by a salvo.*

254

Strasbourg *and a cruiser—destroyed at Toulon.*

Landing ship tank plays the role of junior carrier as a Piper Cub takes off to spot for gunners. Note the small runway deck.

it was planned as a simultaneous operation with Overlord. Because of the long delay, the code name was changed to Dragoon for fear that the other name might have been compromised in the weeks that had passed. D-Day was set for August 15, H-Hour at 8 A.M.

Churchill and most of the British commanders in the Mediterranean opposed the operation. They wanted to land on the Dalmatian Coast and strike up through the Ljubljana Gap in the Balkans toward Austria and Hungary. One of the reasons was political. Churchill did not want the Russians to get into Central Europe first, which, of course, they did.

The South France landings were carried through almost to textbook perfection. Again it was a combined Allied operation in over-all command of Vice Admiral H. Kent Hewitt, USN. There was little opposition on the beaches, and on August 28, only thirteen days after the original landings, the French ports of Toulon and Marseilles were surrendered to General Jean de Lattre de Tassigny and his French II Corps. The corps had been landed on August 16.

For the Americans, there was one truly sad event of Dragoon. Rear Admiral Don P. Moon, apparently overstrained by his duties as Task Force commander off Utah Beach in Normandy, committed suicide on August 5. Admiral Hewitt turned over his command — one of the four attack groups — to Rear Admiral Spencer S. Lewis, a veteran of the early fighting in the Pacific. The commanders of the other three task forces were Rear Admiral Frank J. Lowry, who had commanded the Anzio operation after service in the Pacific, Rear Admiral Lyal A. Davidson, and Rear Admiral Bertram J. Rodgers.

On Operation Dragoon, the Allies also had a support force of small aircraft carriers under command of Rear Admiral T. H. Troubridge of the Royal Navy. No major ships were lost and casualties were small.

With successful completion of Operation Dragoon, the naval war in European waters was over. There still were the German submarines to be dealt with, but that battle was going well. Major units of the American and British fleet began shifting to the Pacific for the showdown with Japan.

The sea secured—the air takes over.

ISLAND BARRIERS DOWN

At the beginning of the third year of the war in the Pacific, United States and Allied forces still were a long way from Tokyo. The Japanese had General MacArthur's forces contained in the eastern end of New Guinea. They still held the Philippines and the islands to eastward that protected their lifelines to the oil and rice of Southeast Asia. More important, the Japanese still had in being a formidable fleet of which reckoning had to be taken in planning any forward move.

There also still was some division in Washington in early 1944 as to the better strategy for the drive against Japan. General MacArthur, with a sentimental obsession with the Philippines, thought the better way was through the southwest Pacific and then up the ladder of the Philippines. And under his command, of course, with the Pacific Fleet in a supporting role. The Navy planners, headed by Admirals King and Leahy in Washington and Nimitz in Pearl Harbor, thought the shorter route across the Central Pacific, through the Marianas to Formosa, the better way, cutting the enemy's jugular vein. The Philippines would be left to wither on the vine. If MacArthur's insistence on liberation of the Philippines en route to Japan was to prevail, then the Navy thought the advance should be two-pronged. And that was the final decision in Washington.

Since Guadalcanal, the strategy of the Japanese had been one only of defense, but they were determined to sell each position as dearly as possible. When an island position was deemed hopeless, they left their forces there to die. This made for a bloody war.

The two-headed drive against the Japanese began first in New Guinea in the late spring after the breaching of the Bismarck barrier and the capture of key positions in the Admiralty Islands to westward. The first big leap forward was to Hollandia, in western New Guinea, the Dutch end of the world's second largest island. The Japanese had built it into a major air base. General MacArthur wanted it for the same purpose.

At this date, April, 1944, General MacArthur had been assigned his own fleet, the Seventh. It was under the command of Vice Admiral Thomas C. Kinkaid, who had been a carrier task force commander in the Solomons and naval commander in the Aleutians when the Japanese were chased out of those islands in the summer of 1943. Allied Naval Forces Southwest Pacific also had Australian and New Zealand men of war with a few small Dutch and French vessels. The largest ship was a heavy cruiser. United States escort carriers gave coverage for amphibious operations. The force was not strong enough to challenge any major Japanese force but it was sufficient for the job it had to do. The United States Fifth Fleet was the shield between all American positions and the Japanese Combined Fleet. It had all the big carriers and the new modern battleships.

When the Hollandia operation was planned, General MacArthur had asked that Fifth Fleet make a sweep to the north, particularly past the Palau Islands, which lay between New Guinea and the Philippines. It was thought the Japanese might have major fleet units there. The Hollandia airfields were within range of land-based American Fifth Air Force, but the Palau Islands were not. In acceding to MacArthur's request for coverage, Admiral Nimitz warned the General that the major mission must remain engagement and destruction of the Japanese Combined Fleet.

In leap-frogging up the New Guinea coast to Hollandia, the Americans bypassed the major Japanese defensive units, totaling a division, and

258

Task force action—a Hellcat warms up.

A battleship pounds island installations.

the landing at Hollandia was made almost without opposition. No major Japanese fleet units had been found in the Palaus, and the American Air Force fliers had so clobbered the Japanese airfield on New Guinea that the Fifth Fleet carrier fliers found little left to destroy. There was no Japanese fleet reaction until MacArthur's forces, moving on up the New Guinea coast, landed on Biak Island late in May. Two efforts were made by the Japanese to reinforce their garrison there, but these were driven away by the Allied cruiser-destroyer forces, and the effort was abandoned when Fifth Fleet began its softening-up air attacks on the Marianas.

Astute strategists, Japanese as well as American, long had recognized the Marianas as a key chesspiece in the Pacific war. Both fleets prepared for a showdown meeting. The odds were not too uneven. In the Fifth Fleet, under Admiral Spru-

ance, were seven large carriers and eight light carriers, seven of the new big sixteen-inch-gunned battleships, light and heavy cruisers, and over half a hundred destroyers. In Japanese Mobile Fleet under Vice Admiral Jisaburo Ozawa were five big carriers, including the thirty-three-thousand-ton *Taiho*, of the same size as American *Saratoga*, and four light carriers, five battleships, including the world's largest, *Yamato* and *Musashi*, eleven heavy cruisers, two lights, and more than two score destroyers.

In air strength, Fifth Fleet had almost a two-to-one edge, in both carrier planes and float planes flying searches from battleships, cruisers, and shore bases — 956 to 473. This disparity, however, should have been offset by the Japanese land-based air. In the Marianas alone they had 172 planes deployed. It was the Japanese expectation that these land-based planes would have severely pun-

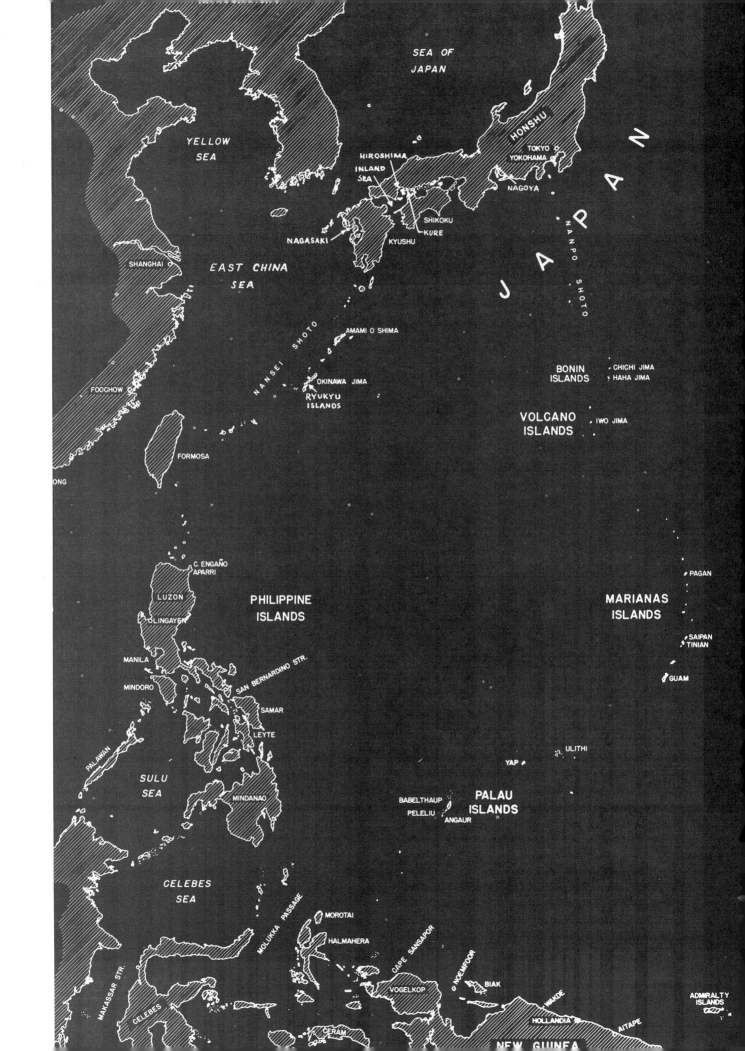

A Japanese fighter explodes under the guns of a Hellcat.

ished the American ships before the carrier pilots and the surface forces moved in to complete the carnage.

The American landings on Saipan began on June 15, and the two great fleets, already on the move, converged on each other in the Philippine Sea.

The ubiquitous American submarines gave the first warning of the Japanese fleet's movements when one saw Ozawa's carrier divisions moving out of Tawi Tawi anchorage in the Sulu Archipelago and another later saw them coming out of San Bernadino Strait into the Philippine Sea. That was the last time any American saw the Japanese, however, until the second day of the battle, June 20. The first day, June 19, the Fifth Fleet fought a strictly defensive action.

Admiral Ozawa, through his own search planes and snoopers from Guam, picked up the American fleet the evening of June 18 and set his course to be in position to attack the next morning. He had his carriers disposed in three divisions, with the light carriers, escorted by his two monster battleships, in the van about a hundred miles ahead of the main striking force. The Fifth Fleet was about two hundred miles west of the Marianas that

Framed in anti-aircraft fire, another Hellcat readies for takeoff.

261

evening, in a good position to push on in for a dawn attack. The commanders knew the Japanese were somewhere out to westward.

That evening there began a series of command decisions that let the opportunity pass. Vice Admiral Marc Mitscher suggested to Admiral Spruance that they continue on to westward to seek contact. Spruance, always a cautious man, rejected it. Earlier Mitscher had suggested to Vice Admiral Willis Lee, the battleship commander who was deployed to westward of the carriers, that if that course was followed there was a good chance that his new battleships could take on *Yamato* and *Musashi* in a night action and the carrier pilots could finish off the fleet the next morning. Admiral Lee demurred and was backed in his decision by

Spruance. Resisted by his subordinate commander, Lee, and overruled by his superior, Spruance, Mitscher had no recourse but to steam eastward, away from the Japanese, and wait for the attack. It began soon after dawn the next morning.

The Fifth Fleet was in the uncomfortable position of having hostile air bases to the east — Guam and Rota — and a hostile fleet to the west. The Japanese had an easterly wind blowing across their decks so they could launch and recover planes without a change of course.

Attacks on the American ships by single planes began soon after dawn, and at ten o'clock, ship's time, the first big attack by carrier plane came out of the west. Mitscher was fortunate in one respect. Since he had launched no attack group,

Japanese bombers are destroyed.

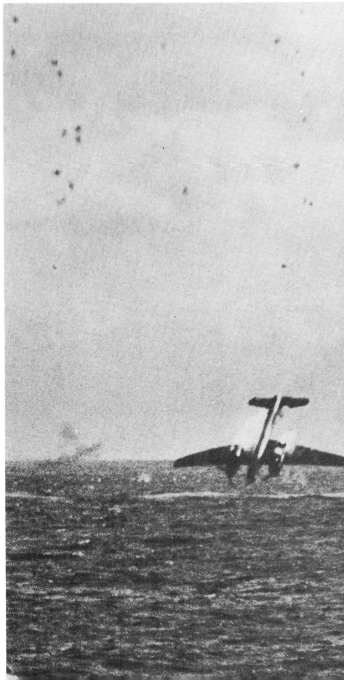

A Hellcat tries to make his flight deck . . .

And there is not much time to get out . . .   But he scrambles to safety.

he had all his fighters available — some 450 of them — to defend.

The first attack was by about seventy-five planes, carrying both bombs and torpedoes. Intercepted some sixty miles out from the carriers, in a matter of minutes all but a handful of the Japanese planes had been shot down. The few that got throught the fighter screen never reached the carriers. They attacked Admiral Lee's screening group of battleships and destroyers but only one hit was scored, a bomb drop on *South Dakota* that killed twenty-seven men and wounded twenty-three but did not impair her battle-worthiness. Three more times during that bright day, the Japanese threw large strike forces at the American ships, but without a single crippling hit.

When the long day was over, Mitscher triumphantly messaged Nimitz in Pearl Harbor that his fliers had accounted for "about 300 planes." For once, the fliers had underestimated the kill. Japanese records that became available after the war showed that only 130 of the 450 planes Ozawa threw against the American fleet that day returned to their carriers, or to Guam or Rota. American losses were 30 planes and 27 fliers lost. The American fliers jubilantly called it "The Great Marianas Turkey Shoot."

While all this was going on over and around the American fleet, four hundred miles to westward two American submaries were more than fulfilling their assigned missions.

Vice Admiral C. A. Lockwood, when the battle impended, had placed a group of his submarines in position to intercept the Japanese forces. Two of them did. One of the four assigned to the area Admiral Lockwood had deduced as on the probable track of the Japanese fleet was *Albacore,* in command of Commander J. W. Blanchard. Shortly after nine o'clock the morning of the nineteenth, he sighted one of the carrier divisions, that led by *Taiho,* Admiral Ozawa's flagship. Closing to under five thousand yards, *Albacore* fired a spread of six torpedoes at *Taiho.* Only one hit, but as it turned out that was enough. It ruptured one or more of her gasoline tanks, and although it did not stop her immediately, she finally suffered internal explosions and sank.

Several miles away, *Albacore's* sister submarine, *Cavalla,* surfacing to have a look around at noon, found herself only a few thousand yards away from a large Japanese carrier recovering planes. Closing to one thousand yards, or almost point-blank range, she fired six torpedoes at her target; at least three hit. The carrier was *Shokaku.* She was much more seriously hurt than *Taiho* and

fell out of formation. Three hours later, while her crew still was trying to save her, she suffered a series of internal explosions, probably of her own magazines, and went down.

When *Taiho* finally exploded and sank, in midafternoon, Admiral Ozawa transferred to the cruiser *Haguro,* from where he directed the rest of the day's operations and gave orders for the next. Because of poor communications on *Haguro,* he had had little exact information as to the day's action. He knew he had lost two of his biggest carriers, but he did not know he had lost most of his fleet's planes and pilots. And what few pilots had returned claimed many ships sunk. He ordered a fueling rendezvous to the northwest for the next morning and planned to resume the battle.

The United States fleet, in the meantime, was doing what it should have been doing the night of June 18: steaming west at its best speed to try and overtake the Japanese carriers. Pearl Harbor had relayed reports from the submarines that one carrier had been sunk and another damaged. (Blanchard did not know *Taiho* had gone down from his one torpedo hit.) Believing that Ozawa

A torpedo-loaded Avenger takes off.

Ozawa's fleet is found—and begins its evasive action.

Weaving and twisting violently—they took a bad beating, losing a carrier and sustaining severe damage to several ships. |265

Sharp watch was kept for downed pilots and crews.

probably had turned back southwest, the American searchers did not catch up with the Japanese until midafternoon. Then they were 275 miles away, almost at extreme range for an attack. But Admiral Mitscher was not going to be denied again. Ozawa had escaped once because of American caution. He was not going to let him get away this time. He alerted his task group commanders when the first report came in, and as soon as the position was definitely determined, he launched an attack group of over two hundred planes, a third of them fighters and only a fourth of their number carrying torpedoes.

The American attack reached the Japanese just at sundown. In an intense twenty minutes of action the light carrier *Hiyo* was hit by at least two torpedoes and sunk. The big carrier *Zuikaku* and a small carrier, *Chiyoda*, were strafed, and both were hit by bombs. The battleship *Haruna* also was hit. None of the three was disabled. Two fleet oilers that had been refueling the fleet were so badly damaged by planes from *Wasp* that they were abandoned and sunk by their crews.

That ended the engagement. Admiral Ozawa, with two of his remaining six carriers damaged, two of his tankers sunk with their precious fuel oil, and his once big air fleet of 450 planes reduced to only 35 operational, turned toward home at his best speed.

While Mitscher still was recovering his fliers the evening of June 20, he suggested to Spruance that Lee and his battleships be sent in pursuit of Ozawa. The carriers were having to steam eastward at high speed to meet the wind for plane recovery. This was carrying Fifth Fleet farther away from the Japanese.

Spruance again gave Mitscher a negative, and it was not until all the fliers had been recovered that the whole fleet turned northwest in pursuit. At Mitscher's insistence, they steamed at only sixteen knots so a sharp watch could be kept for any downed American fliers. Many who had been shot down had been seen to get out safely from their planes when they splashed. This, of course, slowed

Water Buffalo, with Marines, churns toward Tinian Island.

the pursuit. Fifty-nine fliers who otherwise might have perished were pulled out of the water by fleet float planes, seaplanes from land bases, and by Fifth Fleet destroyers.

The vain pursuit of the Japanese, who were making good speed northwestward, continued through June 21. When long searches up to dusk that evening failed to locate the main body or any crippled laggards, Fifth Fleet turned back toward Saipan and a June 22 refueling. Although Fifth Fleet lost a golden chance to wreak havoc on Japan's last group of carriers, they did complete the elimination of Japan's last group of first-class carrier pilots. It was estimated by Japanese sources after the war that at least 445 were lost in those two days of violent action, June 19–20.

While Saipan, Tinian, then Guam were overrun by the Marines and Army, and the big air base built on Saipan from which the B-29's operated in devastating raids until the end of the war, the Japanese never came out to challenge again until the landings on Leyte in late October. Then the four carriers Ozawa took south with him from the Inland Sea in his successful attempt to lure Halsey north had only a few planes aboard and fell easy victims to the American carrier plane strikes.

The great air battle in the Philippine Sea was the last of the war between rival carrier groups. It may well have been the last great carrier battle of all time.

Headed for one of the islands—a load of amphibious tanks.

A downed Japanese bomber sends up its pyre of smoke off
Saipan.

Pennsylvania blasts Guam.

TO TOKYO BAY

After Leyte Gulf, the Japanese surface fleet no longer was a menace. But there still were nine and one-half months of bitter fighting ahead for the United States Navy in the Pacific. Many more men were to die. Many more ships were to be lost.

The first task was to land the Army on Luzon, the main island of the Philippines. The landings were accomplished with minimum trouble, but the Japanese made a determined stand on Manila and in the hills, and it was late January before the fleet could be released.

Then, early in 1945, came the two final steps before invasion of the Japanese home islands: the capture of Iwo Jima in the Volcanoes, southeast of Japan, and of Okinawa, the major island of the Ryukyus chain that stretches southwestward from Kyushu, southernmost of the four Japanese main islands, almost to Formosa.

Iwo Jima was needed as an air base to provide fighter support for the B-29's bombing the home

First landing waves assault the beaches of Leyte.

islands from Saipan in the Marianas, and as an emergency haven for any disabled bombers that could not make it back to their home field. Okinawa was to be the staging island for the final, all-out attack on Japan.

Iwo Jima had no importance except its position. It was almost halfway between the B-29 base on Saipan, and Tokyo — 1,250 miles to the northwest. The volcanic little island is about as unprepossessing a piece of real estate as there is in the Pacific. It is kidney shaped, four and a half miles long and two and a half miles wide. Before the war, a few hundred Japanese scraped a living out of it growing sugar cane and pineapples and extracting sulphur. Its surface is covered with volcanic ash and black cinders, thin and fine, which makes walking more difficult than in sand. An old volcanic cone, Mt. Surabachi, dominates it from its southern end.

The Japanese also had realized its importance, and after the fall of the Marianas in June, 1944, they had begun its fortification. By February, 1945, they had made it about as impregnable as such a small space could be, with subterranean caves and cleverly camouflaged gun emplacements. Its gar-

rison had been increased to more than twenty thousand men.

American attacks on the island had been started the previous December. One reason for the early start was that Japanese fighter sweeps against Saipan were proving too successful. They had been flown from Iwo Jima. The first attack, on December 8, was a joint Army-Navy operation. Fighters and bombers from Saipan first strafed and bombed the two Japanese airfields. Then a cruiser and destroyer force moved in, in bad seeing, to bombard the fields.

Daily bombings and intermittent surface bombardment of the tiny bit of rock and ash and cinder continued until mid-February. Japanese air attacks on Saipan were curtailed but not completely halted, proving again that air and sea bombardment alone cannot immobilize an airfield if its defenders are resolute. Nor did this American activity halt the work of fortification.

The landings finally were set for February 19. Three Marine divisions under the overall command of Lieutenant General Holland M. Smith, who was in charge of all Marine activities in the Pacific, were assigned to the assault. The Navy assembled

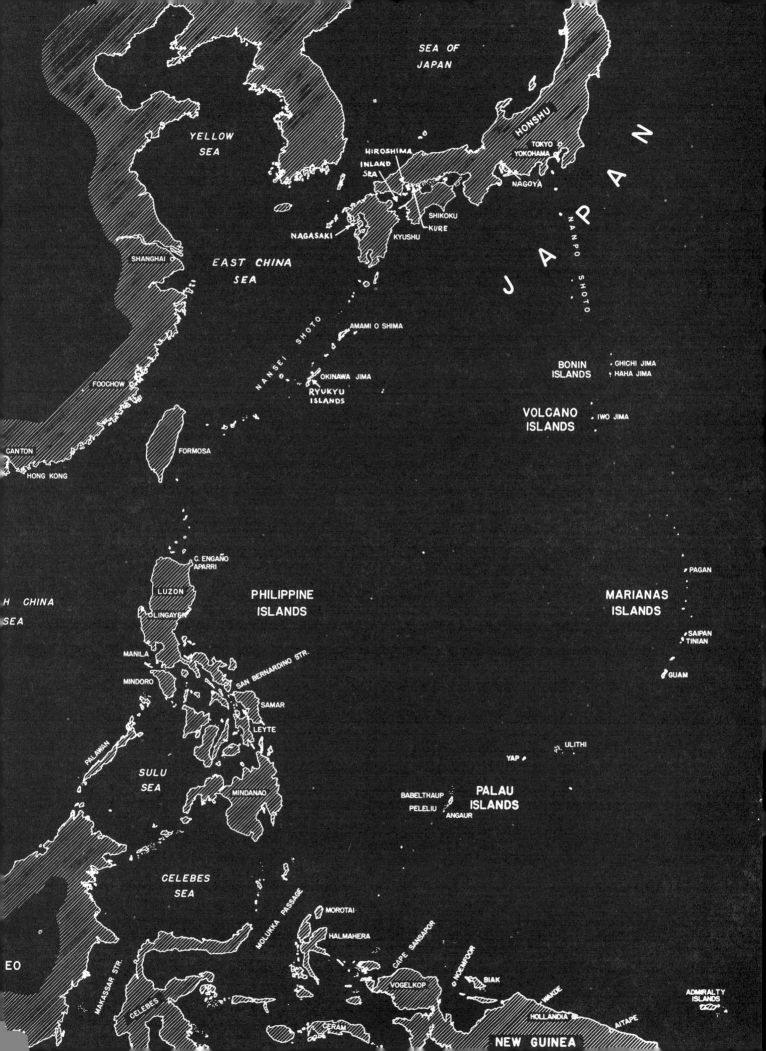

its full combat array under the command of Admiral Raymond A. Spruance, who had relieved Admiral Halsey late in January after the Philippine operation had been concluded.

In Fifth Fleet — which it became when Spruance took over from Halsey — were five carrier groups, with eleven fleet carriers and five escort carriers, and the most impressive shore bombardment group assembled to that time — six battleships (eight on D-Day), four heavy cruisers, one light cruiser, and sixteen destroyers. Among the six battleships were *Arkansas, Nevada,* and *Texas,* which had helped cover the Normandy and South France landings the previous summer.

For three days they pounded Iwo Jima with everything from 20-mm. up to 16-inch shells. The Marines complained later that it was not enough, that they had asked originally for ten days' ship bombardment. That might have saved a few lives. It is difficult to see how it could have substantially altered the pattern of the fighting. The only weapon not used that might have made a major difference was poison gas. A heavy gas that would have seeped into the underground fortifications, making them untenable, probably would have killed or immobilized most of the defenders. Its use never was seriously considered. Poison gases were forbidden under the Geneva Convention, to which the United States subscribed. And no country had used them, so far as was known, since Imperial Germany did in World War I.

Before the landings, on February 19, Admiral Spruance took Fifth Fleet north for a strike by Vice Admiral Marc A. Mitscher's fliers against Tokyo and other targets on the Japanese main island of Honshu. It was the first carrier attack against Japan proper since the Halsey-Doolittle raid in the spring of 1942. Admiral Halsey had long wanted to strike again at Japan, but when the opportunity finally came he was back home, much against his will, being paraded around as a public hero.

Carrier-based raids' results on Honshu.

272

*Battle cruiser **Alaska** fights off her first air attack.*

The attack on Honshu, made on February 16 and 17, was intended not only as a diversion against interference with the Iwo Jima landings, but as a way to "blood" many new carrier pilots who had just joined the fleet. They acquitted themselves well. In two days of operation, often in bad weather, they shot down, or destroyed on the ground, over five hundred Japanese planes, attacked factories in the vicinity of Tokyo, and sank considerable shipping, most of it of small coastal tonnage. The strikes against Japan and against Chichi Jima, also in the Bonins, delayed Japanese air attacks on the invasion forces. None was attempted for twenty-four hours, and then only in small force.

On the night of February 21–22, however, the fleet got a foretaste of the hell that was to come off Okinawa. In a period of three hours, ill-fated *Saratoga*, the escort carriers *Bismarck Sea* and *Lunga Point*, and the net cargo ship *Keokuk* all were crashed by suicide planes. *Saratoga* was so badly damaged she had to return to the West Coast for repairs and was out of action for three months. *Bismarck Sea* had to be abandoned and sank within three hours. Damage to *Lunga Point* and *Keokuk* was not extensive, but the latter lost seventeen killed and forty-four wounded. *Lunga Point* lost no one.

The suicide pilots, the *kamikazes*, had been encountered before, notably off Leyte Gulf during the Philippine landings. There the Japanese first adopted it as a definite technique. Five months later, off Iwo Jima, the *kamikazes* were relied on by Japan as the main defense by air against United States ships. Such suicide tactics required only a man who could fly a plane, and any plane capable of flying that could carry a bomb could be used. The better planes and pilots were not used.

The landings by the Marines on February 19 were made initially without major opposition. But as the first waves began to bog down on the beaches in the black cinders, the intensity of mortar and automatic weapons fire increased. Mount Surabachi, which was honeycombed with gun positions, had both landing beaches under its guns and poured a death barrage on both.

The first day set a pattern. Before the island finally was declared secure on March 26, 5,931 Marines had died or were missing and 17,272 had been wounded. The Navy losses were 881 dead and 1,917 wounded. The Japanese had lost an estimated 24,000, many of them smothered in their caves, which the Marines had sealed. It was the bloodiest campaign in their history for the Marines.

The exact value of Iwo Jima cannot be determined, but it was considerable. During the five months between its capture and Japan's surrender, more than two thousand B-29's made emergency landings there. And no one can estimate how many more were saved from Japanese fighter plane at-

273

Iwo Jima—behind naval barrage, the invasion is on . . .

and nears the beaches, under bristling Mount Suribachi.

Wave after wave they come . . .

and under murderous fire, establish their beachhead. 275

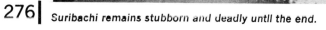

Suribachi remains stubborn and deadly until the end.

tack by their own fighter escorts that flew from Iwo Jima's fields.

While the Marines were making their slow conquest of Iwo, aided to the end by fire support from various navy units, the fast carrier forces under Admiral Mitscher made another strike against the Japanese home islands on February 25, with only minor results because of bad weather. When the weather barred a second strike against Nagoya the following day, Admiral Mitscher took three of his carrier groups to westward and struck at Okinawa on March 1. The American fliers met little opposition and brought back many valuable photographs of Okinawa and other islands of the Ryukyus chain. With Iwo Jima secure and operative as an Army Air Force Base, the preliminaries toward the penultimate step to invasion of the Japanese home islands, the capture of Okinawa, were set in train.

Events now were moving to a climax all over the world. The Russians and Allied Armies were closing in on Berlin. The German surface navy was no more, and the German submarines were being hunted down relentlessly by the "killer" task groups of escort carriers and destroyers in the Atlantic. The Mediterranean now was the *mare nostrum* of the Allies, not of the Axis.

The British, whose early participation in the war in the Far East had been so tragic, were anxious to retrieve some of their lost prestige. Churchill offered Roosevelt elements of the British fleet. There was some hesitation in Washington, but none in Guam, to which Admiral Nimitz had moved his Pacific headquarters the previous fall. He wanted all the help he could get.

Early in March, the British moved their British Far Eastern forces into the Pacific from the Indian Ocean, and on March 20 they became Task Force 57 of the United States Fifth Fleet and came under command of Admiral Spruance. The force was composed of the carriers *Indomitable, Victorious, Illustrious,* and *Indefatigable,* the battleships *King George V* and *Howe,* five cruisers (one from New Zealand), and fifteen destroyers. Vice Admiral Sir H. Bernard Rawlings was task force commander, with his flag in *King George V.* Rear Admiral Sir Philip Vian led the carrier squadron, with his flag in *Indomitable.*

The British were assigned the task of neutralizing the Japanese airfields in the Sakashima Gunto, a group of islands 250 miles southeast of Okinawa, near the north coast of Formosa. They operated with verve and efficiency until late May, providing a shield between Okinawa and the Japanese air forces to the southwest. In addition to strikes on Sakashima Gunto, they also gave attention to some in northern Formosa.

The British suffered a few casualties but lost no major ship. Although several *kamikazes* crashed flight decks of the British carriers, the steel decks of the British ships kept damage to a minimum. The steel deck plating added considerable weight (the American argument against their use) to the British ships. But had the Americans had a choice in the late months of the war they undoubtedly would have traded a few knots of speed for the greater protection the armored decks provided. Planes crashing into an armored deck disintegrated. When they hit the wooden decks of the American ships their bombs frequently penetrated several decks with devastating results.

Before the landings on Okinawa, which were set for April 1, the fast carriers made several strikes at Japan air fields, in which they were joined by the B-29's. United States Army planes from the Philippines joined with British carrier pilots to hit Sakashima Gunto and the Formosan fields, respectively. All these air activities, especially the carrier plane sweeps and the B-29 attacks on the airfields on Kyushu, so upset Japanese operations and plans that it was not until the sixth day after the landings on Okinawa, on April 6, that the enemy was able to muster an effective air attack.

The price for the carrier force was high—*Franklin, Enterprise,* and the new *Yorktown,* successor to the one lost at Midway, put out of action. *Wasp* was severely punished but continued to operate for some time. *Franklin,* the flagship of Rear Admiral R. E. Davison, was hit on March 19 by two bombs dropped by a single plane. They started such fires that she was saved only by heroic work by her crew. She lost 724 killed or missing and suffered damage that reportedly was more exten-

Franklin is staggered by bombs . . .

277

and she begins to list badly.

Impossible?—she survived this holocaust and made it back to New York.

sive than that inflicted on either *Lexington* in the Coral Sea or the first *Yorktown* at Midway. *Franklin* made her way under her own power across the Pacific, through the Panama Canal, and to the New York shipyard in Brooklyn. But she never got back into the war.

In the planning for the Okinawa operation, which was given the code name of Iceberg, one of the more difficult problems requiring solution was that of fueling and ammunition supply. This is always difficult in the open sea, although the United States Navy had developed it to a fine art. So close to Japan, it posed new hazards of surface and air attack.

Vice Admiral Richmond Kelly Turner, the amphibious commander for Okinawa, as he had been for most Pacific landings since Guadalcanal, saw an answer in a small group of islands, the Kerama Retto, which lay some fifteen miles off the southwestern coast of the big island. They had little value in themselves, being small and rocky. But they enclosed roadsteads that could be closed by nets to provide refueling and repair anchorages safe from submarine attack. And the small islands themselves provided good antiaircraft mounts.

Over much spoken opposition, it was decided to seize them before the Okinawa landings.

The British observer at Santiago in 1898 who thought the night illumination of the harbor mouth by American naval searchlights to prevent a sneak run by the Spanish ships "an impertinence" surely would have been speechless had he been present to witness this seizure almost within range of the Japanese guns on Okinawa. That the American admirals could even consider the action is an evidence of the low estate to which the Japanese Navy had been brought less than three and one-half years after Pearl Harbor. Then it possessed the second most powerful fleet in the world.

The landings on Kerama Retto on the twenty-sixth and twenty-seventh of March were carried out almost without incident. Most of the estimated eleven hundred to twelve hundred defenders retreated to caves in the hills, from which they eventually were routed out. One interesting find in the small islands was more than two hundred small one-man patrol boats in which suicide attacks with depth charges were to have been made on the invasion fleet off Okinawa. That plan, of course, died with the seizure of Kerama Retto.

New York moves into position off Okinawa.

279

The troops move to the Okinawa beaches under the flaming guns of the ships.

Rocket ships pour their fire on the Japanese positions.

By D-Day — April 1 — Kerama Retto was a functioning American base and continued as such, with increasing use, until Okinawa was secured. Many badly damaged ships put in there for emergency repair before heading back for Pearl Harbor or the States. Others were made battle-worthy again by the crews of repair ships in Kerama Retto.

On Okinawa when the landings—three Marine divisions, four Army—were made on April 1, there were an estimated 450,000 to 460,000 Okinawans, some organized as militia, and about 80,000 Japanese military.

As on Pelileu, Saipan, and to some degree Iwo Jima, the Japanese chose not to make a stand on the beaches. When the landings began, the Japanese withdrew to well-prepared positions at the northern and southern ends of the big island. As learned after the war in interrogations and from records at Imperial Headquarters, the intent at that time of all island defenses was to make the cost so great that the United States would exhaust its resources and its will and accept a negotiated peace.

The early successes in landing almost unopposed and winning control of the two major airfields did not continue. Each mile became more difficult as the American divisions pressed the Japanese into smaller areas. Before Major General Roy M. Geiger, the Marine commander on Okinawa, declared the island secured, on June 21, 7,613 soldiers and Marines had died, 31,807 had been wounded. Most of the Japanese garrison of more than 77,000 had been killed or had committed suicide as had their commander, Lieutenant General M. Ushijima, who disemboweled himself on June 22. Lieutenant General Simon Bolivar Buckner, the American Army officer who had headed the attack force, had been killed by Japanese shellfire four days before.

On land, the Okinawa campaign was not the most costly or the most bitter. At sea, it was the most deadly campaign of the Pacific war. There was hardly any surface action, none by major ships, for the Japanese had few left. But no armada ever took such punishment from air attack as did the United States Navy in the Western Pacific from April 1 to the last organized *kamikaze* attack late in June. Off Okinawa, the United States Navy had some of its finest hours.

When the Marines came out of France at the

Task force—powerful, mobile, versatile.

Prize of sea victory—lifeline control.

Washington refuels off Okinawa.

end of World War I, they said firmly they would not fight another campaign with the United States Army. After Guadalcanal, where they were almost deserted for weeks, they demanded that they be given their own aircraft carriers and other fighting ships, saying that they wanted no part of a joint campaign with the United States Navy again. Off Okinawa, no charge of nonsupport could be made. That fleet had come to stay. And it did stay, right to the bitter end, unflinching under the most harrowing attack any ships ever took.

Between April 6 and July 29, 30 naval vessels were sunk, most by suicide plane attack, and 368 more were damaged. Many of the latter never got back into the war. More than 4,900 sailors died, and 4,824 were wounded.

Chief sufferers from the *kamikaze* attacks were the little fellows, the destroyers and small gunboats and rocket ships that made up the radar picket line. The *kamikaze* pilots, many of them with scant training, generally attacked the first enemy ship they encountered, and that always was one of the picket boats.

Typical of the ordeals of the picket ships was that of the destroyer *Laffey* on April 16. Of the more than 150 suicide planes that attacked the fleet that day, it was estimated that one group of 40 or 50 concentrated on the one destroyer. Several of the attacking suicide planes were shot down short of target. But *Laffey's* surviving officers plotted twenty-two separate attacks by individual planes during an hour and one-half. Eight of the twenty-two crashed aboard her. She claimed eight of the attackers for her own guns — five-inch and twenty-mm. Of her crew of over three hundred men, thirty-one were killed and seventy-two wounded. She was patched up by a repair vessel off the beach and finally got back to Guam under her own power. But she never got back into the war.

This tactic of a picket line to warn of incoming air attack was a development of the radar age of naval fighting. At Okinawa, they were stationed as far out from the landing beaches as ninety-five miles and as close in as eighteen. The fast carriers, providing cover for the landing forces and the bombardment ships — the old battle wagons such as *Texas, Arkansas,* and *Nevada* and the heavy cruisers—as well as for themselves, also attempted to keep a guard above the picket line. But there never were enough to cope with the mass attacks by the *kamikaze* groups.

There were many Navy tacticians who thought that instead of a passive defense against the *kamikazes* — that is, one waiting for attack — it would have been far better to go in and destroy their nests on Kyushu and Shikoku, the two southernmost of the main Japanese islands, where they had their air bases. Some of the B-29's also might better have been used for saturation raids on Japanese airfields, such as those just preceding the invasion. The Army Air Force opposed this, preferring to burn down more Japanese cities.

Each time that Admiral Spruance did send in his fast carrier forces to work over the *kamikazes'* nests, the effect was immediately apparent, a falling off in the number and violence of the attacks. But only four such sweeps were made from mid-April to mid-May. Then the carriers retired to Ulithi for a rest, something the little picket ships could not do.

In ten major strikes from April 6 to June 22, the Japanese sent 1,465 suicide planes against the fleet off Okinawa and perhaps 300 or 400 more planes in lone attacks. In addition, there were several hundred sorties by Japanese pilots, both Army and Navy, who were not intent on suicide. Most of the latter bombed the airfields on Okinawa or made night attacks on fleet units and harassed the fast carrier forces.

One factor that perhaps deterred Admiral Spruance from sending his carriers in to attack the home islands was the severe punishment they had taken during the invasion. In addition to *Franklin, Bunker Hill* was so badly damaged she was knocked out of the war, and *Intrepid, Hancock,* and *Enterprise,* for the second time in a few weeks, received damaging hits. The attitude apparently was that the carriers were too precious to risk in close attacks on the islands. The destroyers were left to take the brunt. One cynical remark attributed to a high-ranking naval officer was that the United States could build destroyers faster than the Japanese could build planes.

One action during the Okinawa operations that was almost a minor incident was the destruction of *Yamato,* the world's greatest warship, by air attack. She sortied from the Inland Sea with a light cruiser and seven destroyers on April 6, with orders to "annihilate" the invasion fleet off Okinawa. The carrier fliers, who had missed her at Leyte Gulf, caught up with her the next morning and, in attacks lasting from noon to sundown, sank her, the light cruiser, and three of the seven destroyers. American losses were ten planes and twelve men.

On May 27, Admiral Halsey returned from the States, where he and his staff had been working with others on plans for the invasion of the Japanese home islands, and resumed command. Fifth Fleet again became Third Fleet.

Halsey, who was a much more aggressive commander than was Spruance, lost no time going on the attack. He steamed north on June 2 and 3 and sent one of his carrier groups against the

284 | *Two near miss torpedo shots at ships of a task force.*

Kyushu airfields. The fleet got a bad shaking up in a typhoon on June 5, one light cruiser, *Pittsburgh,* losing her bow. But Halsey again sent in one of his task groups on June 8 to work over the Kyushu *kamikaze* bases.

The strength of the *kamikazes* had been expended by that time, however. Only one more major raid was made by them, and that by only forty-five planes, on June 22. The carriers had retired after the June 8 strike to Leyte Gulf, now a major naval refueling and rest area, to prepare for the final softening-up blows on Japan.

Admiral Halsey had been longing for the day when he could sail the Third Fleet against the home islands. No other naval commander was more bitter than he against the Japanese for the attack on Pearl Harbor and none pursued them through the war with greater intensity or vindictiveness. With his flag in *Missouri,* Halsey led Third Fleet north on July 1. For the next month and a half it sailed up and down the coasts of the Japanese home islands.

First targets for the carrier planes were the airfields and shipping in north Honshu and in Hokkaido, northernmost of the four. They had been beyond the range of the B-29's. While the fliers, against almost no air opposition, raked airfields

Fighters up! Looking for Kamikazes.

285

Close—but a suicide attack fails . . .

Yet another tries to crash
as does another.

Mississippi's Kamikaze wounds are healed in a floating dry-dock in the Philippines.

Powerful **Yamato** under an attack begins to list.

and attacked shipping, the battleships, cruisers, and destroyers steamed on firing runs as close as five thousand yards off the Japanese beaches and threw devastating salvos into rail centers, coke factories, and steel mills.

The Third Fleet was still there, doing its will, when the terrible flash of the atomic bomb burst over Hiroshima the morning of August 6 and when the second burst over the port city of Nagasaki three days later. On the same day, the Soviet Union attacked in Manchuria. On August 15, the Japanese finally accepted the terms for surrender agreed on by the Americans, British, and Russians at the Postdam conference.

There had been little doubt about ultimate Allied victory since the Battle of Midway in June, 1942, where the Japanese lost four carriers and many of their better pilots. There had been no doubt at all since the previous October, when the bulk of their remaining major surface ships were sunk in the Battle of Leyte Gulf. American submarines had virtually isolated the home islands and so depleted the Japanese cargo fleet that the home islands war plants were being starved for raw materials. Never before had the importance of sea power been better illustrated, especially for an insular country.

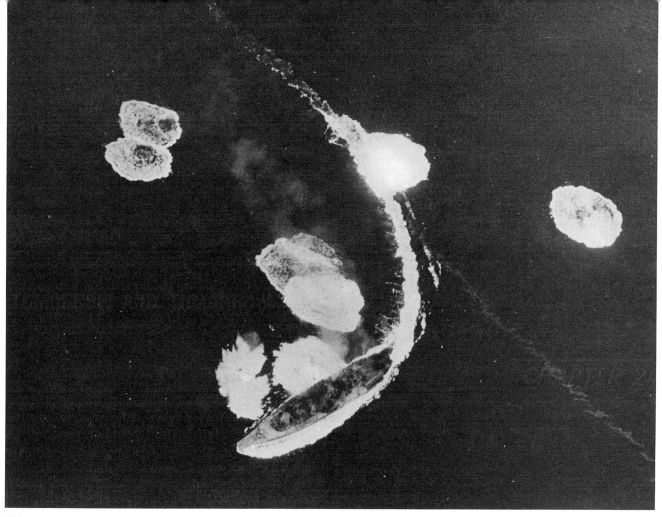

Violent turns will not help.

and vanishes in the East China Sea.

The last of an Empire's navy is destroyed in Kure Harbor, Honshu.

Ise BB/CV?

The Japanese were such a disciplined people, however, and the government's propaganda so expert, that few of them probably were aware how precarious was Japan's position. And there was a suicidal group among the high Army and Navy commanders who would have continued the war to the ultimate destruction had they had their way. Fortunately, Emperor Hirohito earnestly desired an end to the war, and there were enough modern-minded men in the military command to support such a decision and put down the few feeble attempts that were made to imprison the Emperor and proceed with the war to national *hara-kiri*. The inference in the Potsdam Declaration that the Emperor would not be deposed strengthened the hand of the advocates of surrender.

A question that probably will be asked to the end of time is: Was the bomb necessary to bring the Japanese surrender?

In Kure's shipyards at war's end—over one hundred 5-man submarines under construction.

B-29s work on major targets in Japan.

292

Hiroshima

294|

Nagasaki

There is very little evidence that the destruction of those first two bombs converted any of the war-to-the-bitter-end Japanese. And the Emperor and many of his more important advisers already were convinced the war had been lost and needed no such horrible reminders. The entry of Soviet Russia into the war on August 9 would seem to be a more reasonable answer.

More persons were killed in one great fire-bomb raid of mid-March by the B-29's on Tokyo than died at Hiroshima, if number of casualties alone is to be reckoned as an argument. It seems doubtful that many, if any, of the Japanese leaders had any real conception of this new and horrible force that had been loosed on the world. The argument that the two bombs were the deciding factor seems to be advanced more as an excuse than as a reason; advanced by those whose conscience troubles them.

Surrender—and an era ends aboard **Missouri.**

Once the will of the Emperor had become known, through broadcast of the Imperial Rescript on August 15, and an attempt to seize control of the Imperial Guard had been thwarted, the Japanese submitted without incident to occupation.

On August 27, Halsey in *Missouri* led Third Fleet into Sagami Wan, the large bay just south of the entrance to Tokyo Bay, and three days later he steamed into Tokyo Bay and anchored only a few miles from where Commodore Perry had dropped the hook when he opened Japan to the outside world in 1853. On September 2, General MacArthur and Admiral Nimitz received the formal surrender from the Japanese emissaries.

A war was formally ended and with it an era of naval history.

296

TOMORROW AND TOMORROW

When the first atomic bomb-burst over the New Mexican desert early the morning of July 16, 1945, William L. Laurence, Pulitzer Prize-winning science writer for *The New York Times*, said that in that first awesome flash of light he saw either the dawn of a new world or a preview of doomsday. He was not sure which it was. Nor is anyone else.

There probably are only a few men who can grasp the full implications of what took place at Alamogordo in the first controlled applications of the secret of atom-splitting. Every thinking person, however, has been told enough about the principle involved, and the facts of the size of the first atomic bombs, to know that a lot of admirals and generals were talking through their gold-braided, or brass-bound, hats when they said the atomic bomb was "just another bomb" for which a defense could be found, just as one had been for the bullet, the shell, the airplane, and the submarine.

CHAPTER 24

Everyone now knows that space is the only defense against the release of nuclear energy, and we have about run out of space on the earth. There even is in prospect nuclear bombs in orbit that could set fire to half a continent with one blast. The first and only two atom bombs used in war — those dropped by the United States over Hiroshima and Nagasaki in August, 1945 — seem mere firecrackers in comparison with the 100-megaton monsters of the 1960's. Scientists say it is within the realm of possibility some day to launch devastating nuclear bombs from the moon or one of the other planets.

Defense measures, not all of them nuclear, are being devised. So a stalemate beyond that of terror of the consequences may be brought about. As this is written, the near-nuclear monopoly of the United States and the Soviet Union and the knowledge of the leaders of both countries that there would not be much left to the victor either of his own country or of those opposing him apparently has made nuclear war improbable.

Two of the important deterrents to the start of such a suicidal nuclear conflict were naval. They were the missile-firing nuclear-powered submarines of which, at the beginning of 1964, the

Nuclear-powered carrier **Enterprise** *and nuclear-powered cruiser* **Long Beach.**

300

United States had thirty-one in commission and ten more authorized and the U.S.S.R. an estimated twenty-five, and the United States' great fleet of aircraft carriers. The latter were capable of handling and launching supersonic planes with nuclear bombs. They were something the Soviet Union did not have.

The great value of these ships as a deterrent to surprise attack was that both types were mobile. Locating an aircraft carrier on the seven seas might not be too difficult a task, but not an easy one. Locating ten or twenty submarines, some of which undoubtedly would be cruising under the polar ice pack, would be the nearest thing to an impossible task that can be imagined.

In his fanciful look into the future in his book *Triumph*, published in 1963, Philip Wylie had American aircraft launched from carriers and nuclear-armed submarines destroying what was left of the Soviet Union after a Moscow-ordered surprise attack and the Soviet follow-up had destroyed all fixed ballistic missile bases on the North American continent and in Europe.

The book had a ring of authenticity gained in part by the knowledge that just one American submarine with its sixteen Polaris missiles has a blast

Nuclear-powered **John Marshall**

Polaris from under the sea.

power in the nuclear warheads greater than that of all the conventional bombs dropped during World War II.

They were big ships. The nuclear-powered Polaris-armed submarines built in the 1960's by the United States were half again as large as Dewey's flagship at Manila, the *Olympia*. The *Lafayette* class displaced 7,250 tons on the surface and 8,200 tons submerged, to 5,800 for *Olympia*. They could make twenty knots or more when running on the surface and thirty-five knots submerged. Submerged is where most of the nuclear-powered submarines operate most of the time. Nuclear power and new methods of air purification made it unnecessary for them to surface to replenish batteries and change the air for the crew.

It is possible to visualize great undersea fleets putting out from subsurface coastal bases, cruising at terrific speeds to target areas, discharging their nuclear-armed missiles and returning to base without ever having broached the surface of the sea. The carrier displaced the battleship as the capital ship of World War II. Perhaps in the not too distant future the submarine will be the ship that is the Navy's main battle reliance.

Even more frightening for the future of mankind than the nuclear-powered, nuclear-armed submersibles, which, after all, travel at speeds the average sailor or motorist can appreciate, are the unpiloted missiles cruising through space at supersonic speeds for immense distances. Once an accurate means of control is found for them, there

An era is finished.

will be little need of either navies or armies as we know them today. Any war would be fought at distances of thousands of miles and would be over in a matter of minutes, or at least in hours.

Although these new weapons of destruction promise a grim tomorrow for the world, it has always been true that between wars the science of warfare makes slow progress. Only wars, or the immediate threat of them, stimulate activity. In their early stages, wars generally are fought on the general pattern of the preceding one. That was so of World War II. Until the atomic bomb was evolved to haunt the imagination, most of the techniques involved both on land and at sea were only a projection of those of World War I. In any non-nuclear war, the starting weapons perhaps will be improved only in degree over those in use or visualized in 1945, when the last war finally ground to a bloody halt. Which means that for some time the cycle will not have swung full to make the present weapons, and especially those of sea war, obsolete.

For its own national security, and the peace of the world, the United States for the immediate future obviously intends to maintain a strong navy, one capable of moving quickly to any trouble spot, one that is so strong and so modern that any would-be aggressor must think twice before challenging it. The United States still had such a force in 1964, greater in numbers and in fire power than all the rest of the world, including Soviet Russia. And there was no indication of any intent to surrender that primacy. The Navy budget rose from 9.76 billion dollars in 1955 to 15.27 billion dollars in 1963.

This is, of course, only a scanty preview of a possible future war. He would be a very wise man who could see its outline clearly, even if it were to be fought within the next ten years or twenty years. There were some horrible weapons whose details have not been revealed, such as the outline for chemical and bacterial war, either in being or near battlefield use when World War II ended.

This much seems certain. The great naval battles of World War II, especially the air-sea struggle off the Philippines in October, 1944, marked the end of a sea era. Never again will battle line meet battle line in a big-gun duel. Tomorrow's gunnery officer will see his target only on a map. It will be thousands of miles away. What has gone before will seem like a mock battle fought on the floor of the old Naval War College at Newport, R.I. It is a prospect too frightening for sane minds to contemplate. If man is wise, the last war has been fought.

INDEX

Abbreviations and symbols (ship), 6
Abdiel (British fast mine layer), 99
Aboukir (British armored cruiser), 92, 93
Abukuma (Japanese light cruiser) 38, 40, 49, 203, 208
Acasta (British destroyer), 161
Achilles (British light cruiser), 148, 149
Adak, 207
Adams, Lieutenant Max, 30
Admiral Graf Spee (German armored pocket battleship), 147-50
Admiral Hipper (German heavy cruiser), 148, 151, 158
Admiral Nakhimoff (Russian cruiser), 76, 77 *(illus.)*
Admiral Oushhokoff (Russian coastal defense vessel), 80
Admiral Senyaim (Russian coastal defense vessel), 76
Admiral Scheer (German pocket battleship), 148, 158, 161
Admiralty Islands, 258
Adriatic, 86
Ady, Ensign Howard D., 204
Adzuno (Japanese armored cruiser), 76
Africa, 134
Africa, North, landings (1943), 229-38
Agincourt (British battleship), 99
Air attack, *illus.* 273; Pearl Harbor, 177-84
Air bases, Hollandia, 258
Air bombardment, *illus.* 243
Air power, advent of (1910), 137-46 *(illus.)*
Aircraft carriers. *See* Carriers
Airfields, 180
Airplane(s), 18, 28
    Albacores, 174
    Avenger (torpedo plane), *illus.* 143, 189, 264
    B-17's, 145
    B-24's, 145
    B-25's, 40, *illus.* 31, 200
    B-29's, work on targets in Japan, *illus.* 292
    B-98, *illus.* 108
    Baka Bomb (Japanese suicide plane), *illus.* 145
    carrier fighter, 144
    Catalina (later PBY), 156, *illus.* 154
    Dauntless, *illus.* 203
    dive bomber, 142-43, *illus.* 143
    Faery Swordfish torpedo planes, *illus.* 154
    fighter, 172
    Fulmars, 172
    Hellcat, *illus.* 36, 144, 258, 261
    Helldiver, *illus.* 143
    Japanese bombers, *illus.* 178, 261, 262, 268
    Japanese suicide pilots (*kamikazes*), 273, 284
    JU-87's, 172
    JU-88's, 172
    Kawanishi patrol bomber, 144
    land-based, 259
    NC-4 (1919), *illus.* 142
    patrol bomber, seaplane, 144 *(illus.)*
    PBM's, 144
    PBY seaplanes, 144, 180
    Philippines, Second Battle of, 14-16
    Piper cub, *illus.* 255
    scout seaplane, 144 *(illus.)*
    seaplane (1918), *illus.* 140
    skip-bombing, 144
    Sopwith Pup (1917), 140
    Stukas, 172
    suicide planes (Japanese), 273
    supersonic, with nuclear bombs, 301
    Swordfish, 160, 169
    torpedo bomber, 139, 143-44, 156
    torpedo-carrying planes, 169, *illus.* 137
    (first) transatlantic flight, 142
    warfare (naval), 138
    World War I, 139
Ajax (British battleship), 99

Ajax (British light cruiser), 149, 150, *illus.* 148
Akagi (Japanese aircraft carrier), 131-32, 178, 203, 206
Akitsuki (Japanese destroyer), 49
Alabama (old U.S. battleship), *illus.* 141
Alabama (U.S. battleship), 39
Alamogordo, 297
Alaska, 207
Alaska (U.S. battle cruiser), 18, *illus.* 19, 273
Albacore (U.S. submarine), 30, 197, 264
Albacores (torpedo-carriers and dive bombers), 174
Albatross (British seaplane carrier), 138
Albert W. Grant (U.S. destroyer), 40
Alden (U.S. destroyer), 192
Aleutians, 200, 202, 258
Alexander Monormach (Russian cruiser), 76, 79
Alexandria, 168
Algeria, 234, 236
Algiers, 230, 231, 235
Allied Far Eastern Naval Forces, 199
Allied Fleets, North Atlantic, 121
Allied Naval Forces, Southwest Pacific, 258
Almaz (Russian fast scout cruiser), 76, 80
Altmark (German tanker and supply ship), 147, 148, 149
America (U.S. liner), 123
Americal (division of American troops), 200
American Turtle (submarine, 1775), 111
Amora (Russian cruiser), 76
Amphibious operations
    Africa, North, landings (1943), 229-56
    France, southern, 253-56
    Normandy, 239-53, *map* 251
    Operation Torch, 230-34
Amphitrite (U.S. monitor), 62
Anadir (Russian supply vessel), 80
Anderson (U.S. destroyer), 204
Andrea Doria (Italian battleship), 138, 176
Anglo-Japanese Alliance, 132
Anti-aircraft, 140, 146, 191
Anti-submarine patrol, 116, 121
Anton Schmitt (German destroyer), 159
Anzio, 176, 237
Apraxin (Russian coastal defense vessel), 76
Arbrial, Vice Admiral Jean Marie Charles, 163
Archerfish (U.S. submarine), 197
Ardent (British destroyer), 109, 161
Arethusa (British light cruiser), 94
Argentina, 74
Argus (British seaplane carrier), 138
Ariadne (German light cruiser), 93, 94
Arizona (U.S. battleship), 182, 183
Ark Royal (British aircraft carrier), 138, 143, 154, 156, 168, 175, *illus.* 168, 171
Arkansas (U.S. battleship), 121, 240, 246, 272, 283, *illus.* 141, 245
Armament, 31
    Admiral Montojo's Spanish Squadron, 56
    defensive, 18
    U.S., 22
Armistice (1918), 127
Army. *See* individual nations
Asagumo (Japanese destroyer), 49
Asahi (Japanese battleship), 76
Asama (Japanese armored cruiser), 76
Ash can or depth charge (mine), 116, *illus.* 117, 222-23
Ashigara (Japanese heavy cruiser), 38, 40
Asia, 176
Asia, southeast, 31, 257
Askold (Russian cruiser), 73
Assaults, amphibious, Operation Torch, 230-34
Astoria (U.S. heavy cruiser), 204, 207, 211, 212, illus. 211
Atago (Japanese heavy cruiser), 29, 34, 49, 203
Atlanta (U.S. light cruiser), 204, 217, *illus.* 217

Atlantic, war in (1941-1943), 219-28
Atomic bomb, 288, 292, 294, 297, 300, 305, *illus.* 293, 297
Atsutasan Maru (Japanese freighter), 196
Attack and defense (concepts of), 7
Attu, 196, 207, 208, 213, 218
Audacious (British battleship), 93, 94 *(illus.)*
August 10th, Battle of, 73-74; Japanese open fire, *illus.* 74
Augusta (U.S. heavy cruiser), 233, 235, 242, 246, *illus.* 232, 254
Ault, Commander William B., 202
Aurora (Russian cruiser), 80
Australia, 83, 192, 194, 200
Australia (Australian heavy cruiser), 211, *illus.* 213
Austria, 86
Avenger (torpedo plane), *illus.* 47, 143, 189, 264
Aviation, air power (1910), 137-46. *See also* Airplane; Amphibious operations; Carrier
Aviation bases (U.S. naval), 135, 208
Avieri (Italian destroyer), *illus.* 170
Aylwin (U.S. destroyer), 204

B-17's, 145
B-24's, 145
B-25's (Doolittle), *illus.* 200; (Mitchell), *illus.* 31
B-29's, work on targets in Japan, *illus.* 292
B-98's, *illus.* 108
Badung Strait, off Bali, 192
Bagley (U.S. destroyer), 211
Bailey (U.S. destroyer), 208
Bainbridge (U.S. nuclear destroyer, 1962), 24, *illus.* 25
Balch (U.S. destroyer), 204
Balfour, Lord, 24, 96
Bali, 192
Bali Strait, 194
Balikpapan, Borneo, 191
Baltic (the), 72, 83
Baltimore (U.S. cruiser), 51, 52, 53, 55, 58
Baltimore (U.S. heavy cruiser, 1943), 20, *illus.* 21
Barb (U.S. submarine), 233
Barnegat (U.S. aircraft tender), 233
Barham (British battleship), 99, 168, 172, 174, 175; explodes, *illus.* 175
Bartimeus (British naval writer), 176
Bartolomeo Colleoni (Italian cruiser), 170; blows up, *illus.* 170
Battle cruiser, *illus.* 18
Battle Cruiser Squadron (Beatty's), 98-108
Battle of the Tenth of August, 73-74
Battleship(s), 134, 135, *illus.* 259, 303, 304
    1919 (U.S. and Britain), 127
    abbreviations and symbols, 6-7 *(diag.)*
    carrier, *illus.* 49
    Hood, biggest Allied warship, 152
    Japanese, damaged, *illus.* 37
    Philippines, Second Battle of, 14
    pocket battleship, 147, 148
    sections (typical), *diag.* 6
    (the) slugger, *illus.* 14
    world's best, 150
    world's greatest (1944), 33, 34
    world's largest, 259
Bayley, Vice Admiral Sir Lewis, RN, 119, 123
Beatty, Vice Admiral Sir David (Commander in Chief of Grand Fleet), 94, 98-108, 116
Beatty (U.S. destroyer), 233
Belfast (British cruiser), 225, *illus.* 174
Belgium, 127, 132, 161
Bell, Commander Frederick, 129-30
Belleau Wood (U.S. aircraft carrier), 38
Bellerophon (British battleship), 99
Bellows Field, 180, 181
Benbow (British battleship), 99
Benham (U.S. destroyer), 204
Berehaven, Ireland, 121
Bering Sea, 208
Berlin, 90, 276
Bernadou (U.S. destroyer), *illus.* 232
Bethlehem Iron Company (1887), 22
Bethmann-Hollwegg, Chancellor T. von, 96, 113
Bey, Rear Admiral, 160, 224, 225
Biak Island, 259
Biedovoi (Russian torpedo boat), *illus.* 79

Biloxi (U.S. light cruiser), 39
Birmingham (U.S. light cruiser, 1943), 22, 36, *illus.* 23
Birmingham (old U.S. light cruiser), *illus.* 139
Biscay, Bay of, 122
Bismarck (German battleship), 148, 151-57, 168, 224, *illus.* 152, 153, 155, 156; chase of, *map* 155
Bismarck barrier, 258
Bismarck Sea, 140
Bismarck Sea (U.S. escort carrier), 273
Bizerte, 236
Black Prince (British armored cruiser), 99, 109, 246
Black Sea, 72, 94
Blanchard, Commander J. W., 264
Blimp (early aerial anti-submarine patrol), *illus.* 125
Blücher (German heavy cruiser, 1909), 20, 94, 148, 158, *illus.* 21, 87, 93
Blue (U.S. destroyer), 211, 212
Boedicker, German Rear Admiral, 104
Bogatyr (Russian protected cruiser), 73
Boise (U.S. light cruiser), 38, 191 *(illus.)*, 215
Bomb(s), nuclear, 300-301
Bombers, 142-45
    attack (U.S. Navy), 139, 142
    Avenger, *illus.* 143
    Dauntless, at Wake, *illus.* 188
    squadrons, 191
    torpedo planes, 143-44, 156, 169, 182, *illus.* 137
Bonins, 132, 273
Bonte, Commodore Friedrich, 159
Bordeaux, 122
Borodino (Russian battleship), 76, 77, 79, 88
Boston (U.S. light cruiser), 52, 53, 55, 59, *illus.* 56
Bougainville Island, Upper Solomons, 188, 199, 218
Boulonnais (French destroyer), 235
Bovik (Russian battleship), 74
Boyle (U.S. destroyer), 233
Bradley, General of the Army Omar N., 253
Brassey's *Naval Annual* (British): *1899*, 82; *1908*, 84
Browy (Russian destroyer), 80
Brazil, 62, 148, 149
Breakwater sections (floating), *illus.* 242
Brest, France, 121, 122, 125, 151, 224
Brestois (French destroyer), 235
Bretagne (French battleship), 168, 169
Brewster Buffaloes, 205
Brisbane, Australia, 210
Bristol (British 2d-class cruiser), 91
Bristol (U.S. destroyer), 233
Britannia (British battleship), *illus.* 127
British Admiralty, 97, 123, 138
    (and) sinking of *Scharnhorst*, 225-26
    (and) war undersea (1914-1918), 116
British Army, 161
British Far Eastern forces, 276
British Fifth Battle Squadron, Jutland, Battle of, 97-98, 103, 104
British Fleet, Main, and sinking of *Scharnhorst*, *map* 226
British Fleet Air Arm, 139
British Commandos, *illus.* 157, 162
British Expeditionary Force, 162
British Grand Fleet, 16, 92, 95, 116, 121, 276
British High Seas Fleet, 113, 114, 116
British Home Fleet, 88, 148, 151
British Mediterranean Fleet, 142, 166-76
British Royal Air Force, 155-56, 164
British Royal Navy, 14, 24, 88, 113, 116, 161, 162, 210
    1898, 24
    England's life lines, 147-56
British sea and air power, North Africa landings, *illus.* 234
British South Atlantic Squadron, 148, 149
British Third Battle Cruiser Squadron, 98, 103
British-U.S. Grand Fleet, 127
Broke (British destroyer), 163
Brooklyn (U.S. armored cruiser), 62, 64, 66-69
Brooklyn (U.S. light cruiser), 233, 235
Brown, Lieutenant Commander W. L. M., 160
Brown, Vice Admiral Wilson, 188, 189, 201
Brunei, Sarawak, 40
Bryant, Rear Admiral C. F., 242
Buchvostoff, Captain, 77
Buckmaster, Rear Admiral Eliott, 207
Buckner, Lieutenant General Simon Bolivar, 281

308

Buenaventura (Spanish freighter), 61
Buin, 211
Buiny (Russian torpedo boat), 80
Buka Island, Upper Solomons, 199
Bunker Hill (U.S. aircraft carrier), 284
Burnett, Rear Admiral, 225
Bushnell, David, 111

Cabot (U.S. aircraft carrier), 38
Cachlot (U.S. submarine), 204
Cádiz, 70
Caio Duilio (Italian battleship), 138, 176
California (U.S. battleship), 33, 38, 182, *illus.* 183, 184
Callaghan, Rear Admiral Daniel J., 217
Camouflage (ship), 124; convoy, *illus.* 122
Canada (British battleship), 99 *(illus.)*
Canal Zone, 210
Canberra (Australian heavy cruiser), 211, 212 *(illus.)*
Canopus (British battleship), 89, 90, 91
Cape Engano, Battle of, *map* 32, 48
Cape Esperance, Battle of, 215
Cape Matapan, Battle of, 172, 174, *illus.* 173
Capital ships, 131
Carlos II (Spanish armored cruiser), 70
Carnarvon (British armored cruiser), 91, 92
Caroline Islands, 88
Caribbean, 135
Carrier fighter, 144
Carriers (aircraft), 14, 133, 135, 301, *illus.* 16
  battle, 258-68
  battle for a foothold (1942-1943), 209-18
  British, *illus.* 287
  British, steel decks, 277
  Casablanca class escort carriers (1943-1944), *illus.* 146
  Coral Sea and Midway, 199-208
  description, 162
  development, 145-46
  sections, typical, *diag.* 6
  U.S., *illus.* 287
Casablanca, 230, 234-36
Casablanca class escort carriers (1943-1944), *illus.* 146
Cassin (U.S. destroyer), 177; at Pearl Harbor, *illus.* 182
Castillo (Spanish wooden cruiser), 56-58
Catalina (later PBY), 156, *illus.* 154
Cavalla (U.S. submarine), 197, 264
Cavite Peninsula, 55, 56, 59
Cavour class battleship, *illus.* 138
Central Powers (Germany and Austria-Hungary), 96
Centurion (British battleship), 99
Cervera, Admiral, 63-67
Cesare (Italian battleship), 169
Chamberlain, Neville, 168
Chance-Vought Corsair, 144
Charleston (1864), 112
Chase, Lieutenant William A., 204
Chemulpo (Inchon), Korean port, 73
Chenango (U.S. escort carrier), 38
Cherbourg, 240, 252, 253
Chester (U.S. heavy cruiser), 186, 187
Chester (U.S. scout cruiser), 84
Chicago (U.S. heavy cruiser), 211, 212, 214, *illus.* 213
Chichi Jima, 273
Chikuma (Japanese heavy cruiser), 34, 38, 43, 49, 203, 214, 216, 217
Children, German World War I orphans, 157
China, 71, 72, 83, 132, 195
Chitose (Japanese aircraft carrier), 38, 46, 49, 203
Chiyoda (Japanese small carrier), 38, 46, 49, 266
Chokai (Japanese heavy cruiser) 34, 38, 43, 49, 203, 211, 212
Churchill, Winston, 156, 158, 168, 169, 230, 237, 239, 244, 255, 276
Ciano, Count, 234
Cienfuegos, 64
Civil War (U.S.), 22, 70
Clark, Champ, 70
Clark, Major General Mark, 234
Clement (British freighter), 148
Cleveland (U.S. light cruiser), 233
Coal, 14, 123, 125
Cochrane (British armored cruiser), 99
Cocos Islands, 92

Coghlan (U.S. destroyer), 208
Collingwood (British battleship), 99
Collins, Major General J. Lawton (Lightning Joe), 252-53
Colombia, 84
Colorado (U.S. battleship), 131
Colossus (British battleship), 99
Columbia (U.S. light cruiser), 38, 62
Commandat Teste (French seaplane carrier), 168
Commerce raiding, 88, 90, 92, 148
Complement (ship's), education of, 7
Concha (Spanish light cruiser), 64
Concord (U.S. gunboat), 52, 53, 55, *illus.* 60
Connecticut (U.S. battleship), 81
Conqueror (British battleship), 99
Conte di Cavour (Italian battleship), 138, 175
Contentin Peninsula, 252
Convoy(s)
  Allied, and sinking of *Scharnhorst, map* 226
  camouflaged, *illus.* 122
  Murmansk, 224, 225
  U.S. Merchant, *illus.* 116
  zig-zag (maneuver), 124, *illus.* 123
Convoy duty, 122-27; Japanese destroyer, *illus.* 31
Convoy system, 114, 116-18
Conyngham (U.S. destroyer), 121, 204
Coolidge, Calvin, 132
Coral Sea, 138, 211, 279
Coral Sea, Battle of (1942), 199-202, *map* 202; ships lost, 203
Cordelia (British battleship), 99
Cornwall (British armored cruiser), 91, 92
Cornwall (British heavy cruiser), 176, 194
Coron Bay, 40
Coronel (Chilean port), 91, 92
Coronel, Battle of, 88-90
Corregidor Island, 51, 55
Corry (U.S. destroyer), 233
Corvette (British and Canadian), *illus.* 221
Cossack (British destroyer), 161 *(illus.)*
Courageous (British aircraft carrier), 161
Cowie (U.S. destroyer), 233
Cradock, Rear Admiral Sir Christopher, 88-90
Cressy (British armored cruiser), 92, 93
Crete, 175-76
Cristobal Colon (Spanish armored cruiser), 64, *illus.* 65, 67, 68
Cromarty, Moray Firth, 98
"Crossing the T" (maneuver), 76, 77, 104
Cruiser(s)
  British, *illus.* 108, 172, and sinking of *Scharnhorst, map* 226
  French, *illus.* 233
  Italian, *illus.* 173
  Japanese, hit by Halsey's Helldivers, *illus.* 47
  torpedo, *illus.* 156
Crutchley, Rear Admiral V. A. C. (British Royal Navy), 210, 211, 213
Cuba, 22, 52, 61, 63, 64
Culebra Cut, 85
Cumberland (British heavy cruiser), 149, 150
Cunningham, Sir Andrew (Admiral of the Fleet, First Sea Lord and Chief of Naval Staff), 142, 167-72, 174-76, 182, 231
Curaçao, 64
Curtiss, Glenn, 139
Curtiss (U.S. seaplane tender), 178
Curtiss Helldivers, 34
"Cut but not kill" (Japanese tactic), 184
Cuttlefish (U.S. submarine), 204

D-Day, 242, 244, 246, 252, 253, 255
Dace (U.S. submarine), 29, 30
Dakar, 232
Dale (U.S. destroyer), 208
Damage-control practice (naval vessel), 7, 110
  design, problems in, 7
  ship's complement, education of, 7
Dardanelles, 72, 94
Dardanelles Campaign, 139
Darlan, Admiral, 230
Darter (U.S. submarine), 29, 30
Dauntless, illus. 188, 203

Davis (U.S. destroyer), 121
Davidson, Rear Admiral Lyal A., 255
Davison, Admiral R. E., 277
Dealey, Commander Sam, 196
Defense (British armored cruiser), 99, 104 *(illus.)*, 109
Delaware (U.S. battleship, 1909), 84 *(illus.)*, 121
Denver (U.S. light cruiser), 38
Depth charge or ash can (mine), 116, *illus.* 117, 222-23
Derfflinger (German battle cruiser), 94, 96, 99, 101, 102, 105 *(illus.)*, 106
De Ruyter (Netherlands light cruiser), 191-94, *illus.* 193
Design (naval vessel), problems in, 7
Destination North Africa, *illus.* 231
Destroyer(s), *illus.* 24, 158, 171, 224
   1941, 135
   German, *illus.* 160
   Japanese, *illus.* 31, 197
   lays smoke screen, *illus.* 40
   U.S., escort duty, 122, *illus.* 221
   World War II, 16
de Tassigny, General Jean de Lattre, 255
Deutschland (German pocket battleship, later renamed *Lützow*), 100, 148, 150 *(illus.)*
Deutschland (German submarine, 1912), 26, *illus.* 27
Dewa, Admiral, 77
Dewey, Admiral George, 16, 61, 70, 303
Dewey, Admiral George
   Far Eastern Squadron, 51-60
   (aboard) *Olympia*, *illus.* 58
Deyo, Rear Admiral Morton L., 242
Diana (Russian cruiser), 73, 74
Dido (British cruiser), 175
Dieter von Roeder (German destroyer), 159
Dietl, General Eduard, 159
Dimitri Donski (Russian cruiser), 76
Disarmament: and rebuilding, 129-36; Washington Disarmament Conference (1921-1922), 20, 24, 130
Dive bombers, 142-43
Dive-bombing technique (U.S. Navy), 139, 142, 143, *illus.* 37
Dogger Bank, Battle of, 75, 94, 96
Dolphin (U.S. submarine), 204
Don Antonio de Ulloa (Spanish light cruiser), 56, 57 *(illus.)*
Don Juan de Austria (Spanish light cruiser), 56, *illus.* 55
Doolittle, Lieutenant General Jimmy, 145
Doorman, Rear Admiral Karel W. F. M., 192-94
Doran (U.S. destroyer), 233
Dorsetshire (British heavy cruiser), 176, 194; end of, *illus.* 195
Dover, 127, 163, 164
Downes (U.S. destroyer), 177; at Pearl Harbor, *illus.* 182
Dreadnaught (British revolutionary-type battleship, 1906), 82 *(illus.)*, 84
Dreadnaughts (modern), 14
Dresden (German light cruiser), 88, 91, 92 *(illus.)*
Drum (U.S. submarine), 204
Duizend Islands, 194
Duke of Edinburgh (British armored cruiser), 99
Duke of York (British battleship), 151, 224-27, *illus.* 150, 225
Duncan (U.S. destroyer), 215
Dunkerque (French battle cruiser), 168, 169
Dunkirk, evacuation of, 162-66, *map* 163
Dutch Harbor, 207
Dutch ships, *illus.* 235

Eagle (British small carrier), 168, 172
Eagle (British ship, 1775), 111
East of Malta, West of Suez (Bartimeus), 176
Eastwind (U.S. Coast Guard cutter), *illus.* 224
Edison (U.S. destroyer), 233
Education, of ship's complement, 7
Efate, New Hebrides, 200, 210
Egypt, 175, 176
Eisenhower, Dwight D., General of the Army, 166, 230, 236, 240, 242, 244, 246
Elbing (German light cruiser), 108, 110
Elcano (Spanish gun vessel), 56
Electra (British destroyer), 194
El Fraile (island), 51, 55
Ellet (U.S. destroyer), 204

Ellis, Chief Yeoman George H., 69
Ellyson (U.S. destroyer), 233
Ely, Eugene, 139
Emden (German light cruiser), 88, 92, *illus.* 90, 93
Emmons (U.S. destroyer), 233
Encounter (British destroyer), 194
Engadine (British seaplane ship), 140
England, 62, 116; life lines (1939-1941), 147-56
Enterprise (U.S. aircraft carrier), 38, 133, 181, 182, 184, 200, 203-07, 209, 210, 214-16, 277, 284, *illus.* 217
   flight deck, *illus.* 187, 214
Enterprise (U.S. nuclear-powered carrier, 1961), 16, *illus.* 17, 300
Ericsson (U.S. destroyer), 66, 233, *illus.* 63
Erin (British battleship), 99
Escort carriers, 258, *illus.* 42, 221
Eskimo (British destroyer), 161
Espiritu Santo, 210, 215
Essex (U.S. carrier), 31, 38
Eugenio Di Savola (Italian cruiser), *illus.* 170
Europe, 75, 83; invasion of, 239-56
Evans, Joel C., 53
Evans, Rear Admiral Robley Dunglison (Fighting Bob), 62, 81-83
Evan-Thomas, Rear Admiral H., 98, 99, 101-04
Evertsen (Dutch destroyer), 194
Exeter (British heavy cruiser), 149, 191-94, *illus.* 148
   starts her death roll, *illus.* 194
Ewa Field, 180

Faisi, 211
Falkland Islands, Battle of, 88, 90-94, 148, 149
Fanshaw Bay (U.S. escort carrier), 38, 42
Far East, 82, 83, 132, 175, 178, 190, 276
   naval campaign (W. W. II), 194
   Russo-Japanese War (1904), 71-80
Far Eastern Squadron (German), bases, 88
Farragut, Admiral, 106
Fedala, 236
Fire control (naval), and damage, 6-7 *(diag.)*
Fleet Air Arm, 170, 174
Fletcher, Rear Admiral Frank Jack, 186, 200, 207, 210-12, 214
Florida (state), 64
Florida (U.S. battleship), 121
Florida Island, 211
Flying Fish (U.S. submarine), 204
Fifth Fleet cruiser force, 33
Fighting (naval), radar age of, 283
Fiji (British cruiser), 175
Finback (U.S. submarine), 204
Finland, 158
Fiske, Rear Admiral Bradley A., USN, 139
Fitch, Vice Admiral Aubrey W., 201
Fitch (U.S. destroyer), 233
Fiume (Italian cruiser), 174
5-5-3 naval ratio, 20, 131, 132
Force H, at Gibraltar, 151, 156, 168, 169, 175, 176, 232
   three units of, *illus.* 168
Ford Island, 180, 181, 183
Forester (British destroyer), 160, *illus.* 161
Formidable (British carrier), 172, 174, 175
Formosa, 38, 258, 277
Forrest (U.S. destroyer), 233
Fortress Europe (Hitler's), 239, 240, *illus.* 249
Fortune (British destroyer), 109
Fougueux (French destroyer), 235
Four-Power Treaty, 132
France, 24, 86, 116, 123-25, 132, 133, 134, 148, 154, 161, 162, 167, 168, 234, 281
   assault on beaches of, *illus.* 245, 247
   battleship strength (1908 and 1914), 86
   (and) Russia, allies, 75
   World War I, 87
France, southern, amphibious attack on, 253-56 *(illus.)*
Frankfurt (German cruiser), *illus.* 106, 140
Franklin (U.S. aircraft carrier), 38, 277 *(illus.)*, 279, 284, *illus.* 278
Fraser, Sir Bruce (Commander in Chief, British Home Fleet), 225, 226
Frauenlob (German light cruiser), 108, 110
Freighter (Japanese), *illus.* 196

310

French Fleet, 169, 170, 174-76
French Morocco, 230
French Navy, at Casablanca, 235 *(illus.)*
Friedrich der Grosse (German battleship), 99, 103, *illus.* 97
Frigate (British and Canadian), *illus.* 221
Frondeur (French destroyer), 235
Fuji (Japanese battleship), 76
Fulmars (fighting planes), 172
Furious (British carrier convert), 140
Furor (Spanish torpedo boat, 1896), 24, 64, 67, *illus.* 25, 65
Fusan, 74
Fuso (Japanese battleship), 35, 38-40, 49, 203, *illus.* 33
Future (the), 297-305

G-102 (German destroyer), 140
Galatea (British light cruiser), 100
Gambier Bay (U.S. escort carrier), 42, 45, 49, *illus.* 41, 42
Gas, poison, 272
Gato (U.S. submarine), 204
Gavatu, 209
Gay, Ensign George H. (Tex), Jr., 205
Gefechtskehrtwendung (battle movement), 104
Geiger, Major General Roy M. (Marine Commander on Okinawa), 281
General Lezo (Spanish gun vessel), 56
Geneva, 132, 133
Geneva Convention, 272
Genoa, 175
Gensoul, Vice Admiral Marcel Bruno, 168
George V (King of England), 132
George F. Elliott (U.S. transport), 211
George Washington (U.S. liner), 123
German Admiralty, and submarines, 112-13, 118
German Air Force, 170, 172, 175
German Army, 96, 176
German commerce raiders, 121, 148
German Far Eastern Squadron, 88
German gunnery, accuracy of, 101, 102, 106, 149, 152, 154, 161
German High Seas Fleet, 16, 88, 92, 94, 95, 127, 140, 148
   Jutland, Battle of, 95-110
   returns to base, *illus.* 109
German Navy, Imperial, 24, 87, 88, *illus.* 128
   England's life lines, 147-56
   surrender (W. W. I), 127
German Second Scouting Group, 103
German Samoa, 88
German submarine campaign, 111-18, 123-25, 130, 219, 236, 255
Germany, 82, 83, 86
   battleship strength (1908 and 1914), 86
   naval power (1900), 81-86
   naval race with Britain (1888), 20
   Norway, 157-62
   radar, 152
   submarines, 86, 88, 219
   submarines, first to develop, 112
   war undersea (1914-1918), 111-18
   W. W. I, early phases, 87-94
   W. W. I orphans, 157
Ghormley, Vice Admiral Robert L., 210, 211, 215
Gibraltar, 116, 118, 121, 168, 175
Giese (German destroyer), 160
Giffen, Rear Admiral Robert C., 233, 235
Gilbert Islands, 185, 186, 189
Giulio Cesare (Italian battleship), 138, 176
Glasgow (British 2d-class cruiser), 89-92
Glennon (U.S. destroyer), 250
Glorious (British aircraft carrier), 161, 162
Gloucester (British light cruiser, 1910), 22, *illus.* 23
Glowworm (British destroyer), 158
Gneisenau (German armored cruiser), 88, 89, 91
Gneisenau (German battleship, 1926), 148, 150, 151, 158, 161, 224, *illus.* 150, 151
Godefroy, Admiral, 168
Goethals, Lieutenant Colonel George Washington (later major general), 85
Goliath (British battleship), 94
Good Hope (British armored cruiser), 88-90, *illus.* 90
Goodenough, Commodore W. E., 94, 102-03
Graf Spee (German battleship), 56, 150, 158, 224, *illus.* 147-49

Grayling (U.S. submarine), 204
Grayson (U.S. destroyer), 129
Great Britain, 81, 82
   battleship strength (1908 and 1914), 86
   cruisers, *illus.* 172
   disarmament and rebuilding, 129-36
   5-5-3 naval ratio, 20
   France (southern), invasion of, 253-56
   (and) German submarines, 219
   life lines, 112, 147-56
   Marshall Islands, 186
   Normandy, 239-53
   North African landings (1943), 229-38
   North Sea mine barrage laid by U.S. and, *map* 122
   raiders (commerce), 88
   (and) Russia, 75
   (and) supremacy of the seas, 18-20
   war undersea (1914-1918), 111-18
   warfare (naval), 138-46
   W. W. I, early phases, 87-94
Greece, 175
Greenland, 147, 150
Greenling (U.S. submarine), 204
Grenadier (U.S. submarine), 204
Gresny (Russian destroyer), 80
Greyhound (British destroyer), 175
Gridley, Captain Charles V., 56; aboard *Olympia*, *illus.* 58
Gromoboi (Russian armored cruiser), 73, 74
Grouper (U.S. submarine), 204
Growler (U.S. submarine), 204
Grumman Avenger (torpedo bomber), 34, 143, 205
Grumman Hellcats, 34
Grumman Wildcats, 184
Guadalcanal, 129, 199, 209-15, 258
Guadalcanal, Battle of, 216-18
Guam, 24, 70, 132, 135, 261, 262, 264, 267, 276, 283
Guantánamo Bay, 66
Gudgeon (U.S. submarine), 204
Gullflight (U.S. merchantman), 112
Gunnel (U.S. submarine), 233
Guns and gunnery, 134, 135
   automatic calculators, 18
   biggest (1898), 13
   British Navy, 92
   Corregidor, 55
   Dewey's U.S. Squadron, 52
   German accuracy, 89, 101, 102, 106, 149, 152, 154, 161
   Japanese, 42, 74
   muzzle-loading, 13
   Philippines, 2d Battle of, 14
   Russian, 75
   tomorrow's, 305
   U.S. accuracy, 59, 67, 250, 252, 253
   "Y," tosses out its "ash cans," *illus.* 117
   See also Armament

H-Hour, 244, 246, 255
Haguro (Japanese heavy cruiser), 34, 38, 264
Hale, Eugene, 134
Hall, Rear Admiral John L., 242
Halsey, Fleet Admiral William F., Jr., 14, 16, 31, 32, 34-36, 38, 41, 45-47, 185-86, 188, 189, 203, 215-17, 267, 272, 284, 285, 296
Halsey's Helldivers, hit Japanese cruiser, *illus.* 47
Hambleton (U.S. destroyer), 233
Hammann (U.S. destroyer), 204, *illus.* 207
Hampshire (British armored cruiser), 99
Hampton Roads, 62, 63, 81, 83, 85, 116
Hancock (U.S. aircraft carrier), 284
Hannover (German battleship), 100
Harder (U.S. submarine), 197
Harding, Warren G., 130
Hardy (British destroyer), 159
Hart, Admiral Thomas C., 191
Hartzog, Captain, 106
Haruna (Japanese battleship), 33, 34, 38, 88, 203, 216, 266
Harvey, Major F. J. W., 110
Harwood, Rear Admiral H. H., 148, 149, 150
Hatsuse (Japanese battleship), 74
Hatsutsuki (Japanese destroyer), 49
Havana, 62

Havock (British destroyer), 159
Hawaii, 72
Hawaiian Islands, 135
Hayashimo (Japanese destroyer), 49
Heavy cruisers, *illus.* 20; sections, typical, *diag.* 7
Helgoland, Battle of, 94, 96, 98
Helgoland (German battleship), 99
Helena (U.S. light cruiser), 177, 182
Hellcat, *illus.* 258, 261, 263
Helm (U.S. destroyer), 211
Henderson, Major Lofton (of the Marines), 205
Henderson Field, Guadalcanal, 211, 215
Hercules (British battleship), 99
Hermes (British aircraft carrier), 176, 195
Hero (British destroyer), 160, 161
Herodotus (Greek historian), 5
Herring (U.S. submarine), 233
Hessen (German battleship), 100
Hewitt, Vice Admiral Henry Kent, USN (Commander Amphibious Force Atlantic Fleet), 232, 234, 236
Hickam Field, 180, 181
Hiei (Japanese battleship), 178, 203, 213, 216, 217
Hipper, Vice Admiral Franz von, 94, 98-102, 104, 106
Hirohito, Emperor, 292, 294, 296
Hiroshima, 288, 294, 300; after atom bomb, *illus.* 294
Hiryu (Japanese aircraft carrier), 178, 203, 206, 207
History (U.S.), and Spanish-American War, 70
Hit(s)
    aerial bomb, *diag.* 6
    projectile, *diag.* 6
    torpedo, *diag.* 7
Hitler, Adolf, 133, 134, 147-50, 156, 157, 161, 162, 166-68, 172, 219, 230, 240, 242, 246
Hiyo (Japanese light carrier), 30, 266
Hoboken, N. J., 125
Hobson (U.S. destroyer), 233
Hobson, R. C., 86
Hobson, Richmond Pearson, 65
Hobson's *Merrimac* fails to seal it, *illus.* 66
Hoel (U.S. destroyer), 42, 45, 49, *illus.* 43
Hogue (British armored cruiser), 92, 93
Hokkaido, Japan, 285
Hollandia operation, 258-59
Hong Kong, 52, 53
Honolulu (U.S. light cruiser), 177, 204
Honshu, 196
    attack on, 272-73, 285
    carrier-based raids, results on, *illus.* 272
Hood, Rear Admiral H. L. A., 98, 99, 103-05
Hood (biggest Allied warship), 152, 154, 156, 168, *illus.* 153, 169
Hoover, Herbert C., 132, 133
Hornet (U.S. aircraft carrier), 200, 203-07, 216, 217 (*illus.*)
    and Doolittle B-25, *illus.* 200
Horns Reef, 106, 108, 109
Hostile (British destroyer), 159
Hotspur (British destroyer), 159
Housatonic (U.S. fleet oiler), 233
Housatonic (U.S. Union sloop of war), 111-12
Houston (U.S. heavy cruiser), 191-94
Howe (British battleship), 276
Hugh McCulloch (U.S. revenue cutter), 52, 53, 55
Hughes, Charles Evans, 130-31
Hughes (U.S. destroyer), 204
Hull, Cordell, 178
Hunter (British destroyer), 159
Hydroplane, 139
Hyuga (Japanese battleship), 38, 47

Iceberg. *See* Okinawa Operation
Iceland, 135, 147, 150, 220, 221
Idzumo (Japanese cruiser), 76
Illustrious (British aircraft carrier), 138, 170-72, 174, 175, 276
Immortalité (British ship), 53
Imperator Alexander III (Russian battleship), 76, 77
Imperator Nikolai (Russian turret ship), 76, 79
Imperial (British destroyer), 175
Imperial Japanese Navy. *See* Japanese Navy
Impero (Italian uncompleted battleship), 176
Indefatigable (British battle cruiser), 99, 101, 102, 104, 107, 109, 110
Indefatigable (British aircraft carrier), 276
Independence (U.S. aircraft carrier), 31, 38
Indian Ocean, 194, 195
Indiana (U.S. battleship), 62, 66, 67, *illus.* 63
Indianapolis (U.S. heavy cruiser), 189 (*illus.*), 204
Indomitable (British battle cruiser) 98, 99, 103
Indomitable (British aircraft carrier), 276
Inflexible (British battle cruiser), 18, 90, 91, 98, 99, 103, *illus.* 19, 91, 92, 98
Intrepid (U.S. aircraft carrier), 38, 284
Invincible (British battle cruiser), 90, 91, 98, 99, 103, 105, 109, 110, *illus.* 91, 105
Iowa (U.S. battleship, 1943), 38, 46, *illus.* 134
Iowa (U.S. battleship, 1922), *illus.* 134
Iowa (U.S. battleship, 1898), 62, 66, *illus.* 63, 133
Ireland, 119, 161
Irish Rebellion, 97
Iron Duke (British battleship, 1912), 14, 99, *illus.* 15, 96
Isabel II (Spanish light cruiser), 64, 70
Ise (Japanese battleship), 38, 47, 203, *illus.* 49
Isla de Cuba (Spanish gunboat), 56, 57, 59
Isla de Luzon (Spanish gunboat), 56
Isla de Mindanao (Spanish dispatch vessel), 56
Isolationism (U.S.), 70, 136
Isuzu (Japanese light cruiser), 38
Italia (Italian battleship, ex-*Littorio*), 176, *illus.* 170
Italian Army (1943), 176
Italian Fleet (1943), *illus.* 176
Italian Navy, 168
Italian Regia Aeronautica, 172
Italy, 132, 133, 142, 167, 168
    battleship strength (1908 and 1914), 86
    (and) German submarines, 219
    Taranto raid-damaged Italian ships in harbor, *illus.* 171
    W. W. I, 87
Ito, Captain Taisuke, 207
Iwate (Japanese armored cruiser), 76
Iwo Jima, 269, 270, 272, 273, 276, 281
    invasion, *illus.* 274-75
    U.S. Army Air Force Base, 276
Izumrud (Russian cruiser), 80

J. D. Edwards (U.S. destroyer), 192
Jade Bay, 94
Jade Roads, 98
Jaluit, 186, 187
Jamaica (British light cruiser), 225, 226, *illus.* 227
Japan
    battleship strength (1908 and 1914), 86
    bombers, *illus.* 261, 262, 268
    disarmament and rebuilding, 129-36
    Emperor, 292, 294, 296
    5-5-3 naval ratio, 20
    gunnery, 42
    losses at Iwo Jima, 273
    maritime losses, 196
    Marshall Islands, 185-86
    naval power (1900), 81-86
    open fire, Battle of August 10th, *illus.* 74
    people of, 292
    Philippines, Second Battle of, battleships and armament, 14
    Russo-Japanese War (1904-1905), 20, 71-80
    segregation in San Francisco, 82, 83
    strategy of defense, 258
    suicide pilots (*kamikazes*), 273, 284
    surrender (W. W. II), 288, 296, *illus.* 294
    10-10-7 ratio demands, 131, 132
    (and) U.S., naval standing (1933), 133
    (and) U.S., *1904*, 72-73, *1906*, 82
    U.S. strategy against, 257
    warfare (naval), 138-46, 190, 191
    W. W. I, early phases, 87 *ff.*
Japan, Sea of, 74, 75, 80
Japanese home islands, invasion of, 269 *ff.*, 276, 284, 285, 288
Japanese Kamikaze Corps, 146
Japanese Mobile Fleet, 259
Japanese Navy, Imperial, 49, 75, 82, 200, 213, 218, 258, 279
1592, 5
    Coral Sea and Midway, 203-08

Leyte Gulf, Battle of, 29-50
  organized by ship category, 213
  Pearl Harbor, 177-84
Japanese Sho Operation, 49
Jarvis (U.S. destroyer), 211
Java (Netherlands light cruiser), 191-94, *illus.* 193
Java Sea, Battle of, 192, *map* 193
Jean Bart (French battleship), 235, *illus.* 232
Jellicoe, Admiral Sir John (British naval Commander in Chief, First Sea Lord), 90, 94, 97-100, 102-07, 111, 113, 114, 116, 124, 140
Jemschug (Russian cruiser), 80
Jerram, Vice Admiral T. H. M., 98, 99, 107
Jervis (British destroyer), 174
Jervis Bay (British armed merchant cruiser), 151
Jintsu (Japanese light cruiser), 203, 214, 215
John D. Ford (U.S. destroyer), 191, 192
John Marshall (U.S. nuclear-powered submarine, 1962), 26, *illus.* 27, 301
Johnston (U.S. destroyer), 42, 45, 49
Johnston (aviation base), 135
Jones, John Paul, 28
JU-87's, 172
JU-88's, 172
Juan Fernandez Islands, 92
Juneau (U.S. light cruiser), 217
Juniper (British Navy tug), 161
Juno (British destroyer), 175
Junyo (Japanese aircraft carrier), 203, 216
Jupiter (British destroyer), 194
Jupiter (collier), 145
Jutland, 16, 28, 39, 92, 111-13, 130, 140, 148, 152, 169
Jutland, Battle of (1916), 95-110
  fleets and battle areas, *maps* 97, 100, 103-06, 109
  losses, men and ships, 109-10

Kadashan Bay (U.S. escort carrier), 38
Kaga (Japanese aircraft carrier), 131-32, 178, 203, 205, 206
Kaiser (the), and submarine warfare, 96
Kaiser (German battleship), 99
Kaiserin (German battleship), 99
Kalinin Bay (U.S. escort carrier), 38, 42
Kamikazes (Japanese suicide pilots), 146, 273, 277, 281, 283, *illus.* 285-87
  Baka Bomb, illus. 145
Kamimura, Admiral, 74
Kaneohe Naval Air Station, 180
Karlsruhe (German light cruiser), 92, 158
Kasagi (Japanese cruiser), 77
Kashima (Japanese battleship), *illus.* 71
Kashmir (British destroyer), 175
Kasuga (Japanese armored cruiser), 74, 76, *illus.* 75
Katagami (Japanese light cruiser), 203
Katori (Japanese battleship), *illus.* 71
Kavieng, New Ireland, 212, 213
Kawanishi patrol bomber, 144, 187
Kearny (U.S. destroyer), 233
Kelly (British destroyer), 175
Kennedy, Captain Edward Coverly, 150
Kent (British armored cruiser), 91, 92
Keokuk (U.S. net cargo ship), 273
Kerama Retto, 279, 281
Kesselring, Marshal (German Commander in Italian campaign), 237
Key West, Fla., 61-65
Keyes, Commodore Roger, 94
Kiaochau (port), Shantung Province, 74
Kijima, Captain Kikunori, 216
Kimmel, Admiral Husband F., 183
King, Admiral Ernest J., 257
King George V (British battleship), 99, 104, 107, 154, 276, *illus.* 155
Kinkaid, Vice Admiral Thomas C., 31, 33, 36, 38, 39, 45, 258; Seventh Fleet, *map* 32
Kinryu Maru (Japanese transport), 215
Kinu (Japanese light cruiser), 47, 49
Kirishima (Japanese battleship), 178, 203, 213, 217
Kirk, Admiral Alan G., 242, 253
Kiska, 204, 207, 208, 213, 218
Kiso (Japanese light cruiser), 203
Kitkun Bay (U.S. escort carrier), 38, 42

Kniaz Souvaroff (Russian battleship), 75-77, 79, 80
Knight (U.S. destroyer), 233
Kodiak, 135
Köln (German light cruiser), 93, 94
Komandorski Islands, Battle of, 208 *(map)*
Kongo (Japanese battleship), 33, 34, 38, 195-96, 203, 216
König (German battleship), 99, 103
Königsberg (German light cruiser), 158
Korea, 7, 75
Korea (Russian transport), 80
Korietz (Russian gunboat), 73; blows up, *illus.* 73
Kortenaer (Netherlands destroyer), 194
Kota Bharu, 190
Koyanagi, Rear Admiral Tomiji, 43
Krancke, Admiral, 242
Kronprinz (German battleship), 99
Kuantan, 190, 191
Kumano (Japanese heavy cruiser), 34, 38, 43-45, 203, 213-14
Kure, submarines under construction in shipyards, *illus.* 292
Kure Harbor, last of Japanese Navy destroyed in, *illus.* 290-91
Kurita, Vice Admiral Takeo, 32-35, 38, 41, 43, 45, 47, 39
Kurfürst (German battleship), 99
Kuriles, 132
Kurita — Central Japanese Force, *map* 32
Kurusu, Special Envoy, 178
Kwajalein lagoon, 187
Kyushu *kamikaze* bases, 277, 283, 285

Lae, New Guinea, 188, 199
Lafayette class, 303
Laffey (U.S. destroyer), 283; log of, 10
L'Alcyon (French destroyer), 235
Lamberton, Chief of Staff Commander, aboard *Olympia, illus.* 58
Landing craft (U.S.), 244, *illus.* 250
  burning, *illus.* 238
  North African landings (1943), 234, 236
Landing ship tank (LST), *illus.* 255
Langley (first operational U.S. aircraft carrier), 16, 17, 38, 145 *(illus.)*, 192 *(illus.)*
Langsdorff, Captain Hans, 148-50
Laurence, William L., 297
Laval, Pierre, 230
League of Nations, 130, 186
Leahy, Admiral William D., 257
Leavitt, Frank A., 139
Lee, Vice Admiral Willis, 262, 264, 266
Leedstown (British transport), 236
Leipzig (German light cruiser), 88, 91, 92, *illus.* 89
Leviathan (U.S. liner), 123
Lewis, Rear Admiral Spencer S., 255
Lexington (U.S. carrier), 38, 131, 184, 188, 200-202, 279, *illus.* 131, 201, 202; wracked by blasts from internal fires, *illus.* 199
Leyte Gulf, 269, 273, 284, 285
Leyte Gulf, Battle of (1944, Second Battle of the Philippines), 29-50, 288
  four phases of, *map* 32
  landings on, 13, 267, *illus.* 270
  U.S. troops, *illus.* 30
Liberty ship, *illus.* 250
Libya, 175
Light cruisers, *illus.* 22; sections, typical, *diag.* 7
Lingayen Gulf, 53
Lion (British battle cruiser), 94, 99-101, 110, *illus.* 96, 103
Littorio (Italian battleship), 138
Livermore (U.S. destroyer), 233
Lloyd George, David, 116, 184
Lockard, Private Joseph, 182, 184
Lockwood, Vice Admiral C. A., 264
Lodge, Henry Cabot, 86
London (1930) naval agreement, 133
Long, John Davis (Secretary of U.S. Navy), cable to Dewey, *quoted,* 59
Long Beach (U.S. nuclear-powered cruiser, 1961), 20, *illus.* 21, 300
Lorraine (French battleship), 168 *(illus.)*
Lotus Club, New York City, 83
Louisiade Archipelago, 201

Louisville (U.S. heavy cruiser), 38, 39, 186, 189, 204
Lowestoft-Yarmouth raid, 96, 97
Lowry, Rear Admiral Frank J., 237, 255
Ludlow (U.S. destroyer), 233, 235
Luftwaffe, 157, 158, 164, 176, 242; and evacuation of Dunkirk, 162-66
Lunga Point (U.S. escort carrier), 273
Lusitania (British liner), 96, 112 *(illus.)*
Lütjens, Admiral Günther, 152, 156
Lützow (German battle cruiser), 96, 99, 101, 105, 106, 108, 110, *illus.* 96, 107
Lützow (German battleship), 148, 161
Luzon, 30, 31, 33, 36, 53, 55, 70, 269
Lyster, Rear Admiral A. L. St. G., 171

MacArthur, General Douglas, 30, 45, 190, 191, 200, 210, 257-59, 296; Japanese surrender aboard *Missouri, illus.* 295, 296
McCain, Vice Admiral John S., 46, 47
Macassar Strait strike, 192
McClusky, Lieutenant Commander, 205
MacDonald, Prime Minister Ramsay, 28
McDougal (U.S. destroyer), 121
Macedonia (British 2d-class cruiser), 91
McKinley, William, 62
McMorris, Rear Admiral C. H., 183
Macomb (U.S. destroyer), 233
McWhorter, Rear Admiral Ernest D., 233
Madrid, 51, 58, 61, 62
Magellan, Strait of, 91
Mahan, Captain Alfred T., *Influence of Sea Power Upon History*, 22; (later Adm.), 63, 132
Maine (U.S. battleship), 61-62 *(illus.)*
Mainz (German light cruiser), 93, 94
Makharoff (Russian admiral), 73
Makin Island, 186-87 *(illus.)*
Malaita, near Stewart Island, 214
Malay Peninsula, 190
Malaya, 175, 191, 192
Malaya (British battleship), 168
Malta, 172, 174, 176
Maloelap, 186
Manchuria, 75, 288
Manchurian conquest (1931),.133
Mandated Islands, 132
Maneuver, "crossing the T," 76, 77
Manila, 24, 34, 40, 70, 80, 132, 191, 269, 303
Manila Bay, 13, 28, 87, 191
Manila Bay (U.S. escort carrier), 38
Manila Bay, Battle of (1898, First Battle of the Philippines), 51-60, 70, 72, *map* 54
Marblehead (U.S. light cruiser), 191, 192
Marcus Island, 188, 189
Marcus Island (U.S. escort carrier), 38
Maria Teresa (Spanish armored cruiser), 64, 67, 68, *illus.* 65
Mariana Islands, 88, 258, 259, 261, 270
Markgraf (German battleship), 99
Marlborough (British battleship), 99, 105
Marquis de Duero (Spanish dispatch vessel), 56
Marseilles, 255
Marshall Islands, 88, 185, 186, 189
Martinique, 64
Maryland (U.S. battleship), 33, 38, 131, 183, *illus.* 132
Massachusetts (U.S. battleship), 38, 62, 64, 66, 232, 233, 235
Matsu (Japanese battleship), 131, 203
Matsuki (Japanese destroyer), 215
Maury (U.S. destroyer), 204
Maya (Japanese heavy cruiser), 49, 203, 208
Mayflower (T. Roosevelt's presidential yacht), 81
Maynard, Captain Washburn, 61
Mediterranean, action in, 167-76 *(illus.),* map 169, 173
Merchant shipping, 148
Meredith (U.S. destroyer), 250
Merrimac, Monitor engaging, log, *illus.* 8
Merrimac, Hobson's ship, (U.S. collier), 65, 66
Merrimack (U.S. fleet oiler), 233
Mervine (U.S. destroyer), 233
Miami (U.S. light cruiser), 39
Miantonomoh (U.S. monitor), 62
Micheler, Admiral, 235

Michishio (Japanese destroyer), 49
Midway, 31, 135, 138, 186, 203, 213
Midway, Battle of (1942), 203-08, 40, 132, 143, 178, 288, *map,* 207
Midway (U.S. aircraft carrier, 1945), 16, *illus.* 17
Mikasa (Japanese battleship), 76 *(illus.)*
Mikawa, Rear Admiral, 211, 212
Mikuma (Japanese heavy cruiser), 194, 203
Mili, 186, 187
Mindanao Island, 33
Mine(s), 158, 162, 193, 250; depth charge or ash can, 116, *illus.* 121
Mine barrage, in North Sea, laid by U.S. and British ships, *map* 122
Mine-laying (W. W. I), 127, *illus.* 120, 121
Mine Patrol (U.S.), *illus.* 125
Mine sweepers, 246, *illus.* 240
Minneapolis (U.S. heavy cruiser), 38, 189, 204, 217, *illus.* 218
Minneapolis (U.S. light cruiser), 62
Minotaur (British armored cruiser), 99, *illus.* 109
Mirs Bay, China, 53
Missiles, 7, 28, 300-303; Polaris from under the sea, *illus.* 302
Mississippi (U.S. battleship), 33, 38, *illus.* 288
Missouri (U.S. battleship), 285, 296; Japanese surrender (W. W. II), *illus.* 50, 295, 296
Mitchell, Brigadier General William (Billy), 140, 142
Mitscher, Vice Admiral Marc A., 46, 47, 262, 264, 266, 272, 276; Third Fleet, *map* 32
Miwa, Vice Admiral, 195-96
Mobile (U.S. light cruiser), 39
Mogami (Japanese heavy cruiser), 33, 38, 39, 40, 49, 194, 203, *illus.* 205
Moltke (German battle cruiser), 94, 96, 99, 106, *illus.* 101
Monaghan (U.S. destroyer), 204, 208
Monarch (British battleship), 99
Monitor, engaging *Merrimac,* log, *illus.* 8
Monmouth (British armored cruiser), 88-90
Monroe, James, 24
Montevideo, Uruguay, 150
Montgomery (U.S. gunboat), 62
Montojo, Admiral (Spanish commander), 55-57, 59
Moon, Rear Admiral Don P., 242, 255
Moreau, Captain Dias, 68
Morgan, Lieutenant General Sir Frederick E., 240
Morris (U.S. destroyer), 204
Mt. Suribachi, 270, 273, *illus.* 276
Murmansk convoy, 224, 225
Murphy, Robert (Counselor of American Embassy), 230
Murphy (U.S. destroyer), 233
Musashi (Japanese battleship), 14, 33-35, 49, 197, 259, 262, *illus.* 34, 35, 50
Mussolini, Benito, 133, 134, 170, 172, 176
Myoko (Japanese heavy cruiser), 34

Nachi (Japanese heavy cruiser), 38, 40, 208
Nagara (Japanese light cruiser), 178, 203
Nagasaki, 288, 300; after atom bomb, *illus.* 294
Nagato (Japanese battleship), 33, 34, 38, 131, 203
Nagoya, 276
Nagumo, Vice Admiral Chuchi, 204
Naiad (British light cruiser), 176, 194
Naka (Japanese light cruiser), 203
Naniwa Kan (Japanese light cruiser), 77
Nanshau (U.S. transport), 52
Narvik (ore port), and Norwegian campaign, 158-61
Narwhal (U.S. submarine), 204
Nashville (U.S. gunboat), 61, 62 *(illus.)*
Nashville (U.S. light cruiser), 204
Nassau (German battleship, 1908), 100, *illus.* 86
National Industrial Recovery Act, 133
Natoma Bay (U.S. escort carrier), 38
Nautilus (U.S. submarine), 204, 206
Naval Annual (Brassey's British): *1899,* 82; *1908,* 84
Naval powers, three new (1900), 81-86
Naval War College, Newport, R. I., 305
Navarin (Russian battleship), 76, 77, 79 *(illus.)*
Navy, History of Our (Spears), 60
Nazi Navy, 149, 150
NC-4 (U.S. Navy seaplane), first transatlantic flight, 142
Near East, 118

Nebogatoff, Admiral, 75, 76, 79, 80
Nebraska (U.S. merchantman), 112
Nelson, at Trafalgar (1805), 72, 87
Nelson (British battleship), 152, *illus.* 236
Neosho (U.S. oiler), 201
Neptune (British battleship), 99
Nestor (British destroyer), 109
Netherlands, 132, 161
Netherlands Indies, 191
Netherlands Navy, Royal, 192
Nevada (U.S. battleship), 88, 121, 182, 240, 246, 272, 283, *illus.* 183, 241
New Britain Island, 188
New Caledonia, 200
New Georgia, 212
New Guinea, 140, 190, 199, 200, 201, 257, 259
New Hebrides, 210
New Jersey (U.S. battleship, 1942), 14, 36, 38, 46, *illus.* 15
New Jersey (U.S. battleship), 140
New Orleans (U.S. heavy cruiser), 39, 64, 204, 217
New York (U.S. armored cruiser), 62, 66-68, *illus.* 63
New York (U.S. battleship), 121, 233, 279
New York City, first North Atlantic convoy, 116; typical convoy, 123
New Zealand, 83
New Zealand (British battle cruiser), 99
Newfoundland Banks, 124
Newport News, 92
Nicholas (U.S. destroyer, 1942), 24, *illus.* 25
Nimitz, Admiral Chester W., 45, 257, 258, 264, 276, 296
Nine-Power Treaty, 132
Nishimura, Vice Admiral Shoji, 33, 35, 39, 40; Southern Japanese Force, *map* 32
Nishino, Commander Shigeru, 35, 39, 40
Nisshin (Japanese armored cruiser), 74
N.J. Fjord (Danish steamer), 95, 96
Nomad (British destroyer), 109
Nomura, Ambassador, 178
Norfolk (British heavy cruiser), 152, 154, 156, 225
Normandy, invasion of by amphibious attack, 239-53
North Africa, U.S. Army (1942), 176
North African landings (1943), 229-38, *map* 230
North Atlantic, 83, 124, 147, 150, 151, 156, 224
North Atlantic convoy, 116-18
North Carolina (U.S. battleship), 135, 152, 210, 214-16, *illus.* 135, 136, 201
North Pacific, 203, 204, 207, 208
North Sea, 88, 95, 96, 121, 127, 133, 147, 148, 151, 161, 242
North Sea Mine Barrage (laid by U.S. and British ships), 121, 127, *map* 122
Northampton (U.S. heavy cruiser), 186, 188, 204, 217
Norway, 121; British Commandos raid harbor, *illus.* 157, 162
Norwegian campaign, 148, 156-62
Noshiro (Japanese light cruiser), 38, 47, 49
Nouméa, New Caledonia, 210, 211
Novik (Russian cruiser), 73
Nowake (Japanese destroyer), 49
Nuclear energy, 7, 28, 297-305
Nuremberg, 237
Nürnberg (German light cruiser), 88, 90-92

Oahu, 177-84
O'Brien (U.S. destroyer), 215; submarine victim, *illus.* 216
Oglala (U.S. mine-layer), 177, 182
O'Hare, Lieutenant Commander Edward M. (Butch), 188
Oi Sendai (Japanese light cruiser), 203
Oil Pioneer (British tanker), 161
Okhtomsky, Rear Admiral Prince, 74
Okinawa, 269, 270, 273, 276, 277, 279, 281, 283, 284
Okinawa Operation (code name), 279-84
  invasion, 47
  landings, 279
  troops move to beaches, *illus.* 280
Oklahoma (U.S. battleship), 121, 182, 183
Oklahoma City (U.S. guided missile cruiser, 1960), 22, *illus.* 23
Oldenburg (German battleship), 100
Oldendorf, Rear Admiral Jesse B., 39, 40; Seventh Fleet, *map* 32
Oleg (Russian cruiser), 76, 80
Olympia (Dewey's U.S. protected cruiser, 1892), 20, 52, 53, 56, 57, 303, *illus.* 21, 52, 68
Omaha (U.S. light cruiser), *illus.* 253
Ommaney Bay (U.S. escort carrier), 38
Open Door (policy), in China, 72, 82, 132
Operation Anvil. *See* Operation Dragoon
Operation Dragoon, 253-56
Operation Dynamo, 162-66
Operation Husky (attack on Sicily), 236-37
Operation Neptune-Overlord, 240-53
Operation "Sho," 31
Operation Torch, 230-36
Oquendo (Spanish armored cruiser), 64, 67, 68, *illus.* 65
Oran, 138, 168, 169, 230
Oregon (U.S. battleship, 1893), 14, 63, 66-68, *illus.* 15, 64, 68
Orel (Russian battleship), 76-79
Orion (British battleship), 99
Orion (British light cruiser), 175
Orkneys (the), 121
Orzel (British submarine), 158
Oslabya (Russian battleship), 72, 76, 77 *(illus.)*
Ostfriesland (German battleship), 99, 109, 140
Otranto (British auxiliary cruiser), 89, 90
Outerbridge, Lieutenant William W., 181
Owen Stanley Range, 189
Oyodo (Japanese light cruiser), 38, 47
Ozawa, Vice Admiral Jisaburo, 36, 38, 43, 45, 46, 49, 259, 261, 266, 267; Northern Japanese Force, *map* 32; Ozawa's fleet, *illus.* 265

Pacific
  battle for a foothold (1942-1943), 209-18
  early raids, 185-98, *illus.* 185
  invasion, first U.S., 211
  southwestern, *map* 186
  submarines, 195
  U.S. Navy in, 83, 269
  west Pacific island groups, *map* 260, 270
Palau Islands, 258, 259
Pallada (Russian armored cruiser), 72, 74
Palmyra, 135
Panama Canal, 70, 83-85, 135, *illus.* 85
Panzer divisions (Hitler's), 162
Papua, Gulf of, 189
Paratroopers: British, *illus.* 244; U.S., *illus.* 246
Parker (U.S. destroyer), 233
Parrott (U.S. destroyer), 191
Patriota (Spanish steamer), 70
Patrol bomber, seaplane, 144
Patterson (U.S. destroyer), 211
Patton, General George F., Jr., 232, 234
Paul Jones (U.S. destroyer), 191, 192
PBM's, 144
PBY's, 144, 180
Pearl Harbor, 177-84, *illus.* 177, 180-84
  Japanese strategy, 184
  losses, 177-78
  map, 179
  references to, 45, 55, 73, 80, 132, 135, 138, 171, 199, 202, 208, 210, 212, 213, 215, 216, 219, 240, 257, 264, 279, 281, 285
Peary (U.S. destroyer, 1920), 24, *illus.* 25
Pecos (U.S. oiler), 192
Pelayo (Spanish battleship), 70
Peliliu, 281
Pennsylvania (U.S. battleship), 31, 33, 38, 183, *illus.* 139, 268
Pensacola (U.S. heavy cruiser), 189, 204, 218
Peresviet (Russian battleship), 74
Perry, Commodore Matthew C., 80
Perth (British light cruiser), 192-94
Pétain, Marshal, 168, 230
Petrel (U.S. gunboat), 52, 53, 59, *illus.* 60
Petrof Bay (U.S. escort carrier), 38
Petropavlosk (Russian battleship), 73
Phaeton (British light cruiser), 100
Phelps (U.S. destroyer), 204
Philadelphia (U.S. light cruiser), 233
Philippine Sea, air battle (1944), 257-68
Philippines, 24, 132, 135, 195, 257, 258, 269
  floating drydock, *illus.* 288
  U.S. acquisition, 70

U.S. Third Fleet (1944), 13
Philippines, First Battle of (1898), 13, 51-60
Philippines, Second Battle of, 13, 28
   battleships, 14
   landings, 273
   Leyte Gulf, Battle of (1944), 29-50
   vessels sunk, 47-49
Phillips, Admiral Sir Tom (Tom Thumb), 190-91
Phoenix (U.S. light cruiser), 38, *illus.* 183
Picket line (tactic), 283
Picket ships, 283, 284
Piet Hein (Netherlands destroyer), 192
Pike (U.S. submarine), 204
Pittman, Key, 134
Pittsburgh (U.S. light cruiser), 285
Plunger (U.S. submarine), 204
Pluton (Spanish torpedo boat), 64, 67, *illus.* 65
Pobieda (Russian battleship), 74
Pocket battleships, 147, 148
Point Bolinao, 53, 55
Poison gas, 272
Pola (Italian heavy cruiser), 174
Polaris, from under the sea, *illus.* 302
Pollack (U.S. submarine), 204
Poltava (Russian battleship), 73, 74
Pommern (German battleship), 100, 108, 110, *illus.* 109
Pompano (U.S. submarine), 204
Pope (U.S. destroyer), 191, 194; blown out of the water, *illus.* 194
Porpoise (U.S. submarine), 204
Port Arthur, 71, 73-75, 182
Port Lyautey, 234, 236
Port Moresby, New Guinea, 189, 190, 200
Porter (U.S. destroyer), 121
Portland (U.S. heavy cruiser), 38, 204
Portsmouth, N. H., 80
Portsmouth Treaty, 82
Portugal, 132
Poseidon (British oiler), 158
Posen (German battleship), 100
Potsdam Conference, 288
Potsdam Declaration, 292
Pridham-Wippell, Vice Admiral H. D., 172, 174
Prikauguet (French light cruiser), 235
Prince of Wales (British battleship), 154, 190, 191, *illus.* 153, 190
Princess Royal (British battle cruiser), 99, 101
Princeton (U.S. light carrier), 36, 49; burns and explodes, *illus.* 36
Prinz Eitel Friedrich (German armed cruiser), 91, 92
Prinz Eugen (German heavy cruiser), 148, 152, 154, *illus.* 152
Prinz Regent Luitpold (German battleship), 99
Provence (French battleship), 168, 169
Puerto Rico, 24, 70
Puritan (U.S. monitor), 62

Queen Elizabeth's (four in British Fifth Battle Squadron), Battle of Jutland, 88, 97, 98
Queen Mary (British battle cruiser), 99, 101, 102, 104, 107, 109, 110; explodes, *illus.* 102
Queenstown (British destroyer), 174
Queenstown Harbor, Ireland, 119, 121, 122
Quick (U.S. destroyer), 233
Quincy (U.S. heavy cruiser), 211, 212, 242, 246, *illus.* 252, 253

Rabaul, New Britain, 88, 188, 210-13, 218
Radar, 16, 56, 146, 152, 156, 182, 184, 197, 217, 221; picket line, 283
Raleigh (U.S. light cruiser, 1892), 22, 52, 53, *illus.* 23, 59
Raleigh (U.S. light cruiser, 1922), 177, 182, 183
Ralph Talbot (U.S. destroyer), 211
Ramilles (British battleship), 154
Ramsay, Admiral Sir Bertram (Supreme Naval Commander), 239, 240, 244, 253
Ramsey, Vice Admiral Sir Bertram Home, 163, 164, 166
Ranger (U.S. aircraft carrier), 233
Rapido (Spanish torpedo boat), 70
Raunfels (German ammunition ship), 159
Rawalpindi (British armed merchant cruiser), 150
Rawlings, Vice Admiral Sir H. Bernard, 276

Redfish (U.S. submarine), 197
Reina Cristina (Spanish steel cruiser), 56-58, *illus.* 53, 57
Reitzenstein, Rear Admiral, 74
Rekata Bay, 211
Renown (British battle cruiser), 154, 156, 158, 175, *illus.* 168
Repulse (British battle cruiser), 190 *(illus.)*
Resolution (British battleship), 168, *illus.* 169
Retsivan (Russian battleship), 72 *(illus.)*, 74
Reuben James (U.S. destroyer), 220
Revenge (British battleship), 99
Rheinland (German battleship), 100
Rhineland, 134
Rich (U.S. destroyer escort), 250
Richelieu (French battleship), 232; main batteries open fire, *illus.* 229
Richmond (U.S. light cruiser), 208
Rio de Janeiro (German transport), 158
Río de la Plata, 150
River Plate, Battle of, 56
Roberts, Justice Owen J., 183
Roberts Report, 184
Rocket ships, *illus.* 281
Rodgers, Rear Admiral Bertram J., 255
Rodgers, Rear Admiral Thomas S., 121
Rodman, Rear Admiral Hugh, 121
Rodman (U.S. destroyer), 233
Rodney (British battleship), 152, 154, *illus.* 236
Roe (U.S. destroyer), 233
Rojdestvensky, Admiral, 75, 76, 79, 80, 83, 91
Roma (Italian battleship, 1943), 175, 176
Rommel, Field Marshal Erwin, 242
Roosevelt, Franklin D., 28, 130, 132, 133, 135, 188, 230, 276
Roosevelt, Theodore, 24, 62, 63, 80-84
Rossia (Russian armored cruiser), 73, 74
Rostock (German light cruiser), 108, 110
Rosyth, Firth of Forth, 98
Rota, 262, 264
Rowan (U.S. destroyer), 233
Royal Netherlands Navy. *See* Netherlands Navy
Royal Oak (British battleship), 99, *illus.* 107
Royal Sovereign (British battleship), 168
Rundstedt, Field Marshal Karl Gerd von (Supreme German Commander in the West), 252
Rurik (Russian armored cruiser), 73, 74
Russell (U.S. destroyer), 204
Russia, 28, 82, 86, 97, 98, 158, 276, 288, 294, 305
   battleship strength (1908 and 1914), 86
   (and) France, allies, 75
   (and) Great Britain, 75
   Russo-Japanese War (1904), 20, 71-80, 82-83, 86, 87
   (and a) Second Front, 230
   ships (1898), 14
   submarines, missile-firing nuclear-powered, 300-301
   W. W. I, 87
Russian Navy, 24, 88; Russo-Japanese War (1904), 71-80
Russo-Japanese War (1904-1905), 20, 71-80, 82-83, 86, 87
Ryder, Major General Charles W., 231
Ryujo (Japanese aircraft carrier), 203, 207, 213, 214
Ryukyus, 132

S-44 (U.S. submarine), 212
Safi, 234, 236
Sagami Wan, 296
Saginaw Bay (U.S. escort carrier), 38
Saigon, 74
Saint Lo (U.S. escort carrier), 38, 45, 49, *illus.* 43
St. Louis (U.S. light cruiser), 186, 204
St. Nazaire, 122
St. Paul (U.S. auxiliary cruiser), 70
St. Vincent (British battleship), 99
Saipan, 261, 267, 270, 281
Saipan, Battle of (First Battle of the Philippines), 30, 31
Sakashima Gunto, 277
Salamaua, New Guinea, 188, 199
Salamaua-Lae raid, 200
Salerno, 176, 237
Salmon (U.S. submarine, 1938), 26, *illus.* 27
Salmon D3 (U.S. submarine, 1910), 26 *(illus.)*
Salt Lake City (U.S. heavy cruiser), 186, 188, 208 *(illus.)*, 215
Samar (island), 31, 33, 45-47

Samar, Battle of, 45, 196, *map* 32, 48
Sampson, Rear Admiral William, 62-66
Sampson Squadron, 63
Samuel B. Roberts (U.S. destroyer escort), 42, 45, 49
San Bernardino Strait, 33, 35, 38, 41, 45
San Diego, California, 85, 210
San Francisco, California, 63, 82; segregation (1906-1907), 82, 83
San Francisco (U.S. heavy cruiser), 189 *(illus.)*
San Jacinto (U.S. aircraft carrier), 38
San Juan, Puerto Rico, 64, 65, 70
San Juan (U.S. light cruiser), 216
Sangamon (U.S. escort carrier), 38, 233
Santa Cruz, Battle of, 216
Santa Fe (U.S. light cruiser), 39
Santa Isabel Island, 211, 212
Santee (U.S. escort carrier), 38, 233
Santiago, 87, 279
Santiago, Battle of (1898), 61-70, *maps* 66-69
Santiago Harbor, entrance, *illus.* 66
Saratoga (U.S. carrier, 1925), 16, 131, 184, 186, 209-11, 214, 215, 259, 273, *illus.* 17, 131, 210
Saumarez (British destroyer), 226
Savage (British destroyer), 226
Savannah (U.S. light cruiser), 233
Savo Island (U.S. escort carrier), 38
Savo Island, Battle of, 211-13, *map* 213
Sayre, Francis B. (High Commissioner of Philippines), 196
Scapa Flow, Orkney Islands, Scotland (British anchorage), 20, 88, 96-98, 121, 127, 158
Scharnhorst (German heavy cruiser), 88, 89, 91, *illus.* 88
Scharnhorst (German battleship), 148, 150, 151, 158, 161, *illus.* 151, 224; sinking of, 224-27, *map* 226
Scheer, Vice Admiral Reinhard (Commander in Chief of High Seas Fleet), 96, 98-100, 102-10, 113
Schlesien (German battleship), 100
Schleswig-Holstein (German battleship), 100
Schley, Captain (later Commodore) W. S., 62-66
Scorpion (British destroyer), 226
Scorpion (U.S. gunboat), 64
Scotland, 96
Scott, Rear Admiral Norman, 215, 217
Scout seaplane, 144
Scrapping program (ships), 131
Sea power
    battleship strength, comparative tables, *1908* and *1914*, 86
    ratios, 131-32
    U.S., *1898-1964*, 13-28
    U.S. and Japan, *1944* and *1898*, 29-60
Sea Power, Influence of, upon History (Mahan), 22
Sea warfare. *See* Warfare (naval)
Sealion (British submarine), 195
Seaplane, *illus.* 126
Seawitch (British aircraft tender), 192
Second Front, and Soviet Russia, 230
Segregation, San Francisco, Calif. (1906-1907), 82, 83
Sevastopol (Russian battleship), 74
Seventh Fleet (MacArthur's), 258
Sewanee (U.S. escort carrier), 38
Seydlitz (German heavy cruiser), 94, 99, 102, 106, 148, *illus.* 95, 98, 110
Shafter, General (Army commander), 66
Shanghai, 53, 74, 75, 80
Shannon (British armored cruiser), 99
Shantung Peninsula, 88
Shantung Province, 74
Shark (British destroyer), 105, 109, *illus.* 107
Shaw (U.S. destroyer), 177
Sheffield (British cruiser), 225, *illus.* 151, 168
Shell, explosive, 7
Shigure (Japanese destroyer), 35, 39, 40
Shikishima (Japanese battleship), 76, *illus.* 77
Shikoku (island), Japan, 283
Shima, Vice Admiral Kiyohide, 33, 39, 40; Southern Japanese Force, *map* 32
Shimonoseki Treaty, 71
Shinano (Japanese carrier), 197
Ship(s), naval
    abbreviations and symbols, 6-7 *(diag.)*
    aerial bomb hit, 6
    armor plating, 7

biggest Navy (1898), 13
    boilers, oil-burning, 14
    camouflage, 124
    capital, 131
    compartmentation, 7
    fires and firefighting, 7
    flooding, 7
    flotation margin, 6-7
    fuel (1898), 14
    picket, 283
    projectile hit, 6
    pumping facilities, 7
    repairs (immediate), 7
    Russian (1898), 14
    scrapping program, 131
    sunken, *illus.* 250
    torpedo hit, 7
Shipbuilding, 22, 28, 86, 114, 118, 127, 130, 133, 134, 220, 229, 236
Shipping, and war undersea (1914-1918), 111-13
Ship-to-shore operation, and shore-to-shore movement, 231-32, 237
"Sho" Operation, 31
Shoho (Japanese aircraft carrier), 201, 214, *illus.* 200
Shokaku (Japanese aircraft carrier), 30, 178, 197, 201, 202, 213, 214, 216, 264
Shore-to-shore movement, and ship-to-shore operation, 231-32, 237
Short, Lieutenant General Walter C., 184
Shortland Islands, 215
Shropshire (Australian light cruiser), 38
Siberia, 80
Sibuyan Sea, 29, 30, 33, 36, 41
Sibuyan Sea, Battle of, *map* 32, 37
Sicard, Rear Admiral (Commander North Atlantic Squadron at Key West, Florida), 62
Sicily, 169, 176, 236
Sims, Rear Admiral William S., 116, 122
Sims (U.S. destroyer), 201
Singapore, 40, 190-92
Singora, 190, 191
Sinkings (submarine), 220-24
Sisshin (Japanese battleship), 76
Sissoi Veliky (Russian battleship), 76, 77
Sitka, 135
Skagerrak, 75, 97, 98
Skip-bombing, 144
Smith, Lieutenant General Holland M., 270
Smith (U.S. destroyer), 216
Soldiers (U.S.), 1917-1918 and transports, 125-27
Solomon Islands, 199-202, 209, 215, 258, *map* 202
Somerville, Admiral Sir James, 156, 168, 169
Sopwith Pup (W. W. I scout plane, British Royal Navy), 140
Soryu (Japanese aircraft carrier), 178, 203, 206
South America, 83, 148
South China Sea, 38, 152
South Dakota (U.S. battleship), 39, 216 *(illus.)*, 217, 264
Southampton (British light cruiser), 108, 172
Spain, 51, 52, 63, 70, 80
Spanish-American War (1898), 87
    Battle of Manila, 51-60
    Battle of Santiago, 61-70
Spanish Fleet (1898), 18
Sparrowhawk (British destroyer), 109
Spears, John R., *History of Our Navy*, 60
Spee, Rear Admiral Graf von, 88-92
Spooner Act, 84
Sprague, Admiral C. A. F., 41, 42
Sprague, Admiral Thomas, 41
Spruance, Admiral Raymond A., 259, 262, 266, 272, 276, 284
Stagg, Captain J. M., 244, 246
Stalin, Joseph V., 230
Stark, Admiral (Russian commander), 71-73, 230
Steam, and naval strategy, 7
Stewart (U.S. destroyer), 192
Stord (Norwegian destroyer), 226
Strasbourg (French battle cruiser), 168, 169, *illus.* 168, 254
Strategy, 7
    Japanese defense (1944), 258

317

(of) Japanese on Pearl Harbor, 184
Operation Torch, 230-31
U.S., against Japanese advances to Solomons, 199 *ff.*
U.S., for drive against Japan, 257
Stukas, 172
Stump, Admiral Felix B., 41
Sturdee, Vice Admiral F. Doveton, 90, 91
Subic Bay, 53, 55
Submarines and submarine warfare, 92, 96-98, 110, 146, 195-97, *illus.* 26
   1914-1918, 111-18
   American Turtle (submarine, 1775), 111
   anti-submarine warfare, 119-22
   German, 86, 88, 112, 123, 148, 158, 162, 176, 236, 255
   German, and Allied countermeasures, 219-24
   German *U-9* (1914), 92
   German sinkings and losses, 118
   Italian, 168
   Japanese, 193, 195
   Japanese at Pearl Harbor, 181
   Japanese forty-five-ton midget, *illus.* 184
   John Marshall (nuclear-powered), *illus.* 301
   Kure's shipyards, *illus.* 292
   midget, British, *illus.* 227
   North Sea, 96
   nuclear-powered, 28
   nuclear-powered Polaris-armed, 301-03
   Pacific Fleet, 195
   Second Battle of the Philippines, 16
   sinkings, 121, 220-24
   UC, or mine-laying type, 114
   U.S., 47, 135, 264, *1944*, 261
   U.S., and Japanese home islands, 288
   U.S., efficacy of, 195-97
   war undersea (1914-1918), 111-18 *(illus.)*
   (targets of) wolf pack, *illus.* 220
Suez Canal, 75, 94
Suffolk (British heavy cruiser), 152, 154, 156, *illus.* 153
Suicide pilots *(kamikazes)*, 273
Sulu Sea, 30, 35, 36
Sumatra, 191, 192
Sunda Strait, 194
Sunderland, 98
Superb (British battleship), 99 *(illus.)*
Surabaja, 192, 194
Surigao Strait, 33, 36-40
Surigao Strait, Battle of, *map* 32, 44
Sussex (cross-Channel steamer), 96
Suwanee (U.S. escort carrier), 233
Suzuya (Japanese heavy cruiser), 34, 38, 43, 49, 203, 213
Svietlana (Russian fast scout cruiser), 76, 80
Swanson (U.S. destroyer), 233, 235
Swir (Russian repair ship), 80
Swordfish (plane), 160, 169
Swordfish (U.S. submarine), 196
Sydney (Australian armored cruiser), 92
Sydney (Australian heavy cruiser), 170, *illus.* 170
Symbols and abbreviations (ship), 6

Taft, William Howard, 83, 86
Tahiti (French port), 88
Taiho (Japanese aircraft carrier), 30, 259, 264
Takao (Japanese heavy cruiser), 29, 203
Talbot, Commander P. H., 191
Tama (Japanese light cruiser), 38, 47, 49, 203, 208
Tambor (U.S. submarine), 204
Tanambogo, 209
Tandjungpriok, 194
Tanks, amphibious, *illus.* 267
Taranto, 137, 138, 142, 144, 170-72, 182, 199
Taranto raid, damaged Italian ships in harbor, *illus.* 171
Tarpon (U.S. submarine), 204
Task force(s), 186, *illus.* 258, 281, 284
Task Force *38*, 186
Task Force *58*, 186
Tassafaronga, 217
Taussig, Vice Admiral Joseph K., USN, 119-20
Temeraire (British battleship), 99
Tempest (British destroyer), *illus.* 124
Tennessee (U.S. battleship), 33, 38, 183
Tenth of August, Battle of, 74
Terror (Spanish torpedo boat), 64

Terror (U.S. monitor), 62, 70
Texas (U.S. armored cruiser), 62, 64, 66, 68
Texas (U.S. battleship), 121, 142, 233, 240, 246, 272, 283
Thailand, 194
Thompson, Big Bill, 132
Thunderer (British battleship), 99
Thüringen (German battleship), 99
Tiger (British battle cruiser), 99, 101
Tillman (U.S. destroyer), 233
Tinian, 267
Tipperary (British destroyer), 109
Tirpitz (German battleship), 148, 224, *illus.* 228
Tjilatjap, Java, 192
Togo, Admiral (Supreme Japanese Commander), 72, 74-80
Tokiawa (Japanese armored cruiser), 76
Tokyo, 83, 145, 188, 257, 270, 272, 294
Tokyo Bay, 296
Tone (Japanese heavy cruiser), 34, 38, 203, 214
Tongatabu, 203, 216
Tore (Japanese heavy cruiser), 178
Torpedo(es)
   Barham explodes, *illus.* 175
   cruiser, *illus.* 156
   Pearl Harbor, 182-83
   plane-borne, 182, *1923*, *illus.* 137
   references to, 34, 35, 41-43, 45, 105, 106, 108, 114, 123, 124, 127, 137, 139, 144, 154, 156, 158-61, 185, 186, 190, 191, 194, 196, 201, 206, 212, 217, 226
Torpedo boats, 75, *illus.* 76; *Biedovoi* (Russian), *illus.* 79
Torpedo nets, 183
Torpedo planes (bombers), 143-44, 156, 169
   attack (U.S. Navy), 139, 142
   Avenger, *illus.* 143
   squadrons, 191
"Tortoise" ships, 5
Toulon, 255
Tovey, Admiral, 156
Toyada, Admiral (Japanese Commander in Chief), 31
Trafalgar, 72, 116
Transports, 123, 125-27, 129, *illus.* 238
   France, southern, 253-56
   Normandy, 239-53, *map* 251
   North African landings (1943), 234
Treaty of Versailles, 148
Trigger (U.S. submarine), 204
Tri-Partite Alliance, 133
Triumph, 301
Tromp (Netherlands light cruiser), 191 *(illus.)*, 192
Troops (U.S.), plunge to Leyte, *illus.* 30
Troubridge, Rear Admiral T. H., 255
Trout (U.S. submarine), 204
Truant (British submarine), 158
Truk, 213-15
Tsarevitch (Russian battleship), 72-74
Tsingtao, 88
Tsushima Strait, Battle of, 72, 74-80, 82, 84, 91, *map* 78
Tuna (U.S. submarine), 204
Turbulent (British destroyer), 109
Turkey, 94
Turner, Vice Admiral Richmond Kelly, 210, 211, 279
Tuscaloosa (U.S. heavy cruiser), 232, 242, 246
Tyrwhitt, Commodore R. Y., 94

U-117 (German submarine), 140
U-Boats, 125; destroyed, *illus.* 117
Ukeshima, 76
Ulithi, 31, 284
Ullondo Island, 79
Umnak Island, 207
United States
   airplane developed as a navy weapon, 139
   arms and armament, 22
   aviation (naval), 208
   balanced fleet (1908), 84
   battle for a foothold (1942-1943), 209-18
   battleship strength (1908-1914), 86
   disarmament and rebuilding, 129-36
   fighting power, 28
   5-5-3 naval ratio, 20
   (and) German submarines, 219
   isolationism, 70, 136

(strategy against) Japan, 199, 257
(and) Japan (1904), 72-73
(and) Japan, naval standing (1933), 133
-Japanese relations (1906), 82
landing craft, 244
Midway, Battle of, 203-08, losses, 207-08
naval power (1900), 81-86
Normandy, 239-53
North African landings (1943), 229-38
North Sea mine barrage, laid by Great Britain and, *map* 122
Pearl Harbor; *see* Pearl Harbor
sea power, 22, *1898-1964*, 13-28
sea supremacy, 28
ship(s), combatant, 28
shipbuilding, 22, 28, 229, 236
Spanish-American War, 22, 24
submarine warfare (1915), 96, 97
war undersea (1914-1918), 111-18
warfare (naval), 138-46
W. W. I, contributions at sea, 121-22
W. W. I, early phases, 87-94
U.S. Army Air Force, 140, 144, 154-56, 258, 259, 284
Iwo Jima base, 276
Leyte Gulf, Battle of, 29-50
U.S. Army, 70, 218, 267, 269, 283
airplanes, 277
Information Service, 182
North Africa (1942), 176
Pearl Harbor, 182
Sixth (MacArthur's), 30
U.S. Atlantic Fleet (1908), 86
U.S. Congress, 132, 135
U.S. Fifth Fleet, 258, 261, 262, 267, 272, 284
1898, 18
air strength, 259
Asiatic Squadron, 51, 52
Task Force *57* (British Far Eastern forces), 276
U.S. First Marine Division, 209-12, 215, 217, 218
U.S. Pacific Fleet, 47, 185, 186, 200, 213, 215, 216, 257
Battle of Leyte Gulf, 29-50
Pearl Harbor, 177-84
U.S. Marines, 200, 267, 270, 272, 276, 281; losses at Iwo Jima, 273
U.S. Mine Patrol, *illus.* 125
U.S. Naval Intelligence, 208
U.S. Navy, 63, 215, 283
1914, 88
1944 and 1898 contrasted, 29-60
disarmament and rebuilding, 129-36
dive bomber, 143
dive-bombing technique, 139, 142
Dutch Harbor base, 207
losses at Iwo Jima, 273
maintenance of primacy, 305
navy second to none, 82, 130, 136
North African landings (1943), 232-33
Olympia (1883), 52
Pacific, early raids, 185
Pearl Harbor, 182
submarines, nuclear-powered Polaris-armed, 301-03
task forces, 186
torpedo(es), plane-borne, 182, *1923, illus.* 137
torpedo-plane attack, 142
warfare, first battle of modern naval, 13
W. W. I, 119-28
U.S.-Netherlands Force, 192
U.S. Neutrality Act, 220
U.S. Sixth Battle Squadron, *illus.* 120
U.S. Seventh Fleet, 29, 31, 38, 41, 45-47
U.S. South Pacific Task Force, 129
U.S. Third Fleet, 13, 16, 29, 31, 36, 38-39, 43, 45-47, 49, 162, 284, 285, 288, 296
Unryu (Japanese aircraft carrier), 197
Ural (Russian fast scout cruiser), 76, 79
Uranami (Japanese destroyer), 49
Ushakoff (Russian coastal defense vessel), 76
Ushijima, Lieutenant General M., 281
U.S.S.R. *See* Russia
Utah (U.S. target and anti-aircraft ship), 121, 177, 182, 183
Utah Beach, 246, 253

V-48 (German destroyer), 105
V-187 (German destroyer), 94
Valiant (British battleship), 99, 172, 174, *illus.* 169, 236
Vandegrift, General Alexander Archer, 210
Vanguard (British battleship), 99
Varyag (Russian protected cruiser), 73
Velasco (Spanish light cruiser), 56
Vessels (naval), *diag.* 6-7
abbreviations and symbols, 6-7
armored, earliest, 5
damage control, 7
See also Ship(s) and names of individual vessels
Vestal (U.S. repair ship), 178
Vian, Rear Admiral Sir Philip, 276
Vichy France, 166
Victoria Cross, 159
Victorious (British carrier), 154, 276
Victory (Nelson's flagship at Trafalgar Bay), *illus.* 71
Vincennes (U.S. heavy cruiser), 204, 210-12
Vincennes (U.S. light cruiser, later version), 39
Vinson, Carl, 134
Vinson-Trammel Act (1934), 133, 134
Vinson-Trammel Bill (1933), 28
Virginia (U.S. battleship), 140
Virginia Capes, 81
Vittorio Veneto (Italian battleship), 138, 172, 174, 176, *illus.* 170
Vixen (U.S. converted tug), 66, 68
Vizcaya (Spanish armored cruiser), 64, 67, *illus.* 65; explodes, *illus.* 67; wreck of, *illus.* 70
Vladivostok, 73-75, 79, 80
Vladmir Bay, Siberia, 80
Von der Tann (German battle cruiser, 1911), 18, 94, 96, 99, 101, 102, 106, *illus.* 19, 100
Von Steuben (U.S. auxiliary cruiser), 123, 125

Wadsworth (U.S. destroyer), 121, *illus.* 123
Wainwright (U.S. destroyer), 121
Wakaba (Japanese destroyer), 49
Wake Island, 135, 188 *(illus.)*, 189
Waldron, Commander Jack, 205
Walsh, David, 134
War of 1812, 63
Warburton-Lee, Captain A. W., 159, 160
Ward (U.S. destroyer), 181
Warfare (naval), 142
airplane, 138
anti-submarine warfare, 119-22
audacity, 216
Coral Sea, Battle of, 199-202
modern, 7, 18, 28, first battle of, 13
Philippines, Second Battle of, 29-50
science of, 208, 305
submarine (1914-1918), 111-18
weapons, 305
Warrior (British armored cruiser), 99, 104, 109
Warspite (British battleship), 99, 104, 160, 161, 168, 169, 171, 174, 175, *illus.* 159, 236, 237
Wasatch (U.S. cargo transport), 36
Washington (U.S. battleship), 39, 129, 131, 135, *illus.* 129, 130
Washington (U.S. battleship), 217, *illus.* 283
Washington Disarmament Conference (1921-1922), 20, 24, 129-35
Wasp (U.S. aircraft carrier), 209, 210, 214, 215, 266, 277; burns, *illus.* 216; struck by torpedoes, *illus.* 215
Watanabe, Captain Y., 184
Weather, 16-17, 28, 127, 146, 178, 187, 191, 224, 234, 244-45, 276
Weimar Republic, 147
Wellington, New Zealand, 210
West Indies, 63, 64, 92
West Pacific island groups, *map* 260, 270
West Virginia (U.S. battleship), 31, 33, 38, 131, 182, 183, *illus.* 39
Western Front (W. W. I), 122, 161
Westfalen (German battleship), 100
Weygand, General, 230
Wheeler Field, 180-82
White Plains (U.S. escort carrier), 38, 42
Whitworth, Admiral, 161
Wichita (U.S. heavy cruiser), 39, 232, 235

319

Wiesbaden (German light cruiser), 103, 108, 110
Wilhelm II, Kaiser, 20
Wilhelm Heidkamp (German destroyer), 159
Wilkes (U.S. destroyer), 233, 235
Wilmington (U.S. gunboat), 62
Wilson, Woodrow, 86, 116
Wilson (U.S. destroyer), 211
Winooski (U.S. tanker), 233, 236
Witjeft, Admiral, 73, 74
Wolfgang Zenker (German destroyer), 160
Woolsey (U.S. destroyer), 233
Worden (U.S. destroyer), 204
World War I, 24, 87-128, 305
  airplane, 139
  early phases, 87-94, fleets and battle areas, *maps* 83, 85,
    89, 92, 93
  Jutland, Battle of (1916), 95-110, *maps* 97, 100, 103-06,
    109
  mine-laying, 127
  North Sea mine barrage, laid by U.S. and British ships,
    map 122
  U.S., contributions at sea, 121-22
  U.S. in, 119-28
  war undersea (1914-1918), 111-18
World War II, 16, 18, 28, 147-296, 303, 305
  Atlantic, war in (1941-1943), 219-28
  battle for a foothold (1942-1943), 209-18
  Coral Sea and Midway, 199-208
  England's life lines (1939-1941), 147-56
  island barriers down, 257-68
  Japanese Kamikaze Corps, 146, 273, 277, 281, 283, *illus.*
    285-87, *Baka Bomb, illus.* 145
  Mediterranean, action in, 167-76
  Normandy and southern France, 239-56
  North African landings (1943), 229-38
  Norway and Dunkirk, 157-66
  Pacific, early raids in, 185-98
  Pearl Harbor, 177-84

  (to) Tokyo Bay, 269-96
Wotje, Marshall Islands, 187
Wright, Rear Admiral Carleton, 129, 217
Wright Brothers, 139
Wylie, Philip, *Triumph*, 301
Wyoming (U.S. battleship), 121

Yahagi (Japanese light cruiser), 38
Yamagumo (Japanese destroyer), 49
Yamamoto, Admiral (Commander in Chief Imperial Japa-
  nese Fleet), 184, 203, 207
Yamashiro (Japanese battleship), 33 *(illus.)*, 38-40, 49, 203
Yamato (Japanese battleship, world's greatest), 14, 33, 34,
  38, 47, 133, 197, 203, 259, 262, 284, *illus.* 29, 288-90
Yangtze River, 75
Yarmouth-Lowestoft raid, 96, 97
Yashima (Japanese battleship), 74
Yawata class passenger liners (Japanese), 133
Yenessi (Russian mine-laying vessel), 73
Yi Sun-sin, Admiral (of Korea), 5
Yokumo (Japanese battleship), 76
Yorktown (U.S. carrier lost at Midway), 133, 186, 188,
  200-207, 279, *illus.* 206, 207
Yorktown (successor to U.S. carrier lost at Midway), 277
Yosemite (U.S. auxiliary cruiser), 70
Yoshino (Japanese battleship), 74

Xerxes, 5

Zafiro (U.S. transport), 52
Zara (Italian heavy cruiser), 174
Zeppelins, 98, 140
Zig-zag (convoy maneuver), 124, *illus.* 123
Zuiho (Japanese aircraft carrier), 38, 49, 203, 216, *illus.*
  46
Zuikaku (Japanese aircraft carrier), 38, 46, 47, 49, 178,
  213, 214, 216, 266, *illus.* 45, 47